NONDUAL THERAPY

THE PSYCHOLOGY OF AWAKENING

Georgi Y. Johnson

VeReCreations

VeReCreations
info@iamhere.life

Editor: Daniel Johnson

Ordering Information:
Quantity sales. Special discounts are available on quantity purchases by corporations, associations, and others. For details, contact the "Special Sales Department" at the address above.

Nondual Therapy/ VeReCreations. -- 1st ed.
ISBN 978-1-912517-00-8

Can we feel the freedom of a bird? The belonging of a flower? The esteem of a tree? The innocence of a cloud? The purity of water? The peace of a sunset? When we can feel it on the outside, we're already feeling it on the inside. A resonant, healing process is beginning.

"With a mixture of empathy, fierceness and compassion, Georgi cuts straight to the core of an issue."

Mark Wolynn, Author of: It Didn't Start With You

"Georgi's book is a jewel. As soon as I started reading I could not put it down, as I was drawn into an evolutionary process in myself where I came in touch with both the delight and brilliance and with frozen parts of myself - where consciousness is not yet awake to itself."

Renate McNay, Conscious TV

"Encountering this book was a rewarding and nourishing experience. Within a few chapters, I felt a deep appreciation that a book of such richness and depth, of practical yet profound wisdom, was finding its way into my awareness and the world at large.

Georgi clearly writes from a vastness of view and experience, drawn from her own evolutionary journey and her work facilitating others in theirs. Consequently, this book speaks powerful truth, evoking impersonal presence whilst guiding the heart to wholeness. I am heartened to read and receive, and I trust many others will enjoy such a significant contribution to the human unfolding."

Will Pye, Author of Blessed with a Brain Tumor

TABLE OF CONTENTS

Nondual Therapy: The Psychology of Awakening.

PART III
A Curious Universe

This book is dedicated with gratitude to my mother, Pauline Ashby, through whom I manifest, and whose love, care, humor and wisdom are a support and inspiration.

"The legs, for example, of that chair – how miraculous their tubularity, how supernatural their polished smoothness! I spent several minutes – or was it several centuries? – not merely gazing at those bamboo legs, but actually being them – or rather being myself in them; or, to be still more accurate (for "I" was not involved in the case, nor in a certain sense were "they") being my Not-self in the Not-self which was the chair."

ALDOUS HUXLEY

FOREWORD

The place where we sit, deep inside ourselves, will determine the fabric of our reality. It will affect our attitude to what's seen, our feelings and our thoughts. Just the chair of our perception will determine our point of view and our experience, flooding the horizons with its atmospheres.

Where do you sit when you look out on the world? Is it on a throne of authority, or on a prayer stool of humility? Do you sit in stillness, or are you comfortable on the chair of friendliness and belonging? Are you struggling to remain on the same chair, or do you sometimes switch chairs without noticing? Perhaps at work, it's the barstool and in the bar, it's on the seat of wisdom. Perhaps with your parents you're in a high-chair (with a finger on the eject button) and with the partner you enjoy the driver's seat? Could it be that we're switching chairs all the time without knowing it? Perhaps a deeper freedom can be found in the one that can switch the chair of perception according to need?

This book was born to meet the need for a shift in our conception of human freedom in form. It's based on a fundamental world view which is shared by increasing numbers of people from all walks of life across the world. This world view is a result of a wave of collective awakening to timeless wisdom: that consciousness is primary, undivided and unconstrained both in time and space. While each of us is different, we are not separate. Rather, we are all unique expressions of a collective evolution.

When we allow the premise of unity – that it's the same life, consciousness and Source that moves through all different forms – questions remain which are inherently psychological: Why do we feel separate? Why do we suffer? What can we do to experience wisdom and unity? How can we be unconditionally happy?

Thus, the second premise of this book: that our feelings, emotions and states of being are energetically alive, and that they affect the nature of thoughts and our physical health. That is, the way we feel has a causal impact on our health and our state of mind. Emotional suffering, therefore, begs for deeper insight, it should not be ignored. Right now, our shared repertoire of feelings and emotions is impoverished. There are a greater variety of feelings expressed through emojis on our smartphones than in the literature of psychology. Guilt and shame, for example, are conventionally treated as synonymous. But do they feel the same? Are love, peace and freedom just interchangeable words?

When we refine the exploration of feelings and emotions, an infinite scope of sensitivity emerges. This opening of the Felt Sense of living experience has the power to unlock thought patterns that have been conditioned by a limited emotional vocabulary. When our feelings change, the way we conceive reality is also transformed.

In general, where we suffer, there is a sense of contraction or freeze. This freeze creates stress. When the stress is ignored, the contracted energy becomes depressed. Yet it's still there, creating bottlenecks and restraints in the flow of vitality through the body, psyche and mind.

But what has frozen? Where there was freedom, now there is contraction. What has contracted? Thus, Nonduality introduces the principle of our True Nature – the qualities of consciousness that we share and recognize, such as love, peace, joy and freedom.

Our premise is that contractions are frozen forms of those qualities. For example, when we surround a contraction of hatred with unconditional love, a melting occurs which de-contracts the energy.

Out of these insights, a methodology has emerged which is both diagnostic and therapeutic. At first, this work was the result of shared exploration with my partner, Bart ten Berge. Bart has treated thousands over the past thirty years and has a breadth of experience and impact in his therapeutic work which is transformational. At first, we were our own laboratory. We used ourselves as living guinea pigs – researching both the nature of contraction in the psyche and of Nondual Qualities.

The circle expanded to include advanced groups of meditators, colleagues and students. Everyone has brought insight, and in this way, the field of Nondual Therapy has evolved significantly beyond the subtle denial of suffering through a monastic attempt to stay 'Nondual'. The agenda of personal perfection fell away to be replaced by a living celebration of all forms of expression and receptivity. This has truly been a shared, evolutionary project, proving the insight that when teacher and student disappear, learning is happening. For all this, we are grateful.

This book is intended as a support for diagnosis, self-exploration and therapy. We hope that it will be a companion in those moments where it's needed as well as an inspiration. The methodology is in no way intended as a dogma, but rather as a tool to open new possibilities of depth psychology, including the subtle, unconscious and transpersonal aspects of human experience.

We are all expressions of a deeper need which has tremendous intelligence, and our individual purpose is to allow that evolutionary unfolding to be experienced through us. We bless you on your journey through these pages, with the wind at your back and the sun on your face. Every moment released into freedom – even at the most intimate layers of experience – is having a direct positive impact on the well-being of all of us. Thank you for being here, and for allowing the time and space for freedom to manifest through human form.

> *"One's whole being vibrates like strings brushed by an invisible wind."*

PETER RUSSELL

PART 1

A PERCEPTIVE UNIVERSE

"Let's meet purely with presence

and be wholly here to one another

knowing that, in essence, we are the same

knowing that, in being, we are one."

STEVE TAYLOR

Georgi Y. Johnson

CHAPTER 1: INTRODUCTION

"We don't see things as they are, we see them as we are."

ANAIS NIN

What would it be like to live each moment with vitality, belonging, joy and curiosity? What if we could easily access unlimited resources of peace, love and freedom? Imagine the freedom to switch perspectives or points of view, easily moving between one seat of experience and another. We can find ourselves at the seat of insight, or in the chair of universal care; we can move to the launchpad of passion or fall into the couch of relaxation. Rather than burning in a chair of jealousy, being strapped to a seat of fear, or bound to the stark discomfort of greed, we can get up and switch perspectives. Perhaps, if we uncovered this freedom, we would choose to sit where we suffer least, where even the passage of time and the confines of space are impermanent, where it's possible to serve the wellbeing of the whole, of which we are a unique expression.

This book is inspired by the lived experience of the qualities of our True Nature, which are always available, and are especially experienced when we release our minds, hearts and bodies from conditioning. The qualities of true nature, called here Nondual Qualities, are places we sit to become channels to natural and universal wellbeing. These qualities are never far away, in fact, they're deeply close to home – nurturing, sustaining and empowering us moment by moment, with each breath we take and every step we make.

The realization of full human potential involves the evolution of mind. Where there is individual perspective, there is always a dynamic play between individuality and unity. The very concept of individuality is a mental one. In this way, our development presently expresses a crisis of individuality. The mind asks: Who am I? What am I? Where am I? These questions demand sensory answers, which means they are answered by our sense of being alive. From then on, the mind stops dictating experience and begins to follow it. It works as a receiver, reflector and describer of that which is experienced as its own Source – a dimension of experience which precedes all mental functioning. Whereas the mind sees a conflict of opposites, experience allows both sides of a pair. In duality, each side depends on the other in order to be itself.

Nonduality is a broad term which literally means 'not two'. While the term Nonduality can be associated with the ancient Indian wisdom of Advaita, the wisdom of inherent one-ness is found through mystical strains across all cultures of the world. In Western terms, Nonduality is based on the insight that the manifestation occurs through the play of pairs: we have male and female, up and down, left and right. Even when we look at ideals like harmony, symmetry and balance, we witness the play of two. Nonduality doesn't exclude this natural duality but indicates the one out of which the two are born, and the one in which the dance of duality occurs. Nonduality is not a negation of duality, but rather the Source and facilitator of all manifestation. In the words of Nondual teacher Jeff Foster: "The nonduality we speak of is not the opposite of anything... To see what is being spoken of, we must go beyond our ordinary way of thinking and seeing."

Our search to make sense of experience and to find form within physical life is driven by a passion which is universal and at the same time unique. Attempting to contain this tension, our mental conditioning has twisted natural forms of duality into a competition of false opposites: it's 'Me Versus You', 'Author Versus Reader', 'Speaker Versus Listener', 'Black Versus White', 'Good Versus Bad', 'Light Versus Darkness'. This competition between complementary phenomena is illusory. Our right hand is not born to compete against our left hand any more than the in-breath is superior to the outbreath. Competition is conflict, and where we conflict within ourselves, we lose our sense of wellbeing.

Moment by moment, there is potential for compassion, collaboration and celebration, yet part of our evolution is enslaved in a contraction around competition and collaboration. Both are born of evolution and are needed in the liberation of the individual within unity. Yet the energy of competition generates an addiction to conflict in which we grasp towards what we consider desirable and attempt to negate the opposite. For example, we want the pleasure but not the pain, or we want the gain but not the loss. This grasping enslaves us to conflict, which reflects throughout the psyche as energetic contraction. Caught in a hall of mirrors, we invest our vitality in imagined appearances and disconnect from the Source of all duality which is inherently Nondual. One could not become two without the one that feeds, sustains and outlives the dance of two. Two are always formed of the one, which means that all duality is formed of Nonduality.

Therapy is about healing, which is the compassionate movement needed to return to naturalness and wholeness. Nondual Therapy is a process which supports the release of energetic contractions in the psyche back to the Source qualities out of which they were formed.

The process unveils a living, holistic individuality that is dynamically attuned to the needs of the whole. Released of the agenda of personal survival, the individual begins to manifest through the field of possibilities born in each moment, expressing core qualities which are precious and unique, yet which originate from the same inseparable Nondual Source of us all.

Nondual Therapy is not about achieving a status, or becoming a new, improved person. Rather, it's about undoing the web of personality to allow the flow of pure Nondual Qualities through and beyond all forms of the psyche, whether they be broken, twisted or imperfect. Rather than trying to fix the personality, it sees individuality as a precious manifestation of

Source in motion – a flow of unique moments of experience that can be celebrated as part of the evolutionary dance of the whole.

Words struggle to express the suffering of being disconnected from life: the decrease in vitality, inspiration, pleasure and joy; the feeling of being caught in a treadmill of obligation and fear, out of which the only release is the greater fear of death itself. One of the great mercies in this kind of suffering, is that often, we are hardly aware of the pain we're in. Thus, the cliché: "It's better to let sleeping dogs lie." Yet sleeping dogs do awaken, and sometimes with a cry of pain. To put it simply, problems don't go away just because we ignore them. This includes the big problems of who, what and where we are.

It's a tragic paradox that we deny life out of fear of losing that life, yet this is the underlying dynamic that governs much of the human psyche. Controlled by a collective agenda to avoid suffering, we find we are tragically creating more suffering. It seems that suffering is needed as an inseparable part of the evolution of the whole, and as an indispensable part of healing – from the shock and pain of the divisions that are inherent to creation, to the reunion of the manifold within unity. In so many ways, suffering – when allowed – looks like love. Our cry of suffering is the cry for reunion: it is the calling towards home and the awakening of our True Nature. When we repress that call of suffering – which is the precise music of our healing – we also repress the love.

Suffering takes many forms. From one perspective, all experience is composed of suffering. This is because experience is a contraction of our pure nature.

Out of seamless unity, pure stillness or the omnipresence of silence, a need emerges which is a subtle form of primal experience. Experience is a disturbance, a contraction within the whole. In the Jewish Lurianic Kabbalah, creation is described as a process of contraction ('tzimtzum' in Hebrew) in which the infinite contracts to allow the concurrent manifestation of the finite. This contraction of primordial light reveals 'vacant space' or emptiness which is the facilitator of all form. This principle of contraction is found through the qualities of our True Nature. For example, care contracts as possession and abandonment; or purity contracts as shame and disgust. (Section II of this book details 35 examples)

Contraction is uncomfortable, but it's also awakening. This awakening of consciousness reaffirms that this movement, this contraction, is a living aspect that belongs within consciousness. Even if the feeling is of 'nothing', our resting in awareness with that 'nothing' will cause it to expand and differentiate. Perhaps it has a subtle vibration of disappointment in it, or annoyance. Even no feeling is feeling when we stay present as awareness.

Each time we refuse to feel a feeling (that is already happening); each repressed emotion; each moment we distract ourselves to avoid inner discomfort; wherever we pretend to be something we're not to get accepted as what we are; we lose power. This denial blankets the direct sense of self with illusion. It disconnects us from the joy of life and forms a wall, behind which we're isolated and afraid of the future. Much of this is unprocessed, as our sensory system becomes normalized in a state of half-closure, demanding the stimulation of danger, violence, catastrophe or crisis to get the sense of vitality back.

Take some space to check in on what's happening inside you at this moment. That glance towards the inner world is the most important movement we can make: a movement that can transform reality. At first, it can appear that there is 'nothing' there. Perhaps there's a feeling of tightness around the chest, or a restlessness in the solar plexus. Perhaps there are mites of despair; a subtle groan of frustration; or a deeper undernote of longing. Perhaps there's an urge to scream, but for who or what, we never knew, so we never screamed. Often, there is just a sense of numbness. What's going on in this moment in your inner world?

We are conditioned to view the psyche as somehow static: as a fixed thing. We stop making that movement inside, because it seems redundant. "Oh yes, it's me. Nothing changed." There could even be a sense of annoyance, because we already "know" everything that's here on the inside. It can seem pointless or irritating, almost as if we're allergic to the experience of how it is to be alive in any moment. We often don't want to feel what's here on the inside, because it could be horrible, and we anticipate defeat in finding what we secretly expect: that we're made of bad, shallow stuff. It can seem senseless to look inside: the mind will not be able to do anything with it.

Why is this direction switch – from the conscious gaze outside the psyche, to the conscious gaze inside ourselves – so important? Why does it make a difference? First, this switch in attention is a game-changer, because the inner world is not static. It's not a fixed configuration, but a flow of living, pulsating, visceral energy. When our consciousness moves towards it, it comes to life. Movement is accelerated and the subliminal consciousness within the energetic form of the psyche awakens with the promise of reunion with the consciousness moving towards it. When consciousness meets consciousness, it's a reunion. Vitality is released.

This movement of vitality will express itself as the first layers in which we are not free – where our energy is in contraction. That first layer is precisely that sense of annoyance on turning inside, or that sense of restriction, or the feeling of pointlessness. These feelings are the murmurings of the psyche as she is being awakened by the presence of our consciousness. It can be as if a child has been neglected in a room for hours, and has fallen asleep, giving up all hope his mother would come. And then, there is this consciousness at the door, gazing at the child. The child begins to stir, expressing the inner abandonment in which he had fallen asleep: "There is no one here for me. No one is ever coming. There is nothing." He could even turn his face to the wall.

Stay a while with consciousness attending to the Felt Sense of the inner world. Don't try to search, organize or analyze. Just stay a little longer, feeling through the areas of density and space. Notice where there's a feeling of relaxation and space, and where there's stress. Perhaps there are areas where there are no sensations at all. The more we attend to the inner landscape, the more we might notice the effects of our presence. What was a density of energy could now be a stream. Where there was a rough impasse, there could now be a forest of feeling. Where there had been a sense of obstruction, there could now be a sharp physical pain somewhere in the physical body. Where we met an old melancholy, we are suddenly racing with our thoughts after something apparently random. It's all part of the puzzle and all relevant. These are the living effects of turning our attention inside. The inner world is not a fixed entity at all, it's radically alive.

Therapists know that their ability to support a process often depends on their own degree of resilience and liberation – on the ability to contain the process of another without getting triggered by personal issues. So, with a grounded methodology for working with recognizable emotions, energetic contractions and psychological issues, this work is for both therapists and their clients, as a support in creating space for healing to occur.

This book aims to give an overview of the human psyche – in naturalness and in the common areas of contraction. You will learn to recognize how contractions are formed in dualistic pairs, often according to our struggle to contain suffering. Each contraction into psychological duality is formed out of a Nondual Quality that has frozen in manifestation. For example, in the energetic contraction of shame and disgust, there is a call towards that which was frozen: unconditional purity. In this, Nondual Therapy offers a navigational map for the liberation of vitality from the treadmill of suffering. With the critical movement inside, suffering can be transformed to a journey of curiosity, wonder, insight and celebration.

The Dalai Lama has said that the purpose of our lives is to be happy. The purpose of these pages is to open pathways to the happiness which we always were, always are and always will be, at the core of every moment of physical manifestation.

Chapter 2: The Living Psyche

"If only a world-wide consciousness could arise that all division and fission are due to the splitting of opposites in the psyche, then we should know where to begin."

C.J. JUNG

All therapeutic encounters, of any kind, draw on the perennial resource of Nondual Qualities, even when this is an unconscious process. Therefore, all types of therapy, conducted with integrity, are helpful. Therapy involves connection beyond the isolation of the Separate Self. It draws on the healing elixir of awareness, through the art of silence and listening. Conflicts are received, seen and shared, and this has an immediate healing effect.

Before therapy has even begun, the individual has allowed the Nondual Quality of Helplessness, which means they have reached beyond the belief in absolute separation into the wisdom of interdependency and compassion. Resources are passing through the energetic borders of the Separate Self. Therapy involves service, which is also a powerful dissembler of the idea of the ultimately separate individual. A therapeutic process also optimally moves towards shared insight into the unfolding process. These qualities are fundamental to all therapeutic encounters. Nondual Therapy is an evolution of conventional therapeutic models but differs in that it unhooks hypnotic forms of conditioning found in our collective state of mind.

The general field of psychology evolved out of both philosophy and biology. Discussions of these two subjects date back to the early Greek thinkers, including Aristotle and Socrates. The word psychology is derived from the Greek word psyche, meaning 'soul'. While the therapeutic field of psychology has twisted and turned through many streams, the core of the science is found at its origin: the cultivation of a deeper, more alive and integrated feeling of connection with the depths of ourselves, the area the ancient Greeks called "soul". Yet today, many conventional schools of psychological thought relegate the soul as a spiritual concept, operating out of the belief that consciousness is generated in the brain and is limited as a local phenomenon to an individual body. There is an assumed split between 'Spiritual' and 'Human'. This means that the vastness of our True Nature as a living resource is moved to a default position. Nondual Qualities like love and peace are at best fleeting impressions. Consciousness is viewed as functional, not foundational to healing, and healing stops when the personality is again conformed to the consensus of social norms – the collective state of mind.

Conventional therapy tends to presuppose that there is nothing beyond the individual personality. It assumes a back wall to the personality, beyond which there is an abyss, which threatens to rob the personality of both Source and resource. In addition, traditional psychology tends to see the body as an adjunct to the process, rather than acknowledging the holistic inseparability of body, heart and mind. In this, the conditioned mind is invested with the authority and burden of control over feelings, emotions and the physical body, and of course, it inevitably fails. The mind is not the creator of life, it's just one living expression.

With Nondual Therapy, we turn this approach on its head, prioritizing direct experience in the here and now before the agendas of thought. It recognizes the dimension of emptiness (conventionally labelled the black box, unconscious, or subconscious) for its restorative power. It also describes the 'Bardo' phenomena depicted in Buddhism as the experiential dimension between physical incarnations. Found in the emptiness, this is the realm of our core fears – the shadow sides, or inner demons, which directly affect and form our experience of being alive.

Nondual Therapy acknowledges our True Nature as the origin, Source and resting place of all forms of personality. Our True Nature is characterized through recognizable Source qualities, or Nondual Qualities. These qualities are not endpoints, but are like diamonds reflecting the pure, formless Source prior to being. As Nondual therapist and spiritual teacher John Prendacost puts it: "Such openings into a vast shared spaciousness bring a sense of deep peace, great freedom and quiet joy. Clients often report a sense of coming home and of being connected to the whole of life, at least temporarily."

Although known thought patterns and states of suffering can feel like home, clients report a new depth of home coming, which can be more intimate even than the family home. Through disinvesting belief from the personal story, Nondual Therapy addresses the feeling atmospheres around the stories, thoughts and behavioral patterns. When we begin to feel a feeling, it's not a matter of "been there, done that, what's next?"; it's rather a sinking into the ability to remain in experience, and to explore the wonder and refinement of inner sentience. All experience beneath the threshold of the thinking mind opens potential pathways back to the qualities of our True Nature and to increasing ease, peace and freedom.

Below are some of the structures of the psyche referred to in Nondual Therapy. It's important to note that each layer of the psyche is alive and is interdependently rooted in the rest. There is also a holographic principle at play in which each moment of experience – no matter how trivial – has the potential to express the whole. That is, when a structure of Ego takes a hit, it resonates through the layers of Personality and into the Dark Night, and vice versa.

Ego

Ego structures can be both positive and negative, as they move through competing opposites and are born from deeper conflict. Ego is always formed through imagination. Each self-image has a continuum of fear at its core, as the egoic reflection is primarily used to 'check in' on the threat of rejection and as such, is driven by a sense of incompletion and fault.

Ego depends on comparison with others, as well as competition and it therefore arises as a defensive measure where there is trouble between one psyche and another. Ego claims to want to belong, yet through presenting an image based on pretense, it divides us from ourselves and others. Often, this creates a whiplash of self-pity as the feeling of being unseen by others and unappreciated in the world can intensify where structures of ego are strong.

Ego structures move through the dualistic reflex of grasping and aversion to select what we want to be and how we want to be seen from the outside, while keeping a wary eye on what we don't want to be and how we must never be seen. Because of this, structures of ego often present the opposite of what is felt at a deeper layer. Someone with a trauma around humiliation, for example, could present as arrogant, or proud. Someone who is insecure could present as blindly confident. Someone struggling with helplessness will display constant proofs of control. Fear will "put on a brave face." Pain will laugh rather than cry. Betrayal will pretend loyalty to every contract. Rejection will pretend to be unconditionally accepting. To fortify against the risk of exposure, ego structures tend to exaggerate, expressing with absolutist language, such as: everyone, all the time, no one, never.

Ego forms out of the belief in separation; a sense of condemnation; and a seemingly endless sense of lack. It's a cover-up of the imperfect Personality, which seems to be needed, as the Personality is believed to be the essence of who we are. Ego has the dual agenda of creating the best possible self-image, while avoiding worst-case scenarios. The energy of ego is dense, and it can be sensed as a kind of ungrounded, dissatisfied heaviness.

As it has an energetic presence and effect, Ego is not confined to individuals but also can emerge as a field around groups of people. Where the energetic field of Ego is strong in the collective field, it tends to awaken structures of Ego within individuals.

Ego can mask generations of trauma and is rooted in our worst fears. For example, one client said his worst fear was to be condemned unfairly for something that he's not guilty of. What he was describing was an Ego in crisis, which paradoxically occurred precisely when he was most successful. Logic would require the opposite, yet it was precisely this appearance of success from the outside that aroused his deeper sense of illegitimacy. The structure of ego – seeking social acceptance through success – was a survival mechanism to evade a trauma inherited in the Personality. In this case, the ancestral trauma was unearthed in the experience of Jewish persecution where there was too much attention from the environment. Beneath the Ego that sought success as safety was a survival strategy within the Personality to avoid attention to stay safe. Ego is bound up with both the psychology and biology of survival. It's not a narcissistic urge to be blithely dismissed, but a form of contraction born to protect and survive. Its nervous structure reaches deep through the Personality and into the Dark Night of the Soul.

Ego is not something we need to get rid of. On the contrary, where ego starts to play up, we should have a tender curiosity. Ego shows we are vulnerable, perhaps even terrified. Take some time to ponder your own Ego tendencies. What is your greatest and oldest fear, a fear that feels almost too shameful to admit? How do you present yourself to others, when that fear is touched? What is the pain beneath it?

Personality

In our healing practice, it's been repeatedly affirmed that the greatest suffering of all is the suffering of the Separate Self. In terms of spiritual psychology this is the belief that the Personality is absolute: a fixed form and endpoint as to who and what we are. Yet the Personality can be more precisely experienced as a combination of inherited and learned patterns of reactivity. The Personality reflects Nondual Qualities through different patterns of contraction in duality. It's an instrument, but not the origin of the music.

These Nondual Qualities are always here, regardless of differentiation through form or through contractions or trauma. They are not formed in the Personality and are therefore impersonal or transpersonal. They never get lost and they're never injured. All that happens is that they become condensed and clouded through energetic contraction – at the border between ourselves and others. These gardens of suffering divide us from the qualities of our True Nature within ourselves and from the qualities of True Nature outside of ourselves. They consolidate through inheritance and the repetition of habit. Yet at any moment, we can draw on these qualities as resources.

Often, it's when the structure of Personality breaks down that the qualities of our True Nature are revealed. As Leonard Cohen wrote: "There is a crack in everything, that's how the light gets in."

Structures of separate identity and personality gain god-like status and yet like many gods, become impossible to find or define when the search is on. There is nothing stable in the Personality that can be found, held, kept or trusted. The psyche appears as a series of evolving patterns. At most, the nature of our Personality depends on the opinion or attitude of the beholder. That opinion or attitude depends on the beholder's Personality, so we're caught in a perennial wheel of illusion about who and what we are.

At its roots (even though its roots are with our ancestors), Personality is composed of a series of fundamentally narcissistic actions and reactions, drowning in the terror of its own impermanence while clinging to any available tent-peg of identity to preserve itself. In the dimension of Personality, fear is the slave master and anger the guard. Indeed, as it is inherently unstable, insecure and transient, the Personality is fundamentally condemned as a fixed form. Every form of Separate Self is sitting on death row.

The sense of condemnation arising from the deep inner dread of impermanence is inherent to beliefs in the absolute nature of personhood, and this breeds its own state of victimhood. In this, we become disempowered, disenfranchised, devitalized and full of self-pity. We blame outer authorities, our parents, the world or any external 'other' for our suffering. We can even become perpetrators, revenging on the environment for the great injustice of who we are. All this extra suffering – of humiliation, abuse, cruelty and war - when the fatal error has been in believing that the self is separate, and that the Personality is a fixation of who we are.

There has been a lot written about how to become free of the slavery of Ego and Personality. Yet the art is not to get free of Personality, but to liberate the Personality itself. Beneath the thinking, conditioned mind, there is the resting position of pure being. We can be nobody, nothing and nowhere, resting as what Advaita has called I AM. This pure being has qualities as it shines like a sun through layers of form, which always include patterns of Personality and behavior. It creates a natural invitation of contracted forms to unfold. This occurs through experiential pathways of innocence, purity, freedom and other Nondual Qualities described in this book.

Personality is directly and energetically linked to the Source of being. It spontaneously emanates through time and space. When we liberate the Personality to allow this purity of personal manifestation, then what happens is we release the areas where Personality is contracted or traumatized. Contractions still happen, according to protective need, but they are not grasped. If we use a physical metaphor: when we withdraw our hand from a fire it is reflexive and for the good of the whole. Yet a psychological contraction is shocked – the metaphorical hand stays up in the air, even when the feet have moved away from the fire and even when the fire is out.

This is a common misconception. Spiritual seekers often expect that an awakened state of consciousness will forever free them of Personality. This is not true: the Personality will continuously emanate and take form through thought, communion and communication, regardless of whether we believe it as absolute. Belief structures initially reflect where the Personality is most contracted, stalled in time and limited in space. Later, they gain an autonomy through patterns of habit, dictating distortions on perception which confirm the belief. Denial of the inheritance of the Personality is a structure of belief.

We really don't need to hold onto concepts of who, what and where we are. Rather, it's imperative that we uncover ourselves as the Source at the core of all experience. This reunion comes through the experiential trail of Nondual Qualities, or qualities of our True Nature. The deeper we rest back at the source of awareness, the more we recognize these qualities as permeating all experience. Within this profound intimacy with the deeper layers of ourselves, the sense of reunion abounds.

In this, we have seen people with the most horrific life experiences undergo the suffering of total collapse of personhood only to find themselves suddenly and unconditionally free. This is an awakening and freedom that can never be lost, which allows all forms of Personality to emanate and disappear as needed. It's a freedom in which even the deepest suffering cannot block the way home. It's a healing process that turns a despairing wandering through the Dark Night of the Soul into a curiosity, excitement and fulfillment in all experience, even when it's painful.

Others with less fundamental breakages can find it harder to get free of the reflexive habits of personal identification. This doesn't mean that psychological breakage is necessary for spiritual awakening. But at the same time, it certainly need not be an obstacle. As spiritual psychologist Steve Taylor writes: "Spiritual experiences are overwhelmingly positive experiences. They are experiences of rapture, in which we perceive reality at a heightened intensity, feel a powerful sense of inner well-being, experience a sense of oneness with our surroundings and become aware of a force of benevolence and harmony which pervades the cosmos... It seems almost paradoxical, then, that these experiences are frequently induced by states of intense despair, depression, or mental turmoil."

The deeper intelligence of the life force in us will invite the exact experience needed for our liberation, and in this, both therapist and client follow the lead of life, moment by moment, month by month, in allowing the unfolding of Source potential. Sometimes, living intelligence can seem brutal, but that is only when we still believe the separate Personality is at the core of who we are.

The tyranny of the belief in the absolute nature of Personality cannot be over-estimated. The person is inherently empty with no separate existence from the Source. It's a transient effect of the environment and of the evolutionary process through degrees of trauma and resilience which we inherit with our genes. Much of our Personality structure is formed by feedback from other Personality structures. That is, we believe we are that which the world says we are, or even, what we imagine the world says we are.

Of itself, the Personality has little vitality, and there is nothing there to hold onto, even when we want to. Its apparent vitality is life itself which is sourced at a causal layer to all forms of Personality. In practice, when we try to grasp towards the love that moves through the Personality, we're left with neither love nor freedom but with the energy of grasping and aversion – the Source of every contraction. This energy of grasping – like a hungry ghost – is not a pleasant backdrop to the experience of a lifetime.

Much of the Personality is based on an investment of belief in man-made artifacts, because here, we feel in control. We let the streetlamps blind us to the moon and stars, and let the roads they light up become the flat territory of the soul. We want the paper to express on, but don't notice the living trees. We want to be 'someone' but we deny the heredity of our ancestry. We seek creativity without destruction; experience without suffering; gain without loss; relaxation without physical sensation; and arrival without agreeing to being here. It's no wonder we despair.

Yet, to strive to negate our own Personality is as futile as attempting to negate the living manifestation of any form. The belief that awakening depends on negation is akin to the belief that existential peace depends on war, that silence depends on noise, or that space depends on objects. It's an absurdity.

All energetic forms are alive, including our most anesthetized contractions and the denser structures of ego. This means that when they are dying, we can experience ourselves as dying. When they are wounded, they bleed, and we bleed with them. In a wider sense, we could say that where we suffer, the Source of all life, the celestial sources of the universe suffer through us. We are never separate, just as no contraction is separate from the whole.

Yet the fundamental concept of Personality does need revision. When we accept that Personality is just an effect, then we can begin to fall deeper into the cause beneath all effects. We need to let go of the autocracy of Personality and to expand beyond it, but we should never expect it to cease to be. We will carry its changing moods and atmospheres as well as its inherited evolutionary process at least for the rest of this lifetime. But it needs no longer be either a burden or a slave master. Indeed, the Personality we fight to defend is often not here, we are far more in bliss, freedom and belonging than we acknowledge. It's just that the mind projects it there as an artifice of permanence, to evade its own limitations of relativity.

A large part of the tendencies within the Personality are inherited from our parents, together with our DNA. The subject of family trauma has gained renewed popularity out of recent scientific evidence in the field of epigenetics.

Epigenetics is the study of changes in organisms caused by the modification of gene expression rather than alteration of the genetic code itself. It began in 2013 when scientists discovered that certain odors with a traumatic history would trigger a stress response in mice of succeeding generations. Science later revealed the traumas of World War II were showing up in the genes of holocaust descendants. "Instead of numbers tattooed on their forearms, they may have been marked epigenetically with a chemical coating upon their chromosomes, which would represent a kind of biological memory," wrote Natan Kellermann, in the Israel Journal of Psychiatry and Related Sciences in 2013.

In 2016, scientists from Tel Aviv University addressed the open question: can this genetic damage be corrected? Yes, they answered, there is a high chance that healing the trauma in the grandchild, will remove the epigenetic tag, meaning it's no longer passed on. When we successfully release a cycle of trauma, the traumatic tendencies will not be passed on, but resilience to that trauma will. "We don't know exactly why this happens, but it might be a form of biological forward-planning," said Prof. Adam Klosin, who co-authored a paper in 2017 that suggested changes in the environment can impact genes for up to fourteen generations.

What our increased ability to delve into the mysteries of epigenetics is showing us is that the very form of our personalities, as sculpted by patterns of stress, resistance, trauma and resilience, is inseparable from our ancestors. That is, our worst and most inherited fear is probably not ours at all, but a feature of our heredity. With this in mind, the burden of shame at imperfection or the incrimination of unwanted feeling contractions can be vastly reduced. Not only did our Personality not start with us, we have the power to liberate it of afflictions, so that they're not passed on to our children. Our suffering is not a curse, but an opportunity for service.

According to expert in family trauma, Mark Wolynn: "These traumas are important, because they lead us on a hero's journey. We enter the path through introspection, through looking at what's uncomfortable, by being able to tolerate what's uncomfortable, and then by journeying in to what's uncomfortable and emerging on the other side in a more expansive place, using what was contracting us as the source of our expansion. Many of us don't realize that the trauma we are born to heal is also the seed of our expansion."

The fundamental concept of a fixed Personality is illusory, as it excludes possibility of change, evolution and healing. Personality is rather a patterning of stress signals, emotional responses and thought habits. When we believe our Personality is fixed, definitive and unchangeable, we contract the living opportunity of form and transformation. Personality comes to life where there is life; it shines through the light of the qualities of our True Nature; and it transforms through degrees of mastery in bringing those qualities into manifestation through the often-discordant wilderness of the human story.

The more we can relax into the qualities of our True Nature, the less the Personality is a problem. If we let it, it will heal itself according to an ingenuity that is beyond our understanding. Liberation into the freedom of Nonduality is not a movement into conformity, but a release into a Source unity out of which there is a free manifestation of the splendid individuality of any given moment. Nondual Therapy has the power to accelerate this unfolding.

The Dark Night

Between the inherited and conditioned structures of Personality and the qualities of our True Nature, there is a rift. This rift in form is often referred to as the Dark Night of the Soul. It's a region of pure emptiness, alive with all omnipresent resources, yet it can be experienced as hell itself. In the words of Joseph Campbell, "The dark night of the soul comes just before revelation."

The Dark Night is the dimension of the most denied aspects of our psyche. When we throw stuff, memories, situations or emotions "away", this is the "away" we are throwing them into. Jung has described this space as the unconscious (prior to the experience of Opus Mundi or One World), where the shadows of the psyche lurk, seeking energetic reunion with the whole through their reintegration into conscious awareness. This can be the dimension of trauma (separated parts of ourselves) that demands integration. It's the rift in which we can meet our worst nightmares – and liberate them into freedom. Yet there can be tremendous resistance to going beneath the layer of Personality. "People will do anything," writes Carl Jung, "no matter how absurd, to avoid facing their own souls."

Because of the threats anticipated in the Dark Night, rings of existential states shield us off from this realm. These core states are also inherited and tend to be carried collectively in the atmospheres of a family, home or nation. These states include boredom – that drives us away from direct experience to seek egoic distraction in the 'outer' world; states of 'nothing' – not an empty nothing, but a thick, resistant, 'nothing' of energetic denial; states of depression (which can become chronic, as pressure to integrate the whole increases); and states of negativity (in the form of attitudes). Many aspects of Personality are crafted by these states that aim to shield us from the Dark Night.

The Dark Night is where we fall with our consciousness when the known patterns of Personality break down. It's like an ocean under an infinite sky.

But the ocean seems toxic, and the sky seems filled with a dense mist of suffering. The mist will be characterized by a denied part of an energetic contraction: such as betrayal, abandonment, grief, negativity or abuse. These atmospheres become the sky of experience and we breathe them in and out as if they were the baseline of consciousness. The denied parts of experience become like formless gods in this foggy wilderness, and the suffering can seem uncontainable and absolute.

Being in the Dark Night can feel like bleeding out. As if we had an open wound, the energetic pain of broken personhood flows through and out of us. Physical posture and gait will often reflect this energetic phenomenon of bleeding to death. Yet at a certain stage the bleeding will stop, possibly transforming to an endless flow of quality, out of a stillness that is beyond the conditions formally laid down by the stress patterns of Personality.

Compassion, mercy and grace are all needed through these periods of intense suffering, as well as the assurance that it will pass. Attempts to distract from the pain simply defer it, replacing it with the dread of sudden reappearance. In doing this, the therapist has a deep responsibility to escort the pain rather than encouraging denial or distraction. In the words of Bart ten Berge, we need to support our client in "enduring the unendurable." The part of frozen Personality that has died needed to die. We would do well to allow space for grief, regret and even the affirmation of its passing.

As Ram Dass writes: "The dark night of the soul is when you have lost the flavor of life but have not yet gained the fullness of divinity. So it is that we must weather that dark time, the period of transformation when what is familiar has been taken away and the new richness is not yet ours."

A feature of the Dark Night of the Soul is the stubborn continuance of the belief in the Separate Self. This suffering is all about 'Me'. Therefore, time in the Dark Night can be supported by attitudes that undercut the concept of the separate "I", such as gratitude, humility, service and compassion. These are like beacons of light that pass through the illusion of the Separate Self. Gratitude spreads a feeling of loving acknowledgment outwards, beyond the individual. Humility surrenders personal agenda to a greater whole. Service opens a flow of energy for the benefit of the whole. Compassion acknowledges interdependence, and that suffering is not an isolated, private phenomenon. These spiritual signposts can light the way between the suffering residues of Personality and the inner core of our True Nature. In the words of John of the Cross: "In the dark night of the soul, bright flows the river of God."

A prevalent characteristic of the Dark Night is the denial of the Nondual Quality of helplessness. We are born helpless, we die helpless, and in the space between, a core helplessness underlies all experience, including the experience of control. Denial of our inherent helplessness isolates us from universal resources and the support of others. It freezes our receptivity, meaning that it's painful to receive love, support, care and nurture. Without helplessness, we are unable to call for help, or receive it, and without that receptive invitation, our wider universe is unable to respond.

Allowance of our inherent helplessness means we begin to unfold the contracted state, revealing the chorus of need in its precise configuration to the infinite resource of all we are. Whether through prayer or reaching out to our fellow human, the admission of helplessness loosens the belief in the invincible separate Personality. The tired, old barrier of the Separate Self is crumbling.

In the words of Nondual Therapist John Welwood: "Out of our love for another person, we become more willing to let our old identities wither and fall away, and enter a dark night of the soul, so that we may stand naked once more in the presence of the great mystery that lies at the core of our being. This is how love ripens us - by warming us from within, inspiring us to break out of our shell, and lighting our way through the dark passage to new birth."

True Nature

True Nature shines with our deeper purpose, which is to shine. It shines through Nondual Qualities, many of which are described in Section II of this book. From this point, inward, we are out of the normative limitations of physical time and space. True Nature is often sensed where consciousness is free from identity, or when there is a fracture in conventional patterns or habits of the Personality. The process of the Dark Night is about the falling away of all that has obscured the prevalence of our True Nature. In the words of Nondual teacher Adyashanti: "Enlightenment is a destructive process. It has nothing to do with becoming better or being happier. Enlightenment is the crumbling away of untruth. It's seeing through the facade of pretense. It's the complete eradication of everything we imagined to be true."

The movement into freedom fundamentally involves an unfolding of contracted parts of the psyche into the intimacy of pure awareness in which all experience occurs. All knowledge and our very perception of reality depends on experience, and experience arises in a consciousness which is here before, behind and beyond all experience. Consciousness is not a separate thing but is collective and continuous. Even when it becomes obscured through us, the consciousness of others is still perceiving. In the same way, the qualities of consciousness are not separable. Where we can't find happiness within our own psyche, for example, we can allow the experience of it outside of the psyche: in others, in animals, or in the elements. Conscious awareness offers a magical invitation towards the unfolding of contractions in the psyche into the pure experience of our True Nature, which will always puncture the illusion of separation.

Sometimes called essential being, True Nature is at once boundless and intimate, shared and individual. The clarity of certain Nondual Qualities, such as freedom, peace, gratitude, happiness or esteem, can vary from one psyche to another. This is connected to subtler forms of evolution and can pass through family lines. Here, we're not talking about Inherited Trauma but more about inherited evolutionary themes.

In addition to the prevalence of certain qualities in certain individuals, each Nondual Quality can express through the full spectrum of resonance. For example, the peace of the ocean can be subtly different from the peace of sisterly love, which can differ again from the peace of a cathedral. Is there a different quality to love through the female aspect and love through the male?

As there are an unlimited amount of Nondual Qualities (they are all descriptive) and because each individual form is unique, the preciousness of the experience of any individual at any one moment cannot be over-estimated. We are all remarkably special — each drop a unique and miraculous expression of the whole. Yet we're not separate from the whole, just as a teardrop is not separate from water.

To get a sense of the individual expression of True Nature, consider how it feels to be present in a dark room with a loved one without seeing them or hearing them physically. There's no differentiation in pure awareness, yet an original presence manifests as a subtle, individual hallmark of True Nature, making it possible for you to at once connect, and at the same time sense the loved one as 'other' than you.

Many will report sensing the presence of loved ones after they have died, or the sudden Felt Sense of someone close that might be separated through physical space and time. Classically called extrasensory, this sense of presence is integral to our connectivity: there's a communication that goes on without words, normally beneath the threshold of conscious mind. This communication directly affects the way we think about others and our attitudes to them.

Outside of sessions with your client, how do you bring them to mind? Do you picture them in the imagination? Do you think about their story? Do you already build an action plan on how to fix it? How would it be to also blend with their presence — to explore the qualities of True Nature that are expressing through them, and those that are contracted? Could it be that much of the healing process is occurring outside of the therapy space, in a flow of blend and nonverbal communication between you and them?

The more we can attune to the Felt Sense of others, which includes group atmospheres, the more we will get a sense of our own essential being. The more we rest as this essential being without attaching to it, the more we release the power of pure Nondual Quality through all the psyche.

Nondual Therapy is about sharing the qualities of our True Nature, which is at once a celebration and an invitation for contractions to release. In the words of the Irish spiritual teacher Bob Moore: "If you are going to help another person, you have got to have something within you which this person can use. But with your qualities is related to the contact this person is trying to establish to his own qualities. And this is the initial thing, where the whole healing situation begins."

You could think of Nondual Qualities, or the qualities of our True Nature, as channels of heaven towards earth, or from Source through denser vibrations of form. Allowing the connection is key and this allowance involves relaxing our senses, so they can open. It involves a movement out of 'either-or' structures of thinking into the inclusive 'and-and' of direct experience.

When a conscious shift into authentic being is initiated, a natural unfolding occurs of the contractions that limit the Personality. It's no longer critical what we do, but it's imperative to be what we are. Being is recognized as preceding "doing" in every movement.

Source

The more we develop the ability to allow the unfolding of contractions in the psyche, through the cessation of grasping and aversion, the more our True Nature can manifest according to the intelligence of need. Yet the emanation of True Nature, or Nondual Qualities is not something that we can control, create or force. It's more about release or letting go of the instinct to freeze. For example, when we let go of the belief that innocence is lost because we are guilty, the quality of innocence can spontaneously arise, irrespective of guilt. Out of the infinite possibility of vulnerability, a melting occurs through innocence back to source.

Nondual Qualities are powerful and expansive. We can freely identify with them in order to open the channel — for example, we can say "I am bliss"; or "I am pure awareness". Yet if this identification becomes rigid as a contra to areas of suffering, then the freedom and expansion of the quality again becomes stifled. When Nonduality becomes a state that needs to be defended, frequencies of stress and conflict appear in the psyche (sometimes even open warfare).

To truly allow the manifestation of Nondual Qualities, we need to release them. Qualities are here to be shared. Yet we can't give them unless we let them go; and letting go requires consolidation in a deeper Source — a Source from which letting go is possible. This is the Source which Nisargadatta Maharaj called "prior to consciousness" and "prior to being". It precedes all reflection and all experience. It's the innermost tunnel of singularity, the seeing eye which cannot see itself. In the language of Nonduality, it's at once everywhere and nowhere, both and neither.

Beneath all forms of manifestation and experience, the Source is a perennial continuum through all conditions of time and space. It's imperceivable in the same way that an eye can't see itself. It's found in such practices of being aware of awareness; or listening to the listener. It's not an endpoint but a wormhole to unity.

Akin to a black hole that births galaxies, the Source can be known by impressions of itself and by its effects. It can be sensed through its qualities, and by the quickening and liberating effects which are at the same time accompanied by a fearless silencing and a sense of unbreakable stillness. It sounds abstract, yet this singularity of perception is under the nose, in every particle of normal experience – be it transcendental, subtle or in the simplest moment of boredom. Nothing is left out of Source, yet nothing is caught there either. Beyond all fear of division, it facilitates unconditional naturalness with all that arises.

At the layer of Source, the illusion of the Separate Self is gone. The one that is looking is the one that is looking, and it doesn't matter through whose eyes or what is seen. The sense of 'otherness' collapses into an endless play of experience through manifold unity. In the words of Nisargadatta Maharaj: "When the center of selfishness is no longer, all desires for pleasure and fear of pain cease; one is no longer interested in being happy; beyond happiness there is pure intensity, inexhaustible energy, the ecstasy of giving from a perennial source."

Consolidation in Source unity can look like a perpetual, embodied arrival into the mystery of life, moment by moment, which is mirrored by an easiness in letting go and a freedom of consciousness to allow multiple perspectives. It can be noticed in gradual changes such as increased vitality; relief from Ego; an easy emotional intelligence; a deepening relaxation; agility of mind; and a natural ability to attune to the environment.

The more the therapist can relax into the unconditional Source that precedes even consciousness, the more the flow of healing is liberated through the array of Nondual Qualities according to the intelligence of need. Therapeutic agenda is increasingly released as contractions whistle for their own remedies. The therapist follows the client, who follows the contraction, and there is an unconditional unity in the process.

A simple rule would be to say that if you can sense it, feel it, think it, touch it, it's not the Source, but a manifestation or reflection. Its stability, power and freedom are beyond human measure. Yet it's not solid: we can rest and expand as the Source through all layers of experience; and all experience is our experience. A primary resonance of Source through the layers of form is a refined, choice-less, unconditional care. This is why Nondual teacher Rupert Spira has described it as a kind of "loving indifference".

In therapy, consolidation in the timeless, boundless Source of the psyche supports the ability to let go, to let be and to be for real. It allows the release of agenda and the spontaneous emergence of deeper truth. This includes even the agenda to rest as pure awareness or to stay conscious. It requires no effort, as it's an absolute and pre-given unity. We don't need to wait for some sublime attainment to be present as the Source. All it requires is a default position of relaxation in the here and now, following the process with an open curiosity, without expectation or conclusion.

CHAPTER 3: NETWORKS OF LIGHT

"The nondual approach invests in the healing power of the unconditioned mind."

PETER FENNER

Processing the plethora of information through conscious-awareness is the human brain. The brain is the biochemical headquarters of information processing and as such, its service is best described as a receiver. Nondual Therapy rests on the experience that the brain is not the generator of consciousness or experience, but the processor of it. To put it more precisely: the brain is a denser vibration through which consciousness manifests into the physical. In the words of the author of Materialism is Baloney, Bernardo Kastrup: "The brain is in consciousness, not consciousness in the brain."

What this means, is that brainpower is based not on creativity but receptivity; not on doing something or expressing, but on relaxation and opening in curiosity to the unknown. The brain is a receiver, but it also needs to filter information to preserve structure. Like any organ of perception, if there's too much data, or if information is causing too much stress to the whole system, it constricts the flow. It's like squinting your eyes when the light is too bright or pulling your hand away from a fire when it burns you, only with the subtler content of thoughts, feelings and frequencies of consciousness.

According to Kastrup: "This selection process is akin to a 'filtering out' of conscious experience: like a radio receiver selecting, from among the variety of stations present concurrently in the broadcast signal, that which one wants to listen to, all other stations being filtered out."

Think of a Smart TV that connects to a global network of channels broadcasting live. Any channel is possible, but the hardware can only show you one channel at a time. The receptivity to channels brings possibility; the broadcasting involves a narrowing of choice, in which the selected channel becomes, temporarily 'the reality'. The key to this selection of reality is in the attunement, and this requires a meta intelligence which exists outside the box.

Normally, this position is predetermined by physical reflex, or conditioned patterns. But as the brain is encouraged to relax through Nondual Therapy, an opening occurs in which deeper attunement is possible. Think of a radio nob: to decide which frequency we want and to get the most clarity, we turn the nob from left to right, listening until it's exactly right. When we want to switch channels, we turn the nob again, surfing the white noise of confusion, until we pick up the station we need. This movement from left to right is a dance through duality. The listener is a Nondual position – the third point that allows balance to be found and that brings freedom of choice to the selection of live streams appearing in consciousness.

The physical brain and its thought processes operate through polarity: a little to the left, a little to the right. The evolution of the brain to achieve its maximum potential as both a manifestation and a channel of consciousness depends on its relaxation and opening to a field of infinite possibility through attunement. This means we need to be able to relax in the white noise of confusion.

The opening of the mind depends on a movement out of the stress cycles of biological survival, or the opus operandi of fear. Irrational fears are generated through cellular and energetic contractions of feeling and emotion born of trauma, as well as through the influence of the social field. As these contractions are released, we also see a relaxation of the fixed structures of reality as reflected in forms of belief and thought processes.

When habituated thought programs are released, we might at first experience white noise – or the fuzz of confusion before new frequencies of perception take form through the brain. As the client witnesses everything from the disappearance of old forms, to the confusion, and finally the rebirth of new forms, this witnessing can allow for a wider awakening and liberation of consciousness. At a certain stage, even the controlling movement of attunement surrenders to this deeper, unfettered consciousness that brings an inherent genius beyond any 'smartness' of the preconditioned mind.

Neuroplasticity

Historically, we believed that the brain stops growing after childhood. In this decade, science has established that this is untrue. The brain is constantly healing, evolving and opening for transformation. Significant changes in brain mass, connectivity and performance can be encouraged for as long as we live.

The brain is a magnificent receiver and data processor between dimensions of consciousness, including the physical dimension of which the brain is a part. Although we inherit our brains and their conditioned reflexes, these neural pathways are not absolute. The structure of our brain is not fixed. It's formed and influenced most directly by a timeless and infinite source of consciousness, and in this, it can rewire, reroute and evolve through time and space. The brain has a tremendous power to heal its disconnections and to release old software that no longer serves the well-being of the whole.

Neurologists refer to this process of rewiring as neuroplasticity, a phenomenon that is deeply supported by Nondual Therapy.

Neurologist Prof. James H. Austin took a train on the London Underground to keep an appointment. Anyone who knows the Underground can imagine that to the uninitiated, it can be a confusing web, with a multi-colored map of circular routes and dead ends that could evoke the image of a neural network. By mistake, Austin took the train in the wrong direction. He tried to reverse the mistake and found himself lost with no hope of making the appointment on time. Despondently, he ascended one of the long escalators to the surface to try and figure out where he was. Disorientated, he looked around, and perhaps trying to anchor himself, looked up to the blue sky. In that moment, his spirit expanded, and he felt a surge of unbounded, cause-less consciousness. He was lost, disorientated and late according to his personal agenda, but in that moment, he experienced pure, existential freedom.

The brain scientist underwent a spontaneous awakening out of the limited pathways of the conditioned mind. He had metaphorically and literally transcended the limits of the map. The scientist went on to pioneer the bridge between brain science and spirituality, authoring the book Zen and the Brain. In the book he describes that life-changing shift of brain function from thought to experience: "Atomic physicists can tell us in words that we are all derived from stardust. But Zen takes our interpenetration with the universe literally. Its insight strikes as a fact of experience. This deepest truth is not captured in words. Insight information, like a cool drink of water, has an impact at levels beyond reasoning."

At Harvard University's Lazar Lab, a plethora of research is underway exploring the powerful links between practices of mindfulness and yoga, and conditions such as anxiety and depression. Led by Prof. Sarah Lazar, the team was one of the first to publish a paper showing the significant physical changes in the brain that occur with meditation. Through Magnetic Resonance Imaging (MRI), the research reveals that experienced meditators have a thicker cortex than non-meditators, especially in areas associated with attention, interoception and sensory processing. Interoception is the term given for our awareness of inner states – that translates into signals through a diversity of neural pathways. When these signals break down, it has been associated with mental disorders such as anxiety, depression, panic disorder, anorexia nervosa, bulimia nervosa, posttraumatic stress disorder (PTSD), obsessive compulsive disorder (OCD), autism spectrum disorders and others. Thus, a direct link was made between meditation and overall health. Support of the brain's ability to receive information about emotional contraction is fundamental to the physical, psychological and mental wellbeing of the whole.

Loosely used, neuroplasticity refers to this miraculous ability of the brain to reform itself. On the level of neural networks, this is about connectivity, association and identification. From the Nondual perspective, it's about the power to transform our minds out of a predetermined, dualistic system, to access greater, non-discriminating aspects of human potential. It's about the opening of the higher mind that can oversee all duality.

The key ingredient? The disinvestment of our conscious awareness from the belief that thought forms are absolute, that they are fixed, unchangeable and that they decree who or what we are. Out of this third position above binary mind, an unbounded sense of self emerges which is prior to judgement: it's neither susceptible to judgement from the outside, nor is it judgmental. The cultivation of the ability to rest in the powerful, Nondual Quality of choice (Part II, Chapter 1), irrespective of decisions and actions taken – and even while the activity of judgement and choosing occurs – brings a flexibility and responsivity to the here and now that supports neuroplasticity.

To change our minds, we need to allow the insecurity of change. This is an allowance of the impermanence of body, heart and mind that can evoke fear around all that we seek to control. Often, what we want to control is our own worst nightmares. We try to create stability to block the potential shock of something horrible, but in doing this, we try to imagine the horrible to keep it at bay. This involves fixating the world – and the brain's perception of it – to grasp the desirable and to push away the undesirable. But this fixation dulls the brain's ability to perceive. We refuse change within the whole, to prevent our worst fears from springing on us. This refusal of change is a rejection of vitality in the brain and this rejection ultimately enslaves us in stagnating thought patterns.

In neuroscience, the maxim is that: neurons that fire together, wire together. This means that if it's been learned that spiders are a death threat, then neurons associating spiders with extreme fear will instantaneously spark together, even on perceiving a grey ball of wool. The more this happens, the more concrete the association becomes, and the more 'real' the fear appears to be. The more frequently we all react the same way, the more this illusion is shared and appears to be universal. All balls of wool are scary.

Neuroplasticity means we can change the structure of neural networks, possibilities of experience and our subjective reality. It always involves a rising out of the binary form of 'either-or' into the perception of the 'and-and' through the emergence of a third position in the mind that can allow both sides of a duality.

For example, although the arachnophobia has become the road most travelled, it's no longer perceived as the only road possible. New networks can form with the repeated creation of new associations by adding new aspects to the experience. The habitual reaction will stay for a while, but other possibilities are added which disinvests belief and dramatically decreases the biochemical survival responses in the brain. Thought patterns begin to reform, encouraged by a relaxation of the nervous system and effects that reward and support body, mood and mind.

Many thoughts are subconscious – they are active as energetic vibrations before they emerge as language or image. This is because we have been collectively programmed by impulses of fear and survival. Because this programming is fear based, our first reflex is to restrict our consciousness or to close the mind – even to our own reflexive fear responses. This is based on an immature experiential belief around perception – that if you don't look at it, it's not there. It's rather like the instinct of covering our eyes to make the monster go away or covering our eyes to make ourselves disappear.

Because such conditioned networks of repeated suffering are less conscious, they are also less available for transformation. We can't heal something if we are not aware that it's there. What the mind is unable to process will be taken up by the body, reflected in contractions around breathing and movement and processing through physical pain and disease.

In all this, there is an aspect of attending consciousness from above or beyond mind-body activity which is critical to change and transformation. This consciousness offers a continuous third dimension to the binary nature of thought and experience. Without consciousness of the patterns and tendencies of our minds, we encounter difficulty taking new routes.

Imagine that for generations, your family has walked a route to the sea. It's imprinted in your genes. It was walked by both your parents and grandparents. The whole community walks this route. Your feet seem to take that direction by themselves. One day, you get a chance to hang glide above the terrain. You see the well-trodden route to the ocean. It curls, climbs a steep slope, bends backward to avoid some life-threatening this-tles, and then twists back to descend a perilous cliff edge. Even though the ground is smooth, and the way is clear, it goes through a reserve of poison-ous snakes. Indeed, some of your ancestors were bitten and never made it – which is given as a reason for the ambulation up to the cliff edge. The very danger is taken as proof of the need to stick to the same route.

From above, you see another way that leads directly to the sea without complications. It's overgrown with brambles, but it's by far the fastest, safest and easiest. All you need is to walk it and cut out the foliage. Each time you do this, it will get easier. Nobody needs to die. In fact, on this direct route, you get the view of the ocean every step of the way. Your family might think you're crazy and a traitor. They'll warn you about the dangers of the unknown. They'll remind you of the trauma with the poisonous snake. But who would not forge the new path, having seen the terrain from above? Who would not share this easier way with others? The old path is still there, to be used if needed, but other options have emerged. What is needed to access other pathways, unrestricted by the biochemical patterning of memory? Relaxation and the disinvestment from known pathways as absolute through a willingness to release addiction and step into the potential confusion of the unknown.

Neuroplasticity involves releasing the exclusive rights of one pathway and allowing others to form according to new insight. Between one road and the next, support comes from a transcendental position that is not obligated to any path. At first, this unconditional point of view is provided through the attending awareness of the therapist. When we have the support of an awareness unrestrained by fear and the threat of outcomes, predetermined reactions become relativized: they lose their tyrannical hold on reality.

When a therapist is not present, techniques such as mindful breathing, visualizing a triangle, repeating a mantra or blessing, or simply opening the awareness of the physical contact with the feet on the ground can provide a supportive third point out of which to release predetermined patterns. This resting in a third space beyond the terrain of the individual mind unhooks the predetermined, conditioned pathway by adding first one, and then a range of possibilities to the inner landscape. Therefore, behavioral therapy can sometimes be effective. Through discipline and repetition, new behaviors are introduced that disempower the grip of established thought forms. It works from the outside-in, whereas in Nondual Therapy we work outside-in and inside-out at the same time.

Teachings such as the Power of the Now by Eckhart Tolle, provide, for example, a position to encourage neuroplasticity by resourcing the present moment – the 'here' and 'now'. In this book, we describe a range of Nondual Qualities that serve as resources in forming a feeling connection with a freely available aspect of True Nature that is outside the lock of duality. Through the wider freedom of a transcendental point of reference, new possibilities emerge, also at the somatic or unconscious levels.

According to holistic health advocate Dr, Andrew Weil: "Neuroplasticity means that emotions such as happiness and compassion can be cultivated in much the same way that a person can learn through repetition to play golf and basketball or master a musical instrument, and that such practice changes the activity and physical aspects of specific brain areas."

Neuroplasticity takes place in the healing of memories. Here there is some confusion and the idea can provoke annoyance and defensiveness, as there is a clinging to the established story – "What happened, happened! It can NEVER be undone." While this is true, (we cannot undo what has been done), most painful memories are locked in a certain perspective. They involve the re-experiencing of a limited collection of neural networks. Memory tends to reflect a mental contraction where the suffering aspect monopolizes the scene, and the rest is denied.

This is especially true of traumatic memories, where there is a polarization between the content of memory and normal, everyday life. When we let memory come alive in the Now, fresh details reveal themselves in a many shades and colors. The pain can be worse at first. How much more painful is the memory of the bleeding soldier on the battlefield when we acknowledge the backdrop of a brilliant sunset, with a melody of singing birds? Yet this is how memory begins to de-contract as the past comes to life in the Nondual Quality of the Now.

Experiential memory is alive in the here and now. Within these living qualities, memory can expand and focus. It expands to offer that same overview of the terrain but includes the experience of other people or the emotional atmosphere surrounding the event. Deeper layers of experience can be uncovered. For example, the pain beneath the rage: beneath that pain there could be loss, beneath the loss there could be the timeless fulfillment in what has been. When we release our grasp, memory can unfold into life, to allow more of what was there (and what is still here) into consciousness.

Without changing any of the established events of the 'happening', memory increases its plasticity, with new neural networks forming that reveal new perspective, identification, association and possibility. Just one forgotten detail of a traumatic memory can be enough to break open a fixed network. Think of a traumatic event in your life. Ask yourself a random question that you never thought of before, such as: what shoes am I wearing? What am I feeling in my hands? What smells are here? What happens next (after the story is done)?

By domino effect, neurons that associate problems as being fixed, predetermined and unchangeable also become relative. The very movement of transformation means the neuron that shouts "doomed!" in perpetual self-condemnation runs out of bullets. With this, the experience of transformation itself becomes associated not with danger, but with well-being, freedom and strength. Change is allowed, and change can heal the connective freedom of the brain that has been denied. Understanding begins which leads to insight; and this insight into the nature of experience leads to peace.

Whereas neural pathways were previously followed with the agenda of escaping old pain, new networks form under the incentive of freedom. This is supported by the whole body-mind that inherently yearns toward insight, peace and wellbeing.

Both language and verbal thought are coded with duality. Thought has its own resonance of fear and threat. In this, the mind, with its binary programs, tends to support the experience of reality as fragmented. It enhances and dictates the division between the 'I' and the whole, and above all denies the evolution out of its own programs into new dimensions of mind.

It should be noted that the 'and-and' of the Nondual mind does not exclude the either-or of duality, but rather, radically includes it. With this higher layer of mind, consciousness is not caught within the thought or concept, but rather has an almost playful overview. It's as if consciousness were a sun perceiving the whole terrain of thought beneath: it can see both left and right, surface and depth, without getting caught in contraction. Out of higher mind, we can witness thoughts seeding and connecting in silence before they even reach expression. From higher mind, we can truly listen to the miracle of thought – this voice inside the head – and marvel at its capacity. From higher mind, we can also rest in the deeper wisdom of the transience and emptiness of thought. A Nondual position does not cancel out duality, rather, it radically allows both sides of a duality to come to life and to dance in freedom.

All perception, especially visual, is partially a function of imagination. In this way, it's creative. In real time, our imagination can shape the beauty of our rival into awkward ugliness, or the relaxed pose of our bank manager into an embodiment of greed. As the visual aspect of mind is connected so strongly with what we consider 'real' ("seeing is believing"), the realization that seeing is not believing can be unnerving. Yet if we can release the belief that our imagined forms are objectively real, then we will also be able to allow the deepening, enrichment and expansion of creative imagination in the Here and Now.

Mirror Neurons

A foundational premise of Nondual Therapy is that the concept of a definitively Separate Self is illusory. The belief in separation affects not only forms of thought but also patterns of stress, depression and energetic contraction throughout the whole psyche. We can perhaps release the 6idea that our consciousness is separate from the consciousness of others, but it can be hard to allow that also our bodies, minds, feelings and emotions are inseparable from the whole. This is because the intimacy of experience is clearly differentiated from the experience of another, and we believe that difference means separation and that this separation is absolute. On inspection, this belief is incongruous, although pervasive. Does the difference between the fingernail and the finger mean there is an absolute separation between the two? Does the difference between a mother and child set them eternally apart?

In neuroscience, the discovery of Mirror Neurons has brought fresh scientific insights into the inseparability of experience. In the 'eighties and 'nineties, a group of Italian neurophysiologists at the University of Parma comprised of Rizzolatti, Di Pellegrino, Fadiga, Fogassi, and Gallese had the ventral premotor cortex of a macaque monkey hooked up with electrodes to study neurons associated with the control of hand and mouth actions. Each time the monkey picked up a peanut to eat, his brain would cause the monitor to go: "click, click, click". One day, a researcher himself took a peanut to eat, as the monkey watched him. The same sound "click, click, click," resonated through the monitor, although the monkey hadn't moved an inch. The monkey's brain was reacting as if the monkey had taken and eaten the peanut herself. Repeated tests showed that an observed action in another can signal the same brain response as first-hand physical action. The neurons that fired in response to actions taken by someone else's body have been called Mirror Neurons, which display a phenomenon often referred to as 'monkey see, monkey do'.

We can recognize these Mirror Neurons at work: each time we clutch our heads in despair when the footballer misses the penalty; when we're watching a drama on TV; or in any emotional engagement with second-hand situations. They are also at work where we empathize with ourselves through memories of the past or imagination about ourselves in future situations. We imagine the gourmet meal we're going to have in the evening and our mouth salivates. We remember the death of a loved one years ago, and tears come to our eyes. Mirror Neurons are at play in empathic resonance within and beyond the borders of the Separate Self.

As with all neurons, Mirror Neurons multiply according to use. If we don't use them, we lose them. This is where meditation plays a fundamental role in opening the resonant connectivity of the psyche with its whole environment as well as extending the capacity for living experience. The control system over the free deployment of Mirror Neurons is found in the prefrontal cortex – which is the forehead area of the pineal chakra or the third eye. From this area, a quick check is made to the sense perception of the skin surface of the body to establish if emerging experience is local to the body or elsewhere, and based on this, the firing of Mirror Neurons is partially inhibited. Through our prevalent conditioning, if the experience is established as with the 'other', we tend to create distance and restrict empathy. Through bringing relaxation, stability and peace to the region of the prefrontal cortex, meditation will open the possibility of the 'and-and'. Also, I know it's not my body, but at the same time, I am able to share the experience. The duality of 'Me Versus You' is no longer required.

In the words of neuroscientist Prof. V.S. Ramachandran to the Dalai Lama: "Through practices like meditation, maybe you can temporarily suspend the inhibition (on Mirror Neurons), so you are able to genuinely adopt another person's point of view and achieve genuine compassion."

The functioning of Mirror Neurons is not hocus-pocus but a gift of nature. Perhaps you recall watching a dog moving its mouth in rhythm with your own chewing of food. Experience is a shared field, and it's the brain that restricts how much of it we're ready to take in, and what kind of experience we choose to allow. The possibilities of experience are unlimited, but we're so often limited by a combination of fear and belief. For example, we can be simply unable to perceive that which we don't believe is there.

A large part of therapy comes with questioning the allocation of feelings and emotions. This means encouraging the client to take emotional responsibility for the experiences resonating through the psyche. For example, if we walk into a room full of grieving people, does it not affect us? Doesn't grief awaken within our own experience? To make this clear, we are not responsible for the behavior of others, but we are one hundred percent responsible for the effects of the environment on our direct experience.

Often, we will want to blame other people for uncomfortable emotions, or we can get confused as to whether these feelings are ours or from other people. For example, when a client is describing the anger of their partner, it's worth affirming that they also experienced that anger. Anger in the togetherness is experienced by both parts, even if one side is surprised and the other gave the first expression. The couple is sharing a contraction of anger and fear. Just this experiential allowance can open the way to the Nondual Quality of compassion.

Perhaps science will at some stage recognize that these Mirror Neurons – which are found throughout the brain - are about unconditioned consciousness. When Mirror Neurons are empathic to their own vibration of consciousness (when the brain becomes conscious of consciousness), an awakened freedom from form emerges which is directly conducive to neuroplasticity and the evolution of structures of belief. The experience of release, freedom and power that occurs when consciousness is liberated from the filtration system of the brain over the possibilities of experience is what many refer to as spiritual awakening.

This liberation is facilitated first by a deep relaxation of the control centers of the brain through a disinvestment from the absolute importance of thoughts, beliefs and the energetic web of Personality. This disinvestment allows attunement and the emergence of one who can consciously attune to different fields of experience or different atmospheres. In this, attunement depends on the release of the grasping towards either-or structures. Only then can we turn the dial. For example, we can walk into a room full of frightened people and we can attune to the fear in the room. At the same time, and out of freedom, we can also attune to the care in the room, or to the anger outside the room, or to eternal peace in the universe. At a certain stage, control of the tuning system is surrendered as a trust develops in a higher form of attunement arising out of pure consciousness: the instantaneous attunement of perception according to the needs of the whole. This kind of liberation involves the surrender of the belief that we are individually in control, as well as beliefs in judgement. There are no mistakes. Everything has value in the transpersonal play of experience.

The discovery of Mirror Neurons also introduces a scientific premise for the intuitive wisdom of transmission. Spiritual transmission is when an experience is passed between teacher and student without words, explanations or suggestion – simply through vibration. Transmission occurs when there is a strong resonance in a field and the context is safe enough to allow synchronization of the Felt Sense. Operating beneath the threshold of the conscious mind, it involves the sharing of the deeper experiential layers of our True Nature. This has direct relevance for Nondual Therapy as the foundational methodology is based on resonance, and on the understanding that the therapist can only awaken the Nondual Qualities of our True Nature through being themselves consolidated to some degree in these qualities. For example, when a child abuser is confessing the agony behind his behavior, is the therapist able to relax in the resonance of purity? When sitting in a prison cell with a murderer, can the resonance of innocence breath freely, even within all the conditions of guilt?

The baseline of resonant transmission in a therapy session will be found in the ability to relax into the physical body, beyond the grasp of the story, in the Here and Now. This relaxation of the therapist will be transmitted to the client, modeling the deeper possibility of healing. Despite the drama of the story, relaxation is possible in the Here and Now. This is where therapy becomes somatic: the client's body is literally learning new possibilities simply by being present with the therapist.

To take a common example, most people will experience contractions in fear and anger. An anxious client could have learned to repress her natural, boundary-setting reflex of anger as she has learned repeatedly that anger has terrible consequences: people get hurt, she gets punished, relationships get destroyed. This repeated conditioning can create a situation where anger reflexes are immediately translated into a combination of anxiety and self-destruction. The first time she gets angry with the therapist (even though it might be a form of passive aggression), the response of the therapist will give her the signal of whether it's safe to open. When the therapist can directly allow anger, in a relaxed and caring manner, a new depth of trust emerges. There is an immediate modeling of a new possibility which can release vitality that has been habitually contracted, without devastating consequences. But words would not be enough. The body of the client is literally resonating with the relaxation within the body of the therapist, so the client could physically experience for the first time a relaxation in her own body, even when the charge of anger is ignited. This shared experience can be revolutionary for the healing process of the psyche, without the therapist saying a word. The Nondual Quality connected with the contraction of fear and anger is compassion, which is at the core of Nondual Therapy.

The implications of Mirror Neurons and the effect they have on our subjective reality through shared fields of experience can be even greater. Imagine you walk into football stadium in the middle of a match. How does your body and mind react to the roar of supporters in unison? Imagine now you walk into a sacred space such as a church where there are hundreds of people in deep devotion. How does this affect experience? Beyond the four eyes of the therapy session, the effect of synchronized experience can be magnified in group meetings. Here, at the intimate core of direct experience of the individual, the inner borders to the Source can collapse, precisely because of the resonance of the whole. What is true and essential has a powerful pull towards a brain that seeks stability.

When we consider the science of Mirror Neurons, we truly are responsible for one another. In the words of the first President of the Institute for Noetic Sciences (IONS) Willis Harman: "Because of the interconnectedness of all minds, affirming a positive vision may be about the most sophisticated action any one of us can take."

Mirror Neurons play a key role in empathy, but equally they are also involved with introspection and self-contemplation. The ability to have compassion towards oneself, and to be able to take time and space to be curious about the patterns and phenomena within the individual psyche is critical to Nondual Therapy. Here, resonance and transmission are also at work. Yet confusion can ensue. For example, if there is a resonance around the contraction of betrayal and loyalty in our psyche, we will also easily attune to the same resonance outside of ourselves. Our consciousness will be directly attracted to the frequency. When the contraction is seeking resolution or relief, it will lead to a certain tunnel vision: we literally prioritize the resonance of betrayal, for example, over the resonances of love, peace, connection or curiosity that are also here.

A lot of work in Nondual Therapy involves the awareness of these resonant patterns of attraction, and the way that it narrows perception. This involves opening and trusting a deeper layer of perception – the unconditional space of free awareness – which precedes, underlies and outlives all content of perception. Impressions arise and fade through denser forms of awareness, but this purer awareness remains, providing a neuroplastic position through which more possibility and greater freedom can arise.

When Mirror Neurons resonate with Mirror Neurons, we begin to enjoy the liberation of being conscious of consciousness itself, (or aware of our own awareness). We become unfettered by the tiny details of the cruder contents of thoughts and feeling impressions. When we realize that silence, for example, has manifold qualities to explore, our thoughts become less compelling. This mental refinement occurs in the Here and Now, where consciousness is liberated perception from the shackles of time (past programming) and context (a projected situation). The resonance of Beginners Mind, or pure clarity of mind, where consciousness is free of the burden of the story, (and of expectation, projection and conclusion), is also passed between brains through the mirror neuron system. This awake-ness and disentanglement is a fundamental part of neuroplasticity. When the resonance of unrestricted collective consciousness is accompanied with physical relaxation and a sense of safety, the possibility of transformation of individual neural networks out of habitual stress responses increases dramatically.

Autonomic Nerve System

The belief that the nerve system of the body is separate from the brain is directly responsible for the fracture of the psyche into the mind-body split. Autonomic means involuntary or unconscious, which means we have defined the human apparatus of sensory connection with the environment as being a wild card and a threat: it's beyond our free-will, unruly and fundamentally out of control. In terms of mental attitude, this subtle enmity of the headquarters of human perception towards its own interconnected apparatus undermines the sense of wholeness and disrupts integration. The body is 'other' to the brain, and as a source of danger or threat: it's not to be completely trusted. Because it can't be trusted, we are being formed under the collective illusion of brain 'über alles'.

It's possible to check this, right here, right now. Move one hand to touch a part of your body (such as the other hand, the knee, or the cheek). Stay a while with the sense of touch, noticing the sense of touch in the fingers, and in the body part being contacted. What's in the space? Can you sense a subtle attitude towards the body? Try to touch the body with unconditional care, or with a sense of belonging and notice any resistance. This resistance can also emerge as too much effort, frustration or tiredness. Where is the sense of touch? Is it in the hand, or in the 'other' being touched? Can experience be divided? Is the body separate from itself?

This attitude of enmity towards the body generates subtle atmospheres of fear and stress. Stress hormones such as cortisol await activation through any trigger from the environment. When they are released in the brain, they activate the body for freeze, fight or flight. Before they are released, they keep the body in a state of unformed vigilance – as if we were waiting on the eve of war for the first missile to fall.

In addition to the high level of cortisol, neurotransmitters such as dopamine, norepinephrine and adrenaline keep the amygdala charged, generating more fear. At the same time, there is a suppression of short-term memory, concentration, inhibition and rational thought – so that fast survival action can be taken. Yet when stress is ongoing and cause-less, there is a significant reduction in the ability to handle social or intellectual tasks: the brain's abilities polarize into all-or-nothing extremes, and the thousand shades of grey are lost.

When a client is encouraged to honor rather than alienate the spontaneous feedback from the autonomic nerve system, we can often witness this polarization of thought forms into dualistic, either-or structures. This also occurs where they enter a region of unconscious trauma. The Nondual Quality of discernment flips out into polarities of good and evil. For example, the new guy in the client's life with likeable and less attractive traits (all of which show his living humanity), teeters under the judgement call of savior or antichrist. Proportions get lost when something as innocuous as a meeting with the neighbors transmutes through stress into an apocalyptic event: abandonment becomes eternal condemnation; rejection, a perpetual lynching; shame, the burning agony of existence. As these horrors never really take form and complete themselves, the suffering content is excluded from the healing flow of physical time – never completing itself, perpetually repeating and continuously threatening the brain with a hijack of the field of 'reality'.

To put it simply, the more the brain alienates its own gut, legs and arms, the less it can function for the wellbeing of the whole. When thought forms react fearfully to the resource of the autonomic nerve system, direct experience is denied, generating the background continuum of conflict. Mental functioning is impaired through unanchored storms of fear-based illusion. The suffering of highly anxious physical responses feeds back into the illusion of threat and affirms it.

How do we break this vicious cycle? Again, through the relaxation into the qualities of our True Nature, even when our whole physiology is screaming apocalypse.

Whereas we're conditioned to believe that surrender to the nerve system will make us crazy, the denial of sensory input through the magnificent network of the living body is more likely to cause mental imbalance and to compromise the safety of the whole.

Much of the positive impact of Transcendental Meditation is in the behavioral facilitation of the Relaxation Response – the release of the nerve system to a natural movement from sympathetic to parasympathetic. Through the rhythmic repetition of a mantra, a third point of reference is found behind the changing weather of the autonomic nerve system.

According to TM pioneer Dr. Herbert Benson, more than 60 percent of all healthcare visits are related to stress. Stress hormones exacerbate hypertension, headaches, insomnia, irritable bowel syndrome and chronic low back pain, as well as heart disease, stroke and cancer. Chronic stress has a cyclical nature, that can creep up on us. It can lead to fearful physical experiences such as reduced immunity; dryness in the mouth, muteness and difficulty swallowing; cold, clammy skin; shallow breathing and pain in digestion. The physical helplessness in the suffering of these symptoms can in turn awaken fears of illness, insanity and death, which heightens anxiety still further. The net effect is an increased distrust in the nerve system and the freezing of uncomfortable feelings and emotions to try and dictate normalization through the thinking mind. Yet this mental dictation of feeling and emotions is as futile as the attempt of the king that demanded the tide to turn back. It fails, and often the last resort is medication that numbs and confuses our sensory abilities even more.

When we can trust the intelligence of the nerve system in its need to release voltage and retrain itself out of past trauma and into current contexts, it begins to function better as the sensory apparatus of consciousness. This trust involves honoring its needs, and allowing it to find its own balance, without investing in it as an undercover authority on truth or reality. Through practices of relaxation, it's possible for someone with a fear of flying, for example, to relax on the plane and to experience that nervous release of fear in their body, without suffering within it or believing that the plane is about to nose-dive.

Meditation and healing practices are often about allowing the parasympathetic side of the nerve system to do its restorative work. Through a process of pendulation, where one is taken into a position of high tension and from this back to a sense of calm and normalcy, a natural balance emerges throughout the whole nerve system. While the sympathetic is known for 'fight or flight' response, the parasympathetic is known as 'rest and digest'. When one is thwarted, the contraction will play out through the other. For example, the fight or flight response could damage our ability to sleep well. Sleep disturbance will by itself contract the well-being of the parasympathetic nerve system, which will in turn generate more stress. An overactive parasympathetic could mean a client is slow digesting new information, and defaults to tiredness, inactivity and a general retreat from manifestation (including restricted movement, refusal to take risks or difficulty with new activities). An overactive sympathetic will show in a perception of life as a constant crisis and a constant need for drama or emergency to fuel a sense of purpose or direction. In the middle areas, imbalance in one will almost always reflect through imbalance in the other.

In therapy, we will often find clients pendulate between areas of stress and depression. Depression is where the sentient process has been abandoned, because of the havoc the inner conflict has caused for the whole. We just stopped feeling the stuff that brings grief, putting the wounded part of ourselves to sleep. Stress is a natural first response to these depressed areas being touched.

Cultivation of the ability to trust the nerve system in its finely-tuned, restorative swing between the sympathetic and parasympathetic sides of the duality is important. The swing will not always make logical sense.

For example, the client can experience a sudden tiredness and sleepiness just when the core issues are coming forward, or a sudden survival panic at the threshold of liberation. The rule of thumb is to honor the nerve system in its movement of rebalancing while letting the rest of experience relax. It is possible to be relaxed while fear or rage rushes through us, or to relax through and around the frozen areas of depression. The life within the nerve system can even be enjoyed with curiosity at how vitality moves through the physical expression of ourselves at any moment.

To honor the individual nerve system as a part of the nerve system of the body of the universe, we need to find a deeper relaxation at a third position between sympathetic and parasympathetic activities. In this, the Zen practice of mindful breathing is a great facilitator, as breath is both autonomous and can also be conscious.

The nerve system often needs retraining in its reflexes to triggers perceived as a threat to survival. This training is experiential, meaning that the nerve system will only trust the outcomes of experience. In time, the system learns that a phenomenon that could have signaled danger (such as silence) can just as easily signal well-being.

When we breathe mindfully, a third position emerges which is outside of the pleasure-seeking reflex of grasping and aversion. This allows us to relax within the nervous process of attunement and rebalance. In the words of Zen Master Thich Nhat Hanh: "Breath is the bridge which connects life to consciousness, which unites your body to your thoughts."

The more we can relax and see the body as a direct manifestation of the experiential intelligence of life, the more the nerve system is able to open as a channel of information through consciousness. Where there was grey, color emerges; where there were stark polarities, we begin to sense depth and texture; where the mind once dictated polarities of like and dislike, experience comes to life as a sensory field of transformation.

In addition to the enrichment of the Felt Sense, there is an increase of unconditional vitality, wellbeing, clarity, and a greater attunement to the environment which means that the physical body is actually safer. This greater safety arises out of the sense of belonging which is inherent to the body-mind, and which in turn brings a deeper relaxation to the brain, which becomes more supported in its receptivity, creativity and evolution.

Like a flower, the mind opens.

CHAPTER 4: SOFTWARE OF SUFFERING

"We live in a time, a place and a culture in which the cognitive functioning aspects of the brain and mind have been elevated as the pinnacle or place to operate from, at the loss and exclusion of understanding the great wisdom and contribution that the heart brings. And so we've been imbalanced for a very long time."

DARA WILLIAMS

The brain is an interconnected biological form with high responsivity and evolutionary capacity, as brainwaves are electromagnetic frequencies that communicate beyond the borders of the separate mind. This means that, added to the genetic programming that comes with birth, the collective mind has a formative effect on states of being, thought patterns and beliefs. This begins with early learning and is reinforced by the social norms of education and mainstream media.

Submission to conditioning arises out of the themes of safety and belonging. We need to think the same way, and use the same language to communicate, and we need to communicate to belong. If we don't think like everyone else, we risk rejection as an outsider and this pain of rejection reinforces the tendency to conform. We find our sense of 'reality' through each other, but often, there is only a superficial responsibility for the form this 'reality' takes.

Conditioning is not just mental, it's also energetic. Atmospheres of dread, insecurity, anger and stress affect us whether we want it or not. Such energetic conditioning is active where we hold our breath; where our muscles freeze, and bodies feel awkward; where we lose our voice; and when we lie in bed, never wanting to rise again.

Although the impetus behind conditioning is to preserve unity, conditioning is often what separates us from the natural ease of belonging as a unique expression of the whole. Many forms of conditioning contract both the sense of belonging and the depth of individuality, ensnaring the modern psyche in fear. Paradoxically, this means that to release the true power of belonging, we often need to give up on the concept of belonging altogether and weather the fiery experience of rejection and solitude, in order to release the channel of unconditional manifestation from the inside-out.

Where we conform to outer authority, we disconnect from inner authority which is the unconditioned authority of our direct experience. This undermines our sense of truth and generates insecurity. This insecurity is fundamentally based on the illusion of the Separate Self. Only when we believe we are separate; can we be separately rejected. Only when we believe we are a 'thing', is there a 'thing' to reject. Only when we believe in separation, can we appear to be negated. Only when we believe in divided existence does it appear possible to negate, deny or lose the qualities of our True Nature.

Negation: The First Illusion

Nondual Therapy is based on the insight that we're not able to negate anything that we are. As Bart ten Berge states: almost everything is possible, but we cannot un-create. The belief that it's possible to negate any phenomena that emerges in consciousness is fundamentally flawed, as before the belief is even formed, the phenomena has already come to life. We can't undo the past; we can only deny it. We can't undo the flash of rage; we can only repress the next one. We can't undo a moment of touch; we can only disconnect from the memory. We can't cancel the present moment, we can only obscure it. This belief in negation and the resulting mechanism of denial is precisely where we lose our freedom in form, as our energy contracts to a greater density.

We are not able to negate any phenomena, yet we can allow transformation. More specifically, we can allow the transformation of beliefs, reflexes and energetic patterns according to inherent need. We are living beings, and as being is in perpetual motion, it's not stable. Beneath separate identity, our being is radically free, spiraling through and around the core existential qualities of our True Nature such as love, peace, or freedom. These qualities can never be won or lost. They can't be possessed, controlled or held. They can't be increased, decreased or measured. As part of all we are, they can never be negated. Yet the first contraction of our True Nature happens through the belief in the opposite – in the belief in negation, closely followed by the belief in measurement, limitation and control.

We believe that there is love, but also 'not-love'. Yet the very concept of not-love depends on love and is therefore made of love. Because we believe love can be negated, we grasp towards what seems loving and push away what seems to be love-less. But what we're grasping toward are only the effects of love, the love itself can't be grasped. Because we believe love can be lost, we try to possess it. When we believe we can possess or control it, we fear we will lose it. This patterning moves us far away from the only way to connect to love, which is to be in love, as love, unconditionally. Instead, we're left with feelings of abandonment, possession and fear. The belief that love can be negated disconnects us from the love, which is always here, as fundamental to who we are.

This belief in negation even obscures our ability to allow the core of our own existence. We exist, yet we invest in the belief in non-existence. Out of this, comes the impossible striving for the 'right to exist', and the decision to deny others that right. We believe in human beings. Yet we also believe that any 'being' can be negated. Out of this, we find ourselves calling others 'inhumane', stratifying the human species according to projections of fear.

A strong example of the belief in negation is the belief that life can be negated. This belief is so deeply programmed that we spend decades trying to keep life, without living, or without really experiencing how it is to be alive. Everywhere around us we see threats to our 'life'. We never even checked if this life is a private possession or part of everything, everywhere, all around us, that will continue long after this body and this psyche has passed. The belief that life ends is like saying that hot water is forever lost when the kettle breaks. It's a Source misconception.

Based on the belief in negation, we have radically misconceived our True Nature. We believe that care is an obligation that can be forced, controlled and lost. We believe peace is something we need to work for. We believe freedom is only where there are no boundaries. We believe honor needs winning through value and that value is determined by price.

Let's say we have an appointment at the shopping mall at 3 o-clock. This event depends on two limitations – in space and in time. Our appointment can only happen in the set space of the shopping mall and at the set time of three o-clock. The appointment depends on certain conditions of space and time, and these conditions depend on the existence of space and time. Yet we behave as if the unconditional parameters of space and time depend on the conditions. Without that appointment, space and time would collapse. We put the temporal conditions (or contractions) of our psyche in an absolute position and determine that the source of our psyche is secondary. For example, we believe that life can only exist through birth and death – that it depends on birth and death – rather than allowing that the very phenomena of birth and death depends on the endless availability of life. The conditions could never occur without the unconditional space out of which they emerge. So it is with negation: negation utterly depends on something being there before hand, so as to negate it. Negation has no separate reality from all that 'is'.

These consensual beliefs in negation – with accompanying psychopathy, control, denial, repression and oppression – create enormous suffering. Where there has been disconnection, we move into traumatic zones where the sentient connection with our True Nature is forgotten. For example, when our innocence is obscured, it means it can never come back: it's gone forever. When our purity is defiled, it's an eternal defilement. This is like saying that the mud that is in the glass of pure water cancels the water. Through this core conditioning of negation, we espouse beliefs that perpetuate our own condemnation – actively creating isolated pockets of subconscious hell within the psyche.

The belief in the possibility of negation generates a tremendous sense of inner lack, as we lose connection with our own source. Out of this disenfranchisement from our True Nature, we try to recreate those Nondual Qualities through pretense. But the image of the quality can always be shattered, the mask can get ripped away: the created self-image is always under threat. When we wear the quality on the outside, it can easily slip to expose the existential horror (we believe) is lurking within.

So, we try to possess the pretense of the quality still more, tightening our grasp. We decide that for 'Me' to be innocent, others must be guilty; for 'Me' to belong, others must be rejected. For 'Me' to be white, others must be black. By degrees, we have given emotional and sentient substance to an absurd idea – that the individual is eternally separated from the whole both outside and inside himself, and that we are individually divided from each other, from the planet and from the Source of life.

The individual form tries to survive, and this misconception of survival demands perpetual conflict with the whole. In this, the qualities of our True Nature become demonized. They threaten us as ideals that condemn the limitations of Personality. The potent purity of a new baby can cause us to recoil. The unbounded love of an animal can provoke violence.

These qualities shine on and they rattle and shake the areas where they are frozen in the field. The essential qualities of being shine on our perceived defilement and this can make us feel worse still. Qualities can be feared as death traps rather than welcomed as signposts to an inner space where death has no meaning. Just as we grasp towards the end of suffering, the conditioning behind suffering tightens its grasp on us.

Imagine there's a sense of belonging, at the core of any form we could ever take, that can never be taken away, and which can always be accessed through an open, inner door.

How would it be if the love we feel for another was experienced as a love that is never possessed, that moves through us and through all forms and which is never lost?

Can we imagine a peace which is always here, regardless of the condition of heart or mind, regardless of our wars and conflicting cultures? A peace that underlies all winning and losing; all competition and collaboration; all birth and death; and all thought?

Is it even rational to believe that peace depends on the end of war to exist? Or that love depends on the absence of hatred?

Such layers of misconception, with dreadful consequences, are facilitated by our fundamental belief in negation: that we can cease to be. Out of this belief in the choice between being and non-being, existence and non-existence, presence and absence, we go to war with ourselves. Life declares war on life and declares it an endgame.

Consciousness conflicts with consciousness; and experience competes with experience. We split the psyche into pieces and suffer an endless repetition of affliction, when all that is needed is to begin to open some familiar inner doors and to begin exploring who we truly are.

No Time, No Space

A core conditioning is found in the belief that we are definitively separate from each other and from the whole. This perceptive consensus takes differentiation and reframes it as absolute division. It states that we're utterly separate from the Source of what we are; from the earth of which we're composed; from our ancestry; from other forms of life; from the universe; from each other; and from manifestation. The belief in separation gives us an illusion of control and the urge to control is primarily driven by fear. Fear, in turn, can only arise where there is this core belief in separation, so it becomes a catch-22.

This fundamental conditioning of the Separate Self is paradoxically shared by all of us: it's consensual. Because the methodology of Nondual Therapy ventures beyond common conditioning, it could be received as conceptual. Yet all this conditioning – and the conditions of our suffering – are based on the concept of absolute separation – which never stands up to conscious inquiry.

Take some time and look around the space you're in right now. Let your eyes softly scan the objects in view. Are they separable from your seeing? Be aware of the pull of gravity on the body. Is this pull of gravity separable from the feeling of it? Is the pull of gravity on your body, separable from the pull of gravity on all you can perceive? At some time today, take a moment to unconditionally take in another person. Is this other person separable from your experience of them? Is anything that occurs in conscious-awareness separable from the awareness that allows it to be experienced? Is this awareness in you, free of content, separable from the awareness in anyone or anything else?

Thus, the deeper delusion of the modern era: the one belief we all share, that unites each mind in Western culture, is the belief that each human is separate from the rest. The inner world conflicts with the outer. The human world competes with heaven and earth, as if it were separate. We work on ourselves, as if one part were the fixer and the other broken, ignoring the one that has the potential to be aware of both. We criticize and humiliate ourselves, as if we were only the victim and the accuser were some separate, abstract judge. At times it can seem, that even our attitude to the ground on which we stand is one of suspicion and enmity.

Separation is our conditioned default, and based on this belief, humanity is at war with itself. Separation demands us to see an experience as 'other' to who we are. Having made it 'other', we judge it. In judgement, we decide what we want and what we don't. We then try to withdraw consciousness from what we don't want, as if that would negate it. Clearly, to negate what has already been seen in consciousness is a lie. But consciousness brings life, and when it's withdrawn, it can make uncomfortable thoughts and feelings go away (for a while).

Thus, the inner judge or critic is born. Judgement (when taken as an arbitrator of reality) splits the psyche into the stuff it likes and the stuff it wants to get rid of. The desirable stuff is owned, and the undesirable is abandoned. Yet the undesirable is still there, repressed, now with the added suffering of abandonment. A complex of conflict is formed within the psyche, in which experience becomes fractured through apparently opposing and incompatible opposites. This energetic density in turn encourages the belief that all experience should be dictated by the mind. When the mind fails in its grasp of 'reality', confusion ensues, which creates more fear and generates an increasing irrational cleaving towards structures of belief.

Take the example of 'Human Versus Nature'. Nature is ultimately beyond the control of the human mind. Volcanic eruption, hurricane, earthquake, drought or plague can disempower humanity in a moment. We are helpless in nature, just as in birth and death. Because we are afraid, we create a separation. We talk of nature as if the human were not part of it; as if our bodies and minds were not mammalian, as if we have a separate existence from the sun, moon or even the oxygen in the air. Nature is perceived as an unruly 'thing' outside of our cities, and sometimes showing up in the cracks in the concrete. Nature is a threat to our sanity, our health, our homes and our communities. When we're surprised by its power and beauty, we try to grasp the pleasurable aspects and to control the fearful. Most of all, we collectively negate the magnificence of nature by withdrawing our consciousness behind a shield of separation. We see trees in our boulevards as if they were furniture, not living beings. We relegate animals as inferior life-forms, as if life could be measured, rationed and quality tested. We ignore the miracle of our own breathing and attempt to repress and control the spontaneous intelligence of our own bodies.

Yet we are nature itself. It never was separate from our bodies, emotions and minds. We are nature in action. Even the current misconception of the Separate Self is a natural phenomenon – part of the pendulating movement of evolution as the individual expands through unity.

The idea of absolute separation is a fallacy, yet much as we depend on inherent unity, it bothers us. We shrink our perception into the consensually understood concept of separation and deny one of the greatest resources available to the living brain – the resource of its own Source.

Baruch Spinoza put it well: "Whatsoever is contrary to nature is contrary to reason, and whatsoever is contrary to reason is absurd." Yet, we continue to move as if we are essentially contrary to nature. We forgot what it is to shine as the sun; to rage as a storm; to be unbounded as the sky and to express with the spontaneity of birdsong. Collectively, we're resisting life, becoming a natural form, which William Wordsworth called: "the still, sad music of humanity."

It's not enough to separate from the natural world, we're also conditioned into separation from each other. The same formula applies. We withdraw our consciousness from what has already been seen to try to negate it. When that contraction becomes habitual, then we become less conscious. We shutter up the windows of perception in a misconceived attempt to fix our world through censorship of experience.

In this conceived separation between humans, our unconscious shame can manifest as disgust towards our friend. Our subliminal contraction of guilt can show up as an accusation of the government, or another external authority. Our denied fear can explode as rage towards an outer trigger. Our unfelt sadness can color our world with an appearance of cruelty. Our resistance to life breeds subconscious attitudes that are often inherited, such as: "life is grief" or "the world is bad".

All of this is based on duality, and at its core, our first mental judgement is based on the belief in the dualistic opposites of good and evil. This belief has split our psyche through many dimensions, and it is a primary cause of fear.

The more we invest the separated, so-called 'outer' world with the energy of our inner afflictions, the more we depend on the conceived 'other' (our enemies, society, the world). The 'other' is what informs us as to who we are. In this, the Personality becomes shaped by projection. We disinvest from direct experience and invest in the imagined experience of others, to get a sense of who we are. We lose connection with our natural authority and delegitimize our inherent sense of truth.

As we give away power, we biologically experience a loss of vitality. Yet we must continue, so we draw energy from survival reflexes – the adrenaline rush that comes when a lion is approaching – and we must fight or run for our lives. Yet there is no lion and no immediate survival threat, so in time, we burn out through the accumulation of unreleased stress. We freeze inside ourselves, moving into sentient poverty, and we dissociate from direct physical experience.

We are born free as creatures of bliss, compassion, friendliness, innocence and curiosity. Among us, there is a tremendous love and natural belonging. Burning beneath our numbness, negativity and grief is a celebration of life and a passion for being here. All of this is continuously empowered by a universe suffused with peace. This peace feeds, soothes, honors and affirms

us from within. There is purity in our lust; clarity in our confusion; innocence in our crimes; and belonging even in the thralls of rejection.

Our sense of truth, freedom and peace is never lost, yet we have collectively
learned to deny it. We do this, because of resistance to pain and the fear
of suffering. We are still learning the secret melody of our sorrow and the
healing elixir of the truth within our most forbidden emotions. Yet in denying the spontaneous arising of emotion, we also reject the experience of the
Nondual Qualities of our True Nature.

The sword of judgement that divides our experience into good and bad is
both a curse and blessing. The effect of our current mental programming
into all-or-nothing dualities is a fragmentation of the human psyche.
Through the attempted negation of unwanted feelings, we freeze the energy
of life and this creates a density which walls us from the whole, reinforcing
the belief in separation. To liberate the Felt Sense of unity, we need to be
ready to honor these frozen areas of the psyche, and then allow them to
melt back to Source.

As these energetic blocks are made of repressed emotion and pain, liberation begins with allowing feelings to be felt with an open curiosity. It continues with subtle changes in attitude in which we release the agenda to
negate suffering, and rather, begin to appreciate it as an inseparable effect
of manifestation. In doing so, a plethora of secondary suffering can be released as healing through the path of least resistance. When we become
aware of a contraction, the space of awareness opens around the tense area
of density. This space alone brings relaxation and a subtle presence of loving acceptance. In this space, the contraction begins to unfold, merging
with that love. When a contraction melts into love or another Nondual
Quality, there is often an infusion of peace. This sense of peace character-
izes the completion of an evolutionary cycle of form through the human
psyche.

CHAPTER 5: NONDUAL QUALITIES

"When we have a healing situation, then all that happens is that you are brought into a position where it is possible to give to a person, because he has asked for it, more relationship to the experience of depth, a depth that you yourself have already related to."

BOB MOORE

In Nondual Therapy, duality is celebrated. We don't undermine the manifold expressions of life, but rather, we trust the evolutionary pull towards balance and harmony. This healing manifestation can be supported through a loosening of fixated beliefs around our True Nature – the qualities of our being on which even suffering depends. These Nondual Qualities are described by words such as freedom, love, purity and innocence. These qualities, in contraction, express in many recognizable forms of psychological suffering, as detailed in Section II of this book.

Yet it is a paradigm shift. We're invited to recognize the freedom that is present in slavery, or the innocence that lives in guilt. It asks us to recognize the purity of our shame and that hatred is frozen love; just as illegitimacy is frozen esteem; or greed is frozen gratitude.

Like ice to water, an energetic contraction of feeling and emotion will melt back to Source through reconnection with that Source. For example, if we can awaken the innocence around our guilt, the guilt will begin to dissolve – mentally, experientially and in its physical expression. If we can allow a soft love around the abrasion of hatred, hatred by degrees will fragment into the vulnerable and undefended love which is the source of its own shocked venom.

We try to address a fundamental error in causality. Conditioning says that guilt, for example, is in opposition to innocence. It takes innocence and makes it temporal and available to negation. We propose that guilt can only be born of innocence, sustained by innocence, and inevitably, sooner or later, will return to innocence. Without innocence, guilt cannot exist. Innocence is causal to guilt, and it doesn't depend on it. It is not innocent until proven guilty, but innocent, also when proven guilty.

The more we contemplate this within direct experience, the clearer it becomes. How can we even experience guilt without being innocent? If we were ultimately guilty, we couldn't experience guilt – there would be no edge to the experience and no differentiation. It would be like the color blue experiencing blue – it would find no differentiation through which to separate, only more of itself. Only innocence can experience guilt and we could even say that only the innocence which we are is able to experience guilt as a suffering – the suffering of its own contraction.

The qualities of our Being give form to our suffering, and our suffering transforms and heals when it melts again into these core qualities. In the words of spiritual teacher and author Rupert Spira: "Love, peace and happiness are inherent in the knowing of our own being. In fact, they are the knowing of being. They are simply other names for our self."

Nondual healing is fundamentally a process of relaxation, opening and falling back into the essential layers of experience. As energetic blocks or contractions unwind and return to Source, the sky is cleared for a deeper relaxation of the whole system – mental, psychological and physical – into naturalness and health. The release of obstructions can liberate both past and future. It can turn enemies into allies, and fear into physical awakening.

Do we have an essential nature? Or is our psyche formed through the evolution of ethical beliefs and historic events in the environment? The latter might be argued, yet common experience can reveal a qualitative difference between the ethical idea of being kind, and the feeling of kindness itself. One is a dictation of mind; the other is a felt experience of a Nondual Quality.

Many contractions are born from attempts to act and feel ethically – according to inherited beliefs. Those who are forbidden to hate, for example, suffer self-destruction or an exaggerated sense of self-sacrifice. Those who are forbidden to feel shame can be in disgust at the world or the opposite gender. We have been deeply conditioned to forget our True Nature, and to assume that Nondual Qualities are ethical precepts rather than natural arisings in consciousness.

Part of this conditioning states that suffering is inevitable, and that chaos is our default. We grow up with the suggestion that our True Nature (left uneducated) would be wild, destructive, lustful, murderous and perpetually at war. We grow to believe that greed, jealousy, hatred, boredom and guilt are natural, while gratitude, humility, love, enthusiasm and innocence are abstractions that need to be taught. Between the ethical commandment and the suffering of contraction, we lose connection to living experience.

We cannot force Nondual Qualities on the reader, without it becoming another ethical precept. Yet we would like to invite the feeling inquiry. Sure, we should be pure, innocent and loving, but what if we don't feel that way? We have no desire to dictate more feelings, but rather to open possibilities. When we release beliefs in the Separate Self, we could find that these qualities are always here, irrespective of contraction. For example, we can be inherently free and still experience slavery.

It can be hard getting a sense of these Nondual Qualities 'within' ourselves, even though we recognize them. This is because we so much believe in separation. Yet the qualities of being are also here to be explored all around us. Look towards a new-born baby and experience the innocence, freedom, curiosity and peace which is there. Watch the animals – the care that is there, as well as the qualities such as stillness, curiosity, freedom, esteem, honor and connection.

When we connect to a Nondual Quality anywhere 'outside', we are already connecting to it within ourselves. That is, because the separation between inner and outer, or self and 'other' is a mental artifice: we dictate it onto experience. When we witness the peace of a tree, the peace inherent to our consciousness is connecting to the quality inherent to the life within the tree. If we stay in this feeling of connection, the perfume of peace beyond the conditioning of separation emanates the whole.

Much has been written about the power of Nondual Therapy through the sharing of stillness and silence. The ancient Aboriginal culture of Dadirri has for centuries practiced group listening as a healing practice for trauma, as have indigenous cultures of Native America. Eckhart Tolle has taught about the liberation found through the power of the Now, and the healing effect of stillness, just as mystics through the generations have affirmed the restorative and liberating effect of silence. In all these restorations of ancient wisdom to the world of therapy, it's apparent that what was generally considered as 'nothing' – as inactivity or impotence – could be reclaimed as a primary methodology for the deepening of experience, thus deepening the release.

In the emerging world of Nondual Therapy, the power is not in the 'doing' but in the undoing of fixtures and foundations of illusory self through a prioritization of the essential qualities of our Being.

When we listen to the experience of people who have had a transformational Nondual awakening, we can hear many different perspectives. What is described are the qualities of pure being, or what has been called our

True Nature. We will hear descriptors such as purity, freedom, unbounded love, innocence, peace, stillness or freedom. These descriptors strike recognition chords at the core of ourselves. We have an inborn sense of all these qualities. Everyone is talking about the Source of all we are, yet there is still subtle differentiation.

Sometimes, Nonduality presents a formula for the spiritual bypass of suffering which can create new forms of contraction around the duality of 'good' and 'bad'. When we insist on one Nondual Quality as absolute (even if it's pure awareness), we risk undermining the essential need which is inherent in creation and within each phenomenon that arises. Absolutism can recreate the sense of separation behind an energetic wall that is now called 'Enlightened'.

The experience that all phenomena are relative, transitory and impermanent does not negate these phenomena. The need to negate, as said earlier, is the initial trigger of each contraction of form.

Let's take the metaphor of making soup. Every soup contains water, an organic compound (meat, vegetables) and salt. The first differentiation is already there in the raw ingredients of all soups. Further differentiation occurs through the variety of forms. Is a thick chicken soup the same experience as a thin lentil soup? Is it not another experiential universe entirely? How would it be without that differentiation of qualities out of unity? Without the unique and miraculous differentiation within the raw components of the whole? While peace, love and freedom might be core Nondual Qualities, these qualities also express as True Nature through differentiated shades of human experience, such as purity, innocence, belonging and happiness. They are all one, but they are not the same, and each soup of qualities is a healing elixir generated by the unique prescription of the contraction itself.

In this book, we seek to refine some of the formulas of manifestation. Rather than creating a new duality between the 'Nondual' and the 'Dualistic' world of illusion, we seek to show how the one Nondual Source differentiates into Nondual Qualities, which in turn contracts into dualities of the living psyche.

For example, out of the one Source, innocence emerges as a Nondual Quality. This innocence – at the borders between one human and another – partially contracts into the duality of guilt and accusation. What are both guilt and accusation calling for? Innocence. Thus, the energetic resonance of the Nondual Quality of innocence, released around the contraction, will pull the frozen energy of contraction back to Source; into the wider flow of being.

Founder of the Diamond School A. H. Almaas has identified differentiated aspects of numinous experience, such as joy, power, compassion and love – each with its own characteristic physiognomy. The well-known pioneer of alternative medicine Deepak Chopra also discusses qualia, the ineffable aspects of being that make up our conscious perspective. "Qualia," he writes, "allow us to connect everything together through a common property – everything is an aspect of one field of consciousness."

Bob Moore, a leading teacher of healing and inner growth who educated generations of practitioners and was the silent source behind much of the holistic awakening in Europe in the 'eighties, taught extensively about the healing power of qualities. He put forward a critical question at the junction between healing and Nondual freedom, opening many of the paths explored in this book. His fundamental invitation was to explore the relationship between the qualities of our True Nature and healing, asking: "Is there an attraction between our problems and our qualities?"

By taking a holistic plunge into the nature of contraction, through which Nondual Qualities get complicated, and out of which Nondual Qualities offer the midway point to liberation, we can experientially unveil the nature of this. For example, when we can drink from one Nondual Quality – such as the quality of freedom – this quality of itself, will open the field through an interconnected subtle structure of qualia, offering the potential to work with the psyche from the outside-in and the inside-out simultaneously.

According to Bob Moore: "If you are going to help another person, you have got to have something within you which this person can use... this is related to the contact this person is trying to establish to his own qualities. And this is the initial thing, where the whole healing situation begins. Here, areas where you yourself are defective are no longer playing a part, because you have risen to this level of qualities. It may not be all your level of consciousness. At this point in time, it is the level where you are active, and which is producing the attraction from the other person to you. But remember what I said about development: a true contact with that area contains no selfish or ego aspect."

What we are suggesting is an engagement with the subtler areas of human experience – areas that precede all context or story and which can be experienced outside of the conditions of physical time and space.

The release of any contraction – for example, guilt – into the Nondual field of inherent innocence, will of itself bring freedom and peace. If we bypass the sense of innocence, we might well bypass a contraction of guilt. Innocence could lead to peace and release, which will create a resonance through other contractions where peace is lacking. The suffering of this resonance is the invitation for the next stage of liberation. According to Bob Moore: "Spirituality is the combination of all these levels, which takes you into something different, so that you are moving beyond polarity into your qualities. Your qualities are not polar."

By degrees, consolidation happens in the powerful, living resource of our True Nature – the Source of ourselves which precedes and underlies all configurations of time and space. This consolidation is reflected by the brain and nervous system with a fresh openness and relaxation in the present moment. As we begin to come home to our True Nature, the need for structures of Ego and belief falls away, and the Personality moves into naturalness. This flow of transformation through reunion is resonant – meaning it is primarily energetic.

The evolution from one state of harmony to another will be shown by periods of dissonance. The Nondual Quality that allows this evolution – from harmony through dissonance and to a new harmony – is synchronicity, which is the perfect intelligence of need at a causal layer within each moment of change that consists of the causes of that change. In the mind, this will reflect as confusion; in the heart it can surface as insecurity or a sense of vulnerability; in the body it can manifest as awkwardness or clumsiness. These periods of disorientation within normative time and space are deeply healing, signaling an inner transformation.

In the end, and at the beginning, every Nondual Quality is inseparable from the formless, Nondual Source, which in turn is inseparable from any form. Yet the patterning of experience does vary. Human experience varies from the experience of a bird. The experience of one caught in anxiety varies from the experience of the executioner. This miraculous differentiation through experience makes all of us special, yet it doesn't mean we're separate from the whole and it doesn't negate the unity at Source.

The more we can first sense and then become sourced in Nondual Qualities, the more we can contain both sides of a duality to rebalance and evolve. For example, we can contain the energy of the abuser, together with the energy of the abused. Both energies interdepend and are inseparable within a contraction around the Nondual Quality of power.

In a radical sense, every position is a Nondual position. The whole is contained in every detail, just as every detail is found in the whole. Every moment is holographic.

Contractions occur where movement stops, and we neither let go, nor go all the way. When we go all the way in to just one particle of shame, for example, we will realize the purity of shame and our True Nature as purity. At the same time, irrespective of the healing process around shame or disgust, this is a finite process, whereas the quality of purity is infinite: its supply is endless and its nature indestructible. It is available in any moment, regardless of the state of contraction within the persona.

Every Nondual Quality is recognizable to us. Our very ability to recognize a quality (such as freedom), shows that we have been able to experience it. We 'Know' what love is, even though we might feel unlovable. This 'knowing' proves that the experience is there, somewhere beneath the threshold of consciousness, yet still alive.

Feelings can only be remembered by feeling them again - in the Here and Now. This means that even the memory of a feeling brings the energetic resonance to life within the psyche. When the experience is alive, when we experience love – without conditions or context – then any conditions within the body-mind (contractions, heredity) begin to first rattle, then unfold in the healing warmth of that resonance.

This a priori living experience of True Nature means that we have a sensory network that is attuned to the core qualities of life. For example, we have a sense of truth, a sense of belonging, a sense of relief. This sensory ability is critical to working with Nondual Therapy as it proves that no matter how disconnected a client might feel from a quality, such as 'home', they can still sense what 'home' is, and when they allow the sensing, they begin to experience it. The only limitation on experience is the belief in the separate "Me". This ability to allow the experience of 'home', (in this case), is that which opens the psyche to receive the conditions of 'home'. Meaning, when we reconnect with the quality inside ourselves, it will begin to manifest outside of ourselves. This is not magic. We just become more aligned in head and heart with what we need, and the perceptive universe of our psyche begins to move according to the deeper laws of attraction.

Let us stress again the formula of Nondual Qualities. First, they are an inseparable part of who we are, outside of the conditions of time and space which means beyond the body and the individual life story.

Second, because they are a core expression of Source, they are not always perceived. Sometimes a client will say they have no sense of peace, for example, yet the energy of peace emanating from them can be immense. When we are deeply consolidating as a quality, we become one with the quality, and the quality cannot sense itself. Therefore, our concentration tends to naturally move to where we are afflicted rather than to where we are free: pure freedom is often imperceivable.

Third, Nondual Qualities are inseparable from every form of life, including from the pit of our own suffering. They are never left outside of experience, never disconnected, only obscured by the narrowing of our consciousness in its agenda to resist experience.

To bring clarity to Nondual Therapy, we will give some pointers to deepen insight into Nondual Qualities, the qualities of our True Nature.

Qualities are Misconceived

Our experience of Nondual Qualities has generally been reframed by conditioning into a belief that they are in competition with other attributes. Take love, for example. Most will believe that hate is the opposite of love. That would make hate the equal of love and bind us in an endless war for domination. It would mean that love can be destroyed by hate. Yet, when we look to hate, we rarely find it in a field of indifference. It is as engrossed with the object of perception as love. It is formed by the object and is determined by it. Couples can flip from love to hatred in a second. It's much more logical to understand that hate is a frustration of love – frozen love – and to check this with experience. How many people would continue hating if they understood that hate is just another expression of love?

What we are discussing here is a form of 'Quality Complex', where the Nondual Quality (so sorely missed) is pretended as an obligatory aspect of personality. Often this is based on the agenda to avoid negative judgement and associated suffering. For example, we fake love, because we feel we are obliged to be loving, and often when we least feel it as a spontaneous arising.

The confusion of Nondual Qualities within the polarities of the conditioned mind is endemic. The Nondual Quality of silence is experienced by many as a punishment. When generation after generation, voices are silenced under threat of punishment or death, then silence begins to be experienced as oppression: it becomes associated with trauma. Right here, where silence is most repressed in an individual, there is the tremendous potential of liberation when silence is reclaimed in its universal power.

As you move through the contractions in this book, you'll notice references to other examples where Nondual Qualities have been reframed in dualistic terms by our conditioned experience and through the arrogance of the discriminating mind. For example, innocence is childish, and the child is inherently stupid; purity means non-sexual; and more.

Qualities are Evolutionary

Have you ever been deeply inspired, with a million ideas, but felt the impossibility of bringing those ideas to physical expression? Have you determined to give form to the boundless love you feel for your child, only to find the expression of that love frustrated, complicated and limited? This has been described by some as the incredible difficulty in bringing 'heaven to earth' and has led many to give up on the qualities altogether.

Nondual Qualities are evolutionary in the sense that they are not yet freely manifested through the physical dimension. The physical dimension is evolving to let their light shine through. To say it another way, we are in a collective process of Nondual healing.

Mastery of a Nondual Quality means there is resilience; the quality is free to be expressed and enjoyed with or without conditions. Contractions around the quality can occur but they don't stay long as they're not held out of time and space. This means that although we might experience contractions, they don't fixate. This is part of our evolutionary purpose as humans – to move through cycles of learning and healing to allow the pure manifestation of human potential.

Qualities are Eternal and Infinite

Nondual Qualities are unconditional – they exist prior to all conditions; during all conditioning; and after conditions are removed. The first conditions of all form are the allocation of a limited amount of time and space. Expressions such as 'Eternal Peace' or 'Unbounded Joy' indicate the unrestricted nature of these qualities. What this means is that Nondual Qualities exist independently of all contraction.

What is not bound in space and time cannot be possessed, except within the illusion of separation. While Nondual Qualities are everywhere, abundant and ubiquitous, they can't be claimed, manipulated or saved. Bob Moore once said: "Love is a law that operates in such a way that you and I cannot control it. We can only blend with it." This is an apt description of our True Nature is reflected through love. How could we possess what we inherently are?

Our connection with a Nondual Quality can be forgotten, obscured, confused or denied. Yet the quality remains at the depth of ourselves, regardless of changes in the way we connect. We are literally unable to negate our True Nature, we can only temporarily obscure it. In the same way, Nondual Qualities never get damaged, but are at Source of what makes even the concept of damage possible. The inability to lose a Nondual Quality is one of the indicators that these qualities resonate as a living continuum beneath variations in experience.

Qualities are Sensory

Nondual qualities are not created by the mind or thought processes: they precede all form and can be sensed in every moment. They are sensory. Just as we have a sense of sight or hearing, we have a sense of truth, belonging, or freedom. These subtle senses, moving through core recognition, direct the unfolding of contractions back to Source.

All sensory experience occurs in the here and now. Because we can only sense anything where we are right now, sensory effects depend on unconditioned time and space – which is eternity and infinity. Experience is not caught in time: it is always now. Experience is not caught in space; it is always here. Nondual qualities are now – because only in the now can they be experienced. Nondual qualities are here – unbounded and at zero distance – inseparable from all we are. Where else could they be?

The sense organs are not dead-end streets but are channels of information. As the spiritual teacher Russel Williams says, our sense organs are 'organs of consciousness'. When the senses relax enough to open, the channel opens. As a result, Nondual Qualities can be seen, felt, tasted, touched, heard throughout both 'inner' and 'outer' worlds.

Qualities are Inseparable from Conscious Awareness

All knowledge, experience and perception depend on awareness. In this, awareness is primal to the psyche. In its purity, awareness is the Source of Nondual Qualities.

Contemplate how just the awareness of another person can sooth and soften the severity of our suffering. Like the magical kiss of a mother on her child's injured knee, consciousness awakens Nondual Qualities through all vibrations of form, and beckons form back into naturalness and harmony.

Qualities Attract Balance & Harmony

As noted above, dissonance and imbalance can be part of a healing process. Contractions maintain a kind of balance and harmony through contracts. For example, I am the angry one, you are the fearful. When contractions unfold, this balance is lost, and we are confronted with unknown territory. This is when a Nondual Quality could be most perceivable. The quality will pull the energy of the psyche into a new balance and harmony. This is not the movement of rigidification through clinging towards old patterns, but an expansion into natural balance and harmony.

In therapy, it's good to recall that the precise amount of a Nondual Quality that a client is ready to perceive in others, is that which is available to them through inner experience. In the same manner, if they are negating the quality in themselves, they will tend to be cynical about its manifestation outside of themselves. For example, someone who is afraid of freedom in others will often be missing a sense of inner freedom. This can be a good therapeutic indicator, when a client is not yet able to open an inner process, but releases voltage through a commentary on the world 'outside'.

A cycle of healing through a contraction does not end on the 'inside'. We cannot, for example, experience ourselves as inherent innocence, while retaining a belief that others are not. The innocence inside finds completion when the innocence outside is also allowed. That can mean connecting to the innocence within a perpetrator, or within any other external 'demon'. Only when the breakdown of the Separate Self is accomplished in this way is the duality able to dance without any disconnection from inner peace.

To Summarize:

1. Nondual Qualities get misconceived.

2. Nondual Qualities are evolutionary.

3. Nondual Qualities are eternal and infinite.

4. Nondual Qualities are sensory.

5. Nondual Qualities are inseparable from awareness.

6. Nondual Qualities attract balance and harmony.

CHAPTER 6 DUALITY & FORM

"The experience of cosmic unity – being one with the universe – is an extremely powerful healing mechanism. There is nothing in psychology and psychiatry that has come close to it. Unfortunately, we would presently diagnosis that as a psychosis and tell people to stop it. We are interfering with a very powerful self-healing process."

DR. STANISLAV GROF

The world of duality is often spoken about by Nondual communities as a world condemned. To be caught in duality means to be delusional. To be dualistic, means we're not 'awakened'. Yet the division is a natural movement of creation. Splitting through Source is the means through which growth happens, just as through the division into branches, the tree fulfills its potential. It's a mental belief that dictates that when a branch splits into two twigs, the tree trunk is forever lost.

Duality is not a curse but is rather fundamental to creation. We have two legs, two arms, two eyes, two ears, an equal number of toes on two feet. We have above and beneath; in front and behind; East, West, North and South. Duality is creation and is a fundamental structure in the dance of healing and evolution. Yet two will always depend on the one, so that they can be two. The one is never lost.

A large part of our thinking mind is structured through imagination and memory. The moment we open our eyes and look at something, we are the subject perceiving the object: there is the perceiver and the perceived. The moment we are born, there is a self and there is the 'other'. The nature of form is such that our world is organized around the subject-object duality. 'I' (the subjective one inside me) experience 'this' (the objective world).

On being born, I am designated as either male or female. I am one or the other. This fundamental duality of male or female will biochemically, socially and experientially determine the texture of a lifetime until this body dies. But if a river splits into two, does the left branch not contain right just as the right contains the left? The woman contains the man and the man contains the woman. We all contain and express our mothers and our fathers.

We are all manifesting through duality, because that is how the Nonduality of the whole manifests. The art is to come to naturalness in duality; to reunite with the Nondual Source of all duality; and to dance as one within the manifold.

Even thinking happens through the movement of duality or dialectics. The dialectical mind, on encountering the unknown, will put forward a thesis of what this is. The thesis itself will evoke the antithesis of what is claimed – the opposite. Evolution happens where thesis and antithesis transcend into synthesis of the two opposing positions. This synthesis then becomes the next thesis, and so on. It is like a tree following its own branches backwards towards the trunk. Evolution and synthesis demand that we release both the thesis and antithesis – the 'thing' and its absence – so that we can contain both. Free thinking and an open mind always involve a freedom to dance through dialectics.

Consider linguistic forms of thought – the internalized spoken word. We tell ourselves stories. We teach ourselves; we posit explanations and we offer ourselves excuses; we try to compose a script where we're OK. We name things, all things. Why?

The naming of a thing is utterly arbitrary. A table is not inherently a table. Just as you are inherently not your birth-name. These are random syllables strung together to point towards a kind of presupposed 'reality'. We call the furry beast a dog, we don't call it a god. This is because we need consensus to communicate with words. In time, we begin to believe that there is an absolute connection between the word in our head and the thing on the outside. Yet there is no essential connection at all. Without conscious overview, words or thoughts begin to have a life of their own and develop beyond the reach of our influence. Rather than being tools for understanding and communication, they begin to define us. Thought is here to serve us: we are not here to be enslaved to thought.

Words, like vessels, take on energy from the feelings that accompany them. A dog to one person can be a fluffy friend, while the same word to another can contain the horrors of holocaust. We use the same words, but we are often not speaking the same language. This is because we forget how to listen beyond the meaning of the word. We forget how to sense the synthesis between word and object and the effect on the whole psyche. When this deeper listening opens, poetry and creative language comes forward. This is the kind of language through which deeper communion is possible.

When situations are complex or when energy is strong and inexplicable to the linguistic mind, images will often come forward in the forms of memory or imagination, or both. In the news industry, they say a picture is worth 1000 words. This is true also of our visual minds. Imagination and memory shortcut the slow sequencing and inaccuracy of language to throw up a picture or movie that best gives form to the experience, or at least an aspect of it. In this way, the mind can process what can be otherwise hard to contain. But at the same time, this quality of imagination is where we imagine our world and ourselves into being. We invest it with independent reality, when at best it is only ever a representation of living experience at any prior moment in time.

For example, I go to a party and someone is rude, triggering an old pain of rejection, perhaps without even realizing it. Later, I know that I'm going to see him again. I imagine his face in anticipation. Already, his features are uglier, his eyes spiteful, and his body language unreceptive. This image can even distort what I see in real time. That is, when he breezes into the room laughing, I hear contempt in his voice, I see his nose as stuck up, I experience the turning of his shoulder as another deliberate affront. Freedom and compassion are lost. All I see is a monster created by an a priori feeling of woundedness. In self-defense, I barely greet him. I am even sneakily rude. He picks up on this and decides to keep his distance as I'm unfriendly. The wound of rejection has created a repeating situation of rejection in the world, in large part due to imagination. Imagination and memory can interfere with natural manifestation, making what could be simple into a horror of complication.

Horizontal Flows

Emerging as a conscious being in an apparently separate body, the duality of Self Versus Other emerges. This core duality between me (on the inside) and the world (on the outside) is enforced by a web of contractions. Nobody gets free of this, until they can move beyond a belief in the absolute separation between oneself and another, to realize the illusion of a Separate Self. It's there at our birth, and these energetic forms of contraction between ourselves and others only continue to increase in proportion to exposure to the social field.

In the equation of 'Me Versus You', interdependency of form is forgotten. We lose our sense of belonging, togetherness and connection. Yet wherever there is 'me' and 'you', there is always belonging, togetherness and connection. In fact, without 'you' there is no 'me', and without 'me' there is no 'you'. I am your witness and you are mine. In togetherness, we are indivisible.

Togetherness does not eliminate the play between me and you, it just liberates that play. It frees us of layers of Ego and Personality, to relate in togetherness from varying perspectives to all that appears in our shared field. Anger surfaces – a perpetual signature of the Separate Self. There is anger here, in our togetherness. It's neither mine or yours, or it's everyone's and no-one's. Anger is arising here, and we experience it together. Fear arises. It's neither mine nor yours. I couldn't say it's only yours, because how could I know it was here, without experiencing it? If I experience it, it's also mine. Fear is here in the field of our togetherness, and together we move with compassion towards it.

Imagine you are entering a room where there is a group of people listening to one man who is raging about how awful his wife is. At first there is an atmosphere of anger. Within twenty minutes, everyone has become angry. They all shout at each other to get their opinions heard and no one is listening. After the meeting ends, there is still a simmering anger in the room. Everyone decides that the anger belongs to the man (and his wife who clearly provoked him). They shrug off the energy and go home exhausted. Who was not angry in the room? Did the anger channeled by the raging husband ever really belong to him, or did he channel it from some deeper trauma into the bodies of everyone present? Where did it begin? With his mother? With a random, fatal accident long ago?

Whether we choose to or not, we share emotional energies. Our bodies produce goosebumps and our breath becomes shallow, irrespective of what the identifying mind does with it. Even if our response is fear, it is the effect of the same contraction moving through the body and mind. The most we can do is to not interfere and to let it release and integrate according to its inherent energetic intelligence.

Often, what we are unable to contain on the inside, we throw out towards the 'other'. What I don't want in 'me', I identify as being in 'you'. We literally pass our suffering around like hot cakes with varying labels. Few are prepared to hold space for suffering and say: it stops here. Those that can, tend to serve as transformers for the whole.

When we separate ourselves from the field, we can create the 'other' inside ourselves. The higher the intolerance to a contraction, the more likely it is we will place this energy onto the 'other', whether it is another person or 'the other' inside ourselves. For example, in the contraction of shame (me) and disgust (other), we can experience self-disgust, signifying a direct fault line between the part of the psyche we own and that which we would disown. Other examples include self-abuse, self-accusation, self-hatred and self-preservation.

When we are free in a Nondual Quality, we're resilient. We can hold space for the suffering that arises in the field and allow it to pass through without grasping or aversion. Where we are in contraction, it shows us where our awareness is needed. In this way, we are all teachers and students of each other.

This duality of Self Versus Other is also at play in the belief that we are born with a whole new Personality. This Personality, (we're taught to believe), is somehow separable from the body we move in and from the ancestors before us. Research into epigenetics, however, has confirmed what the ancient mystical traditions have said for generations: our ancestors are alive in us. We carry their blessings, their lessons, their resilience and their traumas.

The stress patterns of experience and contractions are passed onto us through the epigenetics of our cells. Our personalities, complete with vulnerabilities, strengths, sensitivities and horrors, are inherited. They are not separate from that of our parents, or from our parents' parents. They are embedded in our genes. Research has even shown that unresolved PTSD is passed from parent to child, as is resilience. It's our task to transform what our ancestors were unable to process, or we pass it on to our children and out to the environment.

Much has been written about Inherited Trauma. In Nondual Therapy, we understand this phenomenon within the wider context of Nondual Qualities. In addition, we expand the epigenetic insights into trauma to include the less extreme areas of contraction. Through human evolution from generation to generation, we are increasingly able to manifest these qualities of pure being on earth, through all dimensions of form.

Healing is happening when heaven can shine through earth and through all dimensions of ourselves, even the most sinister. Individually and collectively, there is resilience. We don't lose connection to our innocence, for example, even when we experience guilt. This means we can relax in the experience of guilt or in a guilty environment. Notice how this resilience opens more possibilities for liberation. If we're relaxed in our contractions, they soften and open easily.

Mastery of Nondual Qualities in the world passes through generations and is part of our biological legacy. We can notice family lines spiraling around a certain quality, for example, power, with multiple perspectives and experiences on where the quality is not free. There will be victims and perpetrators, abusers and abused, and often both at the same time, until the quality of unconditional, liberated Nondual power is mastered.

Couples are often resonantly drawn together through the compatibility of such contractions and could separate when the contraction (at least in one of them) is beginning to release. In addition, their children will often be born with a strong connection to a Nondual Quality around which the shared contraction spins. For example, a father who is 'anger' and a mother who is 'fear' could have a child with a strong connection to compassion; or a mother who is 'desire' and a father who is 'denial' could have a child with a strong ability to find direction.

We are not our personalities. Our personalities are changing expressions of pure Source potential. In a way, they are forming and reforming moment by moment. We are not the contractions that often determine disharmonious forms of Personality but are the Nondual Source out of which contractions of quality are formed. We are not the suffering, but the living Source manifesting through the universe in which suffering is a transient effect. We are not the duality, but the endless Nondual Source that makes all duality possible.

How can you cut a cake into halves without first having a cake? How could the halves of the cake be separate from the cake in its wholeness? Every division depends on wholeness and we do well when we, as a living wholeness, stop depending on division to give permission for life. Form changes. Wholeness remains in every crumb. The cake is a cake, regardless of whether I eat it, or you do. Nothing gets lost, yet everything is free in perpetual transformation.

Vertical Flows

Beyond the horizontal split between self and other, there is also a vertical split. The borders of the Separate Self are found in front of us (the fear of what could happen), behind us (the denial of history and our ancestors), to our left (the contractions around receptivity, the pulling in of the female aspect) and to our right (contractions around activity, the pushing out of the male aspect). They are also found above our heads and below our feet.

Both heaven and hell are perceived as 'other' than the existential dimension of the Here and Now. In general, spirituality is positioned above our heads, in the celestial realms of 'higher' consciousness, angels and God, while profanity is positioned below our feet: the horrors of unconscious mind, the hell-zones of insanity, lust, addiction and suicide. We can fear that if we open ourselves to the spiritual, the profane will revenge us from beneath. Opening is a chink in the armor, a break in the pot, and where there is a crack, not only the light but also the demons can pour through.

So, we seal the pot of cracks and posit God, the soul, consciousness and all ideal forms as 'other' than what we are right now, located elsewhere from where we are right now. The supposed payback for this shielding is that we also get protection from our worst nightmares (for now). Putting our demons away for later generates fear. It keeps us in a stressful vigilance to make sure 'away' and 'later' should not suddenly become Here and Now. This fear-based strategy fails every time, not least at the hour of our death when the walls of the Separate Self start to vaporize as if they never were.

Mystical traditions teach that God is here at the Source of each of us. God is omnipresent, omnipotent and omniscient. How then, could this God be other than what we are? Yet when we objectify God by making it an awesome object to be perceived through us subjectively (or not), we create a separate form which casts a shadow. This shadow is composed of all that we consider 'ungodly', which is often that which is unpleasant to experience or witness. We wouldn't know it's unpleasant if we hadn't already experienced it, so we try and undo the knowledge through denial. This denied stuff gets shafted into the polarity of otherness – into the hell zones below the waist. That's where the devil lives, the hungry ghosts and the horrific nightmares that must never take form. That's also where death is, and the unwanted feelings of betrayal, abandonment, neglect and isolation that are generated precisely through the splitting of the Separate Self from the whole.

When the field of interbeing, or the togetherness and interconnectedness between ourselves and others (the world), is deeply severed on the horizontal plane, then we still have the possibility of transformation through the vertical. But for this, we still need to surrender our belief in absolute separation. This is the birth of prayer, when from the most contracted precincts of being, we call out to the unknown for help. This is the efficacy of the 12-Step Program for addiction, where a critical step is the acknowledgement of a higher power beyond the Separate Self.

Surrendering through the vertical always involves two movements – up and down. That which we think we are surrenders upwards, and in equal amounts that which we think we are not goes to earth, creating an unconscious ocean of rejected experience comparable in power to the posited God above our heads.

The healing is in the movement of surrender to Source, either through vertical (up or down) or horizontal (left, right, before, behind) orientations. Contractions implode internally or externally and move into the flow of transformation. We can surrender our guilt into the perennial innocence. We can surrender our shame into purity. We can surrender our fear into compassion. We can surrender our Separate Self into the one self. We can surrender our separate life-force into the force of life itself.

The lower vertical dimension is also very important as a resource, as it's here that we find grounding and the infinite resource of nature and the earth. When we see the earth of which we're composed as 'other', then we lose this resource. This is a critical loss, because sometimes the disconnection from a Nondual Quality inside us can be severe and can blind us to that quality in other people, as well as shut down the resource of a higher power. Yet nature offers a tremendous Nondual resource.

Can we feel the freedom of a bird? The social belonging of a flower? The esteem of an oak tree? The innocence of a cloud? The purity of water? The peace of a sunset? When we can feel it on the outside, we are already feeling it on the inside. A resonant, healing process is beginning.

The interplay of horizontal and vertical movements of duality are fundamental to form and transformation. It is structural to the perpetual revolution of the psyche, through which all healing and evolution occur. It's supported by the unmoving, yet tremendously alive, Nondual dimension out of which every form, at whatever frequency, emerges.

Contractions are forms, and every form always finds balance one way or another. We may have found balance by investing a negative energy towards the world, so as to feel less of our sadness. In this case, something positive from the world could make us feel unsafe and irrationally sad. We may have denied God to free ourselves from the perpetual feeling of condemnation. But when the wilderness of condemnation begins to suffuse our lives, on whom are we going to call? We may have vested the energy of jealousy in our known enemy, but when she suddenly moves with humility and wisdom, we will be out of balance with jealousy and idolatry until we find a new status quo.

Healing and evolution always include periods of imbalance. Imbalance creates fear and we should be aware of this effect to support the process of transformation.

One could imagine that the psyche is formed as a sphere, in terms of the spatial orientation of our experience. But another way to look at it is as a torus in perpetual revolution and evolution. What was contracted on the inside, later will appear on the outside. A block above our heads, for example, in relation to religion, will be mirrored by a block towards authority expressed through our fellow humans. A block towards nature could be reflected as a contraction around intimacy, or death. All contractions fundamentally reflect a disconnection from our own Source, the innermost center and are therefore formational on the level of perceived reality and attitudes to life.

Psychospiritual Geography
1. Inner & Outer

The decision of what is 'inside' us and 'outside' us is arbitrary. Everything arising in our consciousness is inside. Spatial distance is used to disown, project and deny contractions.

2. Behind

Behind the body is what we can't see, which translates as subconscious. In this, much of what we fear and many of our shadows can be posterior. Behind the body we can also hold what we carry as burdens. Also, our history is commonly placed behind our backs, as well as our ancestry.

3. In Front

Before us is our future, our opening to others, our sensitivity and our vulnerabilities in intimacy and in the social field. Structures of ego tend to be presented in mask form, literally from the neck upwards, affecting facial expression and posture of the head.

4. Left Side

The left side connects with receptivity, pulling in and opening. It tends to represent the female aspect that allows the penetration of inspiration into the circulation of form.

5. Right Side

The right side connects with action, pushing forward and protecting. It tends to represent the male aspect and allows the expression of inspiration into the world.

6. Above the Head

Above us is heaven, God, structures of religious or other authority, wonder and mystery. We are accustomed to seeing infinity only in the sky above our heads, and therefore freedom (out of the body).

7. Beneath the Feet

Contractions around sexuality, intimacy and naturalness will be found in how we touch the physical. Disconnection from nature and the earth is often reflected by difficulties with embodiment, spontaneity, direction and trust.

CHAPTER 7: CONTRACTIONS IN THE PSYCHE

"Suffering begins when you mentally label a situation as bad. That causes an emotional contraction. When you let it be, without naming it, enormous power is available to you. The contraction cuts you off from that power, the power of life itself."

ECKHART TOLLE

Within the evolution of therapeutic language, the word 'contraction' has emerged as a description of psychological suffering. The word 'contraction' brings the dimension of living experience to the foreground. It also has the nature of suffering embedded within it: the cramping of time, space and vitality; and the immobilization suffered when we lose sentient connection to our True Nature. The word contraction indicates at least three layers of interrelated limitation: mental, sentient (feelings and emotions) and physical. It's important to understand that every contraction will be reflected to some degree through all three layers.

When an area of pain inside us is touched, the emotional energy is already rising according to pre-established, inherited patterns, even before our conscious mind gets the chance to process it. Our mental consciousness is often a late comer. But at the same time, when our beliefs are challenged, this can awaken a contraction in feeling and emotion. The mind and the psyche will be equally reactive in the mission to deflect the perceived wounding of the psyche. In this, the physical body is the container, or savior of each contraction – processing mental or psychological distress through contracting muscles and withdrawing perception, which can sometimes express as illness. These somatic contractions will seek reintegration, and from an unconscious dimension, will continue to activate both contractions in feeling and mind, through the release of stress responses.

Through Nondual Therapy, we open our senses to the architecture of our personalities, and the somatic layers that form the Personality, or the concept of who we are. This methodology trusts the intelligence of life as the greatest healer in its natural tendency towards balance and harmony through the resonance of the physical universe. It trusts both the 'inner radar' and the center point of that radar, which is the Nondual Source of all life.

When we can rest in the ubiquitous, unconditional dimensions of our True Nature, contractions tend to fall away by themselves. At first, this can feel like the development of the capacity to stay in pure neutrality or stillness. The space is neither good, bad, nor colored with feeling which could be why we learned to ignore it. Yet it is pure, unadulterated awareness. When we stay in this space, a purification process occurs in which feelings of negativity, guilt, or shame energetically drop away, leaving us naked in the unconditional dimensions. This is also the space of grace, where qualities of our True Nature (such as happiness, innocence or purity) arise spontaneously like blessed winds. In this, our fundamental work as Nondual therapists is in clearance of what we're not. We can trust what we are as True Nature to arise from the whole spontaneously and perfectly according to the deeper needs of the psyche.

As expressions of life, contractions also contain the intelligence of their own healing. They are not to be rejected as afflictions but can be welcomed home as demons that turn to allies. With creative freedom, it's possible to affirm the energetic presence of feelings and emotions as subtle material – with shape, form, temperature and momentum. Because our contractions are living, energetic forms, we can interact and communicate with them.

These energetic forms of feeling are observed playing out at a causal layer to thoughts and beliefs. To put it simply, when there is angry energy, we have angry thoughts. Feelings of love and well-being, on the other hand, birth loving thoughts. Our language even reflects the living presence of contractions. Consider expressions such as "Something is eating me from within," or "I've got a load on my back", or even: "You're killing me."

These feelings exist as energetic substance, and therefore, it's possible to interact with them beneath the threshold of conscious thought. Often, when we release a belief which has been limiting our experience, it's then necessary to address the energetic forms (in terms of inner states, feelings and emotional patterns) that the belief sought to shield. A process only completes when there is the effect of a deepening relaxation in the physical body – as all energetic contractions are reflected by stress patterns through the physical.

When we begin to release a contraction, what was contracted becomes inflated. The compressed information is extracted and revealed in the light of consciousness. The therapeutic task is then to provide the trust to allow this to happen, knowing that just as a contraction can come to life, so will it be able to find its way home. That which can allow the unfolding of a contraction is never bound by the dynamics of the contraction itself. It's beyond the duality of the freeze and in this, the very movement of allowance is a Nondual energetic affirmation.

As feelings and emotions are energetic forms, it's possible to maximize skills of nonverbal communication, in which energetic correspondence or transmission, as well as body language, can penetrate beneath the threshold of conscious reflection. In this, the tyranny of conditioning is undermined. Experience becomes the forerunner, with the mind and verbal communication finding its natural place as a follower of the process.

Too often, conventional psychology tends to move from a premise that life is a kind of chaos that needs to be mastered or controlled through mental instruction, discipline or education. This finds expression in psychiatry and the use of drugs to control behavior. When we can't control experience ourselves, we seek substances from the outside to do it for us. Rather than controlling, we become controlled by the substance. The deeper healing would be to give space for the Nondual Quality of helplessness. Only then is consciousness free to move where it's needed for deeper healing.

While an affliction can be accentuated with a remembered story, the story itself is not seen as the definitive origin, but rather one transient description of a thread of learning that continues until the contracted energy is released and the deeper cause of the affliction is opened. When a contraction releases, unleashing the emotional content that was contracted, it can look like the opposite of healing. The reflex can then be to compress the energy again out of fear of consequences – repeating the original reflex of contraction. Healing support is given when the contraction is permitted to come to life, express itself as whatever, and to manifest in peace. For this, the therapist needs to be free of the associated contraction themselves, at least in the context of the therapeutic meeting. This degree of disentanglement can be achieved as a bottom line through the practice of mindfulness and an embodied resting in the present moment without agenda.

Access to Nondual Qualities can form a bridge to the greater Nondual space from which deeper layers of release are possible. The qualities are not absolute, but they are living, experiential signposts to the Source of all we are – a Source that will exclude nothing and which can never be negated.

Contractions are not the enemy; they are made of the substance of all that we are. This means that they are essentially living beings. It means there is both an interdependence of forms and an equality. The most gross and ugly moment of Ego contains the full sanctity of the whole miracle of creation. It's not inferior and it's neither negotiable nor negatable. It's the whole of True Nature in motion and in transformation. It's energy on the move – precious in its impermanence. Even our worst nightmares are expressions of the absolute on the move towards creative harmony. All we need is to the presence, time and space to allow our contractions to open into the wholeness out of which they are formed. When a contraction releases, the energetic content can find its way back to its Nondual Source: for example, anger gets absorbed into compassion; stress gets absorbed into relaxation; and grief gets absorbed into joy.

Let us state again the basic formula for working with contractions. The first stage is to become aware of them, honoring them for the intelligence within their own vitality. Resting in this awareness expands both time and space. The ability to stay with a contraction sometimes involves moving to a radically unconditional part of ourselves – an existential space of pure neutrality. It's a disinvestment without rejection.

The second stage is to invite the sense of oneness with the Nondual Quality associated with the contraction. We are now expanded even more deeply inwards, as we are allowing both the contraction and the Quality associated with it.

The third stage is to let go of the Quality, and to let it have its own life. At every stage, there is a processing happening to the content of the contraction and its emotional charge. It might be difficult to imagine that in order to feel and release the darkest root of a contraction of guilt, we need to rest in innocence, yet this is so.

Contractions are part of an interconnected web, and they tend to activate each other in hybrid form, deepening, sometimes under the disguise of evasion.

For example, in one session, a client first contacted her sense of personal failure when she compared herself to others. Tapping into the Nondual

Quality of learning lead her rapidly to a sense of shame (which came forward through a verbal diversion). As she tapped into the Nondual Quality of purity, which is associated with shame and disgust, she went colliding into another story about a friend who is a control-freak. Buried beneath this apparently unrelated story about her friend, was the quality that is most contracted: the Nondual Quality of Helplessness. When we arrived at this Quality and deepened into it, she fell silent. In this silence, something essential to the direction of her life's purpose began to unfold. It was a paradigm shift in her healing process.

When we work with Nondual Therapy, we disinvest authority from the contraction so that we may honor it. We give space so that we can dance in duality, but we're not only the dance, but also the dancer, not only the dancer, but also the music and the rhythm; not only the music but also the composer; and not only the composer but also the silence.

When we liberate the dance, we are free to rest beyond the dance: we could even begin to enjoy it.

Here, we offer a list of pointers as to the nature of contraction.

1. Contractions Deny Time and Space

Therapeutically, the introduction of unbounded time and space is critical to Nondual Therapy. The sense of a lack of time and space is at the causal layer of every contraction. It's important to note that the overriding agenda of all who suffer a contraction is to get rid of it as soon as possible. Unfortunately, this repeats the same denial of time and space that is at the origin of contractions.

The healing agenda can cause more contraction through the desire to negate, or to get rid of a problem. Modern techniques of somatic experiencing emphasize techniques of titration – taking a lot of time for little pieces of a trauma. In this case, less is often more. The agenda to deal with the whole thing at once and to become contraction-free can spiral both therapist and client into denial, repression and illusion.

On the other hand, the perennial stability given through the offering of all the time (eternity) and all the space (infinity) through which a contraction can come home to its Source in freedom, brings a formula that will work with all contractions, old or new. Titration simultaneously holds space for healing according to the contraction's inner need, and opens a consolidation in Nondual dimensions beyond form. In addition, it allows the maintenance of another key ingredient of transformation and healing: connection. Just as no city can survive separately from the sky, the earth, and the network of other cities, connectivity is the magic through which reunion and integration of the contraction can happen. When our agenda is expulsion of the contraction, or its eradication, connectivity is broken.

On the level of attitude, this asks for a radical acceptance of suffering, in whatever form, as it presents itself in real time, together with a freedom, softness and curiosity in being willing to take all the time and space to explore its nature from the inside-out.

2. Contractions Claim Autonomy

Because they are separated from the normative time and space of the conscious self-image, contractions become a form unto themselves. Born out of suffering, they continue to affect the overall psyche, forming it through patterns of rejection, projection, denial and grasping. We grasp towards that which appears as the opposite to the contraction, and we project or reject the shadow side. The contraction gains creative power at the causal layers of our perceived reality.

Because contractions are largely autonomous systems, they will be fortressed with structures of belief. Language will include absolutes – such as everybody, nobody, everywhere, nowhere, everything, nothing. These absolutes delineate the playing field of experience. They determine the limitations of thought and restrict the capacity to feel through subtle differentiation. Absolutist language is a kind of violent communication and is often the language through which the contraction speaks, whether about us, others, God or the world.

As contractions are autonomous, they will use any means to prevent violation. In this preventative measure, structures of ego rise that pretend the opposite of the wounding. For example, a contraction around purity will surface through an ego structure that is disgusted at the world; or someone that lost connection with inherent innocence, will accuse others of something.

The apparent autonomy of the contraction also generates grandiosity. There is a palpable sense of superiority around suffering and a killer defiance towards others who dare to trespass. "No one knows what it's like"; "Only 'I' feel this deeper pain".

Often, a contraction can manifest in a cynical pleasure at the suffering of others: "Welcome to my universe." Clearly, contractions of suffering stand as the building blocks of our sense of a fixed, personal identity which in other words is a network of fixed, personal limitations. This personal "I", walled in by suffering, is composed of contractions around the belief in the Separate Self, severed between inner and outer experience, disconnected from others and the environment, bereft of anchorage in the earth or the mercy of the heavens.

3. Either-Or Programming

Contractions are maintained by our mental programming that dictates a division of experience into a series of two-dimensional binary choices. I am happy, so I can't be sad. I am enslaved, so I can't be free. The all-or-nothing, either-or, black or white, good or bad splitting of reality defines our mental programs and our emotional reflexes. It is charged by fear and shows up as fear responses.

The all-or-nothing coding is based on the grasping at an object of perception and a simultaneous aversion towards its shadow. This fundamental polarity is found in every contraction. For example, a contraction around gratitude could manifest in the poles of greed and poverty. We want wealth and we don't want the death-risk of poverty. Yet wealth by degrees becomes impoverished, and poverty begins to look like freedom. The contraction around inherent gratitude oscillates in an argument between the two poles, until it releases back to its Nondual origin – gratitude for all that is. Along the way, we could despise the wealthy and ignore the needy. We'll act out the drama through our lives and through the people in our lives. We'll act it out until the contraction tastes the wisdom of its Nondual Source. From gratitude, we can take time and space for greed, and we can take time and space for poverty. We realize the endless, interconnected dance between the two in which one defines the other. We gain a freedom to be in whatever form arising in the moment. The closed circle of the contraction opens as a spiral of evolution. The energetic charge of the contraction becomes released as vitality returns to the whole psyche.

A therapeutic means to leverage the either-or structures of a contraction is to work with pendulation. A technique of somatic experiencing, this involves opening the horizon of perception to check what else is present. Finding a resource such as a happy memory, or a source of strength in the body, and pendulating between the good spot and the bad spot, has the beautiful effect of relativizing the bad spot. It breaks the skin of separation of the contraction and deflates its absolute status. Also, there is this, also there is that: and-and.

In addition, pendulation between two positions – one the contraction, the other a resource (a 'positive' feeling) – allows the opening of a third position, which is found in the freedom to change perspective, and to be able to move between one type of feeling experience and another. That consciousness which can switch attention is not inherently bound by any form, and with pendulation, the possibility of liberation emerges from the absolute grasp of any form. The freedom to move between states of feeling awakens and integrates through pure interconnectivity. The pleasure in the contraction awakens at the same time as it is made relative, as does the love, the longing and the striving for peace. Movement creates movement and this possibility of movement in and of itself opens the possibility for transformation.

Techniques of mindfulness reflect the spiritual psychology behind pendulation. Whatever is happening in mind, emotion or body, the consciousness is also allowed to follow the miracle of breath. We can be in pain, but also, we are breathing. We can experience pleasure, but also, we are breathing. We can be at the door of existential horror or in a transcendental state of bliss, but also, we are breathing. Breath is a manifestation of the natural flow of form. Taking in and releasing, taking in the present moment, releasing the present moment. The more we are also aware of our breathing; the more vitality becomes available and the more we become conscious outside of the conditions of form. The 'and-and', by degrees, replaces the autocracy of the 'either-or' program of division. Experience comes to life.

4. Contractions can be Anesthetic

At first, contractions can surface as patches of non-feeling. It can seem like there is nothing, yet this is not an empty, spacious nothingness – it is the nothingness of a blank wall, sometimes with a subtle resonance of annoyance. From the outside, it can feel dead; we touch it and there is no response. There are literally blind spots formed within the possibility of experience, including bodily experience. We might not be able to physically feel an area of our spine, for example: the nerve endings lost responsivity.

The nothingness of a contraction is like numbness. It's a depression of form, not a liberation of it. Secretly, the contracted nothing is full of everything.

An insentient contraction is one of the most severe, where the body is already beginning to take the contraction into itself, and to seek resolution through the physical. The lack of Felt Sense, is like a giant no-entry sign to the flow of the psyche, often reflected by a core decision that this doesn't exist (for anyone).

However, the insentience on the inside manifests as sensitivity on the outside. Our client who feels no fear, could be quite occupied with acts of heroism in others, as well as disgusted at others who are fearful. Our friend who claims to feel no shame, will be quite disgusted at certain movies, certain threads of gossip, certain enemies. Whatever is severely contracted on the inside, will be manifesting on the outside. It will be an attractant, a preoccupation, even an obsession. At first, the key to the core contractions of our clients' suffering can be found in the stories they tell of others, or what impressed them on TV. Often the work begins in the field – in their choice of anecdotes, or the kind of content that entices their attention and only by degrees comes home to intimacy of direct experience. For example, a client from England watched the film The Unbearable Lightness of Being and was enticed by the scenes of sexuality and betrayal. For her, the story was all about the impossibility of love. A client from Israel saw the same film, and what gripped him was the Soviet invasion of Hungary and the images of civilians confronting tanks. For him, the movie was about the impossibility of freedom and peace. Two very different versions of the same movie, reflecting quite a different process of contraction.

As the mind relaxes and allows the density of contraction to be sensed in awareness, the contraction begins to communicate. The healing instruction will come from the ingenuity within the contraction itself. In this, an open allowance and receptivity towards the signals from the contraction is therapeutically essential.

Because an area of no feeling begins to come alive in consciousness, the healing process can at times seem to be going backward. The process seems to fail, as the client begins to suffer more not less. Survival reflexes of freeze, fight and flight will occur, and perhaps dissociation. Old, irrational rage can come forward. This can cause a loss of trust in the healing process, and therapeutic support here can make all the difference.

5. Contractions are Living Energy Caught in the Past

Contractions are alive. Just like individuals, they sense the environment, identify threats and fear the pain of intrusion. When we touch them with our consciousness, they are reactive. They are affected by the environment. In the Chöd teachings of Tibetan Buddhism, contractions or energetic blocks are called demons. In the healing system Feeding Your Demons, introduced to the West by Lama Tsultrim Allione, we feed these demons the feeling quality of the fulfilled need which encourages their transformation into allies. Thus, Nondual Therapy is affirmed by an ancient heritage of spiritual healing. The core Nondual Quality is the ally to form revealed through the attendance given to the needs of the inner demon or contraction. In this way, every contraction that can transform through the infinite space of all we are, brings blessings.

When a contraction begins to transform, there is a quickening of energy. It feels truthful, because it is truthful as energy, but it doesn't necessarily have a context in the current situation. The conditions that caused the contraction in the first place – that provoked the anger, horror or despair – are left in the past while the energy comes alive in the present. This is referred to when psychologists talk about 'loss of proportion'.

In Nondual Therapy, no feeling or emotion requires a justification from the outside world to exist. It exists before the mind pins it on an object and it will flow regardless of the authority the mind gives it. Anger is anger. It never needs to be "because of" (the other, the world etc.). Fear is fear. It doesn't depend on an excuse. The attempts to justify negative emotion by putting the responsibility elsewhere is a fatal bypass to emotional intelligence and healing.

6. Contractions are Old Friends

If contractions hurt so much it can be easy to see them as enemies. We want them out of the system, all of them, as soon as possible. But contractions are rooted more deeply than the structures of ego that attempt to disguise them. They are threaded with intimacy. They can hold the unheard rage of the child, or the silent despair of a whole ancestral lineage.

Contractions are also suffused with the suffering and longing of our parents, inherited in our bones and rushing through our blood. When they begin to sing, it is a song of suffering, yet this is the music that could have weathered generations. Contractions are like children calling out to finally be heard, be welcomed, and to come home to the Source. Who would shut the door of life on an abandoned child, bewildered and hungry after decades wandering through an endless night?

We may find ourselves thinking about 'My' contraction. This is an effect of the dualistic mind. Having tried to banish the contraction out of experience, we then try to own it as a personal accessory of suffering. At least if we possess it, it stays separate from the rest of us and remains under control of the Separate Self.

Strangely enough, the idea that 'my' contraction is inherently separate from the contractions of others is also illusory. The anger in one contraction is the same anger as in another. The horror in my house is the same horror in the neighbor's house. They share the same resonance and they communicate like legions of prisoners across the boundaries of time and space.

Therefore, we tend to attract others with complementary contractions. A contraction around trust, for example, attracts a compatible contraction around trust in the other. It's so heart opening to witness our own somatic agony playing out elsewhere! In this, many relationships ingeniously take form for the purposes of healing. Sometimes it looks passionate, often it becomes destructive, but the healing and transformation is anyway happening. How many couples have married out of a contraction around freedom and the right to exist, and divorced out of the same theme?

Contractions are not separate, although they could appear as separate for a while. In the same way, the release of a contraction into the organic whole of our psyche is not separable from a healing of the collective psyche. Movement creates movement. When a little bird sings, the whole universe listens.

7. Contractions are a Protection Mechanism

The only reason feelings and emotions contract spontaneously and reflexively is for the protection of the whole. Contractions literally save stuff for later. They save the love in the grief, the belonging in the rejection, the joy in the jealousy. 'Later' is when the whole form of the psyche can safely process these emotions. Greater warmth and openness encourage release, signaling to the body that it's safe to relax and open. The more we are consolidated in the formless qualities of Nonduality, the more the system is supported to unfold contractions.

8. Conscious-Awareness Effects Contractions

Consciousness is fundamental both in the creation and release of contractions. When an aspect of experience is painful, we withdraw consciousness from it. This reflexive withdrawal of consciousness can be inherited, together with the cellular programming of the body. For example, with the feeling of betrayal: we don't go there; no one in our family ever betrays. The withdrawal of consciousness from the Felt Sense of betrayal separates it from the whole. This is the mechanism traditionally called denial, repression or suppression. The Felt Sense of betrayal is there anyway, we just mask it by manipulating our mental consciousness in other directions. In this way, we develop blind spots. Our disallowance of the sense of betrayal, for example, could create a rigid form of forced loyalty, that generates an explosive charge around the family contract. Although we are ignoring it, there is still consciousness within the sense of betrayal, seeking expression.

By the same token, when consciousness touches a contraction – meaning it acknowledges the feeling which is happening – the feeling begins to awaken. It's as simple as being able to think about sad things and then to cry from it. Consciousness awakens energy vibrations in our system. Transformation accelerates when mental consciousness surrenders to pure feeling awareness, allowing the contraction to be felt and experienced through the body, despite the flow of pain.

In Summary:

1. Contractions deny time and space.

2. Contractions claim autonomy.

3. Contractions form through 'either-or'.

4. Contractions can be anesthetic.

5. Contractions are trapped energy from the past.

6. Contractions are old friends.

7. Contractions aim to protect.

8. Conscious-awareness effects contractions.

CHAPTER 8: TRAUMA

"Our worst experiences can be hugely transformational as working through the agonies of trauma can be an awakening experience into no-self awareness and nondual being. With no judgment and choiceless awareness, our split minds are dropped. We are free to embrace the dazzling mystery of existence in each moment."

GARY TZU

While a contraction is energy that has been repressed in the psyche and progressively desensitized, with trauma we are looking at a deeper rupture from the normative whole. If we were to use the language of medicine, a contraction is a chronic condition. Through repeated movements of denial, the condition develops and worsens over extended periods of time. A trauma is more like an acute condition – like a heart attack or a severed limb. Symptoms appear and change rapidly. When you're in it, it's all-encompassing. There seems to be no way out.

Every contraction has the potential to become a full trauma, just as every trauma will connect to a hybrid of contractions. We can think of it in physical terms. If we deny physical sensations in our left ankle, repeatedly negating information of pleasure or pain, there is a high chance we'll have an accident involving our left ankle. We just won't process its warning signals. For example, if the sense of shame was forbidden in childhood, then we lose the Felt Sense of shame in the environment, in the here and now. The loss of this sensitivity can increase the probability of moving into a trauma of shame and disgust. The young girl doesn't notice or worry that older men are looking at her as a sexual object. She doesn't sense the energy of violation. Her 'shameless' stance has removed the early warning system of the psyche. A contraction based on family patterns has heightened the possibility of trauma.

At the same time, when we carry a trauma, there will be contractions based on prohibition. These contractions are defensive, aiming to ward off consciousness from the traumatic zone. For example, there can be a show of confidence on the Ego level, a subtle contempt on the layer of personality, and a deep fear as the proximity to the traumatic zone is increased. Behavior will also be affected, with possible diversion strategies of humor, hyperactivity and/or disinterest. We didn't even enter the trauma yet. We don't yet know the nature of the historic violation or whether it's connected to sexual, physical, social or emotional violation. Many contractions can be symptoms of a core trauma and can continue to spiral around the trauma until the core imbalance is addressed.

While contractions can play out with even a thin thread connecting them to the Nondual Quality that has become frozen (for example, with issues around rejection), in cases of trauma, that thread has been broken and can be restored only through a progressive reintegration of the experiential dimension of trauma with the experiential dimension of the whole.

Part of what gives trauma its power over the human psyche and what allows it to pass through the genes from one generation to another is that in the splitting off from consensual, normative reality, there is an opening to a greater reality. In the rift between our usual patterns of personality and the traumatic state, there is pure emptiness, alive with the sense of truth. This sense of truth becomes associated with the traumatic state as a foundational reality. In this way it gains a sense of momentous importance. This deeper truth is preserved in energetic memory to help future generations survive.

However, what is inherited is a legacy of incongruous stress responses resulting in a confusion of how to integrate these with a fundamentally safe environment. This confusion separates people still further, as they have no good reason to be traumatized – nothing happened! In April 2017, a study from the Psychiatric Genomics Consortium at Harvard revealed molecular evidence that genetics play a significant role in the probability of getting Posttraumatic Stress Disorder (PTSD) after trauma. This is a game-changer in healing, showing why modalities such as Nondual Therapy – moving beyond judgement to honor whatever comes forward in the here and now – can penetrate deeper than conventional models that focus on personal history and behavior.

Nondual teachers and therapists are increasingly recognizing that we are no more separate from our ancestors as we are from each other or the universe. Trauma is part of our evolutionary inheritance. The personality, together with the body through which it expresses is part of that evolutionary purpose. It is not the Source of all we are, but it is our responsibility. Part of this responsibility is the reclaiming of lost parts of ourselves through reunion with consciously disowned zones of the psyche and the liberation of the Nondual Qualities trapped inside.

Life in the Trauma Vortex

In wholeness, the energetic form of the psyche is like a vortex. In the words of father of Somatic Experiencing Peter Levine: "The vortex orchestrates symptoms to prevent the organism from being overwhelmed by it, and also attempts through devices such as re-enactment to reintegrate that energy in the large flow of experiencing."

The center of the vortex is the eye of perception: the Source of all experience; the seer; the one through whom all sensation occurs. The center is like a perceptive point of singularity, receiving all the impressions that arise in awareness. Like a black hole, it pulls information into itself. When there is a trauma, the energetic material of the psyche is cut off from that whole and a secondary vortex forms – a trauma vortex. Here, the natural flow of receptivity and expression gets thwarted, as the trauma vortex doesn't fit into the current context. As with every vortex, there is simultaneously contraction and expansion. The experience of the person contracts into the duality of the trauma, while at the same time the suffering quality of that trauma expands through all perception. When we're in it, it seems that the attitudes, atmospheres and moods of the trauma fill the whole universe. Yet trauma is formed through the pain of rupture, and this pain is its dominant sentient quality. As Peter Levine says: "The two results of polarization are expansion and contraction, so you have an undulation between the expansive quality of the energy movement and its contraction. That's the normal response of that universe: expansion-contraction. As you go into the trauma vortex you could call that the compression vortex, then the experience is one of expansion."

In trauma, the sense of belonging is lost. This is because of the historic inability to integrate the experiential content of the trauma with the habitual experience of daily life. The trauma doesn't belong, it's severed from the whole, and the whole can't make sense of it. This split is often reinforced by social norms.

For example, a young couple who lost their baby to Sudden Infant Death Syndrome struggled through the process of grief, first because of the horror of the loss, and secondly because of the horror of the people around them. They felt excluded by family and friends through subtle movements of shame, avoidance and denial. Even talk of babies would create an embarrassment, which meant others broke connection. The mother continued working, but she felt she had to constantly guard herself against traumatic triggers: shops with baby clothing, pregnant women, newly married couples. She lost connection to her own sexuality, as this was also a trigger, and the relationship with her husband began to suffer as each retreated behind different coping strategies and a distance appeared between the trauma in one and the trauma in the other. Easily, the shame and blame passed with subtle expressions between them, widening the rift. Yet the same splitting effect of trauma also held the keys to finding belonging again. When they could stand together, facing towards their child, allowing what was shared and the joy that filled the three of them in his short life, they began to belong again, firstly with the child and then with each other. The Nondual Quality of joy became the light that led the way to wholeness inside and outside of themselves. Only then did it become possible to conceive again.

A trauma vortex, like an acute condition, can catch us unawares. It repeats the shock of its own inception. One moment a person is feeling fine, and then he sees a sick dog on the street which triggers his trauma, and then suddenly he is there: inside the trauma tunnel. Another area where trauma shows up is in intimate relationships, partly because both sexual and survival instincts process through the reptilian brain. Sexuality can be confused with abuse, betrayal and abandonment. One moment a couple is having a lovely dinner out at a restaurant, next moment, with the opening of the sexual connection with his wife in a public arena, the husband disappears into a trauma vortex. He loses his appetite, he becomes aggressive, his hands and feet become cold, he doesn't care about the bill, his partner or his future – he feels he has none.

Our inner dimensions of trauma are places of intense suffering. They are characterized by a slowing down of physical movement and a difficulty in both expression and reception. At the same time, there can be a subtle grandiosity. It can feel as if we are standing in the deeper (grim) truth and that others are in illusion. Social interaction can feel like nonsense. It is as if only we know the keener, deeper truth of life. This truth is determined by the Nondual Quality that has been obscured. It can be the quality of life, for example: "Only I know death. Everyone dies. Everyone else is in denial," or it can be the quality of trust: "The world is full of betrayal. Betrayal is the bottom line. Everyone is just out for himself. We're all betrayed." Notice the absolutist language of a traumatic state: everyone, all the time, everywhere, nobody, never. Also, the superiority claimed by the traumatic state over 'others'.

There are always three or more Nondual Qualities locked in a trauma vortex. Chief among these are:

Belonging: the traumatic conclusion tends to be that I don't belong in this world.

Connection: as the trauma vortex, while deeply intimate, is at the same time lonely – the sense of connectivity has broken down.

Peace: as there is an existential conflict between two perspectives of consciousness.

Discernment: the mind reacts with the 'either-or' thinking of survival. The middle way is lost. I am 'good', the other is 'evil'.

Life: trauma is linked to survival and often literally to the experience of death or birth.

Innocence: as trauma brings a sense of condemnation, the legacy of guilt is strong, together with the reflex to blame the outside for the experience.

Purity: especially in sexual trauma, the stain to the psyche can seem to be eternal, never to be cleaned.

In addition, a trauma vortex can move us even away from the differentiation of qualities – into the realm of existential angst. In the words of Nondual therapist Gary Tzu: "I could see that trauma was not limited to experiences of physical, emotional, and sexual abuse, or physical injury or death. It also included experiences of psychic engulfment with no escape, and could even entail witnessing experiences of the absence of existence itself... the non-judgment stance takes us straight to Ego death, and letting go of the Separate Self contraction so the client can drop the split-mind, the grasping at surviving, and rest in being and essence."

Collective Trauma

A premise of Nondual Therapy is that the individual is an experiential entity that uniquely manifests the universal whole: we are one, but we're not the same. Because the individual is inseparable from the environment, there is an interplay between collective and individual trauma. The dualistic thinking of the judgmental mind, as well as fields of contraction and trauma, can play out collectively – through groups, cultures and nations. Yet the solution will always be with individual responsibility. Nondual Qualities are also shared, and unlike suffering, they are an infinite resource. Everyone that moves awakens and reintegrates a traumatic vortex within themselves and offers a tremendous service to the whole. Where there was a resonance of pain, there is now peace and fulfillment. A way home to our True Nature is opened – an experiential pathway in the collective mind. Just the release of these Nondual Qualities into the collective field is a tremendous support and affirmation to others. In the words of Bob Moore: "You are moving beyond polarity into your qualities. Your qualities are not polar."

In the collective field, we are deeply traumatized, and this is partly why we are so destructive towards the planet of which we're composed and why we remain in a perpetual state of war in manifold forms. Collective trauma shows through the force of denial arising from misconceptions around trauma itself. We make it uncommon, on the edge of insanity. If we have a trauma, we learn to be ashamed, and to hide it. From generation to generation we teach our children how to 'steel themselves' in the face of hardship; to keep a stiff upper lip; or to put on a brave face. We rarely admit that without exception, we are all traumatized. The only differentiation is in our freedom of consolidation within the Nondual awareness prior to form. Trauma is at the root in many forms of insanity, addiction, abuse and crime, yet our shared tendency is to reject all perpetrators as "evil" and to pity the victims as weak and inferior.

According to The Sentencing Project, in the last forty years, incarceration in the US has increased upwards of five hundred percent, despite crime rates decreasing. The prisons are overflowing with untreated crimes. Consider for a moment that it's partly the energy of guilt – a deep somatic identification with being 'bad', a perennial feeling of being condemned, a background sense of unworthiness – that causes us to do bad things. What comes first? The guilt or the crime? Conditioned as we are to believe that action makes us 'guilty', we are hardly able to consider attending to the inherited energy of guilt that we carry collectively and experience as personal. It's not the act that makes us guilty, it's the guilt which made us act badly – a guilt that contracted in the psyche long before we could be responsible. As Jung says: "The healthy man does not torture others – generally it is the tortured who turn into torturers."

This sense of being tortured through guilt can come with a horrific pressure on the chest and at the basis of the body. It clamps the buttocks and tightens the throat, limiting both freedom of movement and expression. It narrows the potential of experience and contracts us from others as well as from our own Source. In guilt, we shrink. Suffering this irredeemable sense of inner untouchability, the energy of guilt acts out on the environment. It expresses itself outwardly, seeking to destroy the projected accusers. Why? Because any connection with the world is better than no connection at all.

Our social response is to lock up these misfits and criminals in the ghettos of the guilty, splitting them further from the whole, ensuring that this contraction is passed from generation to generation. It's an epidemic of dosing affliction with affliction, accusing the accused, treating trauma with more trauma. The social field gets split into one great illusory verdict of 'Good Versus Evil'. The fear to fall on the wrong side of the line between insider and outsider prevails. At the same time, for each of us, no matter how much we pretend, the personality we carry is never good enough. We're always guilty and we act as if we can never be proven innocent. To avoid social condemnation we conduct the prosecution, including witnesses, jury and defense in the safer zone of our own thoughts. Judgement follows judgement, and we all await the final reckoning.

Outside of penitentiaries, we have the splitting of ourselves into the sane and insane; the serious and the ridiculous; the smart and the stupid; the winners and the losers; the 'haves' and 'have-nots'; the elites and the masses; the survivors and the suckers; the insiders and outsiders; rising stars and those who are 'going down'; saints and sinners; wives and whores; the cursed and the blessed. We scramble reflexively to become one side of the coin while pushing away the other, flattening the dimension of life into perpetual self appraisal and perpetual failure. The so-called good parts of our personality depend on the bad to be good. Without the good guys, the bad guys cannot exist. Whether outside of ourselves or within our own psyche, there is a perpetual struggle between opposing poles. Yet each side of a duality awakens the other. When we grasp towards the light, the darkness emerges. When we grasp towards a sense of self, we find ourselves disappearing. The more we consider ourselves to be exclusively good, the more our perception fills up with forms of evil. The paradox is that we need the insane people to make us feel sane. They define our assumed normality. We depend on the poor people to bring value to our riches. Our pleasure depends on our pain. The heaven in one corner depends on a hell somewhere else. It was Plato who first observed: "The excessive increase of anything causes a reaction in the opposite direction."

When collective trauma reaches its zenith, the form flips over and the underbelly of trauma begins to take over the social field. Such historic moments can seem like terrifying throwbacks to the past. Where we thought we had secured liberty, democracy and fraternity, we find ourselves again launched into theocracy, genocide and war. The very concept of 'the outsider' carries the familiar, daunting scent of collective trauma. At a certain stage, the disallowed rage and pain of the people becomes uncontainable.

When it's not integrated, trauma will express and release in whatever way it can. It will be both personal and collective, and every shade in between. If the trauma has been about murder, then there'll be murder. If it's been about belonging, there'll be rejection. If it's been about abuse, then there'll be abuse. This is a form of release, but it's a blind process – there's no consciousness in it – so it proliferates and births a future in which history seems to repeat.

The human psyche is enslaved in a dance of duality that will become increasingly contracted in multiple forms of paradox and senselessness until we open and restore the flow of Nondual Qualities out of which every duality emerges. Then there is space for healing; then we begin to dance in the full expression of True Nature through all forms of duality.

Nondual Therapy & Trauma

When we work with contractions, there's the possibility that a trauma vortex opens. This can be fearful but must be received as a healing movement. When the traumatic dimension has overtaken the client's body-mind, however, the methodology changes. A fundamental mechanism of trauma is denial of the experience to preserve the rest of the system. Perhaps for years, the person has been trying to deny, repress or negate an uncontainable experience. This has often been supported by others and their own reluctance to support pain. In this, there has been a withdrawal of conscious time and space from what has been a life-threatening experience. The therapeutic prerogative must therefore be to restore time and space. The client needs all the time and space to let the trauma unfold in a supported environment. Techniques of titration are very supportive: giving time and space by just taking a small detail for a tiny time, or letting events move in slow motion.

As we begin to recognize the trauma zones of the psyche, awareness opens to parallel dimensions within the psyche: the normative one and the deeper one that was born with the traumatic event or through traumatic patterns.

From either universe, the perception of the other is estranged. Often, the only bridge unifying these split parts of the psyche is awareness: in both we are aware. This awareness is timeless, infinite and unbounded. In both the trauma vortex, and in the vortex of the whole personality, there is the formless potential of awareness. Sometimes, all that can be done is to have the client notice that they have moved into a trauma vortex and to let them sense and describe the atmospheres with curiosity. Just this allowance of non-judgmental awareness can have a tremendous healing effect and create a connection in time and space to the rest of the psyche.

As what appears in awareness is also imprinted in memory, it's possible to therapeutically establish a pendulation between the traumatic zone, and other areas of experience. This opens an energetic communication between the trauma vortex and the vortex of the whole psyche. We might not be able to move out of the trauma vortex, but we can expand awareness to include the undeniable rhythm of our breathing in the here and now, or the sensory contact of the feet with the ground. Where there is suffering inside the trauma vortex, we can add to it a visit to a happy memory, and softly move between the two: suffering – well-being – suffering – well-being. Have the client find the location in the body of the vortex, and the place of naturalness and well-being. Where the bodily reflex could have been to freeze, we can move. The movement itself instructs the nerve system in freedom and possibility. When we move, perspectives change. As perspectives change, especially perspectives with a strong emotional charge, then there is an increased consolidation in Nondual awareness that which does not change. The traumatic universe loses its absolutist grip. Above all, our chief resource is True Nature. The emotional content of the trauma will itself indicate the resonance of the Nondual Quality that is needed for re-union with the whole. We can use these qualities as resonant resources, letting the client experience their unconditional arising out of the boundless field of awareness.

Work with trauma can at first seem like a long process, where we visit and revisit the trauma vortex repeatedly, through a cyclical process of healing.

Each movement in and out of a trauma vortex – especially when we are conscious of it – reaffirms freedom of perspective. The same formula applies to all traumas. This means that after the system has learned it, the reunion of traumatic parts of the psyche with the whole will become faster and more reflexive. The nerve system develops trust, dropping many of its warning sirens and protective mechanisms. Healing becomes easier. Still, the therapeutic prerogative is to above all release the agenda to resolve it. As we increasingly consolidate in True Nature, trauma will take care of itself. As therapists, it's important to have unconditional patience, which is so connected to consolidation in the timeless Now. As Lao Tzu asked: "Do you have patience to wait till your mud settles and the water is clear? Can you remain unmoving till the right action arises by itself?"

To summarize, a Nondual approach to trauma involves:

1. Consolidation in unbounded awareness outside of the restrictions of time and space. This is especially important where a client has dissociated into the witness position (often experienced as quite far above the head).

2. Titration: freedom to allow all the time and all the space for reconnection with the trauma vortex and its unfolding within the whole and/or for reconnection out of the trauma vortex with the sentient quality of the whole. Note: if the client is dissociated, all of this is witnessed. Integration will begin spontaneously when the sanctuary of the witness position is allowed and affirmed.

3. Pendulation: softly encouraging the client to alternate between experience within the trauma vortex and experience within the normative whole. In doing so, expression in the form of telling you what's happening is already a pendulation.

4. Discernment: moving beyond judgement and binary thought forms, pointing out the shades of gray and the texture of different kinds of experience.

5. Embodiment: locating the physical area of the trauma vortex and recruiting the support of the rest of the physical body in the here and now. This especially includes introducing the possibility of physical movement.

6. Nondual Qualities: following the need within the trauma vortex and offering the Nondual Quality as an infinite resource that is here irrespective of fragmentation in the psyche. Remember these qualities are present throughout nature and the environment: they are not limited to the 'Separate Self'.

Trauma & Spiritual Awakening

Trauma disrupts the patterns and conditions and forms of our normative beliefs, and in this way, it can be spiritually awakening. As Nondual therapist Lynn Marie Lumiere writes: "Because its effects are so intense and pervasive, trauma can be a catalyst for profound surrender and awakening. I see it as a wake-up call for the human race."

Yet just as trauma can bring spiritual awakening, spiritual awakening can also involve the awakening of trauma. Awakening can come with a high arousal of the nerve system, a rush of vitality and a sense of unlimited possibility beyond the forms of the psyche. It can also be a gradual process of checks, balances and integrations. Whatever form it takes, spiritual awakening shouldn't be confused with its effects. It's not the adrenaline rush, the expansion or the 'high', these are the effects of touching the core of inner, existential truth. To truly understanding awakening, we need to look at what is touched a moment before that expansion of consciousness.

As said before, the personality is not a fixed form, it is a modulating, adaptive flow of patterns. Between these patterns there are energetic rifts that expose the perennial existential emptiness beneath the matrix of time and space. Awakening is an effect of sinking deeply (or falling) into this existential emptiness. When even for a second we touch the existential truth of this underlying reality, sensing its pluripotent power, the nervous system awakens, consciousness expands, and light floods the psyche. Often, the reason we fall into emptiness is because we let go of the habitual resistance to the body, or because of trauma. In the splitting of the psyche, we fall in the formless gap. Ruthlessly, we release possession of the personality, and unfettered consciousness rises through the whole.

While expansion can be exhilarating, it can also offer an escape route from the suffering that led us to surrender into the emptiness. Expansion is naturally followed by contraction – it's the self-regulating mechanism of the psyche. When we can't bare the contraction, we cling to the 'awakened' state and identify with it, bypassing the heart and trying to maintain a split from the psyche. We reject the body-mind as illusory and begin to defend the awakening as if were private property. The more the wounds in the psyche are ignored, the more they vibrate for our attention. This can cause an acceleration into spiritual psychosis or what has been termed by pioneer of transpersonal psychology Stanislav Grof as 'spiritual emergency'. While the visions, psychic information and spiritual journeys made outside of the normal form of the psyche contain insight, it can become increasingly hard to integrate these with the whole. The difference can be like between recognizing the sentient quality of the suffering of Christ and believing that you are Christ. This is a spiritual form of trauma, and here the resolution doesn't come through more consciousness, but through the kind of humility that allows re-entrance into the wounded psyche, and a befriending and embodiment of the physical form. According to author of Mend the Gap Katie Mottram: "ALL crises are potentially transformative. They are all part of a spectrum of an expression of the journey towards wholeness. It looks like mental illness really is starting to be redefined in terms of spiritual experience."

The possibility of spiritual emergency increases when we consider that many become spiritual seekers with an agenda to escape from suffering. The pain of living 'in this world' leads to a rejection of this world, a field of resistance that can continue even after consciousness has been released from a fixed identification with form. It's subtle, but it's still a form of trauma, acting out and legitimized in its poetry through so-called spiritual dimensions.

Imagine that the psyche is an old house, where many rooms are unlit and unvisited. When consciousness is awakened outside of the forms of the psyche, then light floods the whole building. The doors and windows of the house fly open, there is light in every room. Energetically, contractions and traumas begin to vibrate, also awakening to the call of the reunion. If we refuse to hear the call of forgotten parts of the psyche, those aroused parts of the psyche will call us back, one way or another, for healing. We can divide from the forms of body and mind for a while, but sooner or later we will find that the only way out is through.

The awakening of consciousness as liberated from habitual thought patterns will loosen the grip of those conscious, repeating cycles of mind. But what about unconscious patterns? These also begin to vibrate, move and seek release. These unconscious patterns, or trauma vortex, could have been invisible to us for most of our lives – resonating only as a silent state of negativity or an area of background fear that has been with us for as long as we can remember. When working with the emergence of such phenomena from the 'unconscious' mind, we are dealing with somatic experience. In this, the body (the same body which is subject to impermanence, suffering and death) is key. Resistance to the body is a good barometer on states of trauma at a somatic level.

As Nondual therapist Judith Blackstone says, there is a difference between witnessing the body from the mind, and embodiment: "If you look at your hands, you may see them as made of flesh, muscle, bone and blood. You may feel the warmth that they emit or even feel subtle movement within them, which has been called "energy" or "life force." This is how you may experience being aware of your hands. But now enter into them, inhabit them. Feel that you are the internal space of your hands... All of the various parts of the body, and all of the functions of your being associated with the different parts of the body, have a quality, a "feel." We all know what love feels like, or sexual arousal, but even our intelligence has a feel to it, even our sense of personal power has a quality. To experience these various internal qualities creates a shift from an abstract idea of yourself to a qualitative or actual experience of yourself. It produces a sense of authenticity, of being real."

Spiritual awakening is not a rare event, nor is it on the surface a continuous state. Awakening requires illusion – it is an awakening from or to something.

The awakening of consciousness outside of form can be likened to those moments where an underwater swimmer comes up for air, takes a gasp of pure, liberated consciousness, and then returns to the currents and tides of collective illusion. We can't live without those moments, but our purpose here is to swim, to dive, to become one with the water, to dive in order to rise. Only when we venture this do we find that the physical dimension is not a trap, but a portal to boundless freedom. The way out is through.

Because of the rift of pure, underlying emptiness revealed through the fragmentation of the psyche, our traumas represent opportunities for spiritual awakening. The underlying truth in the split between one part of the persona and the other can be recognized as itself a resource – not just an 'empty' space. When we move in the rift between the normal psyche and a fragmented part of the psyche, we touch existential layers beneath and beyond all forms of identity. Traumatic states can suddenly change perception and the nature of experience and this is an opportunity for humility to arise throughout the psyche. It challenges our absolutist beliefs in the Separate Self, and the permanence of personality. Through trauma, we perpetually die to ourselves, and when this movement is allowed, we can also awaken to the rhythm of arrival in the here and now – called by some perpetual awakening.

When a trauma vortex is released and reunites with the experiential center of the whole psyche, there is also a release of a number of contractions. It is not only the suffering content of the trauma that rejoins the experience of the whole, but also the Nondual Qualities around which the polarity of the trauma evolved. When one quality awakens, it has a resonant effect like dominos, releasing the flow of the qualities of our True Nature. Again, there is expansion, not of a vortex within the psyche, but of the whole psyche.

This is the emerging insight of the powerful connection between Nondual Awakening, True Nature and psychological healing. There is a living synergy in this middle way which has the power to transform current therapeutic practices and to bring inestimable relief to many who have been left by the wayside of 21st century stress, medication, materialism and existential alienation. This work is transformative and evolutionary, both for individuals and for our collective future.

In the words of Peter Levine: "Human beings are born with an innate capacity to triumph over trauma. I believe not only that trauma is curable, but that the healing process can be a catalyst for profound awakening - a portal opening to emotional and genuine spiritual transformation. I have little doubt that as individuals, families, communities, and even nations, we have the capacity to learn how to heal and prevent much of the damage done by trauma. In so doing, we will significantly increase our ability to achieve both our individual and collective dreams... Trauma is hell on earth. Trauma resolved is a gift from the gods."

PART II

DANCING IN DUALITY: A QUALITY COMPENDIUM

"It doesn't matter which beach you go to, it's always the same ocean."

YOAD HARAN

Georgi Y. Johnson

FOREWORD TO THE COMPENDIUM

"I have been and still am a seeker, but I have ceased to question stars and books; I have begun to listen to the teaching my blood whispers to me."

HERMAN HESSE

The compendium includes a selection of recognizable contractions, and the associated Nondual Qualities which have been frozen in form. The reader is not expected to wade through them in linear order, but rather to use this section as a reference according to what feels needed at any stage. Each contraction is connected to the rest, and for this reason, work with Nondual Therapy needs to be alive and in the moment. Contractions form in layers, and they are hybrid. This means that when we touch a contraction around shame, for example, we might suddenly find ourselves in a contraction around care.

To dance in duality is to develop an agility to move between perspectives as well as to find the freedom to stay as needed, resting in the Felt Sense of pure experience. It involves following the wisdom of the psyche, which means honoring the intelligence within the suffering. What comes forward can sometimes seem like irrelevant distractions, for example, our client might suddenly change the subject to a story they feel compelled to tell us. Trust it's connected. Relax into the open silence, stillness and receptivity to allow the unfolding through physical, emotional and mental areas, and the wisdom of the connection will emerge.

When working with Nondual Qualities, the most important part is the resonance of the quality – finding that resonance within the shared field with the client – which means attuning to it within ourselves. This resonance will be communicated physically, atmospherically and perhaps suggested verbally. But a directive from the therapist of 'Purity' for example, is not purity if the soul of it isn't free. Our words need to resonate with the Felt Sense of the quality.

Nondual Therapy will always be a pendulation between the core of the contraction and the boundless, Nondual space beyond it. Sometimes, sessions will move towards awakening in the Nondual dimension, beyond the story, beyond the psyche. When we touch our True Nature, this will spontaneously awaken those areas where Nondual Qualities are contracted. Trust the intelligence of need. As therapists, we will do well to take a default position of pure awareness in the here and now. Here, there is an infinite, open receptivity which will bring presence and space for the conscious allowance and unfolding of the psyche. If you meet insecurity, a supportive practice is to breath in the words, atmosphere and presence of the client and to breath our peace.

We hope you enjoy this work, and that the compendium is of service. Whenever the reading gets too intense, just put the book down and move softly inside to let the empathy of the psyche relax into the endless resource of that boundless space inside, through which all peace, fulfillment and allowance are possible. If extra guidance is needed, please feel free to reach out to us through the contact details at the back of the book.

1 SUFFERING, RESISTANCE & CHOICE

The partner of suffering is resistance.

Choice has no opposite.

In choice, resistance and suffering are one.

"The strongest principle of growth lies in the human choice."

GEORGE ELIOT

Pure choice is the Nondual Quality of Freedom reflected through the open mind. The objectification of choice as a thing that we receive, lose, make or take is a critical misconception that sabotages both the freedom of mind and of being. Choice is not a thing that we do: it is a Nondual, experiential dimension of who we are, out of which all activity of choosing emerges. Choice is not the object of selection: it is the dimension out of which selection is possible. Choice is not the decision: it is a living energy of pure abundance and freedom that is here irrespective of decisions, during the consequences of decisions, and after the decision-maker has gone. Decisions are taken, owned or disowned. The Nondual experience of choice is always here.

As this powerful, existential energy of choice is alive and reflects through the physical form of the human brain, the first duality to emerge is between suffering and resistance. The movement towards one or the other is mostly reflexive: choosing happens by itself. Yet our freedom of choice is literally obscured when we believe in the absolute nature of the choice taken: when we believe in suffering (pain) or the agenda of resistance (contraction).

When belief sets in, it attempts to negate the living dimension of choice through mental structures. Belief obscures choice – the space of pure, mental freedom out of which all decisions can be experienced as funda-mentally non-binding and pure. When we believe that we are the doer: that we create our thoughts (rather than receiving them), that we shape our personality or that we are to be condemned for mistakes, the un-conditional power of choice gets obscured. Yet choice is always here, and it never gets lost, regardless of the mistakes made in processes of learning and evolution. As an energy, it doesn't depend on choosing, and is not lost through decisions taken. Rather, choice is the source of our very ability to move in freedom.

Suffering

Processes of change, growth and cycles of form involve suffering. This evolution is an inevitability of manifestation. When these processes of separation of the one into the manifold accelerate, the creative force of love shows up as suffering. Pure suffering is a light so bright that it blinds the eyes. It is a physical sensation so strong, that the organs of sensory perception close. It is a love so strong that the living form of the psyche resists, contracting under the threat of disintegration.

The more we resist suffering, attempting to exclude it from the realm of living experience, the more the belief is affirmed that suffering separates us from the whole. In doing so, the experience of suffering gains the power to obscure the one choice – to allow experience to sing its song in freedom, according to the deeper unfolding of need.

Resistance

Resistance brings its own suffering. The agenda to interfere with the greater need of evolution is ultimately powerless. An attitude of resistance creates conflict with life, with form, with the outer world and with the psyche. Resistance demands an enormous amount of vitality and rather than bringing relief, generates the Felt Sense of resistance, moment by moment.

A natural resistance can bring the dynamics of change into the dimension of time and psychological processing through a series of integrational checks and balances on growth. Yet when this protective reflex becomes hijacked by the agenda to avoid suffering, it landslides into dimensions of ignorance. Even resistance in its naturalness is resisted, and direction gets lost in a senseless wilderness of grasping and aversion.

Choice: Nondual Quality

Can you rest in that bright and powerful ocean of the one choice? Not the feeling when choice is lost through choosing, but before that. Before the decision between this or that and prior to the amputation of potential - even before options are conceived.

Choice is a dimension of freedom in manifestation. Choice is not the moment before action but stays even when actions are taken. How would it be to let the mind rest back as this one, perpetual choice? The feeling of choice; the sense of choice; being in choice; alive. This is choice: the openness, freedom, power and possibility of life; an openly streaming question to which life itself is the answer. Being choice, un-interrupted, releasing even that expectant surge of choosing. Here, we can feel the brightest pulsation of permission to be here and now, for real, without litigation: irreplaceable by any agenda.

Many have lost connection with this Nondual Quality of choice, which is unconditional to any choosing. Yet our manifestation through the phenomena of experience utterly depends on it. Such is its power, that at first it can be hard to allow it and relax within this field of perpetual possibility. Yet each millisecond we stay connected with the living dimension of choice, irrespective of choosing, we gain greater freedom in form. The dance of duality as a blissful expression of life begins.

Contemplations

1. Choose a situation in your life where you suffer. Imaginatively scan the world until you find another person who is suffering in a similar way. Share this suffering with them and notice the effect. Notice also the effects of resistance.

2. Take any situation where you feel you have free choice. Release the situation and experience the feeling of choice as a form of light. Don't get entangled with decisions – they can be taken, or not. Let that light of choice refine and expand, unconditionally, receiving any impressions of comfort or discomfort.

Form does not differ from Choice

And Choice does not differ from Form.

Form is Choice and Choice is Form.

2 BIRTH, DEATH & LIFE

The partner of birth is death.

Life has no opposite.

In life, death and birth are one.

*"Death is not extinguishing the light; it is only putting out
the lamp because the dawn has come."*

RABINDRANATH TAGORE

While birth is generally celebrated, death is collectively dreaded. We project on death a consensual horror and smother it with collective and individual denial. Fear of death is accentuated through conditioning: that life is the opposite of death; or that death is the negation of life. These conditioned beliefs generate a powerful investment in the linear story of beginnings, middles and endings, a story which is "my life". This formula dictates much of our identity – the fixed patterns of who, what and where we are. The twist is that even within this belief in death as the negation of life, there is a secret hope that death of our personal body, mind and story can somehow be avoided – or at least postponed indefinitely - through a disinvestment of consciousness.

The belief that death is the end of life is often announced with full scientific authority. Yet while the appearance of a static, individual body and mind will surely disintegrate, life just as surely continues. It's not a private life – the individual is born and the individual dies – but it is inseparable from the life that we are.

On closer inquiry, the individual including the body and mind, is not in itself a stable entity. The truest thing we could say about it is that it is in constant flux. Cells are dying and being born; thoughts are coming and going; beliefs collapse, evolve and are again newly conceived; behavioral patterns adapt according to inner and outer conditions. Memories evolve, and dreams revolve. We die in each moment and are born again in the next.

Yes, the atmosphere of death can be creepy, no doubt in part due to our conditioned aversion to it. It can feel like a kind of disgust, congealed with a sense of existential shock. This is part of our survival apparatus, but at the same time, it is vastly inflated by collective fields of projection on death. We may meet this atmosphere physically when we walk through a cemetery, attend a funeral or visit a hospice. But if we can sink beneath the astral field of projection, the energy around death is closer to a high frequency of transformation between dimensions, facilitated by a powerful backdrop of peace and release. It's worthwhile to clarify our fear of death. How do you fear death? Is it the suffering? The loss? Is your fear of death existential, meaning, irrational? Perhaps you believe that you don't fear death at all, due to a decision taken long ago not to go there?

For some, death can be associated with the trauma of abandonment; for others, it can be linked to the fear of helplessness. For all of us, there is a degree of existential petrification about letting go or looking over the perimeters of the psyche. The fear of death has many forms. We are so conditioned in denial that death is often conceived as unnatural and disastrous, yet it's all around us. After all, the food we eat is dead or is killed inside us. Death nurtures and supports physical life. Excrement from that process is food for the earth and the trees, which generate more food for mammals. Death is a critical part of the process of trans-formation, not an existential endpoint. Death is not negation, but an expansion into unrestricted life. The death of form is a critical part of the circulation of vitality through the whole.

Birth

Contractions and trauma around birth can limit our ability to experi-ence the birth of each moment in its wonder and freshness. Resistance is pre-coded in subtle forms based on the shock effect of unendurable physical sensitivity during the birth process. The senses – the receptiv-ity of the skin surface, eyes and ears – constrict, obstructing the natural channel of information. These sensory contractions, that restrain the awakening into physical life outside of the womb, include difficulty ad-justing to the crude brightness of physical light, the cacophony of sound, the burn of air on the skin and the sensation of bruising where the body is pulled or carried around.

Sensory potential is also conditioned in subtler ways connected to birth. The stress patterns of the mother's body in-utero and infancy are im-printed on the baby as atmospheric states. Like mist in the clear sky of pure awareness, these can be subtle moods of doom, sadness or shame, for example. They can even be more specific, such as the atmospheres of holocaust; insanity or addiction. Fear of conscious expansion into these formless mists of suffering can cause resistance to arrival in the here and now. Who would want to be reborn into a new moment where the air is initially experienced as toxic?

Resistance to birth, repeating as a template of resistance to the present moment, manifests as a difficulty to accept change. The nervous system reflexively diverts from the "Now" by grasping towards distraction. Yet the distractions themselves are often not random. Areas of social fear or rejection can be masked in thoughts connected with protection. For example, coming into the 'Now', one client with birth trauma that included a recurrent fear of swallowing her tongue, would suddenly be compelled to talk about financial planning. The atmosphere of poverty very much formed the sentient background of her mother's state in pregnancy. This poverty consciousness from the past, held in living contraction, came forward when the present moment was awakened. She was being 'born again' with new opportunity to let the contraction around greed and poverty release into gratitude. When we truly access the present moment – the here and now – we meet the core contractions and states that imprinted the psyche at birth. This is a good thing. The moment we become aware of a feeling or attitude, it is loose from the Source of all awareness, we have deepened as the 'seer' to an inner space which is free from that affliction.

The difficulty in being reborn in the moment, coded by the difficulty around awakening after birth as a separate unit, slows the rhythm of transformation. Opportunities for a conscious refresh are weak and infrequent and there is difficulty allowing change. This difficulty is characterized by a holding onto thoughts, forms and situations to a point of anxiety. While everyone might tell them to "let go", neither the object to release nor the one that needs to let go can be differentiated.

Opening to the feelings of helplessness and shock – which includes a training of the nerve system to relax within them – can encourage the wonder of awakening to the present moment outside of the story of past and future, which can liberate consciousness and the physical senses from the traumatic freeze around birth and human manifestation.

Death

While birth is celebrated in our psychological conditioning, death tends to be a source of dread. Yet both our past physical birth and our future death are contained in each moment, in the now.

The belief in the absolute reality of death as the negation of life generates fear. Fear leads to postponement and denial. Denial is a withdrawal of consciousness from an area of fear through resistance and distraction. It is often confused with courage. Yet it's a fool's courage which allows a conceptual beginnings (birth) and rejects inevitable endings to maintain the illusion of possessing and controlling the story. The story can only ever be a pale and limited reflection of the unfolding of life in the 'Now'.

In the Now, impressions emerge in consciousness. Where form touches form as impression, new form emerges. C.J. Jung expressed this well: "The meeting of two personalities is like the contact of two chemical substances: if there is any reaction, both are transformed." This is true from the micro to the macro, and its understanding will help loosen the grasp of duality. Through all layers of form, we are perpetually dying and perpetually being born.

Transformation is simultaneously the death of an old form and the beginning of a new one. Beginning always leads to ending that always leads to beginning. Life is the energy in which this patterning occurs. Life expresses and receives through perpetual transformation. Said in a different way, creation and destruction manifest interdependently. Birth and death are co-dependent in the nurture of form.

In this, birth trauma will be reflected in fears of death. Imbalances created through the denial of death include obsessive compulsive patterns; difficulty letting go; rigid structures of belief and an addiction to the story, both in controlling the plot and in forcing that story, or reality, on others. The point of view or perspective of individual consciousness becomes rigid and unresponsive. Other perspectives or experiences become polarized as competing enemies, in which only the separate 'I' must be defended as absolute. As the separate 'I' is terrified by death, it threatens death towards other forms. It's 'Me Versus You'; 'kill-or-be-killed'; 'Us Versus Them'. Living form goes to war with living form in the quest to survive. What is the threat that form is surviving? The threat is life. Not death, but life has become the enemy.

The belief in death as a negation of existence splits the psyche, divides us from each other and within ourselves. When we try to kill an experience arising within ourselves, we contract the channel of consciousness. In doing this, death as a concept is at play in trauma and the formation of contractions. The reality of death can be traumatic or even inconceivable, and the trauma of death is recycled and propagated collectively through many forms of horror.

The rotting corpse, suddenly void of human purpose and decomposing back to physical sources, signals the end of a physical life cycle. It is the inevitable transformation and release from form that challenges every layer of identification to let go. Through letting go, contemplation on death in the Now can release unconscious or somatic layers of stress held within the physical body. The release of this stress can feature as the liberating rush of awakening. Consciousness is no longer limited to identification with the body and mind.

It is important to understand the two sides of the movement of letting go – even of our own bodies and minds, and the story expressed through them. For there to be anything to let go of at all, there must be that which is to be released, and that which is holding it. The two are bound through grasping. That which needs to be let go appears at some spatial distance from that which can let go (or not): it is connected by the grasp and takes separate form through the grasping. Grasping is a stress response to the threat of physical death.

When we feel we are falling into the unknown, out of form, there is a tendency to grab hold of anything, regardless of whether it's good or bad. Even patterns of pain can feel more hopeful than the apprehended death in this endless falling through form. Yet when we are falling, and all impressions of external form disappear, what happens? Are we not perfectly still?

When we let ourselves fall through the fear of death, temporal forms lose their grasp, and there's an opportunity to rest as the peace prior to form, unaffected by all transformation. The fear of death releases, which leads to a quickening in energy and a liberation of fields of possibility. Transformation and healing can then occur through multiple layers of form, according to inherent need. Change is allowed through the permissive power of the unchanging, existential core of all we are.

Deathly fear can be so uncomfortable that we become afraid of the fear. This fear of fear can become anxiety disorder, where fear gets a life of its own, without context in the here and now. Every form can die, so no form can be trusted. In this, the deeper need can be to die internally: to die to ourselves. The greatest gift we can give the whole is to give palliative care to that aspect of ourselves which is dying and to support it through the death process.

The depth of healing doesn't polarize life and death and doesn't dance to the drum beat of survival of form at any cost. Deeper healing follows the needs of the whole in the movement of life through beginning and endings, birth and death, creation and destruction, opening and closing, composing and decomposing. It doesn't judge, but invites the expression of life through form at any moment in the cycle.

Contractions around destruction, non-existence, and letting go are all deeply linked with the fear of death arising despite attempts at denial. It can seem paradoxical that heroin-addiction, suicidal leanings, and murderous thoughts and deeds reflect the fear of death. Yet denial of death is at play, through strategies of control. In commanding death, we expect to have a transient grasp on the ungraspable. Yet in the movement of grasping, we are left with the experience of grasping towards illusory forms that can never fulfill us.

Life: Nondual Quality

Every living cell is made up of proteins and as such life science was for centuries focusing on how proteins are created. Not much attention was paid to how those same proteins were destroyed. The bias was on the birth of the protein, not on its death. In the 1980s, three scientists - Aaron Ciechanover and Avram Hershko of Technion, Israel and Irwin Rose of the University of California - began researching into regulated protein degradation. The subsequent discovery of the ubiquitin system won them the 2004 Nobel Prize in Chemistry. The polypeptide ubiquitin, they showed, tags proteins for destruction. Death of proteins, and of cells, is fundamental to the well-being of the whole. For example, if not enough proteins are tagged to die, then cancer can come forward. If too many proteins are tagged for destruction, we see neurodegeneration. Physical well-being depends on the harmony, balance and attunement of the ubiquitin system. It is the free functioning of creation and destruction within the inner universe of a cell that supports the health of the whole living form. Living manifestation requires a natural balance in creation and destruction and between birth and death.

Just as physical cells require a free circulation through cycles of birth and death, so do psychological ones. Birth and death are so interdependent that contractions and trauma around past birth repeat as contractions around future death. This causes a resistance to direct experience, a prohibition against helplessness and a refusal of vulnerability. Experience requires us to open in receptivity which means we must allow both vulnerability and helplessness. When these are denied, experience contracts.

Where there is a contraction around life, there can be difficulty both in action and receptivity. As much as we fear death, we fear surrendering to a form that will die. Contracted experience still echoes the fear of impermanence, however, so deeper denial and greater contraction is needed. Vitality is blocked, and direct living experience becomes increasingly shut down as the mind tries to satisfy the hunger for life with what it believes it can control, and thoughts or activities it believes are safe. Whether this hunger is reached through sexuality, material possession, status, spiritual acquisition, drugs or food, it can never fill the all-pervading absence experienced in the loss of connection to life in the here and now.

Birth and death both call for life. Life is the harbinger of joy in manifestation. In the profound words of Thich Nhat Hanh: "The moment when the wave realizes that she is water, she loses all her fear and she enjoys much more being a wave. She is free from birth and death, being and non-being, high or low, because when we are able to touch our ultimate dimension, we are no longer subjected to fear - fear of being; fear of non-being; fear of birth; fear of death."

Contemplation

Let your awareness sink to the chest area and recall a time when you felt truly alive. Let the sense of life move through the physical body and expand outwards for as far as it needs.

Form does not differ from Life

And Life does not differ from Form.

Form is Life and Life is Form.

3 PAST, FUTURE & NOW

The partner of past is future.

The now has no opposite.

In the now, future and past are one.

"You can touch the future in the here and now, and you can touch the past in the here and now, and you can transform the past and transform the future by taking good care of the present moment."

THICH NHAT HANH

The full potential of healing is found in the present moment. Yet the programs of grasping towards the set stories of the past and averting the unwanted outcomes of the future can radically distract from the natural movement of healing. Language and mental conditioning constantly reaffirm the illusion of time as a linear story, and while many will lack insight into the all-inclusive power of the present moment as the container of both past and future, the therapeutic process – and the language used – can communicate it.

Language in the present tense is the language of direct experience. Even when a client is telling about the past, the shift into living experience can be facilitated through a shift to the present tense. Have the client tell the story as if it is happening now. Rather than: "I walked into the room and saw my husband," encourage them to communicate the memory in the present tense: "I'm walking into the room and I see my husband." This introduction of living experience undercuts the story-based programming of conditioning. It facilitates the shedding of a layer of defense, control and habituation towards what is being told. The present tense brings emotional memory to life, connecting thought patterns and speech to the feelings of the Now.

The same movement into the present tense is also beneficial for stories about the future – and which tend to be areas formed by fear, projection and expectation. When the future scenario is communicated in the present tense, it is already happening energetically, which is a magical movement in which a mental agenda is released into living experience, opening unlimited possibilities for processing repressed emotional energy that is contracted beneath the projection.

Living experience – even the experience of thinking – is happening outside the structural belief of past, present and future. We can only think something 'Now', just as we can only feel something 'Now'. Even when we remember a feeling, or expect a feeling in the future, we are already feeling it in the present moment.

When working with the past and future (in the present tense), it can always be worthwhile to let the experience be also physically reflected in the actual here and now: "What's happening now? What are you feeling in your body?" The relegation to history and the deferral to the future is a reflex enforced by contraction in the present moment. This contraction is already beneath the threshold of consciousness. The present tense is the language of the unconscious, which doesn't adhere to the mental form of linear time. So, touching the physical form of contraction, and relaxing around it is tremendously worthwhile in releasing the net of predetermined mental programs.

From a therapeutic perspective, sessions that are anchored in the present moment which include the freedom to allow each nuance in sensation are effective. When the therapist sits in the Now, they are liberated from the agenda of fixing the issue or saying something helpful. Full presence signals availability and reverberates a trust that invites precisely the parts of the contraction to come forward as a feeling or story which of themselves will offer prescription. The more the therapist can relax in the now, the more vitality is brought to old stories which refreshes them, opening the window of possibilities and perspectives.

Past

Although the facts of what happened cannot be changed, we can spend a lot of energy attempting to rewrite history. This is partly because of the belief that to change who we are and our expected future, we need to get a better grip on the past. Yet the only change possible of the past is through a liberation of perspective that occurs through a willingness to allow the freedom of the present moment.

The past is an illusion in which the same chronological story is repeated. This creates a tiredness and a sense of depression which is appropriate, as this is a freezing of past structures – or a contraction of memory – rather than living memory in the now. The way to work with the past is to recognize that the past is alive in the feelings and emotions of the present. These feelings and emotions have their own intelligence which move beneath the surface of the story.

When working with the past, it is necessary to let the story expand and refine, opening the window for it to be reborn in the present moment.

Notice differences between the story told and the sentient quality of the voice. For example, when they laugh telling you their father died, we can become aware of a significant split between mind and heart which gives a barometer of the state of contraction. Introduce curiosity: seek details outside of the repeated story. For example: What shoes are you wearing? What is the weather on this day? How does the room smell? What happens next? What's going on with others around you?

The past is not limited to the past of our own experience. That experience is inseparable from the experience of our environment and the experience of our ancestors. There is no need to limit our connection to the past with personal events. So much more of the past is alive in us at any moment, together with its learnings, insights and resources.

The nature of the illusion of the Separate Self is that we deeply believe that our story began with our separate identity. The Separate Self resists allowing the interwoven nature of all experience. Contractions rooted intimately in our physical bodies are often born with our ancestors and reaffirmed through our parents and environment. This includes whole patterns of stress and contractions embedded within the personality. When there is a need to delve into the past, it can be liberating to truly go to the past – to the heredity of the contraction that was formed through generations long before the birth of the separate 'I' of the client.

Future

Fear is generated by a displacement of ourselves into the future and as such expresses as aversion to the present moment. Fear is a fast, nervous response. Its function is to facilitate rapid response in real-time to actual threat. Fear instructs the body to act reflexively long before the brain processes what happened. Survival, learning and evolution involve applying past experiences to future contexts. However, when there is a strong aversion to certain types of experience, the thinking mind tries to exclude its repetition from the realm of future possibility. It tries to dictate a form which is less horrible. In this case, it will often keep a constant tab on the worst nightmare, holding it perpetually in a corner of consciousness to attempt to take control of its manifestation. Sneakily, we use the future to grasp at what we resist. This attempt to control what is already anyway present in feeling generates more fear. The irony is that most of the content we fear in the future has already happened to us in the past. We most fear what has already happened, if not directly to us, then to our ancestors. This means the experiential potential is already alive, beneath the threshold of consciousness.

The belief that we control our future is as limiting as the belief that we can control our past. The belief is not free, because the mind is full of agendas and lacks the perceptivity, clarity and insight of the present moment, in which the future will take form.

With fixations on the future, short-term agendas based on strategies to avoid suffering lack wisdom. This is because the receptive part of the brain is out of balance with the active. When we are dictating the desired future, we are not receiving the present environment, including actual dangers. We lose awareness within the environment and this loss of perception ultimately generates more fear.

Now: Nondual Quality

At first, the therapeutic movement into the present moment can feel like withdrawal from deep patterns of addiction. Just the switch into the present tense can feel unreal, insecure, shameful, exposing and violating. Yet here, the therapist's cultivation of a deep relaxation within the here and now can be transmitted to the client. The more the therapist can relax in the present moment, the easier it is for the client to release the addiction to time-based thought and expression. When we don't invest too much in the fixed structure of the story of the client, there is more space to connect to the living experience of their True Nature as expressed through the story. True Nature is not a concept: Nondual Qualities emerge as living power in the Now.

The weaning away from the belief in linear time can bring a rush of bliss with the instantaneous possibility of freedom moving through many contractions at once. In the purity of Now, guilt is no longer here.

Loneliness vanishes as the consciousness liberated from the thinking mind is not contracted around the separate 'I'. A sense of unearned, pre-given fulfillment resonates with truth. It can feel as if nothing ever actually happened in the suffering story of a life. Everything is deeply, purely and irrevocably 'OK'. In these existential moments outside the treadmill of mental time, the person vanishes. Yet then there can be a sense of hollowness – what are we going to talk about then? It's important for the therapist to be able to wait in this. Only the surface has cracked – soon the more vital layers of experience will emerge, possibly through a deeper story, more in alignment with the deeper yearnings of the psyche.

This is especially important when a client has had a recent awakening and has been unable to integrate this in their daily life. When the dust of personality falls to the ground, there can be a movement into spiritual psychosis. The individual wants the rush of liberation back, but not the suffering of contractions. Aversion to regular life can be stronger than ever. They don't want to come down from the conscious 'high'. In this area – the area of spiritual emergency – the work of Nondual Therapy with its insights into the nature of awakening and the Dark Night of the Soul is of critical importance.

By degrees of mental evolution, the personality can learn to release itself into awakening without abandoning itself in the aftermath. The nervous system begins to learn that there is a deep peace in presence, and that letting go of past and future, and the aspect of the personality based on time doesn't have to be accompanied with the adrenalin rush. In doing this, the deeper work of integration and evolution towards embodied freedom can begin. It is a freedom that doesn't need to reject suffering. It is the freedom to be human: transient, impermanent and yet human, nonetheless.

The introduction of the Nondual Quality of the 'Now' is always both awakening and affirming. Consciousness invites, affirms and empowers form, and so the touch of consciousness is a direct invitation for a contraction to unfold. Notice that any feeling reaction could be the first skin of the contraction – including annoyance/frustration, fear, a sudden sense of tiredness or even a sense of blankness (the wall of 'nothing'). Let your client pass through the layers, as if lifting veil after veil. The Now brings an energetic quickening and through surrender to its eternal window, the spatial dimension of the 'Here' comes to life.

Contemplations

1. Recall your earliest memory of trying to go to sleep. Try to find that movement of surrender inside. Close your eyes. Explore if it is the same one that receives the movement inwards towards sleep in this moment. Imagine sometime in the future when you are falling asleep. When you return to the present moment, notice if this timeless one is the same through past, present and future.

2. Find any sense perception (seeing, hearing, tasting, smelling, touching) and relax into it. Let the organ of perception soften or blur. Notice the enlivening of impressions the more control is surrendered. Relax in receptivity to impressions of the Now, noticing where and how perception contracts or diverts from direct experience.

Georgi Y. Johnson

Form does not differ from the Now

And the Now does not differ from Form.

Form is the Now and the Now is Form.

4 Inside, Outside & Here

The partner of inside is outside.

The here has no opposite.

In the here, outside and inside are one.

"The message is that you don't need to go to anywhere else to find what you are seeking."

RAM DASS

The spatial orientation of the client's inner world provides a barometer of the state and density of contraction. All that is disowned, most uncomfortable and most difficult to contain tends to be situated outside at a distance from the client, in the realm of the 'outer'. Yet all phenomena and our reactions to them occur within the awareness of the psyche. We can play endlessly with distance in the definition of the Separate Self, yet freedom in the dance comes when the dance floor is acknowledged as the infinite 'Here' of awareness.

Within the spatial parameters of inside and outside, the persona searches for a place of fulfillment. In religious terms, this could be heaven; from a materialistic world view it could be in the future forms of a holiday location, a better job or a jackpot in the lottery. Yet also in this 'other' place, we store our worst nightmares; as well as the responsibility and authority over our lives.

Abstractions such as 'the world', 'people' or 'life' are often postulated as the outside, splitting the psyche. Yet this is a field of pure projection. When your client says: "The world is a cruel place", this is the voice of inner cruelty seeking expression. It's a movement away from healing, as it abnegates power through the avoidance of direct responsivity. One response could be: "What aspect in you recognizes cruelty?"

The outside, or the 'elsewhere', is the empty Neverland where we position our greatest longings while at the same time throw our aversions.

Just an in the real estate business, the saying goes: "Location, location, location," we are driven by a belief in an illusory 'elsewhere' which will be either free of suffering or in pure paradox, which is the container of all suffering. This can feed the belief that the relief from the suffering we experience here, will come paradoxically where we are not. This belief suspends the movement of healing and contracts awareness. We expect our illnesses to be cured and our problems to be solved, without really allowing them to be here in the first place.

Inside

The belief in a Separate Self depends on a partition between inner and outer worlds. This partition is reflected in the construction of both language and thought processes. The 'I' and the 'Me' is everything from the partition inwards. The 'other', the 'you' or 'the world' begins where the partition of the private self ends.

At the same time, all forms of receptivity (sensory perception, learning, nurture), depend on passage through this partition between inner and outer space. All expression and reception depend on moving through the borders of the private self. We 'take in' the outer world and we express into it.

The energetic borders of the private self are highly volatile. This is because we are programmed to grasp towards what's attractive in the outer world, claiming it as part of the 'inner'; while simultaneously pushing away that which we don't want to identify with, making it 'outer'. These borders are made of the vitality of contraction at any given moment. They are shifting all the time.

When we allow that every form has its shadow, then we can also understand that this can mean the formation of an outer world inside ourselves. Self-disgust (rather than the direct experience of shame), self-accusation (rather than the experience of guilt) and self-rejection are examples of the internalization of the inner-outer split. This inner, estranged 'self', causes a lot of suffering through the sense of alienation. There is isolation within isolation, abandonment or betrayal within the apparently objective context of outer abandonment or betrayal. The psyche is imploding on itself. The battlefield is the body; the weapons are the emotions of the psyche; and the warring forces of the psyche strategize from polarized bomb shelters of the mind.

This can sometimes culminate in suicidal thoughts and tendencies. For example, the voice that says: "I want to kill myself" (Who is killing who?). It's the last call of despair that seeks to get rid of the enemy within, through a futile attempt to finally negate the unwanted parts of the psyche.

Within the context of Nondual Therapy, the outside space also becomes the core inner space when the therapist or outer resource begins to represent the dimension of our True Nature - which is deeper than the structures of personality. When the client is encouraged to rest in the comfortable, familiar, common-place spaces of the psyche, this apparently foreign, inner space, of pure awareness can be revealed as a prevalent resource which is closer to home in each moment of experience.

Awareness of every split between inner and outer demands pure awareness. Without the most intimate awareness of the supposed 'outer' world, the outer world could not exist. This awareness can easily contain psychic opposites, as without awareness, they have no possibility of being. The inside-outside conflict within the psyche, when seen, can help release the addiction to the absolute belief in personality as the ground of *Being*.

When we are aware of two opposing parts of ourselves, a third aspect at a more authentic layer is already emerging. The art of Nondual Therapy is to affirm that third position – a position behind and beyond the conflict. For a while, this third position beyond the split can be embodied by the therapist themselves, but by degrees, the client will experience this unbounded awareness as intimately their own.

Outside

There are many dimensions to the world as perceived as outside to ourselves and all of them depend on the perspective of the perceiver, as well as the limitations inherent to that perspective. For example, if we identify ourselves strongly as a Dutch citizen, then anyone who is not Dutch is an outsider. If we identify deeply with our gender, then anyone who doesn't comply with the structure and content of that identification is an outsider. If we believe we are a generous person, then anyone who is mean is outside. If we base our sense of security within the form of our biological family, then any incoming partner or family member is (and will unconsciously remain) an outsider.

The depth and extent of conflict arising from the abnegation of power inherent to the split between inside and outside can be shocking. Where we position these partitions between inside and outside - both in the vertical and horizontal dimensions - can tell us a lot about the geography of our unconscious minds and our energetic contractions. For some, love is positioned quite far away from the body. When they say they are looking for love, they physically gesture towards a place far away. Love is conceived as external, not as a feeling felt by the speaker. In the dimension of memory, the spatial location of memory is also telling a lot about the degree to which the contracted thought form of experience can enter the experience of the living. A remembered event that is seen far from the body rather than re-experienced from the inside-out, has not yet arrived home into the freedom and intimacy of direct experience, right here.

It's important to note that the placing of boundaries within our environment is a fundamental birthright, which is generally facilitated by the underlying freedom within the 'Here' and the overview that allows us to perceive both 'inside' and 'outside' and the needs of the forms through which we manifest. How could we put a border if we don't have oversight of the terrain on both sides? The ability to put boundaries is a natural movement of freedom, not a dictate of fear. It is inherently free, as the same one that can put clear and empowered boundaries has the freedom to remove them when they are no longer needed.

Here: Nondual Quality

The 'Here' is an infinite Source space where we are eternally located, regardless of movement. Wherever we go, we are here. What changes is perspective. The Here remains. There is no pulse of experience – including the experience of 'others - that can occur in any field other than the most intimate 'Here'.

Pure awareness is infinite: no experience can occur without our a priori awareness in which experience occurs. Yet, also the unconscious aspects of our being, and the non-feeling parts of our bodies are here. In this, the Here is not only the infinite backdrop of conscious mind, it is also the dimension of the subconscious. Even though we blink our eyes, our sight is still here. Even when consciousness is less reflected by the mind, we are still here.

The inside-outside split is reflected in structures of Ego and personality. It is also a key component in difficulties opening in receptivity and blocks in expression. The flow of impression and expression is natural to all layers of form and when that flow – from inside-out and outside-in – is obstructed, the suffering of contractions is accentuated.

When there is a degree of consolidation in the unlimited, universal Here which contains both inner and outer as transient phenomena, then the energetic substance of the Separate Self begins to dissolve, together with accompanying contractions that are based on Self Versus Other, or Me Versus the World. This flow is facilitated by the encouragement of the ability to switch perspectives, or to pendulate between different areas of feeling or different poles of a contraction (for example, pleasure and pain).

The Here at the core of awareness is also the needle's eye through which we can pass from one dimension to another. Only through the Source layer of the Here are we able to release attachment to known contexts and only through the Here can we open to receive fresh impressions.

The infinity of the Here means it is also a space of no-time and zero distance (or pure singularity). This means that even through a pinprick of pain, we can fully release a contraction. Less can easily be more. Infinity means all measurement is impermanent. This is a powerful therapeutic insight, as every energetic contraction depends on an imagined limitation of space.

Contemplations

1. With eyes open, bring your attention to the skin surface of the body, and then to the boundaries of the room or space you are in. Moving outwards from the skin surface, try to sense where the boundary is between you and the outside. Notice the amount of space you give yourself beyond the skin surface, and the shape of the border of the individual sense of self.

2. Close your eyes and ask the question "Where am I?" Notice where you are 'Here', beyond the physical space you are in. (Examples: the 'Here' of an emotion, in connection to a loved one, in the atmosphere of a deeper home)

Form does not differ from the Here

And Here does not differ from Form.

Form is Here and Here is Form.

5 Head, Heart & Body

The partner of head is heart.

Body has no opposite.

In body, heart and head are one.

"The way the Beloved can fit in my heart, two thousand lives could fit in this body of mine. One kernel could contain a thousand bushels, and a hundred worlds pass through the eye of the needle."

RUMI

All experience, all we could ever perceive or conceive, any sense of life or being, involve the physical body through which we live, right here, right now. The experience of our world is inseparable from that which experiences. Matter, as found in the fundamental particles of our physical universe, is an energetic phenomenon. In this, the body cannot be extracted from any process of healing, as each process, through beginning, middle and end moves through the energetic form of the body. What is at issue is not whether the body is sacred or profane, dualistic or Nondual, but what on earth the body is – as the living form through which we manifest.

Whatever we might imagine the body to be, it is not that: our body image is a form of imagination. Whatever we might believe the body to be, it won't cooperate. Our beliefs hang like accessories over a body that has a life of its own and reflexes faster and subtler than any mental processes. Whatever we experience our body to be is experienced through our senses, organs of the body itself. Through these, the body is experiencing its own sensitivity in response to an ultimately unseen cause.

Discussion continues as to whether bodily experience is working top-down – from brain through to the operation of the physical body; or bottom-up – from the physical body up to the processing of the brain. Yet the whole discussion reflects the belief in the split between mind and body rather than allowing that both manifest simultaneously as one interconnected form. The brain and nervous system are part of the physical body.

The physical body is ultimately inseparable from the physical body of the whole universe. It is composed of the same matter and returns to the same matter. It resonates at the same frequencies, and like the electron, it is at once here and not here; simultaneously caught in time and existing outside of time, intimately entangled beyond the conventional thresholds of time and space.

Psychological contractions are reflected in conflict between structures of thought and structures of feeling. This is the highly recognizable split between mind and heart. The heart pulls in one direction, and the mind determines another. The mind attempts to dictate appropriate feelings to the heart. The heart closes to give the mind freedom to play. When the conflict becomes chronic, it is stored within the physical body in the form of pain, muscular contraction and disease. The fundamental duality of head and heart, waking consciousness and sentient awareness, is contained within the most neglected adversary: the body itself, including its blood, sweat, tears and rhythmic tides of sexuality.

Head

Little is understood about the brain. Popular belief is that memory is stored in a compartment somewhere within the blob of flesh. Also, it's believed that thinking takes place specifically within the skull, where the fleshy organ of the brain resides. Most beliefs around the brain focus on the electrical synapses around neural networks. Only a few scientists have endeavored research into the fluidity of the brain, and the inter-connectivity of the whole system through the cerebral spinal fluid, which incidentally, contains the DMT molecule present in medicinal plants and that is associated with journeying between dimensions of spirit. In addition, insights into the functioning of Mirror Neurons has shown that our brains are as directly responsive to the perceived experience of other bodies, as to the perceived experience of our own.

Part of the reason for this collective limitation of mind is the predominance of fear. When we are in a state of fear or stress, Noradrenalin floods the brain cells which makes them slow down and rigidify. We drop connectivity to fulfill the urgent survival tasks of freeze, fight or flight. This fixation of neural networks enforces somatic habit, thought repetition and an endless mental circling through the roads most travelled. New ideas are experienced as annoying. Mental paradox is felt as aggression. The expressions of an open mind seem crazy.

So, we cling to our established thought patterns and structures of belief like children in the darkness of the unknown, unable to move. These contracted thought forms maintain and defend the contractions in our system. This is especially tragic when we consider that many of these contractions – based on survival stress – were inherited from our ancestors and are no longer relevant to the conditions of today.

Above all, the thought forms of conventional mind are based on the autocracy of the separate 'I'. This 'I' hijacks consciousness as itself and struggles to control, define, own or reject all that appears on its horizon. Yet life does not cooperate with this separate 'I'. For some, a liberation from the permanence of identity and the lunacy of the conflictual inner voice is experienced in the form of conscious awakening. There is a realization that consciousness is timeless and unrestrained by identity. This is a rush of freedom that has the power to move us beyond the duality between head and heart. Often, this kind of awakening is initiated through the direct perception of the strangeness or existential miracle of the physical body, beyond mental concept.

Heart

The predominant mind-frame of our time is to consider feelings as mysterious accessories to thought. Feelings and emotions are limited to a few fundamental categories: there is fear, anger, love, hatred, guilt and even with this, the label of love is confused. Yet the spectrum sentience is infinite: there are as many possibilities as there are moments of experience. In addition, rather than being the by-products of thought, feelings determine the nature of thoughts that emerge. When we try to dictate the heart from the head, confusion and disempowerment reigns. It is easy to recall how the deeper longings of the heart come into conflict with the fears and warnings of the mind, and the confusion this creates for the whole psyche.

The belief that feelings can be controlled by the mind is fueled by an agenda to avoid suffering. As we can temporarily ignore or repress aspects of experience, this success breeds the belief that all feelings are created by the mind. That is, if you choose to love another person, for example, then you are obliged to recreate that feeling, even when it's not there.

Our language is littered with examples of mind control. We 'make' peace, rather than allowing the peace that is already here. We 'prove' innocence rather than accepting that innocence needs no proof. We 'guard' purity as if purity can be damaged. We become the directors, producers, actors and audience of our own experience, and in this, life becomes a lonely show with only loose connections to the vast, unbridled Source of itself.

When head and heart dance together, a deep contentment and sense of alignment emerges. Yet for thought and feeling to be liberated from the struggle, the body is needed as the container of both.

Body: Nondual Quality

When every particle of the physical body is 99.99999999% empty, could we say that this emptiness is love? Therefore, that the body is an expression of love? How about peace, freedom, care, innocence? Could it be that this unbounded emptiness that facilitates all physical matter is the dimension of our True Nature, of which matter is a fine and fleeting energetic expression?

How do we know we have a body at all? Through our sense perceptions. Through our sensory perception – our sense of touch, smell, sight, taste and sound – we locate the body. Our experience of having a body at all is entirely dependent on our ability to sense it, or we could say on its sensory capacity. Yet as with feelings and emotions, we are not rationed in sensory perceptions. Beyond the obvious five senses, we have endless others: the sense of gravity, balance, space, orientation, time, temperature, sexuality, pleasure, pain, relaxation. To these, we could add more subtle senses such as the sense of beauty, peace, belonging or truth.

Sensory experience – even of a subtle nature – is not a private affair but passes from body to body through transmission or resonance. When the therapist can rest in the Nondual Quality of the body, the body of the client will be somatically supported through resonance. The more we sink into the experience of the physical, the more we awaken. The more we allow embodiment, the more our minds and hearts are baptized through the pluripotent emptiness which allows the physical dimension to be.

The body is inherently empty: that means that it is open on both sides. It opens to the so-called external world, but also to the infinite dimension within. It is an empty channel in two directions from the world of human feelings, emotions and thoughts (which we could call resonance) towards the infinity and eternity of its own empty Source. It is also an open channel backwards and forwards through ancestral history and towards the generations of tomorrow. In addition, it is a vertical channel. It opens towards the earth, receiving the resonance of the planet and somatically communicating with it, and it opens towards the infinity of the universe.

Contemplations

1. Choose a space in front of the trunk of the body. Position your consciousness in the space away from the body and slowly move with your consciousness towards the body and into it. Stay for a while inside the body, noticing the feeling quality, and then move outside of the body again to the space away from the body. Pendulate like this and notice attitudes of consciousness towards the body.

2. Focus on a body part (such as hand, hip, knee, foot). Bring your attention to the body part and then release the focus, then repeat. Let the mental attention contact the awareness already present in the body part. Allow whatever happens.

Form does not differ from Body

And Body does not differ from Form.

Form is Body and Body is Form.

6 PLEASURE, PAIN & BLISS

The partner of pleasure is pain.

Bliss has no opposite.

In bliss, pain and pleasure are one.

*"Pain and pleasure are the crests and valleys of the waves
in the ocean of bliss."*

NISARGADATTA MAHARAJ

Our first bodily experience of life as impressed on memory is found within the womb. Here, the biochemistry of the mother, including its rhythms and responses, is utterly shared. When the mother awakens with a feeling of doom or depression, the unborn child is at one with the feeling. When the level of cortisol in the blood of the mother spikes, the unborn child also experiences this spiking. Subtle biochemical patterns and reflexes in response to the environment are already being learned at a formational layer of the body. Much of this is experienced as waves of comfort, warmth and safety blending with the deep home of sleep. But something is already happening here.

Something is disturbing the peace. Behind this prenatal biochemical patterning are atmospheres or states of being of the mother.

The birth process is an uncomfortable experience for the baby: culminating in the shock of air in the lungs, a stinging light and a sudden exposure of the skin surface to the external temperature of the rough air. On the other side of birth, peace is found in reunion with the mother and the pure pleasure or merging again with her body and being nurtured in her arms. Where there was physical unity, there is now bliss in the mother's touch. From this moment on, the pendulum between pleasure and pain begins to swing. It is intimately connected with the separation and unity experienced with the body of the mother.

There is a Nondual Quality which prevails in babies during this period of naked infancy. Between the depth of sleep, the shock of separation in form from the mother, and the pleasure in reunion with the mother, there are periods of pure, physical bliss. There is bliss in the opening of the eyes and perceiving patterns of light. There is bliss in hearing sounds; in the touch on the hand; in the kicking of the feet. There is bliss in the rumble of the pushchair and the ability to make sounds that vibrate with that rumble.

As we develop, we lose our connection to this bliss. The grasping towards pleasure, and the attempt to keep it, is balanced by our aversion to pain and suffering. The agenda to control suffering by not feeling it and to maximize pleasure in our lives, gradually numbs the senses. The resistance to feeling pain is also a resistance to feeling anything – simply because we cannot know if an impression is pleasurable or painful in advance of opening to it. Pleasure itself becomes dulled. The bliss of pure sensation that is available beyond the polarity of pleasure and pain gets disconnected as the sensory system by degrees locks down within the energetic form of a Separate Self.

Pleasure

Perhaps the chief illusion about pleasure is that we can seek it out, control it, keep it and defend it. Yet, when we contemplate pleasure, it rarely obeys the prescriptions of the mind.

Even when we take drugs or alcohol to induce states of pleasure, the effect is momentary and dulls with time into a kind of dependency on the drugs to avoid pain. Often, pleasure can be experienced as a temporary relief from pain. How pleasant it is when we are freezing cold to draw close to a source of warmth. What pleasure can be found in eating carbohydrates when we have been dieting for a month. A simple glass of water can give enormous pleasure on a sweltering day. Pleasure can be measured by the relief from pain or discomfort. Pleasure depends on pain, to be pleasurable.

Our desire for pleasure over pain is in a ubiquitous Source suffering. This desire for relief from discomfort creates more discomfort. It knocks out the present moment of felt experience in anticipation of the relief that will come later. We board up the windows of perception and close the doors until the experience of opening them is guaranteed to be a pleasant one. Under the illusion that if we lock down perception, suffering doesn't need to be suffered, we contract experience for later.

Out of a mosaic of contractions based on the avoidance of pain, we can sometimes be surprised by pleasure. It can be very pleasant to release anger. We can take pleasure in crying our eyes out. There can be a sudden, unexpected pleasure in the purity of grief. At the same time, that event in which we had the greatest expectation of pleasure can turn out to be a disappointment. Pleasure cannot be dictated. It can only be allowed as felt experience, as an intricate part of an open sensitivity which always includes threads of pain.

Pain

With tremendous clarity, the spiritual teacher Eckhart Tolle elected to call the areas of emotion 'the pain body'. If we close our eyes and notice our sensations and feelings against a backdrop of infinite darkness, forgetting even the imagined appearance of a body, we will often get a series of patches, hazes, swirls and densities which map out areas of discomfort or pain. This is the pain body: where there is contraction; where flow is lost; where there is blockage or density; or where there is uncommon heat or cold. Even if we bring our attention solely to physical sensations and let them take form in our mind's eye against a backdrop of darkness, we are likely to get a map of pain and discomfort. What this is telling us is that to a large degree, pain defines our experience. Where pain is absent, so are we.

Pain will be at the roots of all contractions outlined in this book. It is a pain that cries out for the Nondual Quality from which it has been disconnected. In a sense, the pain is the baby and the Nondual Quality is the universe of the mother. Pain is not a bad thing; it is the sound of healing.

Resistance to pain doesn't make the pain go away, it simply covers it up. Although we have invented whole classes of painkillers, they don't really kill the pain, they kill the experience of the pain. In a way, they create the conditions in which we can ignore the pain. Used in moderation, external support to ease pain can be merciful, giving us time and space to take in the process in small, manageable portions. But it is a misconception to believe that they make the pain go away. Pain is a message of distress. It is a call for reunion. It wants to come home into the ease of the whole. Covering our eyes and our ears doesn't undo its message. Sooner or later, we will pinch ourselves to check we are still alive.

Pain cannot ultimately be negated, but only transformed towards pleasure, bliss or equanimity. In the words of Carl Jung: "There is no birth of consciousness without pain." Our pain holds the cut of truth and the vitality of life. When we touch our pain in its purity with our consciousness and agree to hold space for it in our awareness, an expansion occurs into the sentient field of healing, in which all forms transform towards harmony. This is because pain can also be experienced as the bliss of being physically alive. The open connection with this bliss is fundamental to the process of transformation from fear to freedom.

Bliss: Nondual Quality

Bliss is unbothered by the duality of pleasure and pain. When either pain or pleasure emerge, they begin to expand through the field of awareness. When we release the agenda of grasping and aversion, the pleasure/pain polarity dissolves into an experience of bliss.

There is bliss in the purity of sensing life beyond the restrictions of form. It's not a bliss that can be contained, kept or held – attempting to do this will drop us again to the sliding scale of pleasure and pain. It is a bliss that expands and refines in proportion to our ability to release it. Wherever we let go of the agenda to control, the bliss of being physically alive is reborn in expanded form. The way to experience bliss is to constantly release the experience of it.

We have objectified bliss through our thinking processes. There is a belief that there is an extreme form of pleasure that can be won through the acquisition of objects from the outside. Conditioning dictates that if there is pain, we cannot know bliss. We delay bliss for later, but later never really comes.

The experiential insight that comes through the realization that bliss is always here, undamaged, unending and irrespective of terms and conditions of pleasure and pain, is fundamental to healing.

Contemplations

1. Relax the body and find an area of relatively more pain or discomfort. Welcome the experience of discomfort. Be curious about the experience of discomfort, inviting it to expand through the body and into the air. Return to the original position of discomfort or pain and notice any changes or shifts in physical experience and/or in attitude towards the physical body.

2. Close your eyes and recall the feeling of bliss from any time of your life. Give the feeling all the space to expand through all the body and the space around the body. Open your eyes and look around. Close your eyes again and observe what happens.

Form does not differ from Bliss

And Bliss does not differ from Form.

Form is Bliss, and Bliss is Form.

7 STRESS, DEPRESSION & RELAXATION

The partner of stress is depression.

Relaxation has no opposite.

In relaxation, depression and stress are one.

"Relaxation is an absence of effort. One does not do anything to relax. What most people describe as relaxation is actually diversion."

RABBI DR. AVRAHAM TWERSKI

Relaxation is a hot product in this era. We watch violence and stress in movies to let the body relax. We absorb global stories of disaster, tragedy and guilt, to keep ourselves relaxed (because it's behind the screen and therefore not 'real'). We build icons and idols that give false feelings of safety through the impression that a higher authority is taking care of us. We design a myriad of drugs and prescribe relaxation over the counter. We build and maintain arsenals of weapons of mass destruction, fight wars and terrorize the terrorists in the name of this elixir – relaxation. We plunder the earth of her finite resources and at the same time poison her atmosphere for the sake of a little bit of short-term ease. We burn with ambition, seek to become someone other than who we are, strive to possess, control, convert or educate one another and work endlessly to keep our imagined enemies at bay – so that we can relax later.

What is this prize – this relaxation – which never really comes but that's found at the core of so much of our striving? What happens when we begin to relax?

What we commonly mean by 'relax' is to move to a relatively lower level of stress. Often this involves distraction from the tensed-up energetic boundaries of the Separate Self through entertainment. Yet distraction is not the same as relaxation, although it can ease the voltage of stress stored in the body, it will not resolve inner conflict.

What happens when we relax? Relaxation is about softening and opening. It's about an agreement to be here, in physical form. Yet the first symptom of increasing relaxation is often pain. As we relax and put our feet up at the end of a hard day, for example, the first thing we notice could be how much our feet are aching, or how the muscles in our neck are clenched. Awareness of this pain is relaxation happening. The wonder of tired feet, the heaviness of the body, the soft nothingness of a mind that has been busy, all signify an expansion of awareness out of where we have been stressfully contracted.

Yet we are more than just bodies. We are also composed of energetic contractions of feelings and emotions. The shame of being proved wrong at the workplace – echoing an old shame from childhood; the stranger on the bus that looks like a dead parent; the sense of isolation around the quest to survive 'out there' in the world of people; all signify deeper areas of stress. Also, these energetic contractions begin to open when we relax.

In this way, relaxation is a spiritual practice and a healing art. It's only through relaxing equally into the areas of comfort and discomfort that the unfolding of the psyche can take place – telling its woes, signaling its pain, and moving still deeper to rest. This multi-layered transformation of stress and depression into peace is vital to our well-being.

Stress

Stress is a deep suffering of always being in the wrong place at the wrong time. It gives a daunting base note of feeling awkward; discordant; not good enough; and always running for or away from something. This births an agenda to improve, or at least to seem good enough to others, which brings more stress. Pretending to be good enough, or keeping up appearances, can be very stressful when exposure can happen through the unexpected.

Stress breeds feelings and beliefs of inherent wrongness or insufficiency. It is the electric fence around the boundaries of the Separate Self, as well as around the contractions and traumas from which we would like to be separated. Often, stress has no definable cause. It can be triggered by certain events – such as the bank manager calling – but deeper resolution is not won by answering the phone. When we begin to relax around areas of stress, this can become increasingly apparent. The reason for stress tends to come later: the stress is there beforehand. This stress has roots in contractions, some of which are unconscious and inherited. The deeper release comes when we can allow the release of stress through the nerve system without conditions, irrespective of actions taken or not taken in the external world.

Depression

Unable to physically run away, or fight, the third fear response can kick in. This is the instinct to freeze. This freezing appears in the form of depression. The depressed areas of ourselves are where we block vitality. In depression, life is frozen through the deadening of inner unrest through denial.

Even after we have withdrawn consciousness from these frozen areas, they still bother us as through our feeling awareness, somewhat like locked rooms in houses that no one ever enters. They surface as feelings of discomfort, generating dreams that seek resolution in sleep when the controlling aspect of mind has ducked out.

As both sense and sensitivity decrease in these frozen, detached areas, we can also become increasingly numb, closing areas of our feeling connection to life. This closure forms a barrier between the inner and outer worlds. Our friends and relatives become 'other' and we, by degrees, become 'other' to ourselves. This alienation, isolation and loneliness can breed more stress and depression. The energetic density of depression causes a feeling of unearthed heaviness. We experience ourselves as separate from life.

Whereas depression is often defined as a complete state, this is the chronic form. In practice, all of us have depressed areas in the psyche. Depression is part of the formula of contraction: we depress what we don't want to feel. Yet when we come into one of these areas – just like when we pass through a thundercloud in a plane – the senselessness can seem to fill every corner.

The healing of depression is found through allowing our awareness to surround the frozen areas of feeling. As with stress, we are fundamentally never depressed 'because of' an external event. While a nurturing, happy environment can be tremendously supportive, the roots of depression precede outer circumstance. When depression comes to life, there is a gradual diffusion of dense energy through the invitation of our awareness. As it diffuses, particles of fear, anger, despair emerge as part of the depressed content. The more we can stay as awareness around the dense energy of depression, even as it starts to diffuse with forbidden emotions and thoughts, the more we awaken. Not in a moment, not in an hour, but with time, a melting of depressed areas of experience occurs.

Again, the secret is in allowance, the allowance of life in all its forms. Healing does not come by refusing to see the affliction. It is always an effect of allowing the affliction into perception, both into our feeling awareness and into our waking consciousness. We cannot heal a disease by avoiding the disease. Healing is not to be found elsewhere, with another authority, a different medication, or with another technique. It is found at the spacious core of the depression itself. The prescription of what is needed is found in the contraction. Where else could it be?

To open to Life, the greatest healer of all, we need to be able to open. This opening occurs as an effect of relaxation. In relaxation, we open like a flower. In letting go, we reconnect with deeper layers of ourselves. In letting go also of these layers, we can suddenly and unexpectedly find we are home, in the formless, living, unrestricted and unconditional space of Being. Depression is the endpoint of the belief in existential negation: relaxation is the starting point of renewed manifestation.

Relaxation: Nondual Quality

Don't delay relaxation. Now is the time to relax, because there is simply no other time. Relaxation is a deepening and expansion into a wider field of awareness that can only happen now. We're programmed to believe in crude either-or fixtures. When there is anger, we can't relax; while we're in debt, we can't relax; while there's suffering in Africa, we can't relax; if that hideous person continues to work in our office, relaxation must wait. This dualistic notion of relaxation is building an inner bomb of stress, that if it can't release, will start to solidify in patches of depression.

Relaxation is a practice that can happen each time we experience anything. Warm wind on the face: relax the body, relax into the experience. Looking at the view across a crowded bus: relax the eyes, relax the senses. Someone is screaming at you. Relax within the screaming. Taking a pee in a crowded shopping center? Take an extra moment to relax into the home of the body. Relaxation is possible together with every fleeting piece of experience. We only lose it because of the way we're programmed. Home comes with us everywhere. We never need leave ourselves to find it.

We're breathing anyway, so relax into it. The breath is a wonderful barometer of our state of stress and distress. When we're troubled, breath becomes more shallow, uneven and often even stops for some moments. By bringing our attention to the flow of our breathing – together with whatever else is happening in any moment – we are signaling with our breathing that it is possible to relax even amid the stress and even when we're depressed.

The key to relaxation is that it is primarily a relaxation out of the programs of mind, this includes restrictions on movement. When we are walking through a depression for example and meet that sense of depression even in the space between our feet and the earth, the challenge is to relax with softness and curiosity into the pain and discomfort of that. When our body is swept with tiredness, relax into the sensation of tiredness. Tiredness is simply the feeling of stress dissolving.

This relaxation into the suffering of what is, means we open more deeply into the perception of what else is here: a hummingbird; the life in the grass, the clouds patterning the sky.

Agree to relax beyond the belief in the Separate Self. The instinct to isolate and to split inside from outside plays a significant part in stress and depression. Just maintaining this belief in the 'I' versus the outer world demands a tremendous amount of vigilance and vitality. It feeds the sense of danger which generates more stress. If we believe ourselves as separate from the whole, we must constantly police the border, which we can rarely soften to ourselves. We can even begin to depend on that sense of threat to manage depression, as stress brings short-term fixes of adrenaline.

As we relax during our day-to-day life, the irrational frontiers of the Separate Self will come forward, as if to remind us of the deadly things that could happen. The art is to not stop relaxing when we meet such stress: to respect our own borders (and those of others), but still allow an energetic relaxation through them. The border remains but the relaxation continues, from the ground up or from the sky down.

Relaxation is not a dull thing. It is the source of rejuvenation which begins with the individual body and reverberates through the whole, supporting processes of healing through body, heart and mind.

Contemplations

1. In a comfortable position in a safe and private space, decide to relax. Notice the falling movement of relaxation and try to surrender to it, regardless of comfort or discomfort. When you reach a floor of relaxation, try to relax into that also. Feel the quality of the floor; become the floor and expand.

2. Scan the spaces around the body and try to sense areas of greater density. Relax around the density and bless the contracted area, noticing its shape, texture, color, sound, smell, taste. Move the attention to

the feet and connect with the sense of gravity. Let your consciousness sink into the earth beneath the feet and rest there.

Form does not differ from Relaxation

And Relaxation does not differ from Form.

Form is Relaxation and Relaxation is Form.

8 WAR, SURRENDER & PEACE

The partner of war is surrender.

Peace has no opposite.

In peace, surrender and war are one.

"Peace is not an absence of war, it is a virtue, a state of mind, a disposition for benevolence, confidence, justice."

BARUCH SPINOZA

Peace is a Nondual Quality that is rarely allowed, and it's often misconceived. The power of peace outlives all conflict. Just as conflict is structural to every contraction, peace is inherent to each conflict. Logically, conflict could not occur except out of the perennial backdrop of peace. This means that the invitation to peace can support the opening of all contractions. Contractions themselves are preservative – they are an energetic means to keep the peace in a certain space, for some time. Yet when a contraction begins to unfold and heal, it is through peace that they are released and the sense of peace signals reunion.

When a conflictual situation is apparently resolved, we can often sense the energetic difference between a forced surrender and true release of agenda. Peace knows no borders, and in this can be experienced as descending from outside the psyche. Through this expansion, what previously seemed like a deadlock unlocks itself with solutions that can appear as if from nowhere. Thankfully, the energy of unconditional peace is a facilitator of new possibilities, perspectives, dimensions, relaxation and existential overview. In terms of the human psyche, peace is precisely the supporting presence that allows us to release structures of the psyche into the flow of transformation.

We often associate peace with the arrival of a new baby or with the hours after a non-traumatic death. When the story is born, peace is here. As the story continues, peace underlies the utterance. When the story is closed, peace remains. Happily, we do not need to wait until our inevitable death to rest in peace. We are already resting in peace, being born in peace, living in peace and dying in peace in each moment.

Peace arrives by invitation, and often just the experiential memory of peace is enough to open the way for expansion through and beyond the conflict inherent to every contraction. Peace is so powerful in its effect that it can be threatening to a psyche locked into the belief that it can create or control reality. While binary thought patterns structure reality through duality and through either-or choices, peace brings the overview that both sides of a duality co-depend. Whether we choose to turn left or right, both left and right continue to interdepend, irrespective of our decisions. Mental conditioning feeds the competition within duality through the belief that it can delete or extinguish the unwanted part of any pair. It wants only good not evil, light not darkness, pleasure not pain. To be at peace is to allow the unwanted partner within every duality, something that the conditioned mind will tend to resist.

Peace inherently allows all that is here, and as such, peace can be feared. Where there is fear, we tend to seek control through definition. Hence, peace gets reframed as conditional – a contract involving defined behaviors that can be implemented by force. In terms of experience, peace is often associated with nothingness, lack of life or the end of life. To draw on the eternal resource of peace, we need to undo this conditioning. Peace is not the absence of life; it is the Source of life. Its potency is beyond any 'thing' the mind could grasp and beyond the mind itself. It is the Source and backdrop to all mental formations and reformations and to all energetic phenomenon.

War

The energy of war is extraordinary in that it surpasses 'normal' everyday experience and promotes the reversal of norms, breaking both consciously conditioned rules and ethics. In this, all psychological trauma is a kind of war zone. Trauma is an area of experience that we are unable to integrate with 'normal' life, including the social field and family arena. As the living experience is left outside of the 'functioning' psyche, it forms a sub universe of its own, with its own game-plans and atmospheres. When we are in a trauma tunnel we can feel far away from normal life, and we can experience ourselves in a state of war with 'normal' life.

As humans, we have put the energetic phenomenon of war in a category of its own, with rules and laws outside of conventional ethics. As one man in a divorce said about care and respect: "That's all very nice, but this is war." When we are "at war", care is frozen and conscious beliefs can flip over into their shadows. Suddenly, lying becomes an asset; cruelty a show of heroism; cynicism a virtue; and killing an act of loyalty. Theft, dishonesty, manipulation and even murder become survival assets within the basic equation of the binary mind, which is 'kill-or-be-killed'. Rule breakers are cheered as heroes and conformists can be condemned as collaborators. There is intense pressure to take an absolute stand on one side or the other, and the consequences of that decision will continue long after the energy of war has passed.

Yet even though we might be suddenly awarded for killing or torturing fellow human beings, the commandment 'thou shalt not kill' still resounds through the psyche. The existential shock of violent death for the soldier is as strong as on a citizen in a time of peace. The shock of mortality and the horror of power is no less damaging to the psyche. When a divorcing couple hurt their children to win custody, they still carry the burden of hurting their children, even after the divorce is processed. The arbitrary rewriting of behavioral codes comes at a heavy and long-term cost to the human psyche. No number of medals from outer authorities can untangle the core of psychic confusion.

When we are caught within the Us Versus Them equation of war, there is an immediate disempowerment. We tend to see ourselves as victims, even when we are the stronger power. Thus, we hear statements such as that of the late Prime Minister of Israel Golda Meir: "We can forgive [them] for killing our children. We cannot forgive them for forcing us to kill their children." While many still sympathize with the sentiment within the parameters of ongoing war, it can also be seen as exemplifying the human helplessness in taking responsibility for the lived horror that clouds all victory when the energy of war rises in the name of separate survival.

The tremendous responsibility deficit left by war presents a legacy of accusation and emotional offloading on the present-day enemy and/or the historic one. In recent years, scientists have suggested that the legacy of war in the form of Post-Traumatic Stress Disorder (PTSD) can be genetically inherited – as is our resilience.

When working with Nondual Therapy, we should be aware that the experience of the perpetrator tends to be the most forbidden from waking consciousness, and therefore the most contracted, especially when the aggression failed. Unlike with victimhood, there is a social environment that resists the release of the experience and its integration into 'normal' life. The repression of the 'bad guy' aspect that is always included in war can surface as nightmares, inner shadows, blind spots and self-destructive behavioral patterns within the client, even when the crime was ancestral.

When we hear our client say: "I hate myself" or "I want to kill myself", we are witnessing a human at war with an inner enemy, where the deeper identification is not with the victim, but with the aggressor – the one that wields power. This state of war will lead to much mental propaganda, behavioral masking and tactics of distraction, avoidance and secrecy. As a last resort, the instinct to destroy the enemy within can become suicidal, as in times of war, the best defense can often seem to be attack.

While the energy of war unearths our habit-based systems of belief, it also unhooks a power that is temporarily free of the normative shackles of guilt and shame: this unrestricted release has a tremendous energetic charge and is compelling to witness. For some, it can even be experienced as a tremendous relief to let all hell break loose. Yet war always burns out in time, leaving its complicated imprints of horror on the psyche, not only for the immediate survivors, but also for future generations.

Often, when marriages break down, this torrent of destructive energy can be witnessed as each side fights the other for property, income and custodial rights. Beneath this war is the fundamental duality of good and evil caught in contraction. If one side is good, then the other will be proved bad, and vice versa through all contractions. If the wife is innocent, then the husband must be guilty. If the husband is pure, then the wife should be ashamed. If the wife is honest, then the husband must be lying. A radical opportunity presents itself in this kind of domestic warzone for the purification of belief structures and an awakening into the inevitability of inner truth, free of the shackles of social authority and the discriminating mind.

Even in the apparently peaceful age of individualism, we are often far more entangled and excited by the energy of war than the energy of peace. In many ways, we are collectively still moving through trauma. The fundamental fight to survive in a time of threat to physical life can be awesome. Yet this old fear of physical threat can show up as the energy of war directed towards anyone who threatens our internal status-quo. In this the energy of survival moves from the physical to more subtle forms: survival of a tradition, a structure of personality, a pattern, or an aspect of Ego. When war becomes a subtler affair, the death threat is not physical but is experienced as existential. This is where we find the horrors which are perceived as 'a fate worse than death', hiding within our worst and oldest fears – fears we hardly dare admit to ourselves.

Through time, the energy of war screams from the core belief in the Separate Self and surfaces as a defense wherever there is a feeling of discomfort. Someone makes you feel inferior, it's war. There is jealousy, it's war. There is accusation: war. The 'other', 'God', the 'world', 'life' or even existence itself takes on the form of the enemy in an unending struggle of suffering perpetuating suffering. Happily, our consciousness is not defined by thought or the survival of personality structures. It can oversee it all and in time, can allow the omnipresent healing power of unconditional peace: that for which every war is fought.

Surrender

The horror of guilt and the burning sensation of shame can be so powerful that we are quite predetermined to identify ourselves as victims rather than perpetrators in any situation. Even when the context has involved direct perpetration, aggressors will often experience themselves as victims. This predominance of victimhood leads to structures in which surrender becomes fear-based, and there is a difficulty to 'stand' for something. While surrender is often hailed as a spiritual virtue, it has also evolved as an affliction of the psyche, showing up as a fear of conflict.

The diversion of the energy of war through the appeasing movement of surrender, is often not enough to release the traumatic charge of war. For the one who has tried to grasp peace through movements of surrender, the moment will come when surrender is no longer an option. The fear of conflict will, sooner or later, magnify the conflict – when the last border is passed, or when impossible demands are made (such as undoing history, or ceasing to exist). If your very existence in any form poses a problem to the aggressor, how is it possible to surrender? How is it possible to not exist, or to have never existed? At a certain stage, surrender of what is demanded by war is no longer possible.

Just as war has often been associated with the male gender or male aspect of the psyche, surrender has equally been associated with the female form. The traumatic split between the sexes, in which women have been historically denied time and space in the collective field of manifestation has cut deep wounds of exclusion. The female conditioning to keep quiet, defer to the husband, to allow her own objectification and control by male authority continues to cause distress between men and women, and is enflamed by the general contraction around sexuality.

In daily terms, the tendency to avoid conflict through surrender leads to many manipulations, games and strategies within the power struggle. The survival movement of surrender is as much built into our physical bodies as is the instinct to fight. When no fight seems possible, an animal will move into possum state – pure surrender. Dissociating from the body, this is the last attempt to deter predators that sometimes lose their appetite when confronted with apparently dead meat – that could have been infected by disease. This state of dissociation is the endpoint of psychological surrender – literally surrendering the time and space of the body and thinning the connection to the body to a mere thread. Dissociation is a known phenomenon in trauma and can be triggered even when a psychological nerve is touched that connects to the trauma.

Surrender, like war, searches for the energy of peace. War seeks peace through possession or negation of the object of conflict; surrender seeks peace through abandonment of the object of conflict. Both movements misconceive peace – as if it were something to be lost or won. Both contain a peace which is always here, and which is powerful beyond all concepts of mind.

Peace: Nondual Quality

Where love can be experienced as light, peace is more akin to the experience of darkness. Yet in the first splits into natural duality, where light is differentiated from darkness, we can sense light as love and peace as darkness. Love and peace dance together through all creation. Soothing, receptive, boundless, powerful, this darkness or peace is a kind of home that allows even the perception of light.

Although contracts and even contractions can support the absorption of peace, contracts are nothing other than conditions. Peace as an energy cannot be enforced from the outside as a form. Conditions may be enforced, but peace not. Peace is always here, never taken away, always available to human invitation. Peace is always now, never yesterday or later. It is infinite in supply and is more familiar to us than home. As peace is inherent to every moment of perception, alive in consciousness itself, it cannot be grasped, kept or controlled. Our only choice is to blend with it into unity, allowing it to coexist and expand through all conditions, whether they formed by dynamics of war or surrender.

Contemplation

Imagine there is a point of light about 30 cm above the head. Out of this point, allow a sky-blue color to descend through and around the body and into the earth. Contemplate the color and its effects, without interference. Move awareness to the chest area and recall the feeling of peace. Release the context of the feeling and invite the energy to expand, sharing it with anyone or anything that appears.

Form does not differ from Peace

And Peace does not differ from Form.

Form is Peace and Peace is Form.

9 FEAR, ANGER & COMPASSION

The partner of fear is anger.

Compassion has no opposite.

In compassion, anger and fear are one.

"One day with compassion is worth a hundred days with-out it."

THICH NHAT HANH

Fear and anger are instinctive energies within the protective mechanism of contractions. They are inherent to the separation of one form into two and are natural in the process of physical creation. Where there is fear, there will be an underside of anger and where there is anger, there will be an underside of fear.

Compassion is a fundamental healing elixir that crosses the energetic substance of the Separate Self. Arising spontaneously, it leaps over the impermanent borders of separation in pure recognition of the commonality of human experience. The suffering inside ourselves is recognized as the same suffering in others, and relief comes of itself as the conceptual lynch-pins of suffering (that it is separate, isolated, excluded and personal) are released. The energy of compassion brings direct release to the tender first emotional layers of separate form – the powerful survival responses of fear and anger.

The emotions of anger and fear tend to be so polarized between victim and perpetrator that we become accustomed to view them as different energies originating from different sources. Yet they go together. It can be so difficult to allow these raw emotional energies to release that we barely experience them in their purity. It is so important to understand and experience that it is the repression of anger that creates violence, not the allowance of it. Likewise, it is the denial of fear that breeds anxiety. Fear and anger are naturally a quick flash of lightning through the nerve system – to put it simply, it's a release of energetic voltage.

Anger and fear are the residues of a painful rupture into separate form, and this rupture is often traumatic. These emotions surround the experience of violation, insecure boundaries and the horror of helplessness. Not least, they originate in the body from the cellular memory of traumatic division.

This pain – or this void-like sense of eternal absence – is already alive. We cannot fear an experience that we have never experienced before. We can only fear the repetition of that which we have experienced in the past. "One is never afraid of the unknown;" wrote Krishnamurti, "one is afraid of the known coming to an end." Often, the repressed conditions of fear and anger feel like home to us, as the survivable status quo. We know the patterns. Trouble starts however, when circumstances cause the old river to burst its well-formed banks.

Both anger and fear are a reaction to the pain which is already here on the inside. It's often not only about a pending violation of the 'other', but more about that which is already suffering within the psyche. Both fear and anger seek to defend against pain, to avoid it being seen or felt. Yet at a deeper layer, both are born out of the pain of separation. How can we at once protect the pain of the 'separate' self and at the same time long to become one with the whole? It's a paradox that seeks the deeper connection found through compassion.

Trouble comes with the belief in the absolute nature of the Separate Self, which is experienced in opposition to the outer world. In the quest for preservation, the interdependent network through which the psyche is sustained is ruptured through hardened shields of distance and isolation. Like a self-fulfilling prophecy, the fear or rage at separation can separate us still further as we become by degrees increasingly sociopathic and alone.

When fear and anger merge, dread comes forward. Dread is a fusion of anger and fear, in a cloud of threatening horror, that moves between and through people. In the social field, it is channeled through aspects of the living psyche that have lost a feeling connection with True Nature and in this, it's a field of primal psychological suffering. Mostly unanchored in the present moment, dread is the source energy of toxic illusion: it is composed of the unhealed horror of memory and the formless threat of what could be. Dread thrives off the belief in the Separate Self and agendas of possession manifesting through structures of control.

Fear

Traditional psychology posits four collective fears. These are: the fear of sex, death, physical illness and insanity. These fears are based on impermanence – the loss of life, virility, health and sanity. All these losses are inevitable, and in this, fear is a rational phenomenon. Sooner or later, we will lose sexual potency. In addition, the 'otherness' of the opposite sex will accompany us to some degree until we leave this body.

Sooner or later, we will physically die. Repression of the fear of death doesn't remove its inevitability. Sooner or later, we will experience physical illness: it is a natural part of our biology. Sooner or later, we will lose mental functioning: beyond normal confusions of identity and/or brain imbalance, physical aging involves the breakdown of mind.

These fears defer the inevitable, but also, when there is awakening into the Now, it can be clear that this pure impermanence – this loss – is already present as a fundamental existential truth. Death is already now, in this moment, not in an imagined future. The split between male and female is also, here and now. All that we are, is now. It's already happening, and it's OK. The energy of dread would have us believe otherwise, though, as fear thrives in the formless threat of tomorrow.

Fear is about boundaries: it's about protecting the physical boundary of the skin surface, but also the sentient boundaries of the psyche. The mind is highly responsive to fear, as it is deeply rooted in programs of physical survival. Yet it can complicate simple survival issues in a spectacular way, by grasping at minute details to predict grandiose outcomes. From the natural physical instinct to avoid pain, fear feeds the agenda to avoid discomfort of any kind.

The mind filters what it sees, and through thought, we edit, amend and censure the content of experience. This brings a short-term sense of power, but also feeds the fear of exposure. It knows that beneath the censorship and the amendments, other spooky, unseen stuff is going on. Thus, it works even harder to keep control, and to establish and consolidate its desired reality. The mind also needs to maintain connection with the object of fear. It constantly needs to monitor the threat, lest it be surprised. As such, the mind is often more preoccupied with fear than contentment.

The energy of fear is connected to conscious awakening which involves liberation from old thought forms. Fear comes when the form is dying. This can transform naturally into bliss, which like fear, also excites and awakens boundaries with the pending release of form.

As in orgasm, the transformation of losing form can be blissful. The shear sensitivity of boundaries expanding to the point of explosion, the adrenaline of pure freedom through capitulation, the surrender to life, brings fear in resistance and bliss in allowance. Always, in and of itself, a new form emerges. Often this is one that is more attuned, natural and responsive to the living energy of the here and now.

The collective resistance to transformation is based on the fear of fear itself. The construction of fear-based, protective fences around fear adds frontier after frontier to the Separate Self. Often, it is no longer clear what all the fear fences are protecting. As the threat takes the unrestricted shapes of nightmare, the energy of nightmare drives the thinking mind in anxious circles around that which must never be experienced.

These empires of fear are the source of the existential angst that often comes forward around a spiritual emergency. In awakening into untethered consciousness, contractions begin to shake in their foundations. In the release of pure, unconditioned consciousness beyond the individual 'I', light also shines indiscriminately through the whole field of consciousness. One effect of light is that it awakens form. Frozen fear comes to life. These structures of fear are the matrix on which personal identity are formed. Together, these inner forms affect the personality. In this, an outcome of sudden Nondual awakening can be nervous breakdown or psychosis, and the great tragedy is that the medical and social choice is often to medicate the patient out of this depersonalized state into socially conformed behavior.

There are three classical fear responses to a perceived threat: fight, flight and freeze. These are survival responses of the human being, but also of the sub-parts of the personality that we call contractions. These responses are natural parts of that process of transformation which are connected to the regulated release of the charge of energy within contractions.

When the freeze or flight instinct fails, especially through the intervention of drugs, the organic cycle of release also gets thwarted. We will release the freeze, or stop running, when we are able to connect to a safer dimension within ourselves. The third fear response – fight – can occur when freeze or flight have failed to bring safety – when we feel existentially trapped. This fight instinct can manifest both as self-destruction and aggression towards other. Here, the individual can become a danger to themselves and/or others, and these are often the cases that get the most psychiatric attention. The fight instinct is deeply connected with the traumatic structure of the inner perpetrator, the abuser, the 'bad guy' in the energy field, which tends to be the most repressed side of every trauma.

The fear responses listed by classical psychology (fight, flight and freeze), are also anger responses. Flight is occurring, for example, in the rageful abandonment of responsibility. Freeze is present in passive aggression or when we 'freeze' someone out through the silent treatment. Fight is unequivocally an anger response in the first degree. In this, we can feel how fear and anger – like victim and perpetrator – dance together in the search for release through compassion.

Anger

When anger has been forbidden as an emotion (that is, when the expression of anger has been repeatedly condemned), it can be frozen to the extent that the person doesn't even 'feel' anger anymore: there can be anxiety and stress even at the scent of anger within themselves or the environment.

Stress, nervousness, irritation, frustration, worry or compulsive thinking are all effects of the denial or repression of anger as well as fear. The powerful, fast energy of anger is pushed down, denied or frozen, and this creates a restlessness on many levels. It's like a bottle neck of voltage awaiting release. This can go into the body, where the cells are forced to hold a charge of unreleased energy (commonly known as the great killer: stress), or it can go into the mind – where thoughts construct realities to try to dictate feelings.

The movement of this powerful, purifying, honest but potentially destructive energy is generally disallowed and feared. Indeed, many are in a cycle of anger at their own fear and fear of their own anger. They are also angry that they are angry and fearful that they are afraid. These twin flames of anger and fear are at the root of severe anxiety disorders and the living hell of panic attacks. Their energetic voltage is so high, that they are found in processes of creation and destruction. They are also found like centurions at the gates of every contraction and at the walls that separate what we know from the vast unknown. They distort our personalities and contort our means to relate in freedom. Through the repressed energies of anger and fear, the field of pure awareness becomes a field with a great sign: "Beware!" – of every conceivable and inconceivable threat. This is hardly an invitation to the experience of life and living, but rather a warning for trespassers, the disenfranchised and the lost.

While our judgements about the emotions of fear are strong, our condemnation of the emotion of anger is even more extreme. Born in the instinct to protect territory, the expression of anger in many circumstances can lead to a consolidation of the divisions between one person and another. It is rightfully feared as it is the energetic source of warfare, abuse, cruelty, violence and murder. Yet the unconditioned energy of anger is closely connected with the natural movement of care and protection.

Taken in slow motion: anger awakens when vulnerable layers of suffering are exposed. Anger is a pain reflex. The anger is rooted in pure suffering, and its agenda is to protect that pain from further injury. In this way, anger is a form of energetic communication which is driven by the need to protect. Although anger is a raw, sublingual form of communication, expressions of anger can lead to communication breakdown. This can open a sense of hopelessness. The core of anger is an open field of existential despair.

Anger can feel incredibly righteous, because in its purity, it has the quality of truth around it. This is partly because as an energetic arising, it is truthfully happening: it is the social oppression or mental repression of this energy which is dishonest. It is also because the pain which is touched, the trigger behind the arousal of anger, is more essential than superficial expressions of fear-driven appeasement and conformity.

There is a lot of light in anger: it's alive, vibrant and vital. It breaks shells to liberate seedlings and splits masks to expose more authentic faces. Because of the quality of truth in anger, its movement can sometimes take form as courage.

Anger gets its bad name when we try to control it, which generally leads to more confusion. We try to white-wash and repress our anger by blaming the world 'outside' ourselves as the cause of it – attempting to find sanctuary in the disempowered form of the victim. Through explanation, justification and condemnation of the 'other', circling thoughts can become like propaganda leaflets repeating the established liturgy stating why the anger is justified. Such liturgies gain hypnotic power through endless repetition and play out socially through attempts to recruit others to the 'right' side.

Compassion: Nondual Quality

The Nondual Quality that supports freedom within the spiraling twin trap of fear and anger is compassion. This is not compassion from a place of superiority, holiness, condescension or charity. It is a reflex that occurs of itself, manifesting the energy of anger or fear through the body in the form of direct action. Compassion doesn't need to be seen and it asks no reward: it happens in and of itself. It has that same atmosphere of truth that is found in the energies of anger or fear. The first opening of compassion is in the wisdom that anger, and fear are collective fields; they are neither the property of the victim or the perpetrator, they are transpersonal phenomena.

Both anger and fear seek the compassion that is always here. Due to the contractions of mind and feeling, this compassion gets severed, disconnected, misdirected and complicated. Yet it is never lost. It can never ultimately be taken away, damaged or compromised. It lives outside of the changing conditions of time and space. We are angry because of compassion, because we care. We are fearful because of compassion, because we care.

The word Compassion is made of the roots 'Com' and 'Passion'. 'Com', from the Latin, indicates togetherness. 'Passion' is synonymous with the word suffering. As such, compassion is the energy that allows differentiation within unity, through which differing forms experience the passion of creation in interdependent togetherness. Difference in form means that the sharing of responsibility is possible. If one form is blind, the other can lead. If one is deaf, the other can listen. These are natural and evident movements of compassion, arising out of a unity that underlies all manifestation through space and time.

Compassion is not a movement of grandiosity, pity or generosity. It's rooted in the wisdom of interdependence: that all forms are interconnected. This interdependence is all-inclusive: it includes the phenomena of the separate self and supports individual uniqueness within unity.

Compassion is supported by the wisdom of non-separation. It arises out of a mind liberated from the program that there is such a lasting attainment as 'separate' happiness. It flows freely when the energetic contractions around private suffering release into a willingness to suffer on behalf of the whole. Unity and togetherness become a living service based on the perception that the freedom, happiness and fulfillment of any one part is utterly dependent on the freedom, happiness and fulfillment of the whole. Compassion dissolves the illusion of separation by degrees, on all levels. When we look at the functioning of individual cells in the body, through intracellular communication, we see that each separate cell resonates with the changing form of other cells, under the guiding parameter of the needs of the whole environment. On a physical level, well-being is an effect of intracellular compassion.

The ability to rest back as a deeper source of compassion during sessions where clients need to release a high voltage of anger or fear is important in Nondual Therapy. Compassion doesn't deny anger, yet it also doesn't buy into the emotional stories that attempt to justify or explain the phenomena of anger. Rather, it recognizes anger as a living energy. Like pain, anger and fear communicate the needs of the psyche for release. The therapist's ability to relax deeply within the charge of emotional energy models to the client the easiness of release. The cells in the body of the therapist are transmitting compassion to the cells in the body of the client through resonance. Even the bodies are not ultimately separate.

The removal of pronouns from an emotionally charged sentence initiates a reprogramming of identification with the luggage of emotion. Instead of 'I' am afraid, or 'She' is angry, try rephrasing the phenomena as "There is fear here," or "There is anger here." If the client insists the anger is sourced exclusively elsewhere, as an example, ask if she also feels a little angry sometimes. Open channels from the caught energy within the contraction of the Separate Self, towards the general field. It is much easier to release the energetic charge of emotion when emotional energy is unpinned from the Separate Self. When identification with emotion is loosened, experience is enabled, and with experience comes transformation.

Emotional suffering will generate the language of absolutes: the 'always', 'all the time', 'everything', 'everywhere', 'everyone'; as well as the 'never', 'nothing', 'nowhere', 'nobody'. These polarizing linguistic constructs are inherently untrue and easily checked against authentic experience. For example: "Are you truly tired all the time? Have you ever experience not being tired, even for a moment? What was that like?" The more we soften the hypnotic language of either-or with the introduction of the language of the middle way, the more we open the living field of possibility beyond emotional entanglement. Go wherever possible for the middle ways of language - the 'and-and' - the sometimes, some places, some people. When they state: "I can't do it," add the simple word "Yet." This ameliorates the either-or construction of the contraction and invites the transformation of patterns in both thought and experience.

Contemplations

1. Recall yourself as a young child at school with many children. One of the children is upset. Watch that child. Notice the feeling that is present in you watching the child suffer without trying to take the suffering away. Notice where you feel the feeling in the body, and let it

move through the body (over the shoulders, down the arms to the hands, or down the body, through the legs and the feet).

2. Imagine any person in your life where the relationship is problematic. With the in-breath, breathe in the totality of the other person (including any emotional reactions you have towards them), and with the out-breath, breathe out compassion (wishing the human form well). Notice the space between in-breath and out-breath.

Form does not differ from Compassion

And Compassion does not differ from Form.

Form is Compassion and Compassion is Form.

10 Despair, Hope & Need

The partner of despair is hope.

Need has no opposite.

In need, hope and despair are one.

*"You have succeeded in life when all you really want is
only what you really need."*

VERNON HOWARD

The question "What is needed?" is one of the most important question we can ask the psyche. The intelligence of need underlies all duality. It is the impulse beneath the dualities of creation and destruction, being and non-being, presence and absence. As we said earlier, contractions occur out of a need to protect. They also release and transform according to inherent need. When we follow the sense of need beyond the parameters of the individual, we move beyond the tyranny of duality.

Both despair and hope are based on separation in time and space. We despair and hope for what we desire in the future and in doing this, we separate from the present moment. We despair and hope for specific forms and in this, we dictate boundaries on space. In this, the individual is denying the infinity and eternity of life as a resource and seeking fulfillment or relief through projection. The conditioned mind is not able to oversee the unravelling of life in its core, so desired outcomes are created through grasping, aversion and the absolute belief in separate identity. Every desired form of the future has a shadow that reaffirms the belief in separation from the whole. The needs of the present moment can only be found within the present moment, through following the sense of need, without agenda, expectation and conclusion.

Hope

In some ways, to live in hope is to deny the intelligence of life. Although hope is prized as a virtue, it denies the present moment by seeking completion in the future.

While there can be a healthy and expansive flow generated by an optimistic outlook, the more energy reaches forward, the less it can relax back into itself, into the pure need out of which hope arises. The more the solution is projected into the future, the less the conscious penetration into the contraction. The resonance of the core of the contraction will be one of need, and we cannot hear it until we first allow the suffering within it. In this, hope can push healing away. In the first place, it defers the healing effect of conscious awareness.

Hope is often born out of a refusal to allow despair. This contraction from despair is born out of a general denial of suffering and a rejection of the painful aspects of being in form. The psychology of hope can become a liturgy that keeps us enslaved to the concept of future redemption through outer authorities. Redemption depends on condemnation, but also affirms it. What can be redeemed today can be condemned again tomorrow.

Hope tends to lack overview, perspective and unity with the whole, and in this way, it can be a last pitch of selfishness and illusion. Often, the chief hope is for the Separate Self to be somehow sustained or revitalized. Denying the suffering that has come forward out of the deeper needs within the personality, hope seeks to bypass painful experience in a way that the personality is preserved and empowered. Where hope has become a compulsive defense of form, the deeper need is often to release structures of the psyche that no longer serve the whole. We hope for restoration, when the need could be to expand beyond the limits of who we thought we were, what we think we are and what we hope to become.

At the same time, hope, in the form of prayer that calls for the unconditional support of a higher power, or for the kindness of other humans, does reach beyond the borders of the Separate Self. So, it's important to check in on how the client is experiencing hope – what it means for them. Hope that 'all will be well' is unconditional and can merge with unconditional trust in a source beyond the Separate Self. This is quite a different movement from hope for a personal outcome that averts individual suffering. The more expansive form of hope will not be moving in denial of despair but will be attuned to it. Indeed, its depth and authenticity will depend on that receptivity.

The paradox is that the more we allow despair, the more unconditional our opening for support from the outside becomes. If we hope for an outcome, we are still trying to command the conditions of form. When hope arises out of the core of despair in naturalness, it will articulate precisely the curvatures of that despair, and in this will open the core of need. Hope as a denial of despair contracts us. Hope as a sharing of the depth of despair with the wider universe creates a resonance which is always answered in some way.

Despair

When experience is hijacked by the agenda to avoid despair, then despair can become the subtle backdrop to all experience, and the untouchable floor of *Being*. In the dimension of the unconditionally condemned, existential despair can feel like the core of all experience. Indeed, this bottomless pit of despair is paradoxically a floor on which whole aspects of personality are built.

The feeling of despair thrives off the core belief in unworthiness. Whatever we do, whatever we think, whatever we feel can only dilute the all-pervading sense of not being 'OK', as is. Through layers of personality and Ego, we can distract, cover up and divert our consciousness from this feeling of despair – for a while. Yet it is always already here, deep within our inherited conditioning: we are condemned just by being born; punishable for breathing air; forever failing in some cosmic test which constantly switches parameters. We are insufficient, never good enough, unworthy.

Where many in the Nondual community will talk about universal presence, or the pure, undivided awareness that is the ground of all being, not many will talk about universal absence. Absence is denied. The argument is that we must first be present, to be aware of absence, therefore absence is illusory. Yet the experience of absence which is part of the expansive feeling of despair can feel more cuttingly truthful than the concept of presence, filling the horizons of our awareness with existential lack. This has an honesty about it that can purify the illusions. In a way, we are deeply disillusioned, which isn't conventionally seen as a spiritual process. Naked, unpeeled and irrefutable, despair has a cutting edge that sees through form, including the varying vibrations of awareness. Yet rather than being untinctured in the manner of pure emptiness, despair is peppered with the belly of our worst contractions. We can feel as if we are in a universal ocean of betrayal or abandonment. It can feel like eternal condemnation. Awareness appears as bereft of any purpose, belief, value or meaning.

It is not the absence of hope that opens despair, but a deeper sentient disconnection from universal need. This kind of despair is exposed when we fall through the web of personal strivings, agendas and hopes. We fall through the experiential veils into the unconditional experience of emptiness suffused with the atmosphere of failure.

This despair is without context, seeming to be ubiquitous, formless and absolute. The surviving parameter in the experience of existential despair is the belief in the Separate Self. Even this boundless despair is still conceived as separate from the suffering of the whole. It is a private suffering but robbed of the comfort zone of known patterns. It can feel like absolute condemnation of the individual: 'I' am the one in the Dark Night of the Soul, forever separate from God, the universe, other forms of life, and the ungraspable source of whoever 'I' am. Even the 'I' seems to be failing and falling through the helpless depths of the pre-conscious.

The first word that clients will use to describe this inner void is often: 'Alone'. If relaxation is possible in that Felt Sense of alone-ness, then sometimes, the first need expressed can be something like: "I need to disappear." This is quite literal. The 'I' - the great hanger on which the personal cloak of identification is hooked - is disintegrating. The client is skirting an ancient and strangely familiar area of the borders of the psyche, where the duality of existence and non-existence appears. Realization of the illusory nature of this duality can open the Nondual gateways of unity.

Our ability to relax more deeply into despair can be at first limited. We grasp, distract, change the subject, or create an urgent, momentously important project. We offer hope to others, where we refuse the despair within ourselves. Yet when we can allow the collapse into the experiential veils of despair, we will fall beyond and beneath despair and crack the fundamental illusions within the dualities of being and non-being; and of existence and non-existence. When we can agree to merge with the living experience of despair, there can be a fast route to the core of many interconnected contractions. So much of human striving through the generations has been based on the refusal to allow the simplicity of formless suffering.

Through allowing ourselves to endure the unendurable, a deeper attachment to experience is released. Experience becomes far less definitive, as it's realized as phenomena arising in awareness within the parameter of conditions; impermanent, changing, full of nuance, composed of flux. This release of the conditions we place on experience, whether it be experience of pleasure or pain, liberates experience itself as well as the deeper authority of universal peace.

When despair loses its power as an experiential deterrent, it is the end of the autocracy of fear. When experience is realized as non-definitive, fear loses its grip on the manifestation of the psyche. Our form is no longer shaped according to the agenda of "that which must never happen" or "that which must never be felt." In this, the separate 'I', directed by agendas of private redemption, begins to break through its skin of limitation, awakening to the infinite field of possibility within consciousness.

The despair in us becomes inseparable from the despair of the whole. The suffering of the whole becomes inseparable from the need of the whole. Even the happiness in us is inseparable from the happiness of the whole. The deeper needs of the here and now on behalf of the whole opens a more authentic form of navigation and direction. The whole itself expands. When despair is allowed, an alchemy of service can be born in which suffering transforms to passion, and energy rises directly in alignment with local and universal need. It can look like a death process of the personality. Yet every death process is, at a deeper layer, a process of rebirth.

Need: Nondual Quality

In Nondual Therapy there is a differentiation between wants and needs. When we use the word 'want', we are referring to desire, which tends to involve fast gratification. For example, a recovering alcoholic might want a shot of gin, but it's not what she needs. Someone suffering rejection might want acceptance, but what he needs could well be to move deeper into the experience of rejection, and to find freedom within it.

Colleagues who have contributed to the evolution of Nondual Therapy have used this differentiation to bring insight into the nature of contraction. Contractions are alive. They are sub-forms seeking resolution within duality, to return to the flow of the whole. The origin of each contraction is protective. That is, contractions are naturally formed and liberated through the intelligence of need.

In Nondual Therapy, we hold space in awareness for the contraction, to allow the continued unfolding of need. When the short-term need for protection is gone, there is the possibility of rebalancing and realizing duality and reuniting with the whole. When the mind can express the Nondual Quality of curiosity, then the question can be asked: what is needed here? When we ask this question to a physical cramping in a body, a story can unfold of the body's own, intelligent prescription. When we ask it to an emotional contraction, the process is the same.

Yet at first, contraction will appear as an enemy and our first agenda will be to 'get rid' of it in some way. This notion of 'getting rid of' infects the whole healing process and sits comfortably with misconceptions that dictate separation from the whole and that negation is possible. Yet the trashing of contractions is inherently flawed, as they are made with the precise ingredients needed to manifest Nondual Qualities through the human dimension.

Take a contraction around grief, for example. To get rid of the grief would be to also get rid of the joy of connection on which the grief is based. Who would want to be free of contraction with a method that aims to existentially eliminate the one thread connecting us to the beloved that has passed away? That essential joy is embedded in the grief: indeed, the grief is made of it. The 'wanting' to be done with grief and to pick up life again might, however, be the first presentation of the contraction. It needs to be heard. The second layer is to ask what the contraction needs. Needing answers through the language of feeling. It can be unhooked from mental agenda. At first, the utterance of need might be a conceptual leap. In the case of grief, it could be: "I need peace". The art is to continue to inquire: if you have that, how will you feel? In showing how the feeling would be, the contraction itself supplies the precise elixir of need. Perhaps the feeling brought forward with the infusion of peace is a need to reunite with the living joy in the connection with the Beloved, outside of time and space.

Whereas what we want tends to be based on agenda and the conditions that appear in waking consciousness, what we need is more tactile, embodied, somatic and resonant. In this, the language of need has the power to uproot many contractions at once by removing certain bottlenecks of energetic flow in the psyche.

Contractions around hope and despair are formed at the edges of the psyche, a moment before reunion with need. In this Dark Night of the

Soul, through which structures of Ego, personality and ancestry can break and reform through choice-less rejuvenation, the strongest guide is universal need. The deeper need, whether it is experiential or connected with service to the whole, always reduces the suffering of the Separate Self.

Contemplations

1. Take a situation where you live in hope. Feel how the body reacts on this, in terms of density of energy or stress. Take a short walk and abandon all hope. Imagine the worst-case scenario and let there be despair. Allow the despair to expand, while bringing your attention to your feet and impressions of the here and now.

2. Take any area of suffering, and let it take form in awareness. Ask the question: "What is needed?" Try to ask the question with feeling, not words. Open to a sentient response. Be patient. When any kind of response appears in awareness, trust it. Ask how the contraction will feel when it gets what it needs. Share the Felt Sense of the fulfilled need with the area of contraction and beyond.

Form does not differ from Need

And Need does not differ from Form.

Form is Need and Need is Form.

11 Expectation, Disappointment & Curiosity

The partner of expectation is disappointment.

Curiosity has no opposite.

In curiosity, disappointment and expectation are one.

"The first and simplest emotion which we discover in the human mind, is curiosity."

EDMUND BURKE

Curiosity is a natural and spontaneous movement of consciousness. We see it through all forms of life. In a way, it is a celebration of all forms of experience, as well as an inherent ability to penetrate the nature of experience. With curiosity, we penetrate the unknown which propels evolution and transformation beyond the conceptual limitations of the Separate Self.

When we are seated in curiosity, expectation and disappointment dissolve into an experience that is here to be penetrated, studied and released, without definitive conclusion. Disappointment can be painful, but it's a melody from their depth of need: the unfulfilled need that is intrinsic to disappointment can bring us to deeper layers of ourselves, to places where we have denied ourselves a resource. Expectation can deflect us from the present moment and generate stress and illusion, but what is the fire behind it? What is it that we're not allowing in ourselves that propels us to grasp towards the future, even to attempt to control the future? Both expectation and disappointment are naturally arising emotions, but where do they begin to dictate our direction, distort our perception and weigh down our sense of well-being? How do they become background states of being?

Curiosity will ask these questions but won't dictate the answers. Beyond conclusions and contractions, the seat of curiosity is alive in the here and now, receiving information without filters through the Felt Sense. It will invite trapped experience to life, and as a seat of perception, will open a channel of transformation.

Expectation

Expectation distorts perception with imagined forms based on memory. Rooted in the impulse to control experience, expectation projects outcomes and actively interferes with direct perception. To live in expectation is to live in a state of vigilance or stress. Stress hormones activate the part of the brain concerned with survival which moves through duality – fundamentally, the duality of good and bad. Born of contractions alive in the present moment, expectation has a subtle way of affirming the same contractions.

When we expect the worst, we tend to create the experience of the worst – even before anything ever happened. If we expect the best, we create the experience of the best, which can involve relying quite heavily on denial to upkeep the projection. The eyes of expectation look outward and, in this way, it is always disempowered. It is as if the contractions within the personality are dialoguing with the imagination in a manner which precludes surprise or shock. This tendency to live in expectation is generally based on pain and a refusal to experience or process that suffering which is already alive within. In denial of suffering, it restricts the vitality available in the resource of the present moment.

Disappointment

Whatever we expect, we will always be disappointed. When we expect our worst nightmare, and it doesn't happen, we can experience a secret disappointment – as we will have to wait a little longer for the release of inner form through physical manifestation.

Often our positive expectations are based on bypassing the suffering of the heart into fulfillment, peace, love and freedom. Because these Nondual Qualities are expected to arrive from the outside, in the future, consciousness is blinded a priori to expanding into them in the here and now.

A feeling of disappointment can be the background atmosphere of a lifetime, which perpetually reaffirms itself each time an external object fails to bring satisfaction. It can be especially poignant when that object has previously awoken a sense of connection with our True Nature. Suffering around repeated disappointment can generate a background state of disappointment that constantly fulfills itself. For example, when parents have promised fulfillment to their children to distract them from the difficulty of the present moment – and later broken those promises – then the pattern of broken promises begins to be expected.

It makes us feel 'at home'. Disappointment begins to feel safer than an unexpected fulfillment.

When disappointment becomes an expectation, parts of the psyche that were alert with anticipation start to freeze in depression as consciousness is withdrawn from form. In this way, the stress of expectation solidifies into a freezing of vitality under the verdict that 'life is disappointing'. The allocation of blame on outer authority further disempowers the psyche, adding to the feeling of impotence in form. Such a client needs a lot of encouragement. They will be reluctant to take time and space. In a way, they have dis-appointed themselves from their lives.

Curiosity: Nondual Quality

The movement of exploration arising out of curiosity delivers its own reward in the form of impressions through the psyche. Curiosity is a quality that moves beyond the judgmental mind - exemplifying the dialogue, flow and evolution inherent to being here, now.

Curiosity liberates consciousness and brings authenticity to the sense of connection. As much as it is active through the penetration of form, it is equally receptive in the unconditional allowance of impressions. It has the power to dispel illusion and invite contractions into life, liberating the flow of learning and insight. In this way, curiosity awakens and can open the excitement of increased vitality that comes with the receptive side of the sense of truth.

Above all, curiosity is needed as the nature of expectation and disappointment and the living contractions in the here and now lead us to displace our direct connection with the deeper layers of who we are.

Contemplations

1. When you experience a sense of disappointment or expectation, be curious about the feeling. How does curiosity effect the stress in the body? Is the body also experiencing curiosity?

2. Practice silent curiosity as you move about daily activities. Both allow the sense of curiosity towards what you perceive, and notice curiosity in other life-forms. When you're resting or can close the eyes, be curious about any thoughts, feelings or sensations. It can be simple, like being curious about an area of stress in the body.

Form does not differ from Curiosity

And Curiosity does not differ from Form.

Form is Curiosity and Curiosity is Form.

12 SADNESS, NEGATIVITY & HAPPINESS

The partner of sadness is negativity.

Happiness has no opposite.

In happiness, negativity and sadness are one.

"There is no way to happiness - happiness is the way."

THICH NHAT HANH

The phenomenon of sadness is inherent to beauty and the impermanence of form. Yet when sadness is refused as if it were a negation of happiness, it forms energetic contractions throughout the psyche. It has an intimate connection with happiness. Indeed, it is born out of happiness and longs for reunion as happiness. Yet happiness can be here behind sadness and together with sadness. Like a sun shining, it continues to shine, irrespective of clouds or densities of atmosphere.

When sadness is refused in its living quality, it affects consciousness with a filter of negativity. The trees can seem to be suffering, the infinite sky can be experienced as a curse, and others can appear as indifferent and alien. When negativity perceived on the outside is filtered with 'rose-pink spectacles' it reflects back as an inner freeze of denied sadness. This sadness and negativity is a vital living ingredient in cycles of form. Just as we experience that there is birth, gain, growth, creation and arrival, we must also experience death, loss, decline, destruction and departure. One is not possible without the other. To deny the 'negative' is to create a freeze in form. Freedom is found when the deeper, unchanging light of happiness can shine through all cycles of form and transformation.

Negativity

Negativity makes enemies of objects of perception and in doing so, rejects the living quality of form. This includes the subtler objects of reflection such as our life story, our personal future or our state of being. Based on negation, negativity attempts to deny life and resists the possibility of healing. The voice of negativity will say: we are born that way; we will forever be this way; this is the way we are. It pulls the flow into an appearance of stasis by freezing form at a distance from direct experience.

Because it can easily become a state which affects consciousness regardless of the object of perception, negativity can filter all we see with subtle resentment, forming a state of Being that can be believed as 'reality' as it appears to be in everything. This belief is further affirmed because when we see the world through negative eyes, the world will tend to respond with negativity. In a way, we evoke the negativity into the foreground of form. When we resist friendship, love and openness, we resist reception of these qualities from the outside-in, and the world appears as unfriendly and closed.

Negativity blocks the outer light from meeting the inner light, partly because the first forms to be touched by the outer light are forms of sadness, which can feel vulnerable.

Sadness

The experience of negativity breeding negativity can lead us to deny our sadness. Ironically, in trying to negate negativity, we negate the feeling quality of sadness. When we agree to feel it, sadness is a fluid deepener of experience towards the more essential layers of perception. Through the allowance of sadness, the heart is aroused, and a deeper, coexistent happiness can be revealed.

As a feeling, sadness depends on the perception of beauty, which in turn, arises out of the core nature of impermanence. Beauty is in the eternal moment that can't be grasped or kept. Its power is found in the meeting point of impermanence and eternity. Like sadness, beauty is fluid. Sadness is intimately linked to the thin line between suffering and love, and when we allow it, it can be the soft light that guides us into the essence of living experience. This guide will always move in two directions – outwards into the world, and inwards to the core of feeling. In the words of Khalil Gibran: "Sadness is but a wall between two gardens."

Happiness: Nondual Quality

When we find the seat of happiness within ourselves, all experience is possible as denial and repression become unnecessary and non-binding. Happiness is by nature unconditional. It shines outward from behind all limitations on time, space and form. Inherently, it doesn't differentiate between pleasurable or painful experience. It is an honest and perpetual celebration of the gift of physical life. We are happy to be alive; happy to experience evolution; happy to express through the whole; and happy to be part of the feeling experience of the whole. This wholeness includes destruction, loss and death. Happiness is the Source vibration of perpetual happening. It is alive at the energetic Source of all manifestation. As form is multidimensional, happiness is here as a continuous Source behind and within all layers of experience.

Within the change, movement and speed of being, forms emerge from happiness and dissolve back to it. In the tension between forms of happening, there is enjoyment of pending reunion of Source with Source. At the eye of the storm, we find the experience of ecstasy. While ecstasy is intense, it is sourced at the core of Nondual happiness that can also be experienced as perfectly still.

As with all Nondual Qualities, it's important to allow the experiential possibility that this happiness is here, together with all forms of contraction. At first, this can feel vulnerable, as if we are abandoning our all-important sorrow by introducing a discordant antidote. Our belief systems often demand that we disconnect from happiness – for example, when we are together with someone who is suffering a tragic loss. Indeed, to dictate happiness on people in pain is discordant. But when we can allow the happiness that is here behind and within the happening, this can support others to reconnect out of suffering to the Source of themselves. Just this allowance brings expansion behind and around the conditions of suffering, without denying anything.

When we can find a connection with this unconditional happiness, we are able to rest back in it, opening a wealth of Nondual resources that release the pressure from afflictions and facilitate healing and transformation. We can be happy to be able to experience sadness. We can be happy to be able to experience the distortions of perception created by negativity. We can be happy because of the space and freedom within experience itself. Happiness is empowering, elevating us out of the conditions of the private self and its conclusions and expectations and reuniting us with the depth behind experience. Around us, everything is happening, yet we are not the happening. We are the still core of happiness out of which all forms appear through a universal dance of duality.

Contemplations

1. Recall any negative thought or belief. Let yourself completely believe in the thought. Notice the effect it has on the body and mood. Contemplate how you would feel without this thought.

2. Move your attention to the chest area and recall a happening that caused a sense of sadness of negativity. Blend with the Felt Sense of sadness or negativity within the body. Give space to the feeling, imagine (at the same time) that there's a bright sun shining from deep inside, near the center of the spine. Contemplate the sense of happiness, and let it expand through the body.

Form does not differ from Happiness

And Happiness does not differ from Form.

Form is Happiness and Happiness is Form.

13. SLAVERY, LIBERATION & FREEDOM

The partner of slavery is liberation.

Freedom has no opposite.

In freedom, liberation and slavery are one.

"The so-called physical senses have been so conditioned to react just within physical structures and not to go beyond them, that we lost a lot of connection to these states of freedom, because we are not able to relate them to a physical awareness, to the use of the physical senses."

BOB MOORE

Like so much of our True Nature, freedom has been misconceived as the opposite of form. We began to believe that freedom can be won or lost; threatened; abused; increased or diminished. We are hypnotized into the experience that freedom depends on conditions, rather than the insight that all conditions depend on a priori freedom. Where freedom is abused, we are left with the energy of abuse. Where freedom is controlled, we are left with the energy of control. Where freedom is threatened, we are left with the energy of threat. When freedom is possessed, we are left with the energy of possession, which in turn enslaves us within patterns of personality.

Between the interdependence of all things and the formation of personality within the conditions of time and space, there is inherent freedom. While this freedom can be experienced as personal, it is the dynamic Source of all personality. It is that which allows the manifestation of all forms, including forms of experience. Change is inherent to form, as is freedom. This freedom can be experienced as so personal that we can confuse it with personhood. Yet freedom is here, regardless of personal form. It is an existential part of us which is alive irrespective of change and regardless of states of being.

The conditions in which we lose the sense of freedom are based on fear. Fear says that we are the form: it limits our identity and perception to the conditions through which we manifest. This identification obscures freedom and contracts perception into the dynamics of personal survival. We lose our naturalness in an ongoing struggle to survive, while having forgot who we are in the first place.

At first, the very scent of this freedom beyond contraction can feel sociopathic: it breaks the consensual habits of the social field. Our ancestors could have spent lifetimes in denial of this freedom, and the release of these patterns can feel like betrayal towards the family. The sense of freedom is often transmitted between us as wild and dangerous, potentially inviting disasters of rejection and insanity. Sometimes, it comes reflexively with the horror of trauma. For example, for someone who has been physically beaten for expressing her point of view, freedom of expression comes with tags of prohibition.

When we access the quality of living freedom untinctured by trauma, deep healing can take place within the patterns of personality, together with a release of blocks in manifestation. In this, the deeper healing occurs when the same freedom experienced within is also allowed within the 'other', even when they are the perpetrator. Again, the allowance of freedom is not to be confused with submission to toxic behaviors. Freedom is not a threat. On the contrary, we will find that toxic behaviors emerge out of a loss of the sense of freedom.

Liberation

The experience of liberation comes forward when beliefs unwind enough for us to realize that we are more than any contraction or pattern of behavior. This includes liberation from forms of identity and structures of authority. The relief, expansion and rush of energy resulting from liberation can give an immediate sense of exhilaration. Yet the energy of liberation is still anchored and dependent on the state of slavery from which liberation arose. Liberation can lead to an experience of freedom, but it is still defined by contraction and caught within polarity. To be liberated, we first need to be enslaved, therefore the experience of liberation depends on the experience of slavery. To be liberated, we need to be defined by the prison. If we are defined by the prison, then the authority of the prison continues despite liberation.

This is an important differentiation between liberation and freedom. Liberation can be exhilarating, but freedom is deeply suffused with the living intelligence of peace. Freedom is here, regardless of the prison. Its realization occurs independently of whether we are inside or outside the prison walls. Liberation, however, can be gained through exchanging one form of imprisonment for another. We can liberate ourselves, for example, from the prison of our marriage, only to enter another prison in the form of another partner based on the same patterns.

Liberation is about movement and accelerates both creativity and destruction. Freedom depends on nothing and is fulfilling in and of itself.

If the rush of liberation is not able to release into unconditional freedom, then a search will begin for other prisons to break free from – within ourselves or in others. This can become addictive – our search is for more prisons to liberate, rather than for unconditional freedom. Thus, some become evangelical after an experience of liberation from a contraction – seeking out other captives and prescribing the remedy. There is a narcissistic element in this, for example, they can make the theme of shame universal, and purity as the one definer of Source.

Slavery

The experience of physical slavery leaves its mark for generations. Dr. Joy DeGruy Leary, author of Post Traumatic Slave Syndrome: America's Legacy of Enduring Injury and Healing, has written extensively about the damage to the human psyche resulting from the severe abuse of power made possible through the objectification of human beings as 'things' to be exploited. Among her insights are those revolving around learned helplessness. This is the phenomena where even when the conditions of slavery are released, the victim continues to embody the known dynamic. As helplessness is seen in this methodology as a Nondual Quality, we would rather discuss learned helplessness as learned submission (see chapter 30). The prison door is open, but there is an inability to move through it. The chains are released, and the instinct is to stay close to the padlock, as if still chained. The slave-master continues to live on the inside.

Repeated trauma around the devastating consequences of liberation can create a situation where the slavery we know is less threatening than the unknown, unconditioned expanse where all horrors could happen. Much religious dogma feeds into this, threatening the condemnation that will come with freedom of individual manifestation. Yet African Americans have given the world a tremendous legacy of insight into freedom within form, pioneering civil rights and – generation after generation – asserting the unconditional birthright of freedom.

At a subtler level, the psychology of slavery plays out in all of us. The slavery of gender-defined roles has impacted both men and women for generations, and although we may live in a culture where gender equality is espoused, the wounds within the psyche continue, with all the internal mechanisms of limitation. In this way, the area of the Mother Wound (the complex relationship to the mother) can affect freedom of identity, expression and connectivity. Within the gender split, the full spread of fear and pain around despair, abandonment and betrayal can play out – both for women and men.

We can also find ourselves enslaved to a culture of consumerism that could be described as a culture of perpetual lack. We can feel enslaved within our imperfect bodies. Slavery can find us helpless within patterns of emotional reactivity. We can be enslaved by ethnicity, social class and employment. Above all, we are enslaved to preconditioned forms of thought and belief through an intense pressure to conform.

Often, even when the chance for liberation is shown to us, we remain within the known prison complex: the trauma around freedom can be so great that it lurks as an inconceivable threat in the shadows of the unknown and the imperceptible. We actively choose for the enemy we know over the antagonistic armies we could fear when we let go of form.

Sometimes we will see clients experience a temporary relief from known patterns of suffering – such as anxiety. For a moment, the contraction falls away. They look at you with amazed eyes, a little bit lost. In the next moment, a compulsion causes them to grasp towards some familiar form, no matter how unpleasant. They can even work quite hard to get back into that trance – the trance from which they sought liberation. Being in a familiar zone of stress is giving them a superficial sense of safety and belonging which feels preferable to the apprehended terror of the unknown.

A vast amount of our mental conditioning enslaves us in the quest to satisfy inner need with things from the outer world. In fact, our conditioning slashes our world into an artificial division between inside and outside of the self. Yet, no matter how much we acquire from the outside, no form can satisfy the deeper inner need to manifest freedom within form. Where this addiction to grasping at content loosens, we will often meet states of boredom or blankness – so conditioned are we to experience a back wall to the psyche. This boredom – packed with insentient, frozen emotion – can drive us out again to seek distraction, keeping us on the treadmill of slavery to the external world.

When personal suffering becomes too desperate, we can also find ourselves biochemically enslaved in spirals of addiction. A tangible substance such as whiskey that alters the way we feel at least gives some sense of relief and a break in the monotony and senselessness of routine existence. Yet it comes at a high cost. The slavery becomes a physical dependence that demands regular use to bypass authentic feelings and emotions. This loss of inner validity and truth further exaggerates the already biological craving for the outer substance. Our opportunity to experience the full spectrum of life by degrees gets lost, as our movements, thoughts and experience become enslaved in patterns of reactivity and stress.

When we find ourselves enslaved, the first movement is to acknowledge the feeling of slavery. Giving time and space to the conditions that surround us brings sobriety and the chance to allow an inner Source of all experience – whatever the Felt Sense of the contraction. Allowance of the suffering of slavery within our experience gives space for the one that allows the allowing - the pure freedom which is here regardless of conditions of form. Out of this freedom comes inner expansion and possibilities appear, including freedom in choice, thought, attitude and form.

Freedom: Nondual Quality

Social conditioning and educational systems implant the belief that if we were to be free, all hell would break loose. If we are free, we will be sexually promiscuous and abusive. If we are free, we will murder. If we are free, we will lie; we will steal; we will become violent. Freedom will bring destruction, to the very fabric of the world we share. If this were the case, then we should indeed fear freedom. Yet is this truly the case? Is evil our True Nature?

It's no surprise that the manipulation of fear and threat are the meta tools of social control. Fear and threat thrive through the projections of unformed horrors onto the unknown. Threat thrives by taking the future hostage and predicting horrific outcomes. As these projected fears are formless, they become all powerful, simulating the elusive nature of a Nondual Quality in that they can't be grasped, controlled or extinguished by the mind. When every movement of change, growth, evolution and healing depends on expansion and release beyond known forms, then it follows that freedom can be apprehended as fearful. Indeed, it could be experienced as an invitation to our worst nightmares. But is it true that freedom leads to disaster? Is our True Nature destructive and compelled to abuse?

The fear of freedom is accentuated by the experience that when we release control, we suffer. Control is a form of denial. It is precisely that mechanism that creates and sustains contractions. Within the psyche, slavery takes the form of withdrawing consciousness from experience in the attempt to extinguish it. We enslave our pain in order to survive. We enslave our anger to survive. We enslave our despair in order to survive. We enslave our shame to survive. We enslave the truth of our experience in any moment to survive. Much of this is already happening by reflex, according to unconscious and inherited patterns.

When we reunite with inherent, unconditional freedom, these contractions begin to liberate. The ecstasy of freedom can then bring a whiplash of a liberated contraction. Intense, irrational shame; rage; terror; despair; or an uncontainable sense of unworthiness. When the miracle of awakening eclipses like this, there is tremendous inner and outer pressure to conform: to contract again through suppression, repression, oppression and overall denial of the living energy of the contraction. In time, the suffering of this denial can become too great. Based as it is on the splitting of the world into conflicting parts, the contraction will explode anyway with all its horrors: the 'freedom fighter' is born, or from another perspective, the terrorist.

While collective slavery often involves group movements of liberation, we are concerned here with the paramount responsibility of the individual psyche for its own direct experience of pain, trauma and inherited patterns of suffering. The freedom to allow pain in its full spectrum of contractions is at the epicenter of healing. When we can truly suffer the enslaved feelings as they are liberated from rigid forms into the flow of time, we begin to consolidate in that boundless Nondual Space which is outside of conditioning.

This is the deeper freedom: the freedom that is here regardless of the conditions of the experience. The more we can rest in that freedom in the here and now, the less we are enslaved to experience itself. The grasping towards pleasure and the aversion towards suffering can be seen without our becoming enslaved to it. As fear and suffering lose status as our navigational tool, a realm of possibility opens. The many colors of suffering become experienced as inextricable to all experience. In this, experience itself takes a back seat to the pure consciousness on which it depends. A transpersonal compass emerges (which can be represented as godly guidance, 'life as the teacher', guardian angels, intuition etc.) and a deeper sense of direction is found.

In Nondual Therapy, it is the therapist who provides that consolidation in existential freedom. Often, when someone is in a process, there is simply not enough space to expand behind areas of suffering. The personality has 'become' the contraction and there is little space between the experience of the personality and the awareness of the personality. The pure permission for the truth of experience in any moment, and the ability to allow its expansion (no matter how taboo) brings oxygen to the suffocation of the psyche. This is especially the case with our most denied emotions, such as jealousy, hatred or contempt.

Misconceptions around the nature of freedom are inextricably bound up with the fundamental belief in the Separate Self. This 'person' is conceived as separate not only from other humans, but also from its own ancestry (mother, father and lineage). It is separate from the other gender. It is separate from the physical dimension, including the physical body, the earth, nature and the universe. It is separate from the spiritual dimensions and the Source of all creation. It is separate from time (beliefs in death and time running out). It is clearly separate in space. Every condition we put on inherent freedom depends on the illusion of absolute separation.

Free choice will be expressed as the ability to navigate through all form, including the layers of binary judgement that are inherent to the mind. It's not restricted as private will. From the perspective of the personality, it is best expressed as "Thy will be done." From the perspective of the inner Source, the deeper insight is: "My will is thy will."

In free will, we can move through structures of belief and freely employ the mind's ability to judge and choose. In free will, we can release the separate 'I'. In free will, the will is not found in concept but in a deepening connection to what is needed – whether it be from within a contraction, within a situation, within the collective human realm or within the universe. Freedom moves through the need that emerges from the here and now, unrestrained by private identity, history or fear of outcomes. It emerges out of the liberated field of consciousness and is no longer enslaved to the survival beat of a Separate Self.

We can observe how psychopathic structures within the personality show some insight around freedom in form. Yet here, the quality of freedom is abused through the split of the imagined Separate Self - in the existential struggle of 'Me' versus 'You'. Enough freedom has been realized to open a channel of creative power (the power to create illusion beyond social norms), yet existential fear is still in control of the psyche. In psychopathy, the psyche is fundamentally split between self and world, with the continuing equation of kill-or-be-killed. Here, what looks like freedom is a deeper slavery to a war between two poles in which the psyche is torturing itself.

Recognition of the freedom that is at the Source of all we are is exhilarating, rejuvenating and healing, bringing a fundamental reset to the psyche and opening the field of infinite possibility. This freedom is never 'other' than who we are. It is never conditioned. A freedom that depends on certain conditions to manifest is not freedom, but the experience of conditions. Freedom is here and now, irrespective of our environment and regardless of any configuration of slavery and liberation. The more we rest as freedom, the more we will notice the personality moving into deeper degrees of harmony and transparent alignment with the living needs of the whole. This alignment of the living personality as it begins to move in freedom is a fundamental expression of our purpose here as humans, and it brings its own immediate fulfillment.

The seat of freedom has wings to fly, without opposition through multiple perspectives, one by one or many at the same time. Its spatial infinity means it brings mastery to the art of living. Everything is allowed, but nothing is binding; nothing is binding, because freedom is integral to consciousness.

Contemplations

1. Recall a situation where you felt caught and with the sense of limitation. See if you can find where the limits are, and how they feel. A shape could come forward: go the core of it. Now, blend this feeling with the sense of being outside of the limitation. Pendulate between the outside and the inside and try to experience the texture of the boundary between the two.

2. Bring the attention to the chest area and move with awareness inside and outside the body, sensing any areas of density. Move awareness up to the collar bone and let it run down both arms at the same time, down to the fingertips. Put a clear turquoise light on the chest area and let it expand around and through the body, upwards to the space above the top of the head. Relaxing in this position, contemplate the feeling of freedom.

Form does not differ from Freedom

And Freedom does not differ from Form.

Form is Freedom and Freedom is Form.

14 ACCEPTANCE, REJECTION & BELONGING

The partner of rejection is acceptance.

Belonging has no opposite.

In belonging, acceptance and rejection are one.

"The human being does not experience; it is experienced.
Consciousness alone experiences."

RUPERT SPIRA

Conflicts around the Nondual Quality of belonging can look like A Game of Thrones. Where we sit is taken to determine how we belong. In family structures and in society at large, so much of lived experience comes down to conflict over who sits where. Take the average family with three children: who sits where at the dining table? Who sits where in front of the TV? Who sits where in the car? Who sits where in the classroom? It can be a battlefield. Where we sit determines how we can relate, how we can express and how we can relax. It says something about us. Where we sit affects how we are seen; it also determines our point of view; and all of this affects the nature of our experience of reality. The form of the chair can signify acceptance or rejection, until we awaken to the impermanence of the chair and the truth of the one who is undefined by the chair. Whenever we sit, we always belong; wherever we sit, we belong everywhere.

Part of our fear of rejection and the striving towards acceptance is a pure misconception around the nature of belonging. We believe it is possible not to belong. This belief causes us to lose our sense of belonging even where we are most at home, for example, with our own families, in our own environment. The sense of belonging is always available to us at any moment, in any context. The more we learn to allow it, the more we will disentangle from the hellish spiral of conformity through the twin trap of acceptance and rejection.

According to a study conducted by the University of Michigan Medical School, that metaphorical stab in the heart registers in the brain in same way as an actual physical stabbing. Research elsewhere into subjects with apparent resilience to the pain of rejection were found to be producing natural painkillers – chemical opioids – into the gaps between neurons in the amygdala, which dampen pain signals in the brain region associated with emotion, survival and instinct. Such opioids, giving the feelings of success and acceptance, determine the amount of pain experienced, whether its cause is physical or emotional. Cognitive-based approaches found to reduce pain, such as hypnosis, acupuncture, distraction and even the placebo response, have been shown to also work through this system of leveraging the neurochemistry of acceptance to antidote rejection. However, while acceptance can generate a sense of award, a tolerance develops which demands ever increasing affirmation to take the edge off the inner threat.

In March 2016, Science Daily reported evidence that mindfulness meditation (bringing attention to a third point, such as the breath) reduces pain without the activation of painkilling opioids. The researchers suggested that meditation, rather than recruiting opioids in the brain, reduces the pain experience through using different pathways of neurons.

The irony is that if we invest in the external circumstance or authorities to give us the seal of acceptance, we also invest in the shadow of rejection. That same authority that accepts you today, can reject you tomorrow. Our state of mind and heart is perpetually held hostage to the unpredictable field of external judgement. While opioids might give a feeling of success, success makes failure a real possibility. We are caught in a spiral driven by a bottomless pit of lack or debilitating insecurity.

Rejection

The pain of rejection can be so intense that we build fences of protection around ourselves to avoid feeling it. Rejection is an emergency, launching the whole system into survival mode. As Dr. Gabor Mate explains: "The very same brain centers that interpret and feel physical pain also become activated during experiences of emotional rejection. In brain scans, they light up in response to social ostracism, just as they would when triggered by physically harmful stimuli. When people speak of feeling hurt or of having emotional pain, they are not being abstract or poetic, but scientifically quite precise."

Often, short-term survival boils down to the raw instinct: 'kill-or-be-killed'. Reject first, to avoid rejection. It's them or us; me or you. Yet at the same time, the experience of acceptance can be addictive, creating an unhealthy and disempowering dependency on outer forms of authority. The compulsion towards the twin sufferings of rejection and acceptance betray the perennial experience of the Nondual Quality of belonging, disconnecting it almost to the point of abstraction.

Long-term, unconscious strategies against the threat of rejection involve anticipation, projection or obsession with the reactions of others; masking the natural expression of feelings and emotions. Such is the threat of the pain of rejection, that it's directly linked to an organization of experience in terms of superiority and inferiority. Within this quest for the survival of the personal psyche, even equality can become an equality complex. The fear of rejection can also lead to a compulsive tendency to compare ourselves to others, to toxic competition. Where rejection is deeply disallowed, we can find that our client has internalized the threat, forming an inner judge and jury that pre-empts the risk of external rejection through self-criticism and condemnation.

It's all far removed from the clarity and beauty of relaxing into the living presence of all we are. The fear can be so great that it's not anchored either in the present time or space. That is, we can spend hours in the comfort of our own beds in mental trepidation about the anticipated pain of rejection that might come tomorrow at the party, or alternatively, that happened previously – perhaps even a very long time ago.

The threat of rejection is a threat of expulsion – from the tribe on which we depend for survival. All the four collective fears of traditional psychology are linked to rejection: the fear of death – in nature, when a herd excludes one animal, it will probably die alone; the fear of illness – illness can be an underlying motive to reject a member of the herd; the fear of insanity – collectively, we reject those judged 'crazy'; the fear of sexuality – rejection games play out between genders and over the gender issue, coupled with vast fields of rejection and projection around sexuality.

In this sense, the fear of rejection would appear to be a meta-fear: more powerful and overriding even than the threat of death. The pain of rejection goes with physical sensations – we literally seize up and contract around the wounding, as an emergency containment measure. It also has a mental sensation in the release of stress hormones that over-activate the brain's control centers and vastly inhibit the firing of Mirror Neurons – so-called 'empathy neurons'. Emotionally, if we let it, the pain of rejection can feel like a hemorrhage of despair – we are literally bleeding out from the center of the chest.

Rejection is linked to trauma. Yet unlike a trauma, in which we break connection with an unwanted aspect of experience due to the pure pain of it, in rejection between people, we feel ourselves to be the trauma within the whole. This is when the threat of rejection appears as an existential threat. The outer world seems to be split between those who belong and those who don't – between insider and outsiders – and we fear being on the wrong side of the border, cut out of time and space.

Aversion to rejection can lead us to reject ourselves in ways that increase suffering. We reject our authentic feelings; repress our voice; conform our beliefs; and rearrange our faces to fit into the environment. Rejection is an arch-creator of most contractions. It is also the source of Ego and pretense: we dress to please the imagined 'other' and we constantly keep watch on the impressions we seem to be making on others. We lose our naturalness, authenticity, harmony and, most tragically of all, our sense of belonging. Intimacy becomes forbidden as we progressively wither through a hall of conflicting mirrors. Life becomes one great game of survival and isolation – but no one ever fired a bullet.

Yet while it seeks to banish, the pain of rejection exists independently in the collective field. Because of this, the first reflex when the pain is sensed can be to reject others. The best defense is attack!

As with physical pain, so it is with the pain of rejection. The moment we allow ourselves to feel the feeling, to recognize the wounding, even without need for objectivity, we create space. That which can allow the feeling is already free from the feeling itself, no matter how intense. A spaciousness emerges through allowance of our own sensitivity, which means we also become sensitive to beauty, to pleasure, to the blessings of the moment which are also here, together with the pain. In this, the tunnel vision of a traumatic state is potentially avoided, or at least reduced in its capacity to get a firm grip. We might have a sense of existential rejection, but it no longer determines our expression and direction. Our universe is bigger than that.

Anything within us that could be rejected is not who we truly are, it's simply an aspect of form. In this way, the pain of rejection can even serve our process of liberation in signaling where we're not yet free of identification and where we still cling to imagined authorities.

Acceptance

The horror of the pain of rejection can lead us on a perpetual quest for acceptance. Seeking safety outside of ourselves, we imagine acceptable behaviors and try to mimic them. We recruit others and attempt to please, contorting or repressing natural expression often to the extremes. All of this is to feel accepted as part of the whole. Yet, when we need to change our form to feel we belong, what kind of safety does that bring?

The attitude of acceptance can be helpful in the whole arena of communication, precisely because the atmosphere of rejection is so devastating. It helps establish rapport and affirm manifestation. Yet in the end, acceptance can also become a power-structure wielding the threat of rejection. That which can be accepted from the outside, can also be rejected. A shadow is cast. Acceptance has no meaning, unless there is a little rejection around.

Acceptance can antidote rejection, but also feeds the belief. Dependency on the acceptance from other people risks keeping us addicted to the rush of feeling appreciated. We need ever increasing demand for reward to numb the pain. This can be a person we admire, or a source of reward in which we seem to receive public applause and appreciation. Yet the opioid source itself does not take away the pain, it simply kills its registration in the brain – temporarily. Physically seen, the knife is still in the chest! In the game of thrones, we can be sitting on the throne of omnipotence, yet for as long as we believe that the throne defines us, there is danger everywhere.

In time, over-dependency on acceptance to numb the pain of rejection will exaggerate the pain of rejection to alarming degrees. We get increasingly acceptance-tolerant, and although there may be all the acclaim of humanity towards us, this pain of rejection grows in equal proportions. We are no longer accepted for who we 'really' are, and we suffer intense loneliness. We feel rejected from our own self-image – one which we can never live up to. Each demand for the wonderful, acceptable side of us, is also an oppression of the "real" us – the one that feels irrationally rejected, cut off, and left alone in the darkness of the soul. Some famous people find their way through this, gracefully opening in authenticity and service to the whole. For others, the inner despair is only revealed to the public through tragedies of self-rejection such as addiction and/or suicide.

When we feel a prerequisite to accept others as they are, without space for altering manifestations of like and dislike, then this can also plummet through conformity to the sense of victimhood. Acceptance will often express as a pretense and will undermine personal boundaries. When we move with acceptance, we often also need to honor our own feelings and emotions within that, otherwise a situation can play out as self-abuse.

Belonging: Nondual Quality

The root of the word belonging is to be in the longing together. It is not an endpoint or a closed circle, but a Nondual position which is always here. It is within this fact of belonging that the game of rejection and acceptance dances. These negotiations around form occur within the field of unconditional belonging and the more we can rest in this inherent sense of belonging, the less brutal the game of rejection and acceptance.

Imagine a typical family structure with the consensual black sheep. She might look, feel and act differently from the rest. The family gets its sense of identity by this black sheep. She begins to symbolize all they reject, and the family begins to depend on that to define itself. Does this family member belong less? Or is she filling a fundamental need in bringing honesty from the shadows of contracted family form?

Without the eccentric professor, the college cannot be itself. It would lose its quality and its richness. The eccentric belongs by itself, without question and precisely because it is manifesting outside the superimposition of standards of conformity.

When we are rejected, it is only possible because we already belong and will continue to belong. Rejection doesn't exclude, it engages the object. Evolution is happening. When we are accepted, it is also because we belong, but sometimes this acceptance is a dynamic that seeks to force belonging and to keep it under control. In this way, inherent belonging has been hijacked by power agendas and conformity.

Every form that exists – including our most intimate expressions of self – belongs simply because it is. Regardless of the feelings or thoughts of others, it is part of the whole. Consider the enormous damage done to the environment through humanity's assumption that it is possible to reject parts of it while accepting others. Also, this movement of rejection is creative. It adds energy to that which is rejected within the field of belonging, because nothing can fall outside of belonging, no matter how much we want it to. The evolution of superbugs in response to the introduction of antibiotics is one clear example of rejection not working out but accentuating that which it claims to counter.

When we relax back in that pre-given belonging on this planet, in this nation, as an expression of this culture, within this group, from this family, then the pain of rejection is vastly relativized. This means that it becomes localized to something that's happening in this moment in a specific context. It's no longer an existential threat.

In our disconnection from belonging (being in longing together), we get confused and fall into the contraction of rejection-acceptance to try and attain belonging. The moment any player in the war relaxes into the field of belonging, an easiness comes forward which is inclusive, not exclusive, one that has space for difference in perspective and that loses its charge of cruelty. This is so very important, as the greatest players in this field of contraction are those who least feel they belong. The perpetrators are often the greatest victims, without even knowing it.

We belong in our bodies. We belong in the ocean of silence. We belong in unity to the space that allows us all to be. We belong as living beings. We belong to nature. We belong as expressions of all that is, through whatever form. No one can take this from us, but we can become desensitized to the experience of this fundamental source of nurture.

Contemplations

1. Let awareness rest in the heart and visualize, recall or contemplate a time or situation in which you felt you truly belonged. Contemplate the

feeling of belonging and let it expand through the physical body. If the feeling gets lost, return to the chest area and gently begin again.

2. Remember or recall the feeling of belonging and let it stabilize. Imagine light on the left hand and the right hand and then on both hands at the same time. Let the feeling of belonging move into the hands. Take your left hand and rest it over the right hand and let the feeling of belonging be transmitted through the skin.

3. Become aware of the space behind the body and let awareness expand there. Position your father and mother behind your back and behind their backs, their fathers and mothers, continuing as much as is natural through the ancestors. Bring awareness back to the chest area and contemplate the sense of belonging.

Form does not differ from Belonging

And Belonging does not differ from Form.

Form is Belonging and Belonging is Form.

15 SUPERIORITY, INFERIORITY & EQUALITY

The partner of superiority is inferiority.

equality has no opposite.

In equality, inferiority and superiority are one.

"Equality does not bring suffering, but the equality complex does... The equality complex says I am as good as her, or I claim the right to be as good as him. But it's only when you know that you ARE her, and you ARE him, that you have harmony and happiness."

THICH NHAT HANH

The notion of equality can seem to be an abstraction which can never be reached in 'real' life. Beliefs around superiority and inferiority, confuse natural navigational tools with the energy of rejection through judgement. Yet the wisdom of equality is deeply liberating from this slavery of hierarchical thought and some myriad contractions of suffering connected with measurement. As Nondual philosopher Pete Sierra once said: "The gates of hell are marked by the words: better and worse, and more and less."

The striving to gain greater status, health, wealth or happiness, can be reduced to one word: striving. Striving is powered by the energy of lack and discontent. This sense of lack is specific to structures of personality and Ego. The personality is not absolute. It is inherently lacking. It knows this and strives to fix that lack through 'self-improvement'. Improvement depends on measurement and comparison: inferior 'Me' seeks superiority.

Each form cannot exist except in relation to all others and is ultimately composed of the same 'stuff' as others. Time and space are relative and impermanent configurations in constant movement. Although we might perceive stasis, this is often an effect of perspective. For example, a mountain could seem permanent, but from the point of view of our sun, the mountains have risen, fallen through time.

The very notions of inferiority and superiority depend on equality. Equality is the invisible center point through which all measurements of less and more are made possible. The phenomena of superior or inferior rest within the precondition of equality. Within the duality of superiority and inferiority a clear example of the mutual dependence of each pole of the duality on the other is revealed. The determination of superior or inferior utterly depends on perspective. A rich woman can experience herself as very poor, when she perceives richer peers, and yet rich when she walks among those who have less. The duality is so strong that we markedly play out the opposite through forms of Ego. A direct effect of her feeling of inferiority will be a mask of superiority when she is with those who are richer than her, and a mask of inferiority when she is with those who have little. There will not be any expression of inferiority without a hidden superiority. Likewise, in every expression of superiority, we will uncover an inner deficiency, or a deeper sense of being 'less'.

When we consider the nature of balance and harmony in form, and the balancing of each duality against its partner within every contraction (for example the balancing between fear and anger), then the core role of equality as the natural resting place to release contractions emerges.

In processes of healing, we will see the duality between superiority and inferiority play out all the way into freedom. The compulsion to measure, compare and to create hierarchies is structural to our conditioning and to our collective conceptualization of form. Each form is unique, with a complete differentiation both in time and space from any other form. It even differs from itself in the moment before. The struggle of the mind to reflect this involves tracking, which involves perpetual comparison. The new experience is compared to older experiences and measured. Our experience is compared to that of others and evaluated.

Part of the mind is conditioned through comparison, competition and hierarchy and in this, the tendency to invest notions of superior and inferior within our independent existence is a powerful one. Yet the investment in either side of this meta duality is a fast route to more contraction. To reject the function and reflex of measurement is of itself a futile endeavor. It would deprive the mind of part of its purpose in freedom. We need to measure spaces to physically move and to avoid danger, measurement is a free part of perception that enables the dance through duality. Yet freedom of measurement can only be found through a disinvestment of belief in the absolute nature of that which is measured. Measurement happens, but we are immeasurable.

The disempowerment of the grip of the inferior-superior contraction is found through cultivation of the ability to relax within the wisdom of equality – even whilst the activity of measurement is happening.

Superior and inferior are part of the dance of duality, they say nothing about who we are. They are the mechanics of an illusion that we use to move through an illusory world. The more we are centered in the wisdom of equality, the easier the flow between balance and imbalance, which can serve the deeper purpose of the collective evolution of form.

Superiority

The contraction around superiority and inferiority will play out to some degree in just about every other contraction. This is because when we move into contraction, we move out of balance with the whole (within ourselves and within the wider environment). The imbalance is contained in contracted form, which prioritizes those contracted feelings as special, (superior or inferior) to 'regular' feelings that freely flow as layers of form. There is a grandiosity in contraction. It is charged, secretly over-invested, and perceived as definitive to who we are. Our pain is more important that anyone else's pain. It's separate and distinguished. Our shame is splendid in its horror (the shame of others is silly); our fear is understandable (the fears of others irrational).

The agenda to be superior is fundamental to the build-up of the masking structures of Ego over the more tender living wounds within the personality. This can take any form. We can be the greatest 'loser'. Our trauma can be beyond the trauma of anyone else. We can claim superiority in our victimhood. Indeed, we can claim an elated status even through broadcasting the core of our experienced inferiority. Belief structures like 'Nobody loves me,' as the ground-breaking work of Byron Katie has shown, inevitably display their opposites – such as no one is worthy to love 'Me'.

Those who tend towards the expression of superiority are often driven by a deep sense of inner deficiency, which propels them into the quest for superior status. The dread behind this is trauma-based, resulting from the agony of the kill-or-be-killed equation. Inferiority means trouble. These patterns of stress can move through generations and will often be reflected from all sides within family structures.

Inferiority

A compulsion towards the inferior position within the duality of measurement is driven by fear of conflict and/or of responsibility. It is characterized by a false humility that seeks peace through an over-emphasis on surrender. This degree of conformity leads to structures of stress and depression within the personality. These structures separate the Source from the flow of life – the flow of reception and expression – which leads to further isolation and depression.

Often, the Ego structures that form out of a strategy of inferiority are judgmental. The disowned anger at others that manifest in freedom, for example, can surface as jealousy, gossip, sabotage and recruitment against the chosen 'offender'. The inferior one will often claim the entitlement of victimhood, and on this basis, an exemption from responsibility.

Those who are caught in the form of inferiority will sometimes be quite grandiose about it. The sense of inferiority can easily feed the 'kill-or-be-killed' equation of the Separate Self – generating conflict between groups, classes or countries. The sense of inferiority contracts the ability to freely express. Someone caught in comparison might, as a child, have loved to sing, but they no longer sing, because others are better than them. They might have a tremendous ability to write, but they will not write a word, because first they need to know that what they write will be superior. Inferiority blocks qualities from expression. It does this because it's so deeply entrenched in the belief in the Separate Self and the possibilities of judgement on this Separate Self called 'Me'.

At the same time, the Dalai Lama has said that if we cannot find equality with another person, then we had better take the inferior position. Every competition is between forms which of themselves have no independent existence. If harmony cannot be found in form, it is indeed better to release the attachment to form. In taking the inferior position in a conflict, we give the full status of form (Ego, wounded personhood) to the other. We release the attachment to the immediate competition, which brings space for movement and expansion at a deeper level. Without a competitor, the competition withers and there is a possibility for collaboration from another depth. Each time we release our agenda around form, a more essential expansion emerges. Miracles can happen when one side simply disarms.

However, when this position of inferiority becomes a rigid structure, and is abused as a strategy for survival and belonging, the genuine opening into the wisdom of humility is replaced by a false humility with whiplash effects throughout the psyche. We can feel tremendously superior about our ability to play an inferior role. We can even experience a superior contempt towards 'the world' that makes us inferior.

Equality: Nondual Quality

The seat of equality opens a channel towards the deeper relaxation into unity within the manifold. The reference point of the wisdom of equality will lead us towards the possibility of finding equality in some way, anyhow at any time. Even with a perceived evil person, we can acknowledge the equality in the physical template of form. He too has a head on two shoulders, with two arms, two legs, with a heart helplessly beating and blood that choicelessly flows through the paths of least resistance. It is always possible to find equality in some way with another human, when we stop grasping towards what makes them better or worse.

When we can find equality with another person (even in a basic way such as 'We both have two arms and two legs'), there is the possibility of dissolving projections. The outer enemy was never really the issue, the deeper threat remains as the imbalance within our inner experience. This enemy within – the superior one that dictates our inferiority; or the inferior one that dictates our superiority – shows a deeper split in the psyche which can cause many projections into the outer world. Both out superiority and our inferiority are perceived through the transcendental point of equality: they depend on it. Without the perennial background of equality, no measurement would be possible at all.

From the seat of equality there is a wisdom which sees beyond the artifice of the Separate Self. Perception through equality penetrates the fundamental law of balance. Even the chair of superiority needs symmetry in its legs for it to be stable.

Out of disconnection from equality, we become addicted to secondary sources that are spatially distant from direct perception: this includes social status and many forms of Ego. This addiction – fired by a disconnection from natural esteem – drives us to seek satisfaction through the outer world: for the higher job, the greater success; the best material possessions; or the ultimate sexual partner.

The wisdom of equality is fundamental to processes of healing. Equality cannot be forced or pretended. It emerges through a willingness to experience the True Nature of form. It is made possible only when we release our deeper layers of attachment to the concept of separation.

Contemplations

1. Take two objects and make a feeling connection with them, contemplating one and then the other. Try to compare one to the other and notice what this does with your energy. Does your consciousness

contract? Is there stress in it? Now, consider another person. Compare yourself to them. Witness how it feels to be compared.

2. Recall someone (or an animal) that you feel is either inferior or superior. Take a Nondual Quality which is easy for you to sense in them. Place yourself into their experience and let the Nondual Quality expand through them.

Form does not differ from Equality

Equality does not differ from Form.

Form is Equality and Equality is Form.

16 ILLEGITIMACY, INJUSTICE & ESTEEM

The partner of illegitimacy is injustice.

Esteem has no opposite.

In esteem, injustice and illegitimacy are one.

*"I wish I could show you, when you are lonely or in dark-
ness, the astonishing light of your own being."*

HAFIZ

Everything we know is based on what we have experienced and all that we experience are phenomena arising within a boundless field of awareness. Within this field, both the objects of perception and the space between them are alive with awareness. This means that the entire universe is both alive and aware. When forms arise through awareness, they are affirmed, appreciated and unchallenged in their existential, value. Spontaneously arising out of awareness is the subtle Nondual fluid of esteem. The sense of esteem is found in the reunion of consciousness with itself, or life with life, or the miracle of being here in a physical body with the miracle or perception.

Esteem is a powerful, expansive energy of manifestation that is here in all we are, in whatever form, because we are. Esteem is in the trees, the mountains and the rivers. It is in the intelligent passage of a protein within a cell, and in the rising and falling of the tides. It is irrefutable. Yet in negotiating splits in the psyche between inner and outer, self and other, our bodies and nature, our individual manifestation and the True Nature of the whole, our unconditional sense of esteem gets obscured.

Contractions around esteem and self-esteem surface wherever forms of the Separate Self break down. Out of esteem, there is a passion to manifest. We feel special, unique and have a sense that our time here is a precious opportunity. Something momentous can seem to be at stake. Many forms of contraction are based on the evolution of the individual within the whole. In this, individuation cannot be forgotten. Yet there is a stage of individuation where individuality seems to be inseparable from limitation. Out of this limitation, we seek to become better, leading to further investment in the absolute form of identity and personality, and inevitably to despair. The paradox is that at Source, it is true that we are all individual, unique, precious and miraculous manifestations of the whole. We are unique, and it is our deeper purpose to manifest that individuality on earth. This is where esteem becomes thwarted, because the outer world can seem to reject our unique individuality, and that rejection gets internalized. The evolution is in the experience that we are miraculous, unique yet interdependent manifestations of one True Nature – or in the famous lyrics of U2: "We are one but we're not the same. We get to carry each other..."

Believing in the authority and judgements of conditioning, blocks around esteem show up as the suffering of illegitimacy and the rage at injustice. These feelings of severe devaluation within the greater whole contract all forms of experience. Sometimes, this can create a fundamentalist adherence to the principle of judgement and the sovereignty of the separate self. Esteem is sought through separation – through 'goodism' (having to be 'good' and not bad), and through 'othering' (seeking a sense of separate self through alienating others). Only when we begin to allow the resonance of feelings and emotions moving through us, do we begin to access again the deeper sense of natural esteem. As a rehab professional told an alcoholic client: "You're the driver of your own life. Don't let anyone steal your seat."

Esteem has a sense of spontaneous living affirmation and unconditional reward. This includes all forms of expression, manifestation and receptivity. It is inherent to consciousness where there is no agenda of judgement. What has been called self-esteem is the same movement within the psyche. We never lack self-esteem; we simply experience contractions around esteem which are created by forms which are not affirmed in conscious-awareness – where form is denied. Often, these contractions are internalized mechanisms arising out of rejections from outer authorities. For example, in the social field of the playground, where the group bullies one child, contractions in esteem can affect the child for years. Sadly, the bullying behavior was probably generated by contractions in esteem within the bullies.

Illegitimacy

Hollowing out and disempowering the experience of form, the pain of illegitimacy has the power to create substrata of the psyche that resonate with inherent fault, untouchability and a subtle loathing that has a depth that causes us to believe that this vile stuff is what we truly are. This secret sense of the 'Despicable Me' surfaces as thoughts telling us that we have no authentic right to manifest and even that our manifestation is hurtful or dangerous to others. Through the suffering of illegitimacy, we can literally experience ourselves as toxic.

Born from the lack of acceptance, affirmation and honor from the 'outside' world, the horror of illegitimacy (not being worthy of taking space, here and now), gets internalized and buried beneath layers of pretense. No amount of certification, legitimization or public applause can alleviate the painful sense of illegitimacy at the core of the psyche. In fact, it can even make it worse as it seems to inflate the lie.

We are all manifold expressions of illegitimacy. We have the wrong body weight; we're the wrong gender for the job we take; we are the children of parents that divorced or died; we were born into the wrong class; or we are of the wrong color or religious faith. Reasons for the shock of illegitimacy abound, with goal posts of legitimacy shifting according to perspective. The inner wound in the psyche tends to attract experiences of illegitimacy, within ourselves and/or others, which feeds the belief in the possibility of existential rejection.

Injustice

Illegitimacy lacks reason and can be perceived as deeply unfair. In this, a rage arises towards the outer world as being inherently flawed and illegitimate in its authority. There is trauma here, as both illegitimacy and injustice have been experienced as survival threats and as causal players in poverty.

This is the rage at injustice. Arising out of the stinging pain of shame and social rejection, the pain of injustice seeks to restore balance through correcting the outer world. This can be destructive and fruitless as it reaffirms the belief in the inherent wrongness of form, birthing ever increasing examples of injustice in the field of perception.

The suffering of injustice awakens other contractions, with emotions of anger, jealousy and hatred. Yet the scream of "It's not fair!" always depends on a forced kind of equality under certain conditions: for example, that children in a family should get identical presents on their birthday. The feeling of 'not fair', precedes the objective situation where fairness is demanded. Yet living parameters shift all the time. Could it be unfair that the mother hugged one child longer than the other? Later, that the other got a longer story at bedtime? In their quest for justice, children exemplify a deep human need for living affirmation in form which is deeply linked to the Nondual Quality of Esteem.

Esteem: Nondual Quality

When we lack esteem, it can feel like we have nowhere to sit inside ourselves. It can be like going into an assembly where everyone is seated, and there's no place for us. We stand to the side, as if invisible, as if we have no right to exist yet we exist anyway. We can feel like a ghost, haunting the lives of others. Insights into the destructive and incapacitating effect of a lack of self-esteem abound in the world of therapy. Yet few have gone deeper to inquire into the felt sense of the unconditional quality of esteem, irrespective of personal identity or beliefs in the separate self.

What is esteem? How does it feel as it arises through the cells, blood and bones of our physical manifestation? How does it affect the energetic fabric of contraction? In its purity, esteem can feel omnipotent.

Esteem is the healing kiss of consciousness to form. It has the feeling energy of the biblical creation in Genesis, when God "saw that it was good." Unconditional, the Nondual Quality of esteem gives an instant sense of legitimacy, power and reward. It's a source of infinite expansion that can include any contraction. It enlivens without grasping; nurtures without control; and releases without attachment.

If it's hard to get a sense of esteem on the inside, then we can ponder it around us. It is important not to be misled by appearances of pretended confidence and the broadcasting of status.

Try connecting to the esteem of a horse as it gallops in freedom, or of a tree with branch tips stretching towards the sun, or of the sun itself, shining choicelessly and unconditionally and regardless of reflection.

When esteem for what we are through all manifestation arises, it is stronger than any limitation of form, yet it blesses and affirms all forms in their temporal magnificence. It perpetuates worth and expands the flow of energy through the psyche, turning problems to opportunities.

Esteem affirms all form as itself, as an energetic source more powerful than any transient judgement. Just as esteem rises through us, releasing the forms of the individual psyche into life, so does it naturally express through an esteem towards others, without compromise.

Contemplations

1. Recall a situation that you felt to be unfair, and stay with that sense of injustice, letting it expand where it wants to go. Find a space in the body where the sense of injustice is less and invite it to support the area of affliction. If all experience carries the sense of injustice, then invite the support of a neutral power, such as an ocean, or the sun.

2. Move attention to the basis of body (pelvic area). Let consciousness affirm whatever appears in sense perception. You can use the words: "Also this is here." Still at the basis of the body, contemplate the sense of esteem and share it with the bloodstream of the body.

Form does not differ from Esteem

And Esteem does not differ from Form.

Form is Esteem and Esteem is Form.

17 Boredom, Addiction & Passion

The partner of boredom is addiction.

Passion has no opposite.

In passion, addiction and boredom are one.

"False gold will only cut your feet and bind your wings,
saying "I will remove your difficulties" when in fact it is
only dregs and defeat in the robes of victory. So run, my
friends, run fast and furious from all false solutions. Let
divine passion triumph, and rebirth you in yourself."

RUMI

A fundamental reflex of contraction is to refuse experience, and in this, to deflect consciousness. The refusal of experience is initially embodied as the movements of denial, suppression and repression. It begins as the instinctive fear of the exposure of pain and develops as a retraction of consciousness from the unwanted energy. The freeze in emotion born from this retraction of consciousness expresses as the field of denied vitality we recognize as boredom. Boredom is not the 'nothing' it pretends to be. It is suffused with denial, annoyance and awkwardness. It is no more at peace than a bottle of soda after it has been shaken. The partner of boredom is addiction – where we seek distraction from the intense discomfort of the 'boring'. Addiction deflects consciousness from the state of boredom to an outer source, often towards an object which is anticipated to give pleasure or relief.

The repressed charge within boredom and addiction is the Nondual Quality of passion. Passion is the power behind greater purpose, beyond the concept of the Separate Self. It is the unadulterated and vital drive of creation through physical form. Because its power is transpersonal, it fires through the hooks of fear and aversion associated with most contractions. Its power is such that it brings excitement and fulfillment just through its own authenticity. In this, the movement of passion, connected to the manifestation of Nondual Qualities, can be a radical healer.

Boredom

A sense of boredom can be the first layer of each contraction and is also often the energetic substance between the personality and the Dark Night of the Soul. This crust of dullness and non-activity is fundamentally defensive. It says: don't come here, there is nothing to be found. Yet if we stay a while in the experience of boredom, what can emerge are the first sparks of anger and fear. There can be an annoyance, a restlessness, or a subtle sense of dread. This is normally when consciousness is withdrawn to pursue pathways which promise most pleasure. When we stay a little longer, the sense of boredom can become almost uncontainable. It is not 'nothing', but a suffering that could lead to a kind of violence, just to feel 'something'.

When the freeze of boredom forms a backdrop to the personality to prevent a falling into the trauma-zone of The Dark Night of the Soul (and the liberating light of Being behind that), then there can be a lot of trapped vitality in the psyche. Such people can talk very fast, be nervous and generally speedy. When they can thaw some of the boredom, letting the dense energy express the anger, fear and longing that has been compressed, an integration begins which relaxes the whole psyche and opens channels for a more attuned flow of expression.

Patterns of boredom, like addiction, are the sentient forms of patterns of stress and release, which are part of the biological drive towards survival. In this, they are inherited on a cellular level and when we can loosen the walls of resistance around feelings and emotions, this can allow a re-patterning of stress reflexes that can transform the personality, from the inside-out. Don't be deterred by boredom: it's not an endpoint but the start of a new dynamic, beyond the known patterns of evasion and dependency that limit personal potential.

Addiction

Addiction is generally associated with substance abuse. However, addiction goes beyond physical substances: we can be addicted to other people, to forms of stimulation, to food or to anything 'out there' that gives us a temporary sense of satiation and relief from the suffering of craving. Addiction is the psychological mechanism that espouses patterns of temporary relief from the unendurable stress suffered on the inside. We are all addicted to collective patterns of thought, behavior and conditioning. These patterns of addiction – in which relief from the stress deep inside us is sought from the world outside of us – have taken authority over our direct experience, and by default, over our sense of truth.

Addiction has an atmosphere, which includes despair, dependency, disempowerment, senselessness and primal rage. The craving for satiation and relief is a distorted form of passion. Yet rather than moving with the alchemy of suffering, passion is identified as sourced in the 'outer' world. Substances or objects on the outside gain authority over inner experience, increasing dependency, imbalance and the loss of proportions.

As the addictive cycle spirals away from our True Nature, it increasingly exposes a sense of lack and unquenchable craving, which in turn generates greater rage and anxiety around the perceived source of satiation. The intense restlessness of an unfulfilled craving, whether physical or psychological, is generated by the field of the unendurable contraction, often experienced within the energetic freeze of boredom.

Some degree of addiction is at play in all psychological suffering. Where this addiction is to a substance, it creates a physical dependency which reinforces the psychological pattern of grasping for relief from the outside. That is, the lack of the substance becomes itself a contraction of suffering. For this reason, it is important to check in on substance abuse with all clients suffering mental unrest. The spiral of physical addiction needs to be released for us to be able to feel into the core contraction of suffering. It is important to understand that both addiction and mental disorder are sourced to trauma (including generational). Yet until the client can feel the benefit of taking the struggle home to the suffering within their own psyche, through withdrawal from the addictive substance, the trauma will not be healed. This is not a movement of control or submission, but rather a movement of trust in a power beyond the perimeters of the suffering, Separate Self.

With addiction, we will meet legacies of stigmatization, shame, guilt and condemnation, and we must be prepared to support Nondual Qualities outside of these structures of contraction. When we try to deny the suffering within a contraction through distraction, it is a movement of control, and the belief in control is generated by fear. It's ironic that many treatments for addiction dictate the restoration of self-control;

addiction is an extreme manifestation of the desire to keep control of our experience of suffering! In the words of addiction expert Scott Kiloby: "Emphasizing 'I should' and 'I shouldn't' thoughts around an addictive substance or activity actually helps keep the addiction around, as it creates a sense of self that seems to have control. If control were truly the answer to addiction, humans wouldn't still be addicted, because everyone is already trying to control addictions. It isn't working."

Passion: Nondual Quality

Passion emerges where a Nondual Quality is released in alignment with universal need. This doesn't have to be a remarkable occurrence, as it happens to all of us daily and is part of our deeper sense of purpose and the release of unconditional vitality to nurture and sustain the whole. Yet the pure potency of passion is often released from the ground zero of disillusionment, the space of burn-out that many associate with despair.

While passion can resemble the rush of addiction, it arises from the Source of life as it expresses through form as part of life, and in this, its supply is infinite. Passion has the power to shake loose the shackles of both boredom and addiction. The seat of passion recognizes impermanence and therefore is intrinsically free of contraction. When we move out of the seat of passion we are unhooked from the restraints of identity, social norms, conditioning and the survival of the Separate Self.

Passion is an unconditional movement through form, guided by the pure power of care. It is the alchemy at the basis of the personality where suffering transforms to love and takes form as service to the whole. The word passion, in Latin, is synonymous with suffering. Often, our passions are born directly within the area where we have been able to liberate a Nondual Quality. For example, in working with orphaned children after we have been to the pit of loss and abandonment ourselves; or in dedicating ourselves to freedom, after we have suffered the core of psychological and physical slavery and found that our freedom propels us through the gateways of slavery and liberation. To put it another way, we could say that our greatest curse, through the alchemy of passion, becomes a blessing to the whole.

Because passion is always of service to the whole, it doesn't get entangled with private identity or reward. It moves beyond the illusion of the Separate Self. Passion doesn't hold back its gifts but lets them express freely – irrespective of acceptance or rejection. Its reward is found instantly in the bliss of its own movement and the joy of togetherness. Passion is the movement of Nondual Qualities into expression, and the simultaneous reception of Nondual Qualities through all the veils of the psyche back to the Source. In this way, passion is an accelerator of both individual and collective evolution.

Contemplations

1. Recall a sense of boredom and be curious about how it feels. Find where this sense of boredom is denser in the body and how it is felt physically. Blend with it. If you like, you can imagine that you are shining a light on the boredom. Notice any effects, such as thoughts, images, physical or emotional responses.

2. Let consciousness expand through the pelvic area and try to get a feeling connection with something you are passionate about. Let the sense of passion be released through the nervous system, without entangling with any blocks or contractions.

3. Contemplate the sense of passion and attend to: a) any Nondual Qualities within the passion b) the sense of need within the passion. Close the exercise by letting your conscious awareness sink deeply within the vibrations of the earth beneath the body.

Form does not differ from Passion

And Passion does not differ from Form.

Form is Passion and Passion is Form.

18 HATE, SACRIFICE & LOVE

The partner of hate is sacrifice.

Love has no opposite.

In love, sacrifice and hate are one.

"Hatred paralyzes life; love releases it. Hatred confuses life; love harmonizes it. Hatred darkens life; love illuminates it."

MARTIN LUTHER KING JR

Love is a well-known yet much abused Nondual Quality. We seek love outside of ourselves, without really knowing what it is. We objectify love: demanding it; missing it; possessing it; and using it to justify all kinds of behaviors. Yet while love is that which drives us as a human species with an intelligence subtler than any thought, it still emanates mystery. Often tainted with the fear of abuse, love remains an unconditional wonder at the core of both creation and destruction.

What is love? Much of what we would associate with love is a descrip-tion of its effects: we confuse love with her footprints. How would we describe the feeling of love? Often, as a warming of the chest area; a sense of expansion; belonging; attraction; or home. Yet these phenom-ena – expansion, opening, attraction and belonging – are the effects of a contraction unfolding in love. They are sentient signals that the form of the psyche is opening, breaking, or melting as an effect of love. Yet our conditioning is to identify with the effects of love as identical to love itself, and because these effects are tangible, we look for their rep-etition as proof of the presence of love. We grasp at the pleasurable effects of love, while experiencing aversion to the unpleasant effects (such as grief). All the time we miss the mystery of love, which is at a causal layer to all its many effects.

Lovers will often see love as embodied in the object of attraction. They (the subject) identify love in the object (the one they love). We tend to see the 'other' as the source of the love, rather than recognizing that the source of love always be in the lover. The effects of love rise and wane according to the healing movement of contractions, and often the beloved is made responsible for the presence or absence of those feelings. There is a subtle arrogance in this. We will say that the 'other' has changed, or we could feel abandoned, or that the love is not the same. Yet we have about as much idea about who the beloved is as we do about who we are. It is sad that one effect of love is the shrinkage, control and dictation of form on that which has inspired that love into form.

The instability of the world of effects creates a tremendous fear around this objectification of love. Love comes with a sense of helplessness, and this can awaken fear and memories of abuse which manifest through attempts to control love – to train, dictate or possess it. When we seek to possess love, we are left with the feeling of possession (grasping). When we try to control love, we feel controlled. When we see love as personal, we are left with the isolation of the Separate Self – the loneliness and estrangement of the individual from all those it claims to love. The universal need to become a channel of love degrades into a personal 'want' to become immune to fear and the pain of loss. Imagine love were a beam of light. What happens when we put our hand there to try and control it?

Unconditional love is a tremendous healer, because love is inherent to awareness and is a ubiquitous element of every contraction. The love that forms the energetic material of the contraction is awakened by the resonance of love around it. Love by its nature seeks reunion of itself with itself, awakening the contracted love into expansion. When ignored, the contracted love will vibrate with a call towards unconditional love. Love seeks itself even from within the restraints of its own conditions. Through love, all is formed; through love all form unfolds; and through love, the appearance of separation is dissolved.

Yet just as light differentiates when it breaks through a prism, love has an infinite spectrum of color and vibration. It also has infinite potential in terms of stillness, movement, diffusion and potency. The one formula to its tremendous genius is that it finds the most unconditional and fastest route towards reunion with itself: faster than the mind can follow. Love can seem to move with incredible power, or to not move at all. Yet these appearances of movement and stasis reflect perspectives of consciousness. Are we moving forward or is the world receding?

One casualty of the objectification and quantification of love through mental conditioning is that we have begun the believe that it is limited in supply. There is not enough love to go around. To receive love, we think we need to be worthy of it. To give love, our love should be pure, otherwise it could be rejected. The objectification of love means that we can compare 'My' love with your 'love', seeing it as sourced in the body, personality or Ego, which means that love is understood as being at least as limited as our current conditioning.

When love is so misconceived, it is not surprising that it often appears as the contracted form of hatred and/or self-sacrifice.

Hate

Perhaps the most injurious way to degrade love is found in the belief that love is in competition with hate. By moving love into the world of duality, an endless war is generated between good and evil, in which both parts move with hatred and call it love. Love is not the opposite of hate. Hatred is one of the most potent contractions of love. Love is there always, but hatred utterly depends on love in order to manifest.

Hatred could be described as frozen love, or love in a state of shock or trauma. Energetic dissonance in the form of rejection or abuse generates an existential threat. Love becomes shocked by conditions. These conditions polarize love within the forms of punishment and reward. When the naturalness of connection through love meets dissonance, pain comes forward. We retract from 'the other' and the love that would have been there in naturalness forms a barrier between one 'person' and the 'next', or a divider between inner and outer worlds. The direct experience of this dissonance is pure suffering.

When we look toward animals, we might witness moments of hatred. These are a kind of communication about safety and boundaries, which can resolve quickly into an atmosphere of peace. Hatred in naturalness is a rapid, energetic signal. It is when we grasp at it that it becomes the brooding, compulsive contraction that we recognize in humans.

Although it can feel cold-blooded, hatred is far from neutral. As much as love, it follows the law of attraction to fix on its target. It focusses consciousness on the object of hatred, charged with frustration, accusation, judgement and condemnation. It actively creates its target as a form of rejection. It is enflamed by the inner pain projected outwardly yet is charged by the agony of thwarted love.

When hatred has been prohibited as a natural reflex, then the client will make the 'other' at cause of the hatred, abnegating power and responsibility. To feel hated is slightly less horrible than to experience direct hatred towards another, and when it's the other's fault, we can still perceive ourselves as 'good'. This is partly because shame at the forbidden emotion of hatred is avoided. But it's a short-term fix. When we externalize hatred as sourced in the other and directed towards the self, we are moving into the area of the persecuted – a structure of identity that can pass from one generation to another. Out of this artificial state of victimhood, we steal a sense of legitimacy for abuse, violence, war and genocide. We exempt ourselves from responsibility, as it is ultimately the fault of the 'other'.

Hatred is a rapid, sentient reflex that is sourced in love. It gains status and separate form when it is denied and seeks justification through horizontal release (through projection on others or on the world). The art is to allow the aversion without identifying with it and without breaking connection with the impersonal, unconditional love in which it is sourced (ourselves). That is, to allow a deeper source of unlimited love to surround and affect the freeze of hatred: to love and hate at the same time. Aversion is a source of information for navigation. In no way does unconditional love affirm or seek to maintain the dissonance of hurtful behavior. On the contrary, it disempowers those behaviors, revealing them as aberrations.

When we can release the external targets of our obsession and begin to surround the ice of hatred within ourselves with the warmth of love, then it begins to melt back to Source. This doesn't render us defenseless, rather, it brings wisdom and peace which are fundamental Nondual Qualities connected to resilience in trauma.

When we are seated in the heart, the 'other' is not the source of love, nor is it the source of hatred. In fact, out of the power of unconditional love, the concept of 'otherness' itself begins to evaporate.

Sacrifice

The identification with being persecuted through the externalization of the source of hatred 'outside' ourselves is one way to avoid responsibility for the unconditional suffering of hatred within our field. When this denial of the energy of hatred is taken to extremes, we begin to move into the partner of hatred which is self-sacrifice. We can so hate the energy of hatred that we would rather sacrifice our deeper needs, the truth of our experience and the naturalness of expression than allow it. While the sacrifice of our short-term desires and personal agendas for the sake of love can be evolutionary, self-sacrifice born from the agenda to keep possession of love will bring misery. Love is taken hostage by a traumatic break in manifestation.

Cultural conditioning has created a tendency for the contraction around love to be more expressed as hatred by men and more as self-sacrifice by women. Yet where there is hatred, there will also be a sense of victimhood and inordinate sacrifice, just as where there is self-sacrifice, there will be an unvoiced vibration of hatred, often in the form of secret contempt.

Where there is a pattern of self-sacrifice, we are witnessing an internal split in the psyche. Who sacrifices who? Is the perpetrator not an internalized form of hatred? Self-sacrifice as a feeling has a sensation of injury, affliction and loss about it. It is quite different from the movement of expansion that allows release or letting go from the limitations of form. It has an inner violence to it. The underground thoughts to this implosion can be along the lines of: "I hate myself"; "I want to kill myself"; "I should be dead"; "I want to disappear."

Where suicidal thoughts (the compulsion of one part to destroy another part), are also prohibited, then patterns of self-destruction can come forward, often looking like suicide in slow motion including eating disorders, cutting, addiction, neglect and chronic depression. In the extreme physical form, the contraction plays out as Suicide Versus Murder, in which the Nondual Quality that is sought is unconditional release.

The energy of self-sacrifice can be suffused with self-pity, resulting from the constant inner humiliation. All this is happening within a severe inner split of the psyche. One part of the psyche sacrifices the other part, or one part hates the other part. There is a split between victim and perpetrator in which the default identification tends to mostly lean towards victimhood. This complicates the natural movement of love. The child that shows his pride in a daisy chain and is slapped by his father, or the teenager in puberty who is sexually shamed by her parents, are examples of the kind of shocked love that can result in the sacrifice of an area of manifestation. These traumas of disconnection petrify the flow of energy in a contraction between inner and outer worlds, and between the personality and its Nondual Source. The freeze between the individual and the whole can starve the psyche of vitality, increasing the addiction to the authority of externalized love.

Identified as the victim rather than the perpetrator, the self-sacrificing personality structure can develop as a thinly veiled strategy to control, manipulate and evade the charge of unrestrained love. As manifestation is muted, personality becomes unstable, lacking affirmation. Every form of personality contracts the moment it is touched. When love is there, it can feel threatening, and trigger a surge of pain. A vicious cycle can take form: the fear-based agenda of self-sacrifice perpetuates more fear as the personality is disempowered; this generates physical and psychological weakness which perpetuates more dependency on outer sources of power.

Within the duality of hatred and sacrifice, we find the fundamental belief structures of Me Versus You; Them Versus Us; or Me Versus the World. In this we are talking about the last line of defense of the Separate Self. These are the contractions that melt when we experience a 'falling in love' and the suffocating division between ourselves and the environment melts into unity. Stress levels decrease; oppressive beliefs subside; and vitality surges as the body and mind relax and open to a source way more powerful than habitual patterns.

Love: Nondual Quality

All that we can see, feel or know is nothing other than the effects of love. The willingness to let our consciousness dive into the cause before the effect – the spacious mystery before the feelings of love – is critical to the allowance of love. When we make this leap in the dark, we release agendas of grasping and aversion. Suffering is inherent to creation, and in so many ways, love is suffering. Therefore, 'letting go' (which is not the same as self-sacrifice) has become a catchphrase. When we let go even of the energetic agendas of seeking love, finding it, getting it and keeping it, we allow the imperceivable intelligence of the source of love itself.

Love creates through division and destroys through reunion. Its power underpins every conflict and each contraction. It combines, confuses and collapses us back into the more spacious dimensions of being. It is inherent to each sense perception and every seeing. It is both the glue of creation and the fabric of form. When one form of love meets another form of love, there is an explosion of love in which only love remains.

Love can give us the power to move mountains and it can leave us faltering in pure vulnerability. It can be a prerequisite to give it, yet a torture to receive it. It is found in the softest touch of the breeze and in the unflinching certainty of emanation. It heals and liberates, makes us feel safe, while infinitely escaping us. Just as it drives us into the world, it calls us home, deep inside ourselves. It is found in every coming and going, beginning and ending, emanation and disappearance, birth and death, yet it will lift us beyond all those illusions.

To gain insight into love, consider the attraction towards the beloved: if we allow this attraction, all the way into the beloved, taking the beloved all the way into the Source of all we are, would we still see the beloved? Would they not be one with all we are? Was this love creative or destructive?

In naturalness, interdependent, interconnected forms move through love and channel it through denser vibrations, all the way into the physical cells of the body and the fundamental particles of matter to a point of absolute singularity where love is no longer perceivable as it is identical with the perceiver.

This is what makes love so difficult to define. What is it that can be at once everywhere and nowhere? In everything and at the same time in nothing? Again, we know love by its effects. When we dive into the imperceivable source of love, those effects accelerate – there is a quickening of transformation.

Just as self-sacrifice longs to belong, love is found in the longing. Just as hatred conspires to stop suffering, love is found in the suffering itself. Love plays out in the dynamic of consciousness at the borders between densities of form: between the Source and the psyche, between the psyche and the body, and between the body and the planet. It is the feeling quality in every touch of form.

It is therefore important to allow this love within the suffering of our contractions. This allowance is radically different to the agenda of 'getting rid' of our suffering. In this way, suffering is not the 'other', it is not a threat, but a lost child coming back to love, as love.

Contemplations

1. Move attention to the chest area and contemplate the sense of hatred, noticing the effect on the mind and body. Without doing anything with the resonance of hatred, expand behind it into an open space of awareness. Let that awareness surround also the area of hatred, without agenda.

2. Recall the experience of love and notice the effects on the body and heart. Release the object or situation of love and invite the feeling of love to expand. Wherever you perceive an effect, release it and let your consciousness dive into the imperceivable cause before the effect.

Form does not differ from Love

And Love does not differ from Form.

Form is Love and Love is Form.

19 LONELINESS, INTIMACY & CONNECTION

The partner of loneliness is intimacy.

Connection has no opposite.

In connection, intimacy and loneliness are one.

"Loneliness is proof that your innate search for connection is intact."

MARTHA BECK

The collective state of humanity includes a shared field of loneliness; an ache of separation from the whole; a longing for reunion or at least communion with something beyond itself.

Loneliness is at the heart of every spiritual seeker, lover and artist. It's even possible to connect with the collective loneliness of humans within the unfathomable, unknown expanse of the universe. It is between man and woman, mother and child, a scientist and her research, the seeing eye and that which it sees. The sheer uniqueness of individual perspective can carry a sharp tinge of loneliness – which is a suffering that can cloud or deter our direct, authentic perception. Seeing things differently, or uniquely, can generate a sense of loneliness, yet this difference in perspective should be celebrated not avoided. We are one, but our individual manifestation is miraculously unique.

The suffering of loneliness is born from a fear of intimacy – its partner in the waltz of duality. This fear arises when there is a resistance to allow what is anyway, already here in the human field: the sense of loss, cruelty, abandonment, terror or betrayal. Can we be intimate with what is experienced as horror? Can we risk intimacy, when it could hurt us?

Like children who cover their eyes in the hope that they'll disappear through not seeing, we split our consciousness from suffering. We refuse intimacy with pain while seeking it with pleasure, thus losing connection with intimacy altogether. Thus, we become lonely, directed by an inner sense of lack towards an outer world that never seems to close the gap. Our refusal to allow intimacy with all the cracks in creation throws up more loneliness, which in its solitary pride whips up more shame and disgust at intimacy. In this way, we spiral into a greater suffering of disconnection from direct experience.

Loneliness

The sense of loneliness is deeply intimate. It arches from the Source of ourselves in a hollow ache of separation from the whole. It has flavors of unworthiness in it. It can be iced with shame and weighted with guilt and (most annoyingly of all) it can have a sense of deeper truth. Indeed, the admitted inner loneliness can have a greater authenticity than the web of projection and illusion that runs between people: it can feel more real to be lonely, despite its suffering, than to pretend a sense of connection.

The lonely can feel left out of time and space. Time left them behind; the world has no space for them; they feel cut out of the rhythms of life and bereft of purpose. The feeling of loneliness can be like a hollow, uncomfortable energy. It can seem to run through the blood and into the bones, causing awkwardness in movement. It clumps in energetic contractions along the spine, often causing back pain and frozen muscles. The body feels heavy in loneliness, as if it were a strange weight being dragged around, with no direction. When the space of loneliness builds up, no words, distractions, or casual conversation seem able to fill that gap.

Loneliness is not only an affliction of the physically alone. Partners can suffer loneliness within their relationships. Family members can meet it behind the curtain of reunion on festive occasions. Children feel lonely in classrooms, packed with action. Often with roots in trauma, loneliness is a contraction formed around the natural polarity of the inner and outer, or 'Me' and the world: its energy gathers in the primal rift created by the belief and experience of a Separate Self. Like boredom, it can be the energetic atmosphere or state that forms like a border between the personality and the Dark Night of the Soul.

It can feel as if only the consciousness of the lonely one there in this loneliness, and this consciousness is believed to be separate from the consciousness of everyone else. Although loneliness in the mind says: "I am excluded," loneliness in the heart says: "I am special." In this, there is a touch of grandiosity and passive aggression towards what is perceived as the outer world. Based on the sense of being 'unseen', loneliness paradoxically dictates that it should never be seen and lives in secrecy, held back from the world.

A first task in approaching loneliness, is to give the feeling all the time and space that has been denied. Time and space are like oxygen to starved vitality. A second task is to express that loneliness through time and space, into the world of form. Tell someone you are lonely, and if there is no one there, tell a tree or an animal, tell the sky. Communicate it. The universe is listening. A third task is to allow yourself to receive the loneliness that seems to be out there in the environment: to take it in and to let it come to life.

Imagine a kind of loneliness that is at one with the loneliness hidden within every human alive today. It's the same loneliness. But don't stop there, let this loneliness include every human that has ever lived, and all those yet to be born. Let it undulate and flow. Let it expand and contract with its own rhythm. Let this awesome human loneliness resonate through the substrata of the earth. Let it radiate into the infinite sky. Let the loneliness have a subtle melody, reverberating through this physical universe and any other dimension. Let loneliness sing, until the word 'lonely' cannot define it anymore.

On the road of self-inquiry, we will travel often through the river of loneliness. We have collectively rejected its surface as a bad energy, a defunct, despicable and despairing space, yet we have confused the energy with the effects of its contraction. We lock up our natural loneliness, masking it, confusing it, oppressing it and pretending it's not there. In this, we create the illusion of loneliness, grossly cemented with beliefs in ultimate separation. As this living Source energy is increasingly layered with masks, unseen, unfelt and forgotten, we begin to deny that it's even there.

Yet even the first layers of loneliness are not 'lonely' in the common sense of the word. Within the suffering of loneliness, we can experience a deep, personal empowerment; and a movement to authenticity and inner truth. In the allowance of loneliness, we move towards our spiritual center, which is not 'out there' in the world, but at the Source of all consciousness. Loneliness burns away the inner structures and constraints that are the by-products of the demands and expectations of others.

If the lonely one can continue into the heart and gut of his or her loneliness, allowing it to arise as a felt sensation in awareness, a kind of alchemy is possible. This is partly because the contracted pain of loneliness is a field shared with the whole. Through allowing our own loneliness, we can release our fear of authority, opening the possibility of greater honesty and expression.

Loneliness has a holiness about it. In its subtle energy, it's a kind of prayer of longing through perpetual creation. When it's allowed, this 'lonely' energy begins to expand through the subtle layers of being. As this energy expands, it naturally connects to the same loneliness in others. As we find peace in the allowance of loneliness, we can increasingly connect with the loneliness in the environment. What happens when two people relax in an agreement to be lonely together? A deeper form of intimacy with life is emerging in which alone, becomes all-one.

Intimacy

For the lonely one, intimacy can be more threatening than the suffering of loneliness. The fear of intimacy, born from wounds in childhood and the social field, is interwoven with every moment of loneliness. In chronic loneliness, there is a refusal to be intimate with an area of psychological suffering. The very sense of loneliness is inviting us into a deeper feeling connection with ourselves. Within the suffering of that self-intimacy, a voice is calling come home, come home, come home! Yet the voice is blocked, as if it were that of an unwelcome stranger. Something, normally a contraction, cannot be shared, and that disconnection causes both pain and stress.

Like the sense of loneliness, intimacy rests on the premise of separation. Yet unlike the natural movement where the excitement of intimacy through different layers of form can be a celebration, the intimacy contraction is caught in the horror of violation. Fear and anger have won the upper hand over the nature of relationship, to the extent that the pleasure of intimacy is sacrificed to avoid abuse or loss. This sacrifice can be reflexive and unconscious as it is often rooted in trauma.

Yet still, life goes on, with unlimited opportunities for intimacy, which are simultaneously sought out and resisted. The individual begins to take half-steps into intimacy, based on conditions. She masks herself as someone else – a fantasy 'person' - so that rejection doesn't hit the inner core of pain. He allows intimacy but only from one person, and only at certain times of the day. She can be intimate with him, but only if he is predictable and acts by her rules. Intimacy itself is conditioned as a happening between humans, excluding nature, animals or the intimate potential of each moment of consciousness.

Out of our fear of intimacy, we armor ourselves against the outer world, and this also numbs our senses, increasing the suffering of disconnection. Openness hurts. In our resistance to intimacy, we compose stories about others to give a sense of control. We tell, rather than ask questions. Receptivity is blocked, and action goes into overdrive, which can be quite uninviting.

The more intimacy is conditioned within the parameters of the 'allowed' and the 'forbidden', the greater the contraction of loneliness. Having decided the 'reality' of how we need the world to be, we begin to dictate that reality on the world, condemning, ignoring or rejecting anything that doesn't conform. In this, we isolate ourselves further. We entrench ourselves away from the here and now of living experience. We widen the rift between ourselves and others through distancing strategies of comparison and competition; and we lose the authentic flow of expression outwards and reception of impressions inward.

All contractions are contractions in time and space of emotional energy. Contractions can also be understood as conditions. Here, we tend to put conditions on intimacy, out of fear of pain. This shrinkage of experience arises from an agenda of what we want to be intimate with, when we want to be intimate with it, and where we want to be intimate with it. These agendas are born of trauma, fear, or collective habit.

The critical stage of the loneliness/intimacy contraction is found in the embedded condition: "I agree to be intimate with you only if I never feel lonely." Whether spoken or not, this is a game of disconnection, where the contraction will become increasingly dense; perception increasingly fragmented, and the physical body decreasingly responsive to the universal invitation to life.

Connection: Nondual Quality

Loneliness and intimacy are driven by the hunger for deeper connection. Connection defines them. Connection is inherent, yet connectivity gets disrupted by grasping and aversion. Connection, like all Nondual Qualities, cannot be created, it can only be allowed. At source, the allowance of the interconnectedness of life requires the release of layers of Ego and identification with the personality. In the depths of connection, the fixated forms of personality dissolve.

Disturbances in the free flow of intimacy and loneliness indicate the need for transformation of parts of these areas, or the release of them. When we allow the Nondual Quality of connection, it can radically change our world view. Connection is not only to other humans but runs through all experience. Rather than being an assortment of separate things, or psyches, or humans, or life forms, we experience a vast, interconnected web in which nothing is left out.

When we consolidate in the Nondual Quality of connection, there is no dependency on intimacy, although intimacy depends on connection. Loneliness also can only exist through connection. If we didn't have an inherent sense of connection, we could not suffer loneliness.

When we relax in the inherent connection between forms, there is no perception of 'other': connection is here regardless of experiential content. Unity manifests through webs of connectivity. Even the felt sense of disconnection is connected: the connection is just suffused with suffering.

In the twin-trap of loneliness and intimacy, the therapist supports the client through the Nondual Quality of connection. Loneliness can be an easier sentient zone to allow than intimacy, where wounds can include sexual abuse or rape, childhood trauma or a deep loyalty to toxic family patterns that forbid intimacy and naturalness, promoting pretense as a strategy for survival. At the same time, clients who have developed an addiction to intimacy – sexual or otherwise – are often in 'flight mode' from that dreaded zone called loneliness. The raw energy at the bridge of separation into individual sentient form is at once dynamically lonely and intimate, and held within an indestructible truth of connection that can be denied for a while, but which is never lost.

Contemplations

1. Choose an inanimate object that you feel connected to, and a person in your life. Connect with the object and then with the person. Release both object and person and try to relax in the sense of connection without object.

2. Relax inside yourself and contemplate something or someone in your environment or within yourself with which you feel you have no connection at all. Stay with the contemplation for a while, then move the contemplation to your ankles: left ankle, right ankle, and both at the same time, returning to the one with which you felt no connection.

3. Connect to a memory of childhood (pre-puberty). Explore the sense of connection experienced at that time. Explore the sense of connection between you and that child.

Form does not differ from Connection

And Connection does not differ from Form.

Form is Connection and Connection is Form.

20 Jealousy, Idolatry & Humility

The partner of jealousy is idolatry.

Humility has no opposite.

In humility, jealousy and idolatry are one.

"Do you wish to rise? Begin by descending. You plan a tower that will pierce the clouds? Lay first the foundation of humility."

SAINT AUGUSTINE

The contraction of jealousy and idolatry is a harsh one, formed out of an absolute belief in the primacy of personality. Self-image is taken as definitive and is commodified within the parameters of comparison and competition. Personal worth is equated with existential value, and therefore, the stakes are high. If your personal form is received as 'less', you lose value; if your personal form is affirmed as 'more', you are entitled to privilege.

It's notable that the first commandment in the bible is: "Thou shalt have no other gods before Me." According to the bible, when Moses was given the 10 commandments - which would form the foundations of modern civilization - he came down from Mount Sinai to find the people of Israel intoxicated and violent and worshipping a golden calf in the place of God. The rage, cruelty, violence and jealousy that possessed the Israelites in the thralls of idolatry at the foot of Mount Sinai led Moses to despair in humanity. He smashed the tablets. They had to be given a second time.

The quest to become something, to succeed, to survive or to impress others is a quest that inherently falls short of our True Nature. As Nondual teaching has repeated: What you are looking for is the one that is looking. The deeper wisdom of humility is that all which can be perceived is not absolute, including the structures of the self. No thought, feeling or experience can exist in separation, but each is an expression of a deeper awareness. Why? Because whatever can arise in our consciousness utterly depends on that same consciousness. If we can see the 'form', we are not the form: we are the one seeing. Forms come and go, the seeing is continuous.

Jealousy and idolatry dance together in the perpetual investment in personality as an estimable form that dictates our human value. Both are bound up with addictive grasping towards success, reward and privilege. The same personal rivalry that resents the happiness of another human, has the potential for unwarranted destruction and cruelty. Paradoxically, the contraction often indicates a depth of disconnection from the purity of personal manifestation. When we move with humility, the scope of personal manifestation widens - to be big, we need to be generous.

The Nondual Quality of humility brings the relaxation needed to release attachment to personal structures and to disentangle from the patterns that hold us hostage. It can do this, because humility says that whatever I perceive myself to be, I am more than that – I am the one that is able to perceive. When personality is thus deflated an inner space opens that can flow more easily with the needs of the present moment, regardless of separate agenda.

Jealousy

Jealousy is a taboo emotion, although it is everywhere among us. It can be experienced as a stinging, irrational hatred with a consistent drum beat of wishing bad for the 'other', or a sharp, continuous pain that seems impossible to release. As it is taboo, it can also be surrounded with clouds of dread. Jealousy gets us out of center, bringing a kind of soullessness, as if we have no value. It's infused with fear, loathing and rejection. It resists being named and moves through the shadows. Gossip and toxic stories are often laced with the energy of jealousy, seeking to deny responsibility through recruiting others towards a consensual negative reality about the target. This is the breeding ground of toxic competition, lies, pretense and manipulation, and can often lead to social ostracization. No one is immune to this, as jealousy is a transpersonal energy that affects the atmosphere before it is defined within the parameters of 'who is jealous of who'.

When there is jealousy between people, this subtle, toxic energy also affects the target of jealousy. It can be as much a suffering to have jealousy come your way, as to feel jealousy towards another. It is infectious. The same pain can resonate through the system of both subject and object. People who attract a lot of jealousy, in time, learn to disentangle from the field through simply not touching it. Those who are liable to be jealous will go from one object of jealousy to another under the misconception that fulfillment is somehow possible through the destruction of the perceived competition. Personal manifestation gets lost in the obsession to control the manifestation of others.

Born from a sense of lack, jealousy distorts perception. For example, we can experience intense jealousy towards our neighbor because he just bought an expensive car. We don't care that his son was killed in a terror accident and that he cries himself to sleep every night. The expensive car defines him. We want the thing the other has 'got' but not all the conditions around it. Asked whether we would want to change places with the target of our jealousy (including the whole package of suffering which is inextricable from their success), most would decline.

Jealousy is linked to the belief that qualities are in limited supply. It moves with the belief that if the other were to lose the quality, then it would be available for the taking. In this way, it has a close connection to the contraction of poverty and greed, to which the Nondual Quality is gratitude. Through investing in these gross levels of materialism, fueled by perpetual comparison and competition, jealousy perpetuates the inner sense of deficiency that is found at its Source. It also generates a collective field of jealousy that prohibits individual expression, lest the success of that expression be also condemned to jealousy. Jealous personalities dare little on their own behalf.

Idolatry

Where we find a contraction that manifests with the emotion of jealousy, we will also find various forms of idolatry. Idolatry is the inflated worship of a thing perceived as 'other'. This object is seen as containing all our hidden promise, prayer and yearnings for fulfillment. It involves the objectification or dictation of the forms of life, in which various subjects worship at the feet of the object. The object could be a rock star with a lousy attitude and lots of bad habits, but this won't deter the compulsion to idolize. The inner experience of the idol is irrelevant to the idolaters, who seek to fulfill their fantasies through projecting them onto him.

Like jealousy, idolatry is blind, moving through sliding scales of inferiority and superiority. In the case of the rock star, the idol is posited as vastly superior to the crowd. The personality of the one idolized gains godly proportion, especially if they are suddenly killed. Yet such an idolized personality is surrounded by jealousy, manipulation, flattery, pretense, opportunism and a startling lack of living care towards the genuine need.

Humility: Nondual Quality

The Nondual Quality of humility has been demeaned into a structure of abuse, which has led it to be equated with 'humiliation'. This is far from the natural humility of being that is inherent to form. The misconception of the quality of humility has bred legions of egoic forms based on false humility: self-negation, self-sacrifice and difficulty in manifestation. When humility is used as a stick to beat the other with, it gets associated with guilt, shame, deception and a loss of self-esteem.

Humility is not about self-effacement. Its nature is subtle and profound, with the potential to open the Felt Sense of our unique presence, or the individual expression of True Nature. Humility reflects as the wisdom of impermanence. This means that personal survival instincts are relativized through a deeper consolidation in Nondual Qualities. With humility, we drop belief in the definitive nature of the chair on which we sit. But we don't smash the chair, rather we rest back in the more expansive chair of perception behind it. Humility doesn't make us small, it allows us to be infinite. It opens the horizons of consciousness.

Humility is intrinsic to form. All manifestation has the inherent wisdom of impermanence. Unstable and transforming, manifestation arises from a greater Source and will return to it. The wisdom of impermanence supports living fluidity, and the dissolution of the suffering of separation. Humility acknowledges the whole history that has created the forms of the present moment, as well as all the futures embedded in the present moment. It is rooted in the direct experience of oneness.

When we suffer the afflictions of jealousy and idolatry, we are also deeply imbued in the wars of competition and comparison. The charge of competition and measurement depends on the objectification of self. It demands that we see our self as a measurable 'thing' that can be compared to other selves, which are measurable 'things'. The fixation of the self as an object is dislocated from the living, fluid nature of self. When the self is a 'thing' that can be compared, it is also a 'thing' that can be destroyed. This means that even the concept of this separate object we call 'I' is constantly living in the shadow of death.

The strength of authenticity within the naturalness of humility releases this charge. All forms are non-absolute and do not exist in isolation. No form is fixed except for a brief excerpt of linear time. Humility has a softness, sweetness and is gentle, yet it also has incredible power, as it directly draws on the Source of the whole.

Contemplations

1. Connect to the feeling of jealousy at any time in your life and be curious about the nature of the feeling, let it tell its sentient story. Connect to the feeling when someone is jealous of you and do the same. How do the experiences of being jealous and receiving jealousy differ? How are they the same?

2. Connect to someone or something that is idolized and relax into the feeling experience of idolization. Notice the direction of the feeling, and the spatial position of you in relation to the object that is idolized. Now

imagine that you are the one idolized. Notice the Felt Sense of the energy. Expand the feeling of being idolized and be curious of its subtle undertones.

3. Recall a situation with others that bothers you. Let the personal atmosphere in the situation expand as much as it wants. Now, bring the attention to the body. Zoom out from the body as if by satellite image, seeing it first as small and then imperceivable on the surface of the planet. Zoom out from the planet until it is small within the milky way. Zoom out from the milky way until it is tiny in the universe. Return to the body and connect with the subtle vibrations in the feet. Notice the space between the feet and the ground and move a little into the ground.

Form does not differ from Humility

And Humility does not differ from Form.

Form is Humility and Humility is Form.

21 BETRAYAL, LOYALTY & TRUST

The partner of betrayal is loyalty.

Trust has no opposite.

In trust, loyalty and betrayal are one.

"Be what you are. There is nothing to be afraid of. Trust and try. Experiment honestly. Give your real being a chance to shape your life. You will not regret."

NISARGADATTA MAHARAJ

Overshadowed by the sword of condemnation and suffused with the existential agony of the Dark Night of the Soul, the psyche can be formed, controlled and destroyed within the nightmarish experience of betrayal. Often, the prerequisite of loyalty to something forms the floor on which the psyche is composed, and the collapse of loyalty or the experience of being betrayed can be part of a deeper awakening to human potential.

Loyalty contracts are based on duality and often arise out of a shadow-land of conflict. These contracts can be conscious or subconscious and are formed through patterns of habit and expectation. For example, when two people become friends, there is already an unspoken contract that one won't slander the other, without breaking the contract of friendship.

We often make contracts to empower ourselves against conflict, which means they can be based on a perceived threat. When the contract begins to determine the freedom of authentic expression, it begins to shrink the psyche and generate disconnection and deceit. Often, such loyalty contracts are reflected as rigid beliefs and energetic contractions shielded by fear. They can be inherited with our DNA, based on past trauma and reaffirmed through education and the pressure to conform. For example, if we experience joy at a funeral, we break a social contract – we betray a social form. This can make loyalists and traitors of us all, depending on perspective.

Loyalty that arises out of fear and threat reaffirms the sense of the Separate Self, with the potential to disconnect us from our True Nature. The payload of the emotional suffering experienced as betrayal is held in a contract of duality – or to say it another way – in contraction. Contractions around purity, innocence and belonging will all shake where the floor falls out on loyalty. Yet what is it that we're loyal to? The partner? Parents? Children? Ancestry? Religion? Culture? The nation? Inherited ethics? Our physical well-being? Humanity? Ourselves?

When words like loyalty and betrayal are being used to condition the human psyche, feelings around abandonment and possession will be in the background. Beneath this will be a simmering crisis in individuality in which boundaries are sought through contraction, exclusion and separation. To allow the unadulterated impressions of the here and now, a deeper consolidation is needed in the Nondual Quality of trust.

Betrayal

The experience of betrayal can come with a deep sense of horror. It can feel as if the gut of the heart has been cut out, such is the sense of severance when a contract is broken. As both our belief structures and the energetic forms of personality are held together through a network of contracts, when we are betrayed, it can feel like a part of us has been amputated. The Felt Sense suffuses both perpetrators and victims. It can feel like a fate worse than death, invalidating purpose, pleasure and passion. As it often represents breakage within the psyche, there can be a suicidal resonance around it. Guilt and shame are residents to this contraction, and fear is the landlord – irrespective of who betrayed who.

Sexual betrayal can come with an epigenetic legacy of Inherited Trauma. The termination of the loyalty contract of marriage historically carried the prospect of poverty, banishment and incarceration, with all its accompanying social stigma. Betrayed women that couldn't consider or risk such domestic catastrophe would continue the appearance of married life, attempting to contain the violation of intimacy at the womb of vulnerability, through numbing the senses and closing the heart. On the other side, women that betrayed could be interned as insane or become social pariahs. Even today, banishment and/or death is a common punishment for female betrayal in many parts of the world – even when that 'betrayal' amounts to complaining about domestic violence or 'immodest' speech or dress.

Men who betray find themselves further excluded from the heart of the family, condemned by wife and children and sleeping in a bed of fundamental sexual shame. Seeking reunion with the female, he betrays the female, seeking relief from the sense of inner condemnation, yet actually increasing that suffering. Lies and deception to attempt concealment further disempower him, widening the sense of isolation, abandonment and disconnection. There seems to be no way home. Shame, disgust, guilt, accusation, loneliness, unwanted intimacy and dread suffuse the field of togetherness. The (often sudden) cascade into these multiple afflictions can obscure purity, love, peace and even fundamental care. It is a contraction that can make behavioral monsters out of victim and perpetrator alike.

Yet, at a deeper layer, betrayal can have a bright side to it. Systems, contracts and power-based codes of conformity such as marital, social, religious or political structures are rarely based on living experience, but rather on fear-based attempts to dictate form onto life. In this, the form of the individual is already in contraction. The concept of loyalty can impose severe limitations on the authenticity of experience.

Often, we have a contract with toxic family structures as well as with power-based, tribal structures of authority. For example, the contract could be that we never talk about how granddad liked to indecently touch the children. Would not a betrayal of that contract be a deeper loyalty? Sometimes, clients will leave therapy because they fear they will betray the contract they have with their parents – contracts often formed by trauma and which have the underlying dictate: to belong, you must be loyal to the lie. Reframing family systems to honor the love, peace, and a priori belonging that is here, irrespective of damage and fear, can be critical to a healing process that will affect many more than just the individual in therapy.

Loyalty

The feeling of loyalty is different from the demand for loyalty. The feeling can have a warmth in the belly, a sense of belonging, and a deep relaxation into the sense of home. The demand for loyalty from the other, however, is often based on fear of loss and the abuse of power. It is the same when we demand that others trust us, and feel betrayed when they can't or won't. Loyalty is often concerned with possessive agendas which inherently limit freedom of form. Demands for loyalty come with the threat of betrayal. If you are not loyal to the prescribed form, then you are a traitor, you are unworthy of belonging to the whole.

All movements towards integrity and authentic self-expression can shake up contractions around loyalty. Contractual loyalty can feel like a slow death. It can exclude adventure, passion and risk, reducing vitality and fogging perception. Designed to preserve the living connection, contractual loyalty can lead to disconnection through tiresome habituation. In addition, if it is not challenged from the inside-out, a comfort zone of loyalty can easily get shaken from the outside-in. Stuff happens.

No act of loyalty, like no act of betrayal, leaves the world without footprints of horror. This is because at its root, loyalty is based on threats from the perceived 'outside'. The very concept of loyalty demands belief in the threat of betrayal: that is, it affirms betrayal. Loyalty seeks an unreal exclusivity over experience. In addition, it creates distance from the object of loyalty.

To what could we be loyal if it is not an entity which is inherently separate from who or what we are? Can the mental concept of loyalty close the gap we experience between ourselves and another, or is a deeper awareness of unity needed?

Often loyalty conflicts are initiated in childhood, where the child finds itself caught between the conflicting authorities of two parents. Loyalty is rewarded, betrayal is punished, if not explicitly then in implicit ways: the parents withdraw consciousness from the child. Dancing within this duality of betrayal and loyalty requires consolidation in existential trust. Our core authenticity depends on it.

Trust: Nondual Quality

Trust, like other Nondual Qualities, has been abused through power games of the Separate Self, to such an extent that it is generally misconceived. The external demand that we trust the other, or the authority, depends on the belief that trust is a feeling that can be created. This undermines true trust and replaces it with subjugation. The individual's direct experience is wiped away to conform the individual to a stronger power. While we might be able to say the word 'trust' and take a big leap in the dark, this is not trust but a search for it. Trust itself has no fear in it: it's as strong as all that exists. The art is not to move with trust, but to be the trust.

Trust, like truth, is not a feeling designed in the first place for the 'other'. Hijacked in the split of the Separate Self, many will demand that they be trusted, as if trust from the outside could bring them trust on the inside. This is a movement of power between one form and another, or an attempt to dominate the shared direction. It's not trust which is demanded, but subordination and conformity. The demand for trust is often generated not by strength but by fear. It often displays a lack of inner trust or confidence. It implies inner distrust. Contractions around the suffering of the separate self generate pain and vulnerability, causing us to demand that the sense of trust be provided by the other.

Power is not a dirty word and is itself a Nondual Quality. Emergency situations can require temporary surrender to the stronger party for maximal survival, such as a child to a parent, or a client to a caregiver. Yet this surrender is possible out of an inner, existential trust, in the first place: an existential trust that connects to the living trust in the other, allowing the shared form to be unconditionally supported.

Feelings of loyalty and betrayal seek trust and depend on trust and are composed of frozen trust. They long for a trust which is so irrefutable that the very concepts of betrayal and loyalty evaporate.

There is a perennial trust that arises when we are anchored in dimensions beyond form. It is always present, outside of linear time, and untouched by action and reaction. This kind of trust is foundational to the freedom of being. It moves beyond the fear of death and breeds confidence and mastery in being able to deal with whatever manifests, and to evolve through it. Unconditional trust can allow the motile truth of experience. It doesn't need to grasp or push anything away. It is here, irrespective of possession and abandonment, gain and loss, or pain and pleasure. Trust is also trust in the contraction – as it manifests in the here and now. It is the unwavering inner presence that can allow transformation.

If we're confused, then it is possible to trust the confusion. Confusion doesn't arise out of nowhere. When we don't trust our confusion, we run to an outer authority to tell us what to think. In doing this, our true experience gets relegated to the guess work of others. When we can sit in trust with confusion, confusion tells its own sources, revealing the sentient roots of conflict. When the conflict of duality emerges, an attunement will begin towards a space of synthesis and a deeper harmony. The seat of trust facilitates this attunement.

One might think that this kind of trust isolates us from other people and society – reducing them to mere fleeting impressions. But this is not the case. A direct formula in the ability to be in trust is the ability to connect with that same space of trust in others – to trust them from the inside out. The trust in us tunnels to the trust in the other, and as such a connection beyond conditions is formed which can withstand all weather of experience. This connection facilitates the sharing of living energies without polarization. Trust opens the ongoing possibility of communication which is unconditional to contraction (we can always communicate the nature of our experience). Trust is the bedrock of communion and the foundation of true community.

Contemplations

1. Softly move the focus of attention to the pelvic area, including soft tissue and bones, and sink into the sense of hot or cold around all physical sensations. Inwardly say the word 'Trust' and observe its effect.

2. Close your eyes and imagine light over the chest area, letting your sense of sight and sound sink into the body. Relax there for a while and contemplate the Felt Sense of trust.

3. With eyes closed, feel the surface area of the neck, face and head, including the back of the head. Move your awareness to the brow and relax there. Visualize a night sky and visually relax into the infinity of darkness. Contemplate trust and notice where there is a gap between the individual sense of trust and any answer from the infinite night. Make a movement of trust towards that gap.

Form does not differ from Trust

And Trust does not differ from Form.

Form is Trust and Trust is Form.

22 SHAME, DISGUST & PURITY

The partner of shame is disgust.

Purity has no opposite.

In purity, disgust and shame are one.

"I took my diamond to the pawnshop, but that don't make
it junk."

LEONARD COHEN

Shame is directly connected with the light of consciousness. When consciousness exposes that which we don't want to be seen, there is a painful shock of shame. Consciousness illuminates, reveals and exposes parts of the living psyche which we try to conceal. Shame and disgust show up in the painful rift where we split the psyche in an attempt to deny or negate experience. In this, the felt sense of shame can also hold a promise: of healing, revelation and liberation of multiple contractions within the unconditional light of consciousness. While we deny our core suffering, it nevertheless at the same time deeply longs to be 'seen'.

The emotion of shame is an effect of the belief that the differentiated form is ultimately separate from the whole. When shame is unbearable, we spit it out in the form of disgust.

The contraction of shame and disgust thirsts for purity: it is made of shocked or frozen purity and has severed itself from the power of this purity through the belief that purity is forever lost. When we allow the experience of pure shame or pure disgust, healing begins within the field of pure experience.

Shame

Shame is a light emitted out of the intense pain of exposure. It's not heavy, but hot and rapid, charged with unbearable vitality. It is reflexive and happens faster than the conscious mind can control. Notice that in the Garden of Eden, shame is ignited prior to guilt and condemnation. The contraction of shame from the pure light of our True Nature is its own punishment. It is a direct split in consciousness between the individual form and its living Source.

The feeling of shame is one of sudden exposure or the shock of revelation in the light of the consciousness of the perceived 'other'. Even when we are ashamed before ourselves, the energy represents a severe split between the exposed vulnerability of a separate or disallowed 'self' and the consciousness which perceives it.

Shame is alive in the here and now, yet most of the time we won't feel it, as it is habitually anesthetized through protective structures of Ego. When we are touched at further depths, however, it will begin to resonate. Responses can be rapid, involuntary and physical: the cheeks flush red, the throat tightens, the pelvis freezes, buttocks tighten and there can be a terrible sensation of burning or freezing in the upper chest and/or pelvic area. Body movements include covering up: the crossing of legs, aversion of the head, the covering of the lips and face, and the twitching of the eyes. Yet although shame sings her song in rapid tongues, she is not so easily released. An energetic contraction of shame can stay for lifetimes and be passed consciously or unconsciously from generation to generation. In some families, the experience of shame can be totally prohibited. This is partly because it hurts so much: we shut down and stay shut.

The origins of many contractions of shame are found in childhood. Incidents around bodily needs, sexuality and the collective family attitude towards the eyes of the 'world' all seed shame in the infant psyche. Parental rejection and educational methods often confirm layers of shame through public humiliations intended to conform behavior.

In addition, our social awkwardness in addressing cruelty and suffering within the family domain often encourages more shame in areas from incest, divorce, through to childhood illness, grief and loss. In the dynamic of collective repression, shame is a key weapon. This means that the traumatized are often traumatized again through contractions of shame generated by the raw fear in the familial and social environment. Pretty soon, a child learns that the feeling of shame signals a horrible isolation. He or she learns to distract, conceal, hide or to freeze the Felt Sense of purity altogether.

Yet, beneath these covered layers, the contraction of shame remains. In a way, part of the vitality and life force of the organism is trapped in the perpetually burning flames of hell. This hell is made of pure isolation, untouchability, rejection and is supported by the illusion of static perfection. In general, no one wants to feel it for long, so the energy is cast out towards the 'other'. In the words of Adam, in facing the Godly light of his own Source in the fire of shame: 'Eve made me do it.' In the words of Eve: 'It was because of the snake.'

Disgust

The energy of shame can be so sharp, hot and hellish in its experience that the reflex is to get rid of it. This revolves around contraction retraction from the 'other' and often revenge on the 'other'. It is like spitting the 'other' out. This is a biological reflex to spit out the poison of shame. The stomach contracts, the vomit reflex sets in. The body goes hot and cold: disgust is taking form.

The movement of repulsion can have a time-lag, or it can be instant that is, the moment another even comes close to a contraction of shame, the threatened one attempts to throw the energy out of his own system in the form of disgust. This can be such a repeated reflex that the living sense of shame is no longer even accessed, all that is experienced is disgust towards the 'outside'.

As shame and disgust play out within family systems, it's easy to watch the passing of disgust between one family member and the other. In childhood, it can be a game. Later, it becomes deadly serious. It's almost as if a burning ball of fire is passed from one corner of the dining table to another. Often, such a family will designate a scapegoat as a final recipient of the shameful energy, if not a willing human being, then another family member such as an animal. Other families, to give the internal scapegoat a break, will designate the foreign neighbors, or the tax man as the pet hate. Often the scapegoat themselves will seek out a more vulnerable victim on which to pass the disgust. It seems that someone needs to hold the shame/disgust, for the 'whole' to keep its chin up.

On a global scale, it is possible to see how unhealed shame plays out to horrific proportions. How easily the shaming of the whole population of Germany of World War 1 could be transformed into a collective disgust towards the Jews, gypsies, homosexuals and disabled, who were considered 'other' to the pure Aryan race. This disgust was not just dictated, it was experienced by many, as the contracted agony of shame began to release at the expense of the 'other'.

Yet we don't need an 'other' to play this game of shame and disgust. The whole drama also takes place within our own psyche. When you meet someone with self-disgust, you meet someone who underneath that, is burning in existential shame. At some time, the psyche split, and one part of the psyche was radically disowned. Between the frying pan of self-disgust, and the fire of shame, the disgust came forward as a biological attempt to expel the toxicity. Disgust towards a distanced part of the psyche hurts slightly less – there is even some authority in it.

Unfortunately, a return to purity is often sought out through shaming behaviors which can be abusive. Drinking oneself silly on Christmas Day at the house of the in-laws might help release the shame, but afterwards, the flames of the fire can burn even brighter. Indeed, a whole range of addictions, from substance abuse through to pornography, compulsive talking, to food disorders, all have their roots in the twin contraction of shame and disgust. The engagement relieves the agony of separation in the short term, although in the long term, it tends to make the experience of isolation worse.

A central arena of the contraction of shame/disgust is in the dimension of sexuality. From Genesis until today, the split between male and female is a natural duality in creation and as such, is also suffused with the pain of separation. The 'otherness' of the opposite sex, from the physical through to the emotional and psychological patterning carries with it an easy reflex of shame and/or disgust, as well as a legacy of trauma. This tends to get played out through fields of sexuality and power. It is not for nothing that sexuality has been historically and religiously defined and condemned as impure.

Often in the shadows of the gender politics of shame are revenge rapes sexual abuse and incest. There is little rationality in it, although the strategy often involves an abuse of the word 'modesty' in an insistence that somehow the woman (as an object) is the cause of the shame entangled within the man's desire and is therefore an appropriate target of disgust. The prescription is that women should be modest – they should cover up naturalness – they should be ashamed, especially in the realms of expression, sexuality and power.

Ironically, the shaming of sexuality, also entangles the energy of shame with trapped sexual energy. This merger of sexuality with shame can affirm the belief that sexuality is inherently shameful. We will even meet those for whom only shameful forms of sexuality are arousing - sexual purity (in unity with body, heart and spirit) ceases to be exciting – it can even cause disgust. This can mean that sexual acts must be increasingly shameful, disconnected or cruel to still be arousing. In this, humanity is birthing a great shadow along the hell-way of sexuality and trauma, where generations often follow in procession. The global porn industry thrives. Sexual purity is conceived as abstinence and the denial of bodily sensation. Yet is it possible that true sexual purity involves the pure experience of the rhythms, longing, release and peace in the sexual and sensual fields – fields which are fundamentally part of our living biology?

In spiritual psychology, the dance of shame and disgust around sexuality can be sourced in the agony of separation found in the Mother Wound – which is so deeply connected with complications around naturalness, helplessness, nurture and attachment. The mother is synonymous with the universe. To the new born child, she is the alpha and omega of his or her experience. Her world, including her awareness, energy patterns and yearnings are shared by the baby. There is no separation, and often the first shocks of sentient separation involve pain and shame. It's a separation that can be biochemically experienced in unity with the mother, already in utero.

Purity: Nondual Quality

The spiral of disgust and shame arises out of the belief in the separate self: the absolute separation between the self and the 'other' (whether the 'other' is another human being or an inner persona). This disconnection is rooted in the belief that purity can be lost forever. It hides in the shadows of perfection and behind the mask of social norms.

Shame and disgust both crave this purity. Their agenda is purity. They seek it out. The whole energetic contraction of shame is composed of purity that was severed, rejected and thrown back into separate form in a kind of existential shock. When the contraction of shame and/or disgust is fed the energy of purity, the purity within the contraction begins to sing and return to Source. The more it de-freezes into unconditional purity, the less the cement of separation holds between one individual and the whole. Bringing the existential energy of purity towards the energy of shame and disgust is a high note of healing, from the core of the Mother Wound out into a purification of consciousness on all levels.

As with all Nondual Qualities, purity is not an abstraction. Purity contractions can feature with fully charged emotion on the domestic homefront, including the most innocuous environments such as loading the dishwasher, small-talk, map-reading. The panic to control the conditions around purity can be rife, leading to exaggerated and grandiose scenes that later seem to be surreal in their loss of context and proportion. The average control freak is often standing on a floor of shame.

As a Nondual Quality, purity cannot be grasped, defined, kept, won or lost. Purity is unconditional and indestructible. It is beyond the conditions of time and space which means that it is essentially formless and non-physical. Purity is an activator of the capacity to sense life unconditionally, whether it is the purity of anger or the purity of peace. When an experience purifies, it transforms, releasing limitation and re-uniting with its unconditional Source.

As shame is such an arch emotion reflecting the initial reflex to cover-up our human authenticity, to hide and to separate, it is natural that purity would be a Nondual beacon lighting the way home. Are we ashamed of the purity of our feelings? Do our emotions disgust us? Can we allow them the pure impurity that is there in their authentic energetic emergence?

Imagine a purity which is always here, at the Source of all we are. It has always been here and can never be taken away. All manifestation is inseparable from this purity. We breath it in with the oxygen and breath it out. It is pure because it is, in simplicity, all that is, as it is. This purity is not separate from you, nor is it separable from you. It is an inextricable part of all that we are, all that we have ever been and all we ever will be. It is the light within our sight; the silence within our thought and the stillness within every movement.

Through sexuality, this purity is the channel to new physical life, the purity of touch and the purity of a baby. As such, our sexuality flows through purity and in purity each conception occurs.

This purity is indivisible. No amount of shame, or disgust can ulti-mately divide this purity from itself. It's not ours to claim or to keep, yet we will never ever lose it. It's as unquestioned as a sun burning and shining its light through an infinite universe. It can be seen in the eyes of a new-born child, or the hand of an old man on his deathbed. It resonates through animals and trees, the blue of the sky and the empty darkness of the night. It pervades the moment between each thought, and the space before, behind and between every feeling. In purity, we are one, and through purity we belong also to ourselves.

Purity as a Nondual Quality is not a structure but a living aspect of who we are, behind patterns of Ego and personality. When we begin to relax, and reunite with the living energy of purity, even our worst moments can be recalled and experienced from the seat of purity as Source purity in perpetual motion. To quote Thomas à Kempis: "Purity and simplicity are the two wings with which man soars above the earth and all temporary nature."

Contemplations

1. Tune in to a sense of purity and relax into it. Inwardly say the words "I am purity" and notice the effect it has. If the effects become uncomfortable, move into the sense of unconditional purity again.

2. Imagine a downwardly facing triangle beneath the feet and fill it with light. Invite that light to purify, even beyond what we can visually imagine. Let the light rise into the body and through the empty spaces.

3. Connect with the purity within another person, animal, plant or object. Let the purity expand around them. Move back to the sense of your own inner purity. Pendulate between the purity within yourself and the purity within the other.

Form does not differ from Purity

And Purity does not differ from Form.

Form is Purity and Purity is Form.

23 GUILT, ACCUSATION & INNOCENCE

The partner of guilt is accusation.

Innocence has no opposite.

In innocence, accusation and guilt are one.

*"True innocence is the innate capacity of the heart to
openly meet whatever is appearing when it appears, and
to see it truthfully for what it is."*

GANGAJI

Structures of reward and punishment; judgements of good and evil;
and verdicts around condemnation and redemption play out at
the core of the psyche, perpetuated by the dualistic belief systems
of the binary mind. The contraction of guilt and accusation is intimately
linked with the collective contraction of condemnation, redemption and
the Nondual position of salvation (the essence of experience, which is
always saved). They are enshrined by religion and encoded in the archetypes that seek to make sense of life.

Is our existence here a punishment for some fatal flaw in who we are, or is it a reward, which we should cherish in all its manifestations? Are we doing time as a punishment for a crime we unwittingly committed, or are we in time as a precious opportunity? When there is good fortune, how often do we hear the murmur: "I must have done something good." Or when there's misfortune, the question: "What did I do wrong?"

The consequence of falling on the wrong side of the sublime sword of judgement can be dire, as they play out at a formational layer through the whole of the psyche. The core sense of an inner lack, untouchability or inherent unworthiness suffuses the Dark Night of the Soul. It can feel like we are falling into a bottomless pit: irredeemable; eternally condemned; banished; and severed from the whole. The threat of this experience can be deeper than the fear of death and is found at the origin of beliefs in hell. Many would rather freeze all movement in states of depression than fall into this Dark Night between the loss of persona and the unveiling of our True Nature.

Clinging within contractions of guilt can seem preferable to ultimate condemnation, yet even when we cease to cling, the energy of guilt clings to us. Confused by many as conscience, the contraction of guilt aims to protect the whole psyche from falling into the Dark Night, attempting to negate the inner sense of evil. Yet guilt doesn't rest, it seeks resolution and balance and often release is sought through accusation. Both guilt and accusation seek the inherent innocence which seems to be lost. Guilt is suffered through innocence, and when we attack the other with accusation, we are often seeking the innocence in them which we fail to access within ourselves.

Guilt

Many are born into an inherited sense that they must 'make it good'. This belief, that the onus is on the individual to pay some debt of correction to an injured world can be generational and will always indicate a contraction around guilt and accusation: the world is not good (accusation) and it's up to me to fix it (guilt); or, I'm not good (guilt) and it's because of the world (accusation).

Guilt is one of those dense, energetic substances in the psyche that persists as an active contraction, even when we might have had parallel experiences of awakening. The contraction is ancient, collective and often compulsive. It's passed through the genes as patterns of stress and trauma. It can be alive in the skeleton of family structures, and in the rift between male and female. Its dark resonance can be sensed through unfinished grief processes. It arises wherever bad things happened, and no one could stop it from happening. Whose fault is it? Who should have prevented it? Although we can easily think of children as innocent, so often we seat them in the chair of guilt.

Guilt is regularly confused with responsibility and the deeper sadness of regret. It freezes action and creates bad action, seeking to act out inner dissonance on the world. A guilty person – or a person born guilty or faulty, as all of us are – will be in conscious and unconscious conflict with the world. Survival is the name of the game. The world is the executioner of the guilty person, and as such, the world is the enemy. The inherent sense of fault will at some stage be expressed by doing 'bad'.

It's a great irony that our prisons are filled with people who were guilty long before they committed a crime; and for whom guilt was reaffirmed rather than introduced with a verdict. Many criminals were born guilty and could never prove their innocence. That is, they were born through trauma and into trauma.

What is guilt? Where is guilt? Is the body guilty? Is it the dirty fingernails? The wrinkles around the mouth? Is the mind guilty? Is it the ault of our bodily odors? Our eating habits? Our sweat? Our fear? The thought that shouldn't have been thought? The thought that was never thought? Is love guilty? Are we guilty of emotions that happen before we can stop them? Are we guilty for not conforming, not pretending, not feeling good? Could we always be guilty for failing to prevent a bad thing? Does the destruction of a body take guilt away or does it spread it around?

Guilt is definitive and cumulative. Wondrous acts will not remove the guilt of past crimes. Accusation gives temporary relief, but when we obsess with the evil in others, we are obsessed with evil. Stories of victimhood don't wash away, because our misfortune could have been a punishment for our own inherent wrongness. Why else would we suffer if not because we deserve it? We could try surrendering to guilt. Put up our hands and confess: "It was me. I did it." This doesn't really work either, as it can be a whole other trip into egoic structures in which the separate 'I' is endorsed as the great cause of suffering. This guilt empowered 'I', guilty even of being born, can play out as a grandiose manipulator: everything that happens is because of Me. These are thought forms that appear in early childhood when the child sees itself as responsible for all the chaos (Step on a crack, break your mother's back). This magical thinking makes the Separate Self as ultimately to blame for all disaster, which can repeat through contractions of guilt throughout adult life.

Surrender to the chair of judgement doesn't work because judgement is based on illusion. It thrives through the illusion of negation – the negation of innocence. Second, judgement arises out of the illusion of the Separate Self. Third, it demands the illusion of external authority. Fourth, judgement arises out of the illusion of 'Good Versus Evil'. Surrender to the guilty verdict is also ineffective because we could still be guilty of surrendering to the wrong authority. How do we know what's true?

Experientially, each side of a judgement depends on the other side to exist. There can be kindness in cruelty, just as there can be cruelty in kindness. There can be reward in punishment and punishment in reward. When abusers have moments of mercy, these moments reaffirm their power. How can you repeatedly beat someone down, if you don't also lift them up for the next beating? The concept of absolute, either-or divisions of reality is a mental prescription superimposed on life. These black-and-white divisions simply don't stand true in the realm of living experience.

How does guilt feel? It can be experienced as a dense, sticky block. Like rotting wood oozing decay, brittle, yet gluey. At more essential layers, meditators have reported a kind of quintessential evil or badness. One described the Felt Sense of guilt as: "Dirty, ashy, corpse-like psycho-toxins that get into the blood and move around the body." Guilt can be experienced as both heavy and amorphous. It literally pushes the head down as if a weight were on the neck, compressing the chest and weakening the flow of breath. Love tends to move around its obstruction, like water around a rock. But to let guilt begin to breath in freedom, a more precise Nondual elixir is needed: that of powerful, potent, uncompromising, unconditional innocence.

Accusation

Embedded in contractions of guilt is the belief that innocence is dependent on form. In this case: if the other is guilty, then I can be innocent. Again, we see the either-or split. If you are guilty, that means I'm OK. If you're dirty, then I am clean. If you're black, then I can be white. If you're evil, that makes me good. This binary psychology forms the reason why, in the quest to seek relief from guilt, we swing to the other polarity: accusation. This badness is too big to be only 'mine'. Evil is everywhere – it can't be only 'Me' – I was tempted, I was provoked. The horror at fault overrides the border of the Separate Self, which means it's also yours. In fact, wouldn't it take a whole load off my chest if it was only yours? What a temporary energetic relief to decide that the badness can only be 'other' than all I am.

Where there is accusation of the other, there is also a contraction of guilt. Aroused by fear and propelled through the energy of righteous rage, accusation is a way to release the charge of fault on the 'other'. The best defense is often attack. Rain down hell on the other, and perhaps hell won't rain down on me. With accusation, we depend on outer evil to bring inner relief: we need the 'other' to be bad. We want the bad guys, so we can be the good ones, and the dynamic accelerates, because all the bad guys on the planet can't ultimately release that nasty, secret core of perennial guilt. In this, the felt sensation of accusation can at first feel powerful, but soon gets a resonance of weakness and whining.

Guilt arises out of a sense of inherent condemnation. Out of this void of shear failure, we express our sense of condemnation outwardly. We condemn the world again and again. With heroism, we try to fix the failed world, to make it better. Yet each attempt to fix it rests on the foundation of a priori condemnation. Only something that is broken needs to be fixed. This is a core contemplation for healers and impassioned change-makers. Could they be investing in perpetual condemnation through the constant affirmation that the world is bad? When we witness humanity's attempts to 'fix' the world through the centuries, have they really made it better, or have they made a mess? When we approach our client with a preconceived agenda that they are not OK, precisely as they are, do we risk setting up a dynamic that invests in their belief in unworthiness? Still more, if we draw our feeling of OK-ness from our clients' not being OK, are we not increasing the contraction of guilt between us?

As with the macrocosm, so with the microcosm. Self-condemnation breeds the energy of inherent fault. Attempts to fix our personalities to make them good enough can often create more mess. What is needed is not an affirmation of badness, but a shift out of the duality of Good Versus Evil.

The feeling of accusation can include a sense of empowerment and authority, but at the same time, it leaves in its trail a sense of slavery. The energy of accusation tries to balance the energy of guilt in the body by contorting the form from an inferior, lowly position (body slumped, head bowed, chest contracted), to a superior, magnanimous position. The accuser lifts his face upward, crooking the neck in the other direction with an expression of contempt. With nose pointing skyward, shoulders are lurched back, and the chest is pushed outward. The voice takes on a nastiness whittled of naturalness, as if a supreme, unearthly judge were speaking. The finger points and stabs the space around its victim with an emblematic violence of penetration. There are no middle ways. All details only prove the case in hand, and the case is one of a priori condemnation.

The compulsion to judge and to condemn the other – with all the cruelty in its trail – is a direct result of a difficulty in allowing the energy of guilt and in realizing the innocence behind both guilt and accusation – an innocence which is never lost.

Innocence: Nondual Quality

Heaven weeps with innocence and its tears are called humans. Should we apologize for being born? Should we feel guilty for being here, taking up space and time? Is life a reward or a punishment? We are born through innocence; we die through innocence; creation is innocent; existence is innocence. The human body as an expression of nature is innocent. At the beginning, middle and end of every cycle of cause and effect, humans are innocent creatures, innocent even in the confusion of guilt. We are innocent, and we are responsive.

We are affected by events, whether we consciously allow the effect or repress it. The purest form of responsibility is to allow the energetic response which is happening anyway. There is no guilt, no condemnation and no judgement needed in this: just an allowance of what is anyway already here in movement.

We are innocent irrespective of our actions. We are innocent in our guilt complexes and we are innocent in our compulsion to condemn each other and the planet. The innocence precedes the formation of our personalities and outlives them. It's never lost, it just gets obscured by dense clouds of illusion, created by a mind that has not yet evolved out of an addiction to conflict.

Innocence is often banished by our mental precepts into the domains of the weak, childish and mentally inadequate. It has a bad name. Innocence means we get cheated, manipulated and abused. Innocence makes suckers of us all, and no one wants to be a sucker. We have misconceived innocence as an idealistic failing that thwarts our chance of survival. If we don't see the threat in the hammer, we're going to get hammered. Because of this, we lost our feeling connection to a Nondual Quality that is characterized by a high vibration of omnipotence.

Innocence is often identified as the state of being prior to trauma. When trauma comes, many say, we lose our innocence. Innocence is lost, and trauma takes hold of reality. One moment we are innocently doing our own thing, living, breathing, thinking our thoughts; next moment – WHAM – our innocent bubble explodes, and some unexpected horror happens like a car accident, sudden death, or some other violation or loss. For a while, we are shocked out of innocence. Yet conditioning tells us that this disconnection is the deeper reality, that Innocence is the illusion.

We can feel guilty about innocence, and we can condemn it to the point of prohibition: "You're too innocent for this world." (For innocent, read: stupid; ill-adapted; gullible; childish; irresponsible; dim-witted; retarded; fanciful; disconnected; foreign; herbivorous, inexperienced, inferior). In our innocence, we get traumatized. Or is it because of our innocence that trauma happens? Were we guilty of being too innocent? Should innocence therefore be condemned? At least, through residing in the complicated map of diversions, excuses and penalties that threads together our guilt complex, we could find ways to stay far from Sucker's Street? After all, the whole world is guilty of something, and therefore the whole world is perceived as a threat to the separate psyche.

Innocence is not for cowards: it is one of the most potent Nondual Qualities. It resonates through the bones, flesh and blood of the physical body, reverberating through the cells of the body in open resonance with the vibrations of the environment. Contrary to belief, innocence is never lost, it is integral to consciousness. It is a light that is so potent that it can hardly be imagined through the physical mind. When we bring innocence into the contraction of guilt, then the contraction begins to vibrate. At first it can seem like horrific feelings of guilt are coming forward. Yet they come into consciousness to be shed of binary structures through the powerful elixir of innocence. They are exposed at the core of their own mental fallacy.

Even when we have done wrong, innocence is not lost. It is precisely the continuation of innocence that makes the guilt painful. If innocence were lost, guilt wouldn't be a problem. Guilt is made of innocence, as is the energy of accusation. It calls for innocence, it seeks it out and holds it up as a mirror of its own Source. If we allow the innocence, the guilt complex, over time, will begin to shed its layers, shell by shell, back to its Source.

Innocence is not weakness of mind either. The innocent mind is akin to what the Zen Buddhist tradition calls 'Beginner's Mind'. Luminous and clear, it can perceive directly, unfettered by expectation. It is unlimited in its refinement as it doesn't cling to impressions as permanent. Out of innocence, there is space for all that is occurring.

Each return to the seat of innocence refreshes the quality of perception, literally clearing consciousness of its dullness. When we find a connection with inherent innocence inside ourselves, irrespective of social judgement, crime, guilt or feelings of unworthiness, that connection rapidly perceives the innocence on the outside. The voltage within accusation and condemnation is reduced. Innocence is everywhere in consciousness with a light which is more authentic than any temporal form.

Contemplations

1. Relax the basis of the body. Let your breathing find a natural movement. Remember a feeling in which you felt or feel guilty. Let the feeling of guilt be here together with the in-breath and out-breath. Bring attention to the innocence of the in-breath and out-breath and the space between in-breath and out-breath.

2. Invite the feeling of innocence directly, or through imagining something we consider innocent (a newborn baby, a puppy, a flower). Relax into that quality of innocence. Give that feeling quality a light of any color. Move with that color to the center of the forehead and softly touch the brow with innocence. Do the same with both shoulders, hands, hips, knees and feet. Let the quality color of innocence flow through the feet into the earth.

Georgi Y. Johnson

Form does not differ from Innocence

And Innocence does not differ from Form.

Form is Innocence and Innocence is Form.

24 Possession, Abandonment & Care

The partner of possession is abandonment.

Care has no opposite.

In care, abandonment and possession are one.

"Imagine you're walking along and you see a plant com-
ing up through the ground, or a kitten, or a dog, whatever
it may be – and your heart opens out. Mettā is already
there, spontaneously, without a single thought taking
place. So why do we have to seek it?"

RUSSEL WILLIAMS

Nondual teachings often stress the need to be free of grasping and aversion: this is a master-key of Nondual Therapy. In the dance of duality, we tend to grasp what we desire and averse what makes us suffer. This is how contractions are formed. Behind the dynamics of grasping and aversion are the root psychological dynamics of birth and the break in attachment from the mother. That is, grasping and aversion come forward with the first psychological emergence of the self as separate from the whole. In this emergence, the inner world conflicts with the outer, and the 'Me' is born as a separate form. The birth of the Separate Self is the birth of the sensation of 'otherness' which provokes feelings of discomfort, separation and abandonment. When physical warmth, comfort, togetherness and unity are restored, the suffering of this "otherness" evaporates.

The Separate Self has an agenda to get the unity back by repressing, denying or destroying the 'otherness'. Later, the otherness gets identified as (also) the source of reunion (the (m)other takes the baby and feeds her). In this, the mechanism of grasping and aversion towards what is perceived as separate from the self is set up. The contraction of possession and abandonment is in play, searching for the Nondual Quality of care.

The experience of abandonment and the fear of abandonment can be hellish: a hollow, quaking, gut-wrenching sense of loss. Both abandonment and possession are looking for the Nondual Quality of Care. When we abandon the abandoned, a natural care will emerge out of the emptiness, in and of itself. When we possess all the way, we become one with that which we seek to possess, and separation disappears. Care is unconditional: it's not about obligation. It's not a command, but a natural flow through the interconnectedness of all forms.

Possession

The experience of possession can at first come with a hopeful high. The allure of that which we seek to possess is still sensed, and we seek to keep it. Yet everything crumbles in our grasp and we're left with just the experiencing of grasping through the air, wondering where the magic went. So, we seek to possess more, or dictate the conditions we think will restore the Nondual Quality. Yet one of the key determinates of a Nondual Quality is that it can't be possessed: the qualities of our True

Nature are formless, moving through and beyond the conditions of time and space. When something is truly ours, can we possess it? Doesn't the very notion of having to grasp at something reinforce the sense of separation? If we were to truly take it in, moving all the way with the energy of pure possession into zero distance, would we not become one with that which is seen, vanishing it out of perception?

Possession promises to make us secure, yet by degrees undermines our sense of security. The addiction to possession is formational in our addiction to the belief in the absolute nature of our personality. We try to possess the best personality, just as we try to possess our lives. This generates a hunger, because possession, just in the movement of grasping, draws out of the peace of our own center.

The greater the energetic habit of possession, the greater the threat of loss. In an atmosphere of constant threat, we must keep our grip tight on that which we seek to possess and keep. We spiral increasingly out of our center as that which we seek to possess begins to possess us. This can be experienced as a fearful slavery in an intense contraction which is wholly unanchored in the here and now.

The possessive spouse, as well as the spouse who is possessed, generate a cloud of suspicion within the most intimate meeting points of relationship. This suspicion blinds us, which can expose inner spaces of abandonment.

When relationships are based on possession, there can be rituals of control, interrogation and manipulation which often lead to lies and intense power struggles. The more possession fails to deliver a sense of safety from abandonment, the more demanding it gets. It requires constant validation to feel safe and seeks to bind the relationship in limitation. Yet with each new bond, the free expression of love, belonging and trust is further obscured.

Abandonment

The sense of abandonment can feel like falling into an amorphous zone of horror, and because of this traumatic imprint, we dread it. Often just the threat of abandonment can be enough to mobilize survival systems on levels of body, heart and mind. When we move into the relatively formless dimensions of the Dark Night of the Soul, the sense of abandonment plays a key role in the belief in the fixed personality or separate self. We seek to possess ourselves as a 'person' to avoid that shadow of abandonment at our backs. As this doesn't work, we try to improve the person, to make it better, more worthwhile and safer. This also doesn't work. The sense of abandonment is never satisfied with a brilliant person – no matter how much she shines; she can still be left alone.

Lost in time and space, forsaken by god, bereft of inspiration yet still here, the abandoned one ghosts the activity of life, experiencing it as superficial or deluded. Yet out of a state of abandonment, there is still no freedom from the armor of personality. It is rather like believing we can be free of our own shadow. No matter how we shake ourselves up, or how many times we change our outfit, it still follows us around. No amount of acquisitions, material or spiritual, are ever going to fill that void. Even the greatest satori of liberation experienced out of personality is likely to be followed by a deeper immersion in abandonment. You can't take away absence by filling it. The absence is always here.

Freedom within the horror of abandonment comes when the belief in the Separate Self and the autocracy of personality collapse into the realization that anyway, I am still here, as pure awareness. Seeded in experience itself and behind the veils of the Dark Night of the Soul, this awareness is alive with universal care.

When I walk with a client through the wilderness of abandonment, I often ask the question: "When a child cries alone in her room at night, who hears her?" Invariably, they will answer "No one". I have rarely heard the answer that the child hears herself cry. Yet how many of us can remember the strange sound of our voice crying out in the dead of night, heard by us, and at the same time heard by an inner Source much older and vaster than our local sense of self? Are we truly abandoned? Isn't there a Source to all we are, that is here, unconditionally listening to every breath, thought and wisp of experience, which is prior to the very concept of abandonment? Is that Source separate from any other Source? Does not even The Valley of the Shadow of Death depend on it?

Wounds around abandonment can express in abandoning behavior. The inner hell of abandonment can break the ties of personality and family ties, liberating us to 'walk free' through paths of destruction. Often, the abandoned become abandoners. They would rather do that than get caught in possessing or being possessed. They can abandon by betrayal, physically walking away or by inwardly collapsing into spaces of isolation. They break connection with form. When the sufferer of this contraction is a parent, it can lead to varying degrees of neglect towards children.

When the abandoned one abandons and when the possessor finds they're possessed, the deeper need is for reconnection with the Nondual Quality within the contraction – a quality that in its sweet refinement suffuses even the Dark Night of the Soul. That quality is unconditional care, beyond the artificial confines of the Separate Self.

Care: Nondual Quality

The Nondual Quality of care has been confused with the demand that we 'take care of' (the activity of caretaking), or that we 'be' caring (assume a certain attitude). Yet the forcing of care is a disguised form of control. So often, caretaking is part of the social negotiation that goes on to try to avoid insecurity. If people need us because we take care of them, then they can't abandon us, right? This kind of caretaking can often be driven by unresolved contractions around guilt and neglect that often lead the caregiver to burn-out, flipping them into rage attacks and/or abandoning behaviors: "I have to take care of myself now!"

Likewise, the accusation of being uncaring or selfish carries a weight of social condemnation and rejection, with all its sentient suffering. This can obscure the connection with an unconditional care that is always here, inherent to our feeling awareness – a care which isn't fabricated but is a natural arising. When we feel forced to take care out of the fear of being abandoned, then we increasingly become enslaved to the fear of abandonment and disconnected from the actual sense of caring. Our self-sacrificing acts of care seem unseen and unappreciated and the feeling of existential abandonment increases anyway.

The quality of care is not caught in the perimeters of measurement, it's inevitable. We care the moment we're aware of something, whether we try to block the quality or not. We care when we give up and say we don't care – often even more. Care surrounds us and suffuses all of nature. It's inherent to the interconnectedness of all phenomena. We care because we are aware.

We're taught to believe that care is an activity done by the 'I' in the play between subject and object. But it is not like this. The separate 'I' tends to mostly interfere, which means a restriction of the spontaneous expression of care. Care is inherent in the object, in the subject and the consciousness that unites them. It is inseparable. It arises of itself, spontaneously and authentically, the moment the idea of subject as separate from object subsides. It can arise as anger, as fear or as tenderness. It's unconditional and free. We don't need to earn it and we don't need to do anything with it: it's here as integral to our True Nature.

To take the seat of care is to experience the flow of presence in the here and now, beyond the illusion of the Separate Self. Imagine the touch of a mother as she caresses the cheek of her newborn child, and the bliss this awakens in the experience of the baby. This is the power of care: healing, penetrating and affirming the inherent connectivity of forms. When we touch any object with care, care moves through us and it is possible to experience this as bliss. This includes the touch of our feet on the floor, the touch of the wind and the touch of our perception.

It is the care within all contractions that attracts our attention. It is the unconditional care within our awareness that moves to the contraction and invites its unfolding. Care calls out for care. It is care that leads us to be cruel and care that leads us to be kind. Care is behind our anger and equally behind our fear. Care is in our jealousy and in our idolatry. It seeds our sense of loss and affirms our sense of gain. It is here when we are receptive, taking in the world, and it is here when we express our qualities into the world. We often lie because we care, we hate because we care, and we reject because we care. It is the subtle intelligence behind the whole cycle of creation and destruction. It is the soft floor of the sentient dance of dualities.

How to experience unconditional care? The more we relax into pure awareness, allowing ourselves to be aware that we are aware, without grasping at anything that arises in the field and without pushing anything away – the more we can release even the concept of awareness itself – the more we can notice a fine resonance of care which is inseparable from awareness. It has a sweetness and familiarity which is beyond words. It impregnates every mite of experience. Yet it's never far away. We will all find it in the loving atmosphere of parents, our caregivers, even if riddled with contractions. We can find it because we were conceived through it. We can find it in contemplating the perfectly imperfect symmetry of a flower. We can feel it through our own touch on our bodies, or when we touch any material object. It resonates through all experience, of any kind. Care is at the root of suffering and a return to this boundless care is our destiny.

True care is choice-less. It's not in our power to negate it, because this care is boundless and more fundamental than any temporary mental, emotional or psychological form.

Contemplations

1. With your hand, touch any inanimate object with care. Notice the resonance within the touch and how the allowance of this resonance affects the body.

2. Recall any situation in which you believe you possess someone or something. Really take in the thing you seek to possess, as deeply into yourself as you can. Truly open to all that it is, and let it become your universe.

3. Give yourself a radical permission not to care. Whatever agenda, responsibility, stress or obligation that comes forward, abandon it. Keep abandoning until there is nothing left. Relax as the awareness of that space, without caring about the relaxation, the awareness or the space.

Form does not differ from Care

And Care does not differ from Form.

Form is Care and Care is Form.

25 Grief, Preservation & Joy

The partner of grief is preservation.

Joy has no opposite.

In joy, preservation and grief are one.

"Grief is always with us. But so is joy. The greatest mistake we make is to assume that if we have one, we can't have the other. Both make up the totality of human experience."

JOHN E. WELSHONS

Grief doesn't die. It is energy that waits, timelessly preserved as natural contraction, until it can re-enter the flow of transformation. It is not uncommon to find, for example, that anxiety disorder is rooted in unprocessed childhood grief. The same goes for obsessive compulsive disorder, anger issues and addiction. The shock of complicated grief can also pass through generations, patterned in epigenetic stress reflexes in the DNA. It is, after all, deeply connected with the resilience and intelligence within the fundamental drives of physical survival and the preservation of form.

The instinct to preserve form is powerful. Yet the compulsion to preserve form can often be bound to an inability to grieve, or a stalled grief process. For example, the need to follow fixed routines, to keep a specific order of objects in the house, or to adhere to specific plans regarding the future can often reflect unprocessed grief. The positing of the one that died as somewhere 'out there', far away from the self, is a subtle way to try and preserve form – to freeze or control it – rather than to allow the living energy of physical loss into awareness.

Many believe that grief is about letting go of the past. Yet it's more connected with letting go of the future. The past stands, as a preserved series of happenings. There is history of shared experience, connection and joy. The essence of this history transcends the border between physical life and death. When someone dies, what is really lost is the future. This is accompanied by the loss of opportunity and expectation.

When we are deeply caught in the instinct to preserve, the future is pre-established. The story is already written. The sentient content is already decided. When physical death breaks this timeline, the future collapses, including all its subtle agendas connected with other contractions (for example, the agenda to become free of guilt or to restore connection).

Both grief and preservation seek the joy of the living. This is the joy of togetherness in physical form. Processes of grief and the release of physical form will depend on processes of preservation. It can be very hard to say goodbye to something which has no form. Preservation gives form to the lifecycle that has completed: when we can find form, we can relax into the joy of the formless. In this existential joy, not only the past, but also the present and the future are redeemed through the undivided power of True Nature.

Grief

The experience of grief surrounds the irrevocable certainty of physical death, and can become associated with it, or even interchangeable. When we think of death, how often are we rather contemplating the agony of grief? The confrontation with the mystery of death is a direct opportunity to open towards the unknowable, which means it has a powerful potential to awaken the more essential layers of living experience.

The event of death is loaded with dread, horror and the energy of trauma. It's seen as bad. To some, just the word 'death' is the bottom-line proof of the invalidity of life. When we move with our loved ones who have died through a process of physical separation through death, grief can be the doorway that indicates parallel dimensions of life, often suffused with synchronicity and joy.

Resistance to the threat of death generates some of the horrors found in the Dark Night of the Soul. These frequencies can be so sinister and charged that when asked, many will respond saying the fear of losing someone close resonates as a fate worse than personal death. The one that dies is gone, leaving the beloved forsaken, waiting on a metaphorical death row.

This is a result of the interdependency of all of us. When someone close dies, a process is initiated beyond our control which transforms who we are, who we thought we were and who we thought we were going to be.

Just as each birth and each death is unique, so is each process of grief. Such is the impact of a death on social structures, that it's almost too clinical to label the resulting acceleration of transformation as a 'process'. As such, this is a subject to be handled with great tenderness and care. More than ever, it is imperative to give all the time and space to each movement the client makes – even if the process will take a lifetime. At the same time, it's important to be vigilant of the social pressure to stop the process, as it brings discomfort to others. Many clients will internalize this judgement, which will stop the flow of transformation through all the shades of experience.

Death or loss of a loved one can move beyond contextual loss, to trauma in belief systems, with a crisis in trust; revealing core issues around God, life and purpose. It's a Dark Night of the Soul in the clear light of day. With guidance, it is also a tremendous opportunity for awakening and freedom.

Grief processes potently reveal the circulation of birth and death. This is a core circulation of energy. The sun rises, peaks, sets and becomes imperceivable. The planet moves through the cycles of spring, summer, autumn and winter. The cycle of coming into physical life, leading to physical manifestation, followed by a letting go and returning to Source ready for the next cycle is structural to the beauty and freedom of every moment. The personality itself is moving through this cycle. Where the flow between incarnation, expression, reception and the release of peace is thwarted, we find our contractions, which is where personal evolution is happening.

Grief processes embody this flow through the raw physical body, that contains all the contractions of the psyche and all the concepts of mind. They shake up and loosen the holistic network, bringing the vitality of the core of human experience. At the same time, as whole structures are released, a lot of light shines through. Our client needs to be encouraged to welcome and allow that light, as it is this pure consciousness that will guide them to the reunion with joy.

Preservation

When someone we know dies, it can seem that everything is lost, forever. Death has a finality that sits perfectly with binary mind – that affirms that beginnings and endings are absolute. This is the program of linear time: the story line. Conditioning states that all experience is defined and held within a two-dimensional story based on time: beginning (birth), middle (life), end (death). When death comes, the story is finished. The death knell is therefore taken as the end of togetherness, and of shared fields of love, peace, freedom, manifestation and joy. It's all over. It can almost be as if it never was.

In the face of a death, the instinct to preserve can become over-riding. Grief – charged with the passion of life and the helplessness of loss is itself a form of preservation. It slows down the perception, sheltering the content so that it has space and time to release from the somatic layer of the body through the patterns of familiarity, rituals and thought.

In the dance between grief and preservation, grief often comes in waves, breaking through the areas where form is preserved. We can repeatedly, suddenly remember that the beloved is dead, as if for the first time, experiencing the full shock again. These waves, and the natural rhythm of them, express a protective psychological mechanism that uses preservation to process what can feel unbearable: the sublime existential fact of our physical and psychological mortality.

Preservation begins to take a ritualistic role when it comes to funeral arrangements, sympathy cards, memorial services and the official forms given to grief. Yet in the shadows, none of this can encapsulate the immensity of the loss or the severity of the disconnection suffered by the mourners. It can be hard to dispense with clothes and personal effects that belonged to the one who has passed. There is an instinct to preserve. Sometimes, mourners can refuse to let anyone use the room that was occupied by the beloved, holding the space as if there would be a return. This is preservation.

These movements of preservation can support the process of grief. Yet they can also begin to block it. This is because the one that was lost cannot be contained in his old pair of shoes, or in a candle-lit shrine at the corner of the room. He or she cannot be reduced to a gravestone or a memorial plaque. The living joy escapes the form. This joy is essential to the connection, and when the emphasis is on the preserved form, the joy in the beloved gets obscured.

In addition, there are many contractions that can be awoken by grief such as fear-anger; guilt-accusation; shame-disgust; condemnation-redemption. These contractions form the energetic stuff of separation, between our sense of self and the world; between our personality and/or essence; and between ourselves and the beloved that has died. When we are in the contraction, the essential presence of the beloved becomes further obscured from awareness.

The instinct and feeling of preservation of form is intimately rooted in unconditional care. It longs to come to peace. In this, it can become an ally in a grief process when recruited with wisdom. The preservation energy can be used to preserve the opening of the crack in the wall of separation – an opening that allows the living light of joy to come through. We can preserve the space through which we are one with the beloved. We can even continue to share joy with the beloved through wider dimensions of form.

Joy: Nondual Quality

As children play together, we can witness the greatest source of enjoyment: the free interplay between forms in the playground of our world. There is even enjoyment in their conflicts. Springing spontaneously from the core of life, joy is a direct effect of recognition and reunion. Beauty – when the beauty of being sees itself reflected in external form – naturally brings joy. New life brings joy. Liberation from restriction even the restriction of physical form) brings joy. Reunion brings joy. Death is also a return to joy. Have you ever noticed the feeling of relief that can be there in the background after someone has died? We tend to deny it as it seems inappropriate, but could it not be the sharing of the relief of the beloved that has passed out of the restrictions of personal form into existential joy?

It's possible to enjoy almost anything: even the most horrific experiences secretly carry a backdrop of enjoyment. We enjoy truth, we enjoy our lessons on this earth, we enjoy witnessing the deeper layers of how life moves. In short, our True Nature is to enjoy life and each other, for better or for worse. Is it possible to enjoy grief? Is it possible to enjoy preservation? To enjoy pain, loss and sadness? These questions are akin to asking: Is it possible to enjoy life? When enjoyment is unconditionally here, what happens to the contractions of suffering? Do they not momentarily become relative to the vast expanse of our True Nature?

Often those walking the intertwined path of grief and preservation will unexpectedly find themselves surprised by joy. This joy is at the source of all connection and manifestation through manifold forms. How would we grieve the loss of the beloved without sharing this timeless joy with them?

The experience of joy can sometimes be followed by an experience of intense contraction – a whiplash into those areas in which we are not yet free. This is because the intensely alive vibration of joy awakens the energy trapped within contractions. It is especially the case in contractions of grief and preservation, when beliefs about the finality of death and the absolute nature of separation forbid the freedom of joy.

Healing always involves a release of attachment to the exterior world and a surrender to the inner world. Along the way, we meet contractions. Each time we're surprised by joy from within the Dark Night of the Soul, we gain more courage to move deeper into the gold-mine o all that is. In this, any experience our client has had of unconditiona joy is a timeless resource in guiding the way inward to a reconnectio1 with the sacred trust of the living.

Contemplations

1. Relax the body and bring awareness to the chest area. Attune to th Felt Sense of one who has died and let it refine – as if they were presen in a dark room. Take one Nondual Quality that shone bright througl them and sense the quality. Let the atmosphere of the quality expand and go wherever it's needed.

2. Begin with your attention at the lower back and pelvic area. Let you1 feeling awareness rise to include the lower chest area. Visualize tha1 there is a bright sun behind your back, emanating joy, shining uncon- ditionally through you, irrespective of physical form or contractions ir the psyche. Try to rest back as that sun.

Form does not differ from Joy

And Joy does not differ from Form.

Form is Joy and Joy is Form.

26 LOSS, GAIN & FULFILLMENT

The partner of gain is loss.

Fulfillment has no opposite.

In fulfillment, loss and gain are one.

"Live, dear friend, live this day, this ordinary day, this sacred day, this one and only day, knowing that in some incomprehensible way it has already fulfilled your deepest longing."

JEFF FOSTER

L oss and gain dance together through all dimensions of form. The contraction is inherent to the experience of change and transformation. In each moment, we lose and simultaneously gain: one moment dies to birth the next. Just as the death of a cloud signifies the birth of rainfall, or the breaking of a seed signifies the beginning of the tree, the old births the new. The loss of the water in the kettle is the birth of steam. The loss of the mountain is the birth of the valley. Our car can gain huge distances, but it will lose petrol. The loss of identity is the birth of freedom of identity. This is the nature of transformation.

Loss and gain are negotiations that take place through the borders of the Separate Self. Beyond the limitations of the personal 'I', existential polarities unfold. Emotions around loss and gain appear out of the mystical discovery: "I am nothing" and the parallel experience "I am everything". Between the 'nothing' and the 'everything' is the something: a particle of form, and in the world of form we are perpetually gaining and losing. This is indicated through the Buddhist wisdom: form is emptiness and emptiness is form. In the something, the everything and the nothing are one. In the something, there is the miracle of life.

Like the shore of an ocean, where tides rise and fall and where each wave destroys itself before being pulled back into the ocean, loss and gain move through us in a constant flow according to the evolutionary need of the whole. This is reflected in the famous quote of Nisargadatta Maharaj: "Wisdom says I am nothing. Love says I am everything. Between these two, my life flows."

Every form is some 'thing' and being something is part of our essential evolutionary purpose as humans. Yet something suffers the cycles of loss and gain. It is always a formulation of creation and destruction, which means that psychologically, it is accompanied by the emotions of gain and loss.

In the domain of personality, the sense of gain experienced through status is shadowed by a sense of lack. Gain inherently carries its own loss and therefore is accompanied by the fear of loss. Although we may believe that our personality is who we are, or that the physical body is what we are, we also know that this will die. The more we acquire, the more we will lose; the more we gain, the more there is to die.

When our client is caught in contractions of gain and loss, we're looking at a general resistance to change. Transformation is blocked as it's conceived as negative change: it's fearful and full of risk. This is because the sense of unconditional fulfillment has been numbed by fear.

Gain

Gain can be a pleasure, yet it can also be part of a cycle of suffering. The relief from the suffering of loss inherent to the pleasure of gain can set up the dynamics of addiction. It also can hold the personality in a sense of endless background lack. Because just as loss can seem to be a bottomless pit, so is the need for more gain. The curse of 'never being enough' can generate a desire to acquire more and more forms of an increasingly dense nature. We can get a better spouse, a bigger house, a more expensive car, more money in the bank, more status and more friends. We can binge on all the goodies in the house, but this doesn't take away the sense of inner lack and can even perpetuate it.

So much of gain is based on fear and a lack of access to the Nondual positions of gratitude, trust, need and fulfillment. The contraction of loss and gain is riddled with paradox: drives us to seek belonging by trying to be different from everyone else; to build fences around our houses in order to be part of the town; to have a higher income than others in order to feel equal worth; and to destroy others in order to experience 'more'.

Weight watchers will not see gain as a positive thing. Here, loss is suddenly the positive attribute and gain the negative. Eating disorders often reflect the compulsion to control natural processes of change through the pathology of gain and loss. Control gives a temporary sense of relief from the fear of physical helplessness which is often rooted in trauma.

For many, gain can also show up as another kind of affliction. To gain something, we need to be able to receive it. The receptive aspect of ourselves is the most vulnerable and helpless. Receptivity requires openness and relaxation, which require trust. To gain love, we need to be able to relax in the feeling of being loved. It can be surprising how confrontational the experience of receiving love can be. The same goes for money or fame. Although we might believe we want it, the reception of it can be unnerving: money brings responsibility and fame invades privacy. For those who find comfort in dependency, the empowerment of wealth can bring up the fear of abandonment.

Gain is a pleasure, but the pleasure is in the feeling of receiving, not in the object received. The pleasure is in the relaxation and in the connection. When gain is accompanied by grasping and a desire to keep, to hoard and to defend, it can become a curse. It can lead to a psychology based on possession that spirals into increasing degrees of illusion.

Loss

Processes of loss, like processes of grief, spin around the wisdom of impermanence. It is not for us to judge the impact of any loss on another person. It can be something as apparently innocuous as losing a piece of jewelry which triggers a cascade of unfelt feeling around former unprocessed losses. As therapists, it's important to relegate the judge that measures the justifiability of emotions around loss. While a loss of proportions gives us an indication of traumatic origins, it is not for us to dictate what feelings should be there. Every process of loss is in some way also a loss of proportions. It's embedded in the nature of the loss of that which was held in time and space. We literally lose proportions.

Each loss contains within it all the other experiences of loss encoded through the structure of the psyche and patterned in epigenetic codes through our cells. One small loss in real time can open the giant ontraction around a tragic loss in the past, including the past of our ancestors.

When we deny loss, and seek only gain, we form the shadow of a loser. The more we identify with gain; the more loss will haunt us. For some, he greatest nightmare is that they will lose everything. Yet what can happen is that when they lose everything, is that they have nothing left to lose and are liberated from a lifetime of fear and vigilance: they simultaneously gain everything.

While loss is a big happening in the form of physical life, especially from he perspective of the loser, it is also the closing of a cycle of form. When form closes its cycle, a great feeling of peace can descend. In peace, we release, or perhaps when we release, there is peace.

The experience of loss is an inevitable part of living through transient forms. Finding peace within it will strengthen the wisdom of impermanence, increasingly revealing that existential core of all we are that can never be lost – the Nondual Space of unconditional fulfillment.

Fulfillment: Nondual Quality

Is it possible to feel fulfilled in every moment and through everything we touch? Could we experience the everything in the nothing and the nothing in the everything and rest in the fulfillment of that miraculous space where the something, everything and nothing are one? What shift in consciousness is needed to allow a deepening into an unconditional space beyond the contraction of gain and loss? Could it be that everything we need for fulfillment is right here, right now, arising out of the sense of fulfillment itself?

The sense of fulfillment tends to get denied by general conditioning. We are conditioned to seek fulfillment from the outside world, rather than

within the inner sense of abundance. We often allow the experience o
fulfillment based on external conditions - the 'only if' or the 'only when'
There is often a latent belief in limited supply: meaning that if we agree
to experience fulfillment, that which fulfills us could be withdrawn, and
we might then be left lacking. Fulfillment is often seen as an endpoint
a cessation, meaning that progress will stop, perhaps even that life will
stop. If we're fulfilled, we'll lose our passion. Conditioning says that i
you're fulfilled, you don't need anything anymore. So, we defer fulfillment and invest instead in the sense of lack, just in case we might need
more, later. Yet each moment full of lack, births a next moment full of
lack.

After we have cultivated the ability to rest in the sense of the Nondual
Quality of fulfillment inside ourselves, it is then possible to again turn
our attention to the outer world and to perceive it through the lens of
fulfillment. Notice how the quality of perception becomes more vital
and more alive.

To admit the sense of fulfillment can be a paradigm shift out of patterns
of suffering. Fulfillment is the start, the arrival and the journey. It is
the purpose. It is the drive. It brings a perpetual flow of abundance,
beyond the parameters of the Separate Self. Fulfillment is the well-
spring out of which everything takes form and into which everything is
released. It is the ceaseless fountain of contentment and wellbeing.

For this reason, it's important to realize fulfillment as a Nondual Quality. We are at once the need and the fulfillment of that need. It's happening with every moment of consciousness. It's perfect in its process.
Our lack is already fulfilled. Our gain is already fulfilled. Our misconceptions are already undone. We are that space of wholeness to which
nothing can be added and from which, nothing can be taken away.

Vhat does fulfillment feel like? When we source the feeling, we can otice how we expand through a space that was already here. How eaceful it is; how alive. In this space, we are losers and winners, perctly imperfect, beautifully flawed and ecstatically wounded. Nothing eed be altered, and no 'thing' stays the same.

Contemplations

. Contemplate something you would like to gain and ask yourself how ou'll feel if you get this. Let the body answer with the feeling itself, nd let the feeling expand through the whole physical body and into he earth.

. Create a natural flow of mindful breathing. With the in-breath, agree o gain, with the outbreath agree to lose. Notice the spaces between inreath and out-breath.

Form does not differ from Fulfillment

And Fulfillment does not differ from Form.

Form is Fulfillment and Fulfillment is Form.

27 GREED, POVERTY & GRATITUDE

The partner of poverty is greed.

Gratitude has no opposite.

In gratitude, greed and poverty are one.

"To see clearly is to be grateful – to simply notice that life is a gift, eternally present and infinitely abundant. To perceive things as they are, is to be grateful. I have discovered it works both ways, if I am suffering in some confusion, feeling gratitude allows a clearer perception of life as it is to resume."

WILL PYE

Within the contraction of greed and poverty there is a severe conflict between the personality and its environment, as well as a suffering of dependency on the outer world to fulfil the inner. The outside is believed as the only source of that which must fulfill the inside. But no matter how much is taken from the outside, the hollowness on the inside remains, or even expands.

Both poverty and greed are driven by a sense of 'never enough': a seemingly endless inner lack that exposes the intrinsic instability of personality. Inherent to the sense of poverty is the sense of inferiority before the world. Implicit with the emotion of greed is the sense of privilege; the world 'owes' me more. Often, the poles of poverty and greed switch: I must have more than my share because historically I have had so little. I have less because others have so much more.

Contractions of poverty and greed rest on the simple evidence that wherever we are seated, we don't see ourselves but rather see the sitting positions of others. Filled with the experience of others, we think that if we could have the next chair, or the superior position, we would be more comfortable.

Unable to rest back in the wonder of experiencing the place where we are sitting at any moment in time, we seek to acquire more or better, according to what we imagine is experienced by others. In this, experience is radically limited to what we see on show in the environment. It's a radical shrinkage from the boundless experience of unconditional being. Yet our conditioning has programmed us with this interminable sense of lack and dissatisfaction. To quote Game of Thrones: "I swear to you, sitting on a throne is a thousand times harder than winning one."

The Nondual Quality of gratitude is a beacon of light that can guide us through the Dark Night of the Soul, or out of the despairing core of any energetic contraction. The energy of gratitude is expansive and expands the field of conscious awareness beyond forms of contraction. Gratitude is perceptive: it opens consciousness and affirms the essential benevolence of all experience. When we are seated in gratitude, the miracle of being here begins to unfold from the inside out, with an endless flow of universal abundance.

Poverty

The suffering of poverty is among us, if not in our neighborhood then in the next. The physical lack of food, shelter and warmth tangibly threaten physical survival. When poverty is adjacent to wealth, it can feel as if the individual has been cut out of space and time. This horror of exclusion is like a death knell, with many accompanying contractions in shame, condemnation and despair.

The physical experience of poverty can be traumatic, affecting generations. While most of us in the developed world have our basic needs met, poverty can be part of the legacy of Inherited Trauma. The nervous response to the specter of poverty can be panic. The threat of poverty can feel like the shutters being drawn on life. We are threatened with losing stability, health, status, legitimacy and the ability to protect our families. Because the trauma of poverty can be passed from one generation to the next, we can continue to suffer poverty contractions in the psyche, even when we are affluent. Even when we win everything we feel like losers. Even when we have a safe stash of money in the bank, it seems never to be enough to make this dread of poverty go away.

Our client might appear to 'spoiled' or deeply lacking in gratitude, obsessed with safety and caught in an unending sense of 'never enough'. Here, it is worthwhile to look back into the family history: who experienced poverty in the family, and what were the traumatic consequences? The horror of being left out in the cold, bereft of income and shelter can be alive in the present moment, even when physical conditions are fine. Sometimes, all that is needed here is recognition of the inheritance, and gratitude towards the ancestors for living that challenge.

'art of the contraction of poverty is intensified by spiritual impover-shment – the feeling of discontent on the inside and the conditioning hat drives us to seek fulfillment through consumerism or through a)etter partner, job or city. This internal sense of lack arises when we ιre deeply invested in the personality as absolute. Of course, the per-ιonality is never good enough: it's just a temporal flow of behavioral)atterns. Personality cannot bring us nurture, fulfillment and safety – t can only bring us its own impermanence. When we disinvest from the ;linging to our own reflection, that same impermanence is the blessing)f healing potential. Yet when we believe deeply in our own separation, ;he personal form is perpetually impoverished.

Greed

When our basic needs are fulfilled, the irrational despair of poverty can manifest as greed. The dependency on forms from the outside to fill the ;aps on the inside can spiral into a viciousness in which the single-pointed focus is on the acquirement of 'more'. The obsessive nature of ;reed can cause cruelty, abuse and ignorance. Yet the one caught in a contraction of greed and poverty is compelled to continue by an inner ιnrest that is fired by an interminable lack of satiation.

When it comes to food, the contraction of greed can be expressed as eating disorders such as binging. There is a kind of rage in taking in as much as possible, beyond borders, that is linked to a prior experience of not having enough. There can also be a background where a lot of control has been put around food. The family dinner table can be a perfect barometer of the stress around food that could reflect a family contraction around poverty and greed.

The emotion of greed is also related to the contraction of craving and repulsion (which can be sometimes felt as physical agony in the belly). Both spiral into an almost formless sense of hunger, or the feeling of a bottomless pit inside, which is perhaps what the Tibetans refer to when they talk about the dimension of the hungry ghosts. This can descend into addiction, in which the psyche is helplessly controlled by substances from the outer world, substances that in themselves generate a deepening of the demand for 'more'.

The psychological suffering of greed can lead to a commodification of ourselves and others. The contraction is deeply caught in comparison and competition, enslaving the psyche to hierarchies in which measurement is absolute and value determined from the outside-in. We literally talk about how much we are worth, or our right to exist, as if both value and existence could be traded. When we eat too much, our extra body weight brings no barrier to the impermanence of life. In the same way, excessive greed destroys its object through consummation – the object of desire is lost.

When we consider the contraction of greed and poverty, we can find a vast difference between what we want and what we need. There is no question that we all need food, warmth and shelter. What we want tends to be more destructive, grasping for short-term relief from psychological discomfort in which overview is lost and the narcissistic illusion of the Separate Self thrives

Gratitude: Nondual Quality

Much damage has been done to our freedom to experience natural gratitude by the obligation to feel grateful. How many of us were told as children that we should eat food we didn't like because people are starving elsewhere in the world?

The demand for gratitude is contrary to the Nondual Nature of the quality. Too often, the demand for gratitude thinly veils a demand for submission. Gratitude cannot be forced, obliged or ordered: it's a atural and authentic arising, closely associated with unconditional ove. Telling our client to be grateful when they are caught in a contraction around poverty and greed could hit a traumatic thread. It can be more effective to move around the trigger, for example, by telling hem that you're grateful that they are able to share the deeper layers of pain. Gratitude has a resonance, it's contagious. Precisely where they re unable to receive gratitude, we will find the contraction around vhere they are unable to express it.

The expansion of gratitude – in appreciating what is present beyond he borders of the perceived private self, softens the partition of isolaion between one 'I' and another. It brings connection to the field of solation, collaboration to the field of competition and unity to the field of division. Gratitude is an offering beyond the private self, that directly pulls the quality out of any given situation. Thus, it dissolves fear and alleviates the addiction to comparison.

Gratitude can be present irrespective of the nature of experience. It is available whether the experience is pleasurable or painful. All experience is a gift to the living universe, and the universe – on receiving a gift – says thank you. In this, the energy of gratitude supports the evolutionary process of the whole. This brings immediate relief in the area of the suffering of the Separate Self.

Sometimes, it is precisely the energy of gratitude that opens the possibility of transformation. If we feel discomfort around receiving from the other (for example, in the form of humiliation) then returning the gift with the gift of gratitude can restore a sense of balance and equality. On the other hand, if we feel that others are obliged to 'serve' us, then we can suffer arrogance and superiority. Also here, the energy of gratitude can bring relief and open the possibility of harmony.

Sometimes it can seem like life is a school of hard knocks and that w have little to be grateful for, but this is itself a contraction of gratitude Poverty consciousness and greed says there is nothing here for 'me' an subsequently distorts perception. Gratitude notices the vast gifts whicl are perpetually also present in every moment of being alive. In th words of the Dalai Lama: "Inner contentment doesn't come from havin all we want; but rather from appreciating and being grateful for all w have."

Contemplations

1. Let consciousness move around and inside the body. Notice wher there is a sense of lack or poverty. Investigate the lack and ask it wha it really needs. Allow any response in thought, feeling or body.

2. Relax the body. Imagine anyone or anything that is expressing grat itude towards you. It can be a person, an animal, a plant or even ¿ kitchen surface. Open to receive that gratitude inside yourself and no tice where there is resistance.

3. Regress to a time you felt grateful and contemplate the feeling. Re lease the person, thing or situation you felt grateful for and stay witl the unconditional sense of gratitude. Move with the sense of gratitude to the physical head and let that feeling move downwards deep into the pelvic bowl and then to both feet and into the earth.

Form does not differ from Gratitude

And Gratitude does not differ from Form.

Form is Gratitude and Gratitude is Form.

28 Good, Evil & Discernment

The partner of good is evil.

Discernment has no opposite.

In discernment, evil and good are one.

"If time is not real, then the dividing line between this world and eternity, between suffering and bliss, between good and evil, is also an illusion."

HERMAN HESSE

Our True Nature is benevolent. Benevolence is intrinsic to all Nondual Qualities: they are expressions of well-being and they wish well for form. We are expressions of a benevolent universe. There is no opposite to this. The belief that there could be an opposite of this pluripotent benevolence is a deep cause of suffering. The more we cling to the seat of goodness, the more we endorse the seat of evil. Why else would we cling so hard to being good, if we did not deeply trust the power of evil?

The split of human perception into subject and object is deeply and somatically expressed as the competing archetypes of good and evil. W seek the good we shun evil. We identify ourselves as good while striving to become free of evil. Perhaps one of our darkest fears is to be con demned as 'evil' – to fall outside of the social consensus of 'good'.

Good and evil is a fundamental duality on which structures of religious political and social control take form. In the splitting of our collective consciousness into the polarities of good and evil, our greatest fears are born. These fears are both towards the outer evil that could destroy u. and towards the inner evil – that which we must never allow ourselves to become.

Beyond the duality of good and evil is the perception of 'otherness' One origin of consciousness perceives another origin of consciousness through varying densities of form. In that moment of perception, the absolute perspective of the seer is lost, identification is made with the form, rather than the identical consciousness, and the possibility of con flict arises. The seer identifies itself as good, while the 'seen' is defined as evil. This works both ways. Each side identifies itself as good and the other as evil.

The belief in a war between good and evil splits the core of our experi ential universe, hijacks our intrinsic purpose through the energy of con flict. Our mission is to defeat evil and to make it all good. In the name of 'good', we become destructive. Embedded in this fundamental duality is the inherited consensus that 'the world' is evil. This can emerge as a belief that the world is intrinsically bad, and we are here to help fix it. It can also surface as a belief that because the world is basically evil, we might as well join it.

The problem is, that when our foundational point of view is that the world is bad, we affirm and solidify a reality that the world is bad. We perpetually condemn the world out of the misconception of judgement, even before we allow ourselves to experience it. When our collective starting point is that the world is bad, then we surely don't want to fully experience this badness, lest we become bad ourselves. So, we start to interfere with direct experience. We replace experience with the wish to first make it better, so that it is fit for us. Or we push away pain and try to grasp towards pleasure. Yet without opening to experience, our attempts to deal with the world are happening in a darkness in which we don't know what we're dealing with.

This dynamic is ultimately an inner dynamic. The human psyche ceaselessly condemns itself through a subliminal, imagined war between good and evil. This war rests on the fundamental judgement of intrinsic evil, or original sin. It draws on a subtle verdict that our True Nature is innately bad. If our True Nature is evil, then all the Nondual Qualities presented in this book are illusory. The deeper reality is unending, universal war – against the depth of who we are.

The bottom line is that living experience is not to be trusted, because evil could emerge here. We contract from life and the Source of our own vitality. In this contraction, we also form a wall between ourselves and others, to keep evil away. Yet this conception of a Separate Self is not enough to give a sense of safety. We can still sense the evil in the air: we breathe it in and it runs through our blood.

We suffer loneliness, despair and a sense of abandonment from behind the protective wall of the Separate Self. Out of this suffering, we are compelled to seek togetherness. But how to protect ourselves from the evil that could blow through when we open the doors to our fellow humans? What can defend our 'good' psyche against the wicked energies of the earth or our bodies? How can we open to God, and be sure that Satan won't jump through the hatch in the attic?

Again, the splitting of our experiential world into good and evil depend on the perception of 'otherness'. If God is 'other' than who we are, the God has a separate form from us, which means it will cast a shadow c all that God is 'not', or all that we don't want to associate with God That shadow will be identified as evil. If the earth is 'other' than wh we are, then the very bones of our body threaten us with possession an betrayal. Our own body is an alien trap, where we get caught. If ou fellow human is 'other' than who we are, then enmity will be an under lying precondition of all connection.

Judgement would seem to be at cause to this perpetual sense of con demnation. Yet judgement is nothing other than an unevolved, auto cratic cousin of the Nondual Quality of discernment. Where judgemen sees black and white, discernment can sense the whole spectrum of colo and contour.

Discernment is innate to consciousness and is reflected through eacl particle of the body and mind. Each time we use our senses, there is somatic discernment or attunement. Each decision engenders the free movement of discernment. Every movement through time and space involves discernment. Our direction through a room, through our family relations, through the social field, and through the physical life cycle demands the use of discernment.

When discernment becomes judgement – which is binary thought within the duality of good and evil – our thoughts get formed by fear. Mani festation is impeded and the connection to free will is severed.

The primary agenda of being 'OK' is born, resting on the premise that we are not 'OK' in naturalness. The very question of 'OK-ness' rests on the belief in the Separate Self that could be judged. Within our own psyche we split into the accused, the accuser, the witness, the jury and the judge. This sentient and mental drama drives the purity of living xperience out of consciousness, clouding connection and generating pri-ate illusion.

Good

The agenda to be good is not as holy as it at first seems. Such is the xtent of suffering through depression, anxiety, guilt, shame and self-destruction through this apparently praiseworthy agenda, that some-imes it appears that the problem is not whether our client is 'good' nough, but whether they are 'bad' enough.

The fatal crux is that the striving to be good rests on the a priori as-umption that we are bad. If we were innately good, there would be no striving. If we don't exert ourselves through control, repression and uppression, we will express that evil into the world. In striving to be ;ood, we fail before we even begin. In striving to do good, we disinvest urselves and the environment of goodness. We are trying to make a lifference to something that we only experience blindfolded, deaf and lumb, because we have already decided its nature should be 'other' han what it is.

Before we even begin, we have judged the past, present and future as ad. It should not 'be' as it is; it should be made good. This judgement as already disconnected us from the unconditional experience of the nvironment which means we have lost the opportunity for true dis-cernment. Through discernment, we can recognize the benevolence of Nondual Qualities running through all forms of contraction.

It's the good inside us that can perceive the goodness which is appar-ently outside of us. In the same way, it's the evil in us that can perceive the evil outside of us. We cannot know 'evil' without resonating with it. Indeed, goodness utterly depends on evil, in order to be good.

Without this contrast to itself, it would simply be unconditional experience. Goodness is defined by evil and therefore needs it to affirm itself

The agenda to 'be good' demands that we seek out evil and sometimes aim to conquer it by whatever means. The cruelty of the Spanish Inquisition is just one example of how this can take form in the most cynical of ways. The more we seek evil to affirm our goodness, the more we fill the psyche with the experience of evil. The duality flips over, as our consciousness becomes filled with the horrors of the night, many of them sought out from the environment, and many more imagined. We breathe in evil, we touch it everywhere, we notice it in every corner. Our world becomes evil and the goodness in us shrinks to a lonely church tower shaped with the letter 'I'.

When we tell our children that they are good to reward conforming behavior, we begin to seed the belief that goodness needs to be proven in the world – that the child's benevolence is not inherent. When we reject them for their anger, selfishness, jealousy, playfulness or neediness, we are showing them the 'evil' inside themselves. Children learn young that to 'be good', they must behave with obedience, otherwise they are 'bad'.

There is already damage here but add to this that the parent's judgement of the child within the parameters of good and bad often have little to do with the child's behavior. Highly stressed parents with social fears, addictions and mood swings will often react on their children according to their own states of suffering with little direct relation to the child's behavior. From the child's viewpoint it can be all rather random, which further generates a perennial sense of condemnation.

The child seeks to 'be good' in order to reconnect to the parent who is at once their universe, and their own means of survival. Often, this involves the repression of vitality, spontaneity and naturalness. This kind of goodness is paralyzed by the threat of rejection and directly severs the child's connection with his or her own authenticity and vitality. The goodness is a mask, birthing an inner sense of unworthiness.

Evil

One person's heaven is another person's hell. When someone who has fallen into the consensual definition of being a 'bad guy' looks at the 'good' people, he sees a bunch of fakers. Although he is designated evil, he sees through their pretense at goodness, and because he has this insight through the masks of goodness, he is more honest, which means that he is the good guy. Whistle blowers on the consensual 'good' are often condemned as evil. Even when they're later championed as great lights of integrity, they will have rarely escaped this stage of collective condemnation.

Even in the writing of these words I can feel the reactivity of readers. What about Hitler? What about child abusers? What about terrorists? Animal torture? rape? Is this not evil? Is it right to deny it? Isn't it our overriding human duty to confront it, to protect ourselves, to lock them up? Can we let a holocaust just happen?

The error is in the belief that evil exists somehow independently from good, or as separate from the whole. In this way, it's possible to believe that another person is intrinsically evil and that out of this evil, will do evil to others. To suggest otherwise can provoke righteous rage and cause people to hate you. Notice how the poles switch over?

When we feel into the energy behind the questions arising out of the horror of 'evil', we will find the shock of pure pain, accompanied by reflexes of fear. This pain or uncontainable suffering is at the core of the projection of evil onto the other. It should be remembered that hatred is composed of pure suffering, as is jealousy, rage, cruelty and many of the other classic qualities of evil. What is needed is a deeper understanding of boundaries to confine destructive behavior and protect the pain from being violated so it can heal. The wisdom of boundaries comes with discernment. Human territory is a living terrain with many dimensions and infinite possibility. It's not the judgement of good and evil that will keep us safe but living discernment as to the nature of the landscape, with all its weather.

When we move deeply into contraction, especially through the repression or denial of our natural boundaries of physical survival such as anger and fear, we lose the sense of our True Nature and of the wider environment. This is the nature of contraction: it by degrees loses sensitivity, from decreased sentience all the way to total numbness (a blindspot, nothing exists there). This decrease in sensitivity blocks the natural feedback of care towards the extremity of suffering. Yet the numbness resonates a lie: it brings its own kind of suffering. Out of the density of contraction, a scream of rage or pain can be heard. Acts of 'evil' can liberate the contraction, wrenching down the curtains of conditioning and tearing down social norms. The pressure to release these bonds can be so great that we move beyond the fear of physical death and the other parameters of fear and threat. From the inside out, the expression of pain screams in the world without restraint, often in terrifying form for the consensual whole. Evil acts are a wakeup call to unhealed trauma: such trauma will wait generations if necessary, to re-enter the flow of healing and transformation.

When contractions are collective, we have what could be called 'the machine'. The machine is exemplified by the blind systems of government, war, profit or exploitation that have evolved through the short-term survival interests and the greed of the many. Although these forms are man-made, no one is responsible. Although the machine can perpetrate evil and injustice on others, it is unconscious – a spiraling mass of cause and effect destroying everything in its path. A good example of his is the machine of the holocaust. Collective irresponsibility depended n a billion refusals of personal responsibility. Everyone was just obey-ng orders in the striving to do better and to be 'good'. A wave of ollective injury overpowered the whole.

he belief in evil demands distance from the object we believe to be vil. It depends on abstraction. We can consider child abusers to be vil, until our own teenage child is convicted of child abuse. We can onsider war criminals to be evil, until we hear the firsthand account of omeone who describes their father who served in the gestapo. We can elieve terrorists to be evil, until we move close and feel their imbalance nd disconnection from esteem.

These words in no way remove our necessity to put boundaries, preserve orm, and kill if needed, to be of service to the needs to the whole. The hapter on war, surrender and peace already introduces some pointers nto the deeper dynamics involved in collective evolution. Yet our afety, life and survival is actually more undermined by our belief in he war between good and evil than our transcendence of that belief.

When we can reside in the unconditional dimensions of ourselves, the limensions beyond the conditions of time and space, then discernment allows us to navigate the minefields of duality. Experience can be a patterning of good and evil flavors, yet good and evil are interdepend-nt, a play of form, not a definition of who we are, or who anyone else s.

The moment we open to living experience, evil dissolves into pain. This s not a treatise to forgive all psychopathic murderers, but an invitation o relax this core duality within our own psyche by giving space and time to the Nondual Quality of discernment.

Discernment: Nondual Quality

As we begin to release the belief in the polarized forces of good and evil
the Nondual Quality of discernment begins to emerge. Beyond the dualistic parameters of judgmental mind, the openness to directly perceive
through deeper layers of form emerges. This perception liberates our
consciousness into degrees of expansion through our own psyche and
the environment. It relieves the deep suffering of perpetual condemnation which is often the perceptive floor of projections into the 'world'.

To be of service to any situation, or to meet any need, we must allow
that need to be there in the first place. When we reject experience from
our consciousness, or when we have an agenda to 'get rid' of certain
flavors of experience, then we are in a poor position to be of service to
it. It is as if a doctor decides your foot has cancer and without exami-
nation, proceeds to amputate the leg.

The natural quality of discernment allows us to uncover a causal layer
of affliction, by first receiving the history – the story told by the patterns of the pain. It means we can recognize that pain as perhaps repeating in other parts of the body, through connected symptoms. It
means we're able to ask that pain what it needs to relax again into the
whole.

Discernment is a quality that can dance through duality. It uses judgement, checking the left, checking the right, measuring pressure, measuring relief, but it remains in the first place receptive to all effects. It is
always in movement, at no stage making conclusions and at no stage
narrowing the view with expectation. It is the act of perceiving itself,
through layers of form: a movement that is only possible when we are
free of the agenda to deny what we see. Discernment is not conclusive
but is continuous, penetrating to the core of form.

Take the classically evil emotion of jealousy. Satan is jealous of god. What is this jealousy? What is this vibration? Discernment rests in the feeling of jealousy with curiosity. What is this? How does it move? If we expand it more, how does it taste? How is it connecting to the whole? Is there love in the jealousy? Is there pain? Is there despair in the jealousy? What does the jealousy need? What is it seeking?

Much of this book has been written through processes of discernment. When we begin to move with discernment through the human psyche, we can reach the most intimate layers and give them space. We can contact the living core of suffering and the longing for reunion within it. We're able to allow contractions to direct us toward freedom, rather than letting them dictate limitations as if they could never be lifted. Discernment is the end of the resistance which is at the source of every contraction and which forms the walls, floor and ceiling of the suffering, Separate Self.

Each form flowers through space, time and infinite discernment. Every unnecessary contraction can release through discernment with an awesome precision according to the intelligence of its historic formation.

Contemplations

1. Close your eyes and connect with the pull of gravity, letting the body relax. Take someone or something that you consider to be either good or evil. Blend with the sense of goodness or evil. Notice the awareness which is behind the sense which is neither good nor evil. Are we aware also of this awareness?

2. Close your eyes and imagine there's a soft pillow behind and around the head that is absorbing all thoughts or mental activity. Bring your attention to the forehead and gaze into the nothingness, which is there, until the nothingness relaxes and expands. If any image comes forward,

allow yourself to move with discernment through the image, easily changing the angle of view and/or proximity and distance.

Form does not differ from Discernment

And Discernment does not differ from Form.

Form is Discernment and Discernment is Form.

29 ABUSE, VICTIMHOOD & POWER

The partner of abuse is victimhood.

Power has no opposite.

In power, victimhood and abuse are one.

"When the power of love overcomes the love of power the world will know peace."

JIMI HENDRIX

Where you find a person who is abusing power, you will also find a victim of power abuse. In the dance of duality, one of the most injurious areas of contraction is around the Nondual Quality of Power. Contractions around power are born through the belief in the Separate Self and they propagate suffering and trauma exponentially. The belief that power can be seized, controlled, created and maintained is birthed at its roots in the belief in the Ego as an absolute form, which is absolutely separated from the whole. As universal power moves through the psyche, it's identified as 'mine'. We try to keep, control and command power, claiming power over power, just to keep the illusion of the Separate Self alive.

The dance between abuse and victimhood can be one of the most complicated contractions to work with, as it is interdependently linked with all other forms of expression and receptivity. It can include the guilt of the abuser; the shame of the abused; the rage at victimhood; and the fear of perpetration.

When working with people, or even reflecting on the collective dimensions of cultural trauma, we will see that there is a dogged allegiance to the healing and support of the victim. Yet the roots seeking release in this contraction will always also include the energy of abuse. There can be no victim without abuse. Yet our client will often refuse to admit the energy of abuse, or the inner perpetrator, and therefore the contraction is unable to come to peace.

The position of the abuser is distanced as an embodiment of evil. The energy is thrown out, repressed and denied. If this continues, the victim will by degrees begin to express as the perpetrator. The denied shadow will take form.

In an act of abuse, the energies of both abuser and abused, perpetrator and victim are alive in the flow of power through distortions of form. Power is seeking release through the combination of two forms. It doesn't recognize the Separate Self. In the aftermath of abuse, both forms carry the whole energetic charge. Healing involves releasing the whole energetic charge, regardless of which side of the coin we are escorting – the victim or the perpetrator. Both are injured by contractions around power.

Between the abuser and the abused is a shared field of abuse. Between the victim and the perpetrator is a shared field of perpetration. Out of these fields of horror, the contraction of power awaits release.

Abuse

Whatever they did, our client is likely to identify with the victim posiion and to reject the position of the perpetrator. Even when the fact f perpetration is acknowledged, it often comes with an excuse ('because f...'). This means that the energy of victimhood lurks beneath the fact f perpetration. Perpetrators are 'bad', and victims are often seen as good'. This means it can be very difficult to allow the fullness of the xperience, which can delay the healing of trauma.

Difficulties around the energy of abuse can show up as:

1. Depression: a total refusal to feel the feelings. This is a kind of existential lock-down, often because the charge of guilt or shame associated with the admission of the experience is too unbearable (the forbidden sense of badness, being wrong or evil).

2. Mutism or Refusal to Communicate: the shock of the destructive impact of unchecked power can cause an incremental refusal to bridge the rift between the Separate Self and others.

3. Anxiety and Panic: the client immobilizes themselves in fear of becoming an abuser, according to somatic triggers. The repression of inner power creates a charge which surfaces as pure fear, and fear of the fear which is anxiety.

4. Manipulative behavior: the client releases the charge of power through back-stage manipulation, evading responsibility through schemes and agendas.

5. Grandiosity: the victim, empowered through the power of being the good one in the Good Versus Evil paradigm, assumes a position in which it's forbidden to make them suffer in any way. The cause of this suffering is always the 'other' and thus, even in minor

instances, the 'other' should be condemned with the full wrath o righteousness.

6. Rage: contractions around power can surface as fits of rage whe the voltage becomes so intense that it explodes connections, mos significantly, where the connection is intimate and therefore per ceived as invasive/violating.

It's clear that in this section on abuse, we're talking simultaneousl about victim and perpetrator. The fundamental drive of the perpetrato is to do good, or to put the world to rights. Yet this drive rests on th wound that the world is unsafe, dangerous and at risk. In this, abus forms the floor of the contraction and often fulfills itself through ex pression in the 'world'.

Abuse brings the binary equation of 'kill-or-be-killed.' As this trauma tized psychology internalizes, it can seek release through suicide, wher the psyche is both killing and killed. Grace comes where there is per sonal disempowerment utterly aloud, with a call to the universe beyon the Separate Self for help.

Work with abusers is hard. Although they ooze victimhood, behavior i formed by the dictate that they must never again be a victim. Ther will be a tremendous rejection of Nondual Qualities, such as helpless ness, esteem, care and belonging. We could meet layer after layer o agenda based on the terrified need to control reality, not only subjectiv reality, but also the realities of others. Don't be trapped into thinkin this is only about psychopaths, areas of abuse are alive within all of us

The art is to allow time and space for the victim within the perpetrato and the perpetrator within the victim, gently unhooking any identifica tion with personal power. Above all, there needs to be the facilitatio of trust in the Felt Sense of the client in the here and now, over strat egies of blame and beneath the radar of the social contracts of morality

Victimhood

The scapegoat; the sacrificial lamb; the crucified; the eternally wronged: these are the archetypes of the victim. Together with the stinging shame and the endless falling through the dimension of the forsaken, the victim feels unseen; misjudged; deceived; misunderstood and abandoned. Victimhood can become both an attitude and state of being, emanating a subtly resentful sense of disempowerment and self-pity.

The flow of quality expression as well as the ability to receive impressions in the here and now is slowed by constant security checks. To release the forbidden voltage of power, the victim will sometimes take up outer causes to save 'other' victims. The conflict becomes projected on the outside and enacted with great emotional charge and intensity. In this, the victim finds the license of righteousness to become the perpetrator: acting out on others to fix the 'world'. While this can be a strong drive that can answer the collective call of suffering, where the victim has the upper hand in the psyche of an individual, it is often more conceptual than of practical help.

Projected victimhood becomes an excuse to avoid touching the inner world. Often, we see that when freedom is experienced for a moment, or there is a deep meditation in which the whole dynamic of action and receptivity gives way to a softness and vulnerability, the voice of the victim comes forward. "How can we all sit here and meditate when there is a war going on (elsewhere)?"

The victim needs to learn to sense and allow the Source of unbounded power within themselves. The purification of this power and the courage to allow it to flow into and through the psyche will depend on the constant reminder to release the sense of the Separate Self or the isolated 'I', which is a complex network of beliefs and identities, often in conflict and mostly imbued with pain.

Power: Nondual Quality

Imagine a power that is freely available and that can never be wounded or taken away. Timeless in nature, this power is alive with universal potency in every particle of matter; every cell; every vibration; all waves of light; and at every speed and frequency. The only limitation on this unbounded power is that it cannot be divided or annulled. We can never be free of it, as it is the substance of all we are. This power cannot be claimed as "mine" or as "yours", it is universally experienced as it is fearless and indiscriminate. It is intensely alive.

The only freedom we have with this power is to resist it – for a while. Power doesn't mind if it's resisted, it is alive anyway, regardless of what our conscious minds, our energetic or physical bodies decide to do with it. When this power is perceived as "other" than what we are, it creates fear. Yet allowing it to move through us can also dramatically excite the nervous system, if we identify with its effects.

Of all Nondual Qualities, power is perhaps the most abused, misconceived and misinformed. Without power, no form can exist at all. This includes forms which are outside the landscape of waking consciousness and this is what fuels the drives, instincts and forms of unconscious mind.

Yet, power is implicit to waking consciousness. Consciousness itself is power and it empowers all that arises within it. The human brain can direct consciousness: to make choices about where to focus in the collective field awareness. This gives consciousness a creative power that has been popularized by schools advocating that we can 'manifest our reality' through conscious will. This misconception around power obstructs the freedom of power as an agent of healing. It rests on the belief in a Separate Self, an objectified person and an attainable 'reality' (a reality that can be fixed, held and/or controlled). Where the unstable, ransient personality is empowered as absolute, its wants and desires nevitably come into conflict with those of other 'persons'.

The universal power that moves through all forms becomes contracted when we identify with it. Personal power gets pitted against external power ('the world'). Divisions between success and failure, winners and osers, haves and have-nots emerge. This culminates in the basic precept of: "Me first". This is based on the illusion of an ultimately Separate Self and is overshadowed by the condemnation of inevitable death of separate identity. It's a power game that's lost before it began: everyone is abusing, and all are abused.

Power is everywhere. It is also the vitality caught within areas of contraction: indeed, it's the Source vitality of all forms. This is regardless of whether we're conscious of the contraction or not. Where there's less consciousness of a contraction, there's a likelihood that the power voltage will become embedded in the physical body through stress, tension and areas of numbness. In this, we see the somatic roots of disease. In pondering this, we can notice how the symptoms of illness show up as the body's attempt to heal itself through releasing the contraction.

A key area where power gets entangled and contracted is in the core duality between male and female. In the field of sexuality, physical 'otherness' is embodied as the opposite sex. Fears, contractions and misconceptions around sexuality and the belief that females are receptive (victims) and males are active (perpetrators) form traumatic rifts between gender identities. The abuse of power takes many forms between the male and female, through various known and unconscious contracts. The male-female, abuser-abused formula runs through cultures and through generations. When we break the consensual gender contracts between the sexes, it can often feel like a betrayal of our birth families and our ancestry.

To allow power as a Nondual Quality to move unhindered, we need consolidation in emptiness, humility, stillness and peace. It's a paradox that the more we allow ourselves to be empty in perception, not grasping or pushing away any phenomena, the more powerful we become. The less we believe in personal power, the more the personality begins to express universal power. The less we restrict power, the more power flows through the forgiveness, peace, love and unity which is inherent to all we are. Each particle of experience liberated into the flow of power is a service to the whole. The intelligence of the form itself will titrate the movement of power, if we allow it.

Contemplations

1. Let yourself move into a relaxed awareness of your breathing. Recall a situation in which you felt yourself a victim. Release the memory and stay with the sense of victimhood, scanning the body to sense where it's strongest. Return your consciousness to the breathing, and now check if you can find a sense of the inner perpetrator. Again, find where this sense is strongest in your body and let it expand. Close by returning to your breathing and letting the body relax into the pull of gravity.

2. Take a natural phenomenon that feels to you to express pure, unconditional power. Contemplate the phenomenon, the atmosphere, rhythm and vibration. Blend with it, letting it move through and around the body and psyche. Take note of any effects.

Form does not differ from Power

And Power does not differ from Form.

Form is Power and Power is Form.

30 CONTROL, SUBMISSION & HELPLESSNESS

The partner of control is submission.

Helplessness has no opposite.

In helplessness, submission and control are one.

*"Be helpless, dumbfounded, Unable to say yes or no. Then
a stretcher will come from grace to gather us up."*

RUMI

We are born in helplessness, we die in helplessness, and in between we are inherently helpless. All the qualities of our True Nature are intrinsically helplessness: they shine indiscriminately like the sun. During our physical life cycle, we have an opportunity to manifest these qualities, yet pure manifestation often depends on surrendering agendas of control. We often need to get out of the way of ourselves, in order to shine.

Resistance to helplessness is generally born from trauma, through which the charge of fear and the horror at impotence has not released. This means that to move to the roots of trauma, we need to reclaim help lessness not as an enemy, but as a universal resource. We will mee helplessness in every moment of transformation, and the meeting can be a tremendous relief and a blessing. Through the allowance of core helplessness, we are able to release the resonance of need that will facil itate the core of transformation. When we allow our fundamental help lessness, a relaxation occurs, and there is an opening. Out of this opening, expansion becomes possible in which the (often grandiose) agendas of control and the conditions we put on the kind of help we want are released.

Paradoxically, there is enormous power in helplessness. This is not individual power, but the flow of universal resources through the psyche The psyche is empowered by the power that flows from our True Nature. In this, helplessness is not a horror, but a living ground of being that allows the perception of infinite possibility. Through reconnection with our pure, unadulterated, universal helplessness, patterns of fear-based control can evolve into the wisdom behind mastery. Whole new dimensions born.

Control

The conscious agenda to keep control of our lives is deeply conditioned. In sneaky ways, we believe we control our sleep, our breathing, the healthy functioning of our organs and our feelings and emotions. When the body fails to submit to our agendas, we divorce ourselves from the body or psyche, feeling betrayed. This sense of betrayal and violation is often associated with helplessness, so we blame ourselves for not keeping better control.

Built into the attitude of control is the tendency to think that others become sick because they did something wrong; and that we suffer because we deserve it. This births an endless striving for this impossible standard of controlling the uncontrollable, through whatever means. Often, it means we seek to control others, to get them to fit into the mental agenda. Yet the agenda to keep control is born to fail. This is because we lack the knowledge or experience of that which we seek to control. We expect to get a grip on it, win its obedience and dictate its form, without knowing what it is in the first place, and without knowing what we would do with it, having gained control. Based on history and future expectation, controlling agendas can radically miss real threats and opportunities arising in the present moment.

The feeling of control can be pleasurable and relaxing in the short-term, but it can easily become a source of stress, as control is never absolute. Any sense of control depends on the narrowing of perception to a small slice of life which seems to be controllable. When we are deeply contracted in structures of control, the window of consciousness narrows and becomes obscured by fear, flooding the system with stress.

Control issues are an evolutionary bump in the movement towards the kind of control that can ride the wave or sail the boat in harmony with the forces of nature: a control that depends on the admission of fundamental helplessness within the omnipotence of natural forces. This deeper control, born of the total surrender of the mind into the core of receptivity and the relative play of activity, would better be called mastery. It's spontaneous, alive, attuned, and allows all that appears in awareness.

Submission

A way to rewrite the word submission could be sub-mission: that is, there is a controlling agenda beneath the threshold of consciousness.

When we depend on submission to survive, we feel controlled by the unexpected, oppressed by outer forces, and fundamentally disempowered. Our survival reflex to keep control gets castrated by a deep confusion around guilt and responsibility. Bad stuff is happening, and it's because of us, because we failed to keep control. So, in our unworthiness we abnegate control to what we perceive as a stronger entity. We submit the psyche and move with sub-mission. If mistakes are made, it's not our fault; and if cruelty happens, then we are victim not perpetrator.

Submission is an attempt to evade the horrible responsibility that comes with the belief that we're in control. Instead, we give control to a strategic 'other'. It's not helplessness, but a strategy to avoid the private suffering – a more manipulative form of control. When we have moved into a state of submission, we become disempowered, and parts of the psyche become frozen in stress and depression, which can lead to existential angst as we doubt our right to express and play in the world of form.

Both control and submission can dance freely in duality: there is a time and place for both. Sometimes we need to take control, for example when driving a car. Yet we would be very bad drivers if we didn't admit our helplessness in the face of the unexpected. Sometimes we need to submit, for example, when we are a passenger. Yet we all know how annoying a back-seat driver can be.

Helplessness: Nondual Quality

In the section on Freedom, we refer to the phenomena of learned helplessness. This is indeed an important area of psychological insight. Yet in this context, it could be preferable to see this phenomenon as 'learned submission' or 'learned slavery'. Helplessness is not learned, it's ntrinsic. It's the ground zero of the human psyche, and a doorway to ore transformation.

Even in spiritual circles, helplessness can be seen as an affliction – a orrific state of despair that signals pure defeat of the spirit. If we feel helpless, we've failed; we need to get rid of it; we need to restore a sense of control. This misconception generates more stress which incapacitates our responsivity in mind, heart and body. Yet most of how we associate with the suffering of helplessness comes from an association made through trauma. We learned that extreme pain, violation and death go together with helplessness, and we even blame the helplessness or the disaster. What is generally conceived as the horror of helplessness is in fact the horror of horror: it's the resistance to suffering and he suffering of resistance. The quality of helplessness, stripped of association, is none of this.

To try and clear the Nondual Quality of helplessness of its bad name, let's give some examples. Is it possible to experience an orgasm without allowing helplessness? Is it possible to give birth or be born without helplessness? Is it possible to create? Is it possible to sneeze, or even swallow? How does it feel when we helplessly burst into tears, and the depth of grief shakes through our psyche? To laugh spontaneously, helplessly, kissed by joy?

We can watch a ping-pong game, in which athletes seem to have a brilliant degree of control. Yet this is not control, but a mastery that comes from the surrender of the controlling mind to its intrinsic helplessness. How would they be able to hit the ball or anticipate angles at such speed if they were thinking it through and deciding the ball's spin, as well as their interception in advance? The mind and energetic psyche fully surrender to the experiential intelligence of the body. The mind is just a witness, anchored in a quality of helplessness which is literally powerful beyond belief.

When we admit our helplessness, then the Separate Self surrenders it agenda to 'do it alone'. Admitting helplessness brings a relaxation tha allows the resonance of a need to expand. When we are in contraction the quality of helplessness has the power to unearth the floor of th contraction. The suffering which is there has a resonance that wil awaken the universal resource of our True Nature.

Where there was resistance and suffering, choice emerges; where ther was fear and anger, compassion comes to play; where there was confu sion and agenda, consciousness clarifies. Where we allow the sense o helplessness, the 'other' and the Separate Self meet, merge and disap pear into one truth alive with infinite possibility.

Contemplations

1. Write a list of some areas in your life you feel you can control. On a second page, make a list of areas where you feel controlled. Close you eyes and move between the Felt Sense of control and being controlled Close by relaxing into the weight of the body, noticing areas of density and resistance.

2. When you come across a situation in which you feel helpless, take some time to go inside. Allow the sense of helplessness and let it expand Perhaps an even deeper situation of helplessness will come forward. Dc the same, layer by layer. Let the sense of helplessness expand into the universe and relax.

Form does not differ from Helplessness

And Helplessness does not differ from Form.

Form is Helplessness and Helplessness is Form.

31 LIES, HONESTY & TRUTH

The partner of lies is honesty.

Truth has no opposite.

In truth, honesty and lies are one.

*"The opposite of a trivial truth is false; the opposite of a
great truth is also true."*

NIELS BOHR

The energies of lying and honesty interdepend within all atmospheres of communication. Both dance around the truth, attempting to penetrate, control and express it. Yet both are tools in the dance of illusion. Illusion deepens in direct proportion to the split between one part of our psyche and another. For example, if we hear a sound and we tell ourselves again and again that we don't hear it, we're splitting part of ourselves (the mind) from another part (our sense of hearing). When the manipulation of these splits based on fear-driven agendas to keep control intensifies, we get used to the dissonance, and lying begins to be less conscious, and can even be taken as a form of honesty. When there is stress around the split inherent to the illusion, we generate the energy of a lie. When we are more at one with the illusion, there is the energy of honesty. This gives us a good barometer for the density of contraction. Often, it's actually the lie emerging into consciousness which can break open the sense of truth whereas honesty can show an intention to reaffirm illusion.

Honesty tunnels inwards to more essential layers of experience, guided by the sense of truth which is intrinsic to every moment of being. Yet honesty, in a way, is a purer form of lying. It's still based on an illusion of a truth that can be known and held. The best liars can seamlessly communicate their 'truth' without dissonance. Too often, honesty is held as an ethical standard, or an attainable attribute. Consider the statement: "He is an honest man." Where is the truth in this? Does it mean he doesn't steal? That he's uncomplicated? That his style of communication defines his humanity?

Communication always depends on at least two points of view, or two perspectives on 'the truth'. This includes the way we communicate with ourselves in our inner world. Self honesty is the first step towards clearer, uncompromised communication which is fundamental to our shared evolution out of the dualistic mind. Yet when there is a belief that the truth being communicated is absolute, rather than descriptive then communication becomes dualistic and caught in the agenda to conquer one 'reality' with another.

When we talk about lying and honesty, we generally refer to language: more significantly, the relation between a sign and the signified. Between the word and the thing, meaning arises which is entirely subjective. Word and object only appear to be married to each other. The underlying atmosphere, for example, of resistance or denial, or openness and vulnerability, offers a deeper sense of meaning than the word itself. When we say that "He is a man of his word," what we're saying is that he word dictates reality, and that this man is subservient to this dictation. He gives his word that the parcel will arrive tomorrow. Yet the ostal van crashed and landed in a ditch. What happened to his word? Clearly, when we are talking about honesty, we are looking at the level f intention beyond the fulfillment of contract.

When we move from lingual to sublingual forms of communication such s body language or tone, we begin to rely even more on our Felt Sense. How far do our words express our feelings? When we communicate, are re understood, or do people hear what they want to hear? Are we in ontrol of communication at all?

or example, if I say the word 'mother', you could either take it with eelings of love and nurture, or of abandonment and betrayal. Its meaning would be found in the tone, context and listening agenda. These gendas are based on emotional associations with motherhood. The word 'mother' itself is arbitrary. The sense of truth arises through sentient resonance. Truth itself is not an endpoint but a journey.

When listening to a client, we can open the Felt Sense towards the eeling quality of words as well as towards sublingual communication. Certain words have a charge, whereas others can sound like a repeated iturgy. When we hear a story of intense horror told by rote, in a monotone, or when someone tells you their child died as if it's a minor event, here's a dissonance. This dissonance shows a split between thought and eeling, which indicates the state of contraction. The Felt Sense is important here. The objective meaning of the words spoken is secondary o the feeling content expressed. This feeling content will be the sentient uter layer of the contraction. For example, when someone jokes that heir mother overdosed, that nervous energy of humor is alive on the uter perimeter of the contraction, together with its attempts to find ion-dramatic social expression. As the contraction opens, we are going o meet this nervousness, insecurity and fear, (that was masked in the laughter). That means that rather than pointing out that the feeling i inappropriate, we will rather point towards that feeling by asking, fc example: What's in this laughter? What's the Felt Sense behind that Rather than getting caught in the spoken lie, we follow the sense c truth within the deeper emotional undercurrents.

Often the words express the opposite of the emotion. For example: "I'r not afraid," coming from a woman who feels obliged to show courage Or: "I don't care about my child's alcoholism anymore," coming from father who despairs of losing his son. Again, sourcing of the feeling con tent in the here and now will liberate the verbal lie.

The opening of the sense of truth is critical, to Nondual Therapy. Trut] is not a fixed thing, it's alive and unconditional. It's a sense that call us into deeper and more authentic layers of experience, an inner com pass through networks of contraction. As we touch the intimacy of pai within a contraction, a vitality is released which can liberate limite structures of belief and break the monopoly of autonomous program within the conditioned mind. Here, we can find a sentient differentatio between suffering and pain.

We suffer where we are distanced from truth, when swaddled in blan kets of denial. This is the suffering of illusion: a suffering in which fals truths have been used to cement the lie of negation, dividing us fron the core of our experience, from others, from our history, our future an from the unique miracle of all we manifest.

The living pain that we uncover through the vitality of truth bring power. Dissolving the cement of the Separate Self, it reconnects us t all we are. It's awakening, rejuvenating and has the strength to set u free.

Lies

Can we be honest about the lies we tell ourselves? The word 'lie' is heavily loaded, and that's why we chose it. We could have used the word miscommunication, but this would not have carried the weight of social and ethical condemnation of the word 'lie'. This is important: as here are many lies told about lies, just as there is a terrific inability to be honest about being honest. To lie is to suffer a sense of guilt, condemnation and social rejection. No one wants to be caught out as a liar: Satan, after all, is cited as the father of all lies. Yet from one perspective, lying is intrinsic to communication.

As said in the first section of this book, Ego structures are surface contractions formed out of vulnerability in the personality. Insecurity, for example, could be masked through Ego with an appearance of self-confidence. The Ego presents the preferred side of a contraction within the psyche. It overcompensates what's felt as a survival threat through a shield of pretense. These deceptions, bluffs or lies aim to create a perception from the outside-in of success, to avoid the threatened failure on the inside. In addition, the presentation of a controlled image means we can feel less threatened by rejection – if the image is rejected, we're still protected as it's not who we really are.

Some family cultures lie as a matter of habit, while still demanding honesty to maintain control. For example, in the family of one client, lying was severely prohibited. As a child, the client had learned (like so many of us) that honesty is goodness, and she strived to be 'good'. Then one day, at dinner with the extended family, she told that her mother had said that Uncle James is a cross-dresser. This was honest and 'true'. Silence and shame fell over the table. The little girl had done something terribly wrong, but she wasn't sure what. Later at school, the teacher asked the class if they were enjoying the story. She put up her hand and answered that the story was boring. She was sent out of the class.

Honesty, to some degree, seemed to be as punishable as lying. He mother told her she was 'tactless'. The child was left confused in th whole area of communication.

These kinds of inconsistencies and complex patterns of lies and honest; within the parameters of communication can be even more damagin; when a child is caught between a mother and father. Whereas there ca be some habituation to the family patterns of communication throug the duality of lies and honesty, when the perspectives of the parent polarize, the world of the child can be ruptured. Sometimes both par ents expect the child to lie to the other side, while both expect honesty Whichever way the child turns, he loses. In general, it can be challeng ing for children to figure out when they're supposed to lie and whei they're supposed to be honest. Too easily, the virtue of honesty ca become a crime.

Further confusion around the ethics of honesty can result from genera tional trauma. In times of war, deception becomes strategically advan tageous and even ethically commendable. There are times when a lie can save lives: for example, to lie about being Jewish during The Holo caust. But survival has many branches, including financial survival; so cial survival; survival in a job; or survival of the Ego. In an unsafe world, which is full of abuse, confusion, persuasion and miscommunica tion, the instinct to lie can be strong. Everyone lies anyway, so the best defense is attack.

When lies are told, truth is still present. It's true that a lie is being told. There's truthfulness in the energy of a lie. There's truth in the painful substance of that thick energetic veil of separation between one psyche and another. All the underlying causes and history behind the lie are also true in that moment. Truth never gets left outside.

t's important to introduce the sense of truth to the field of lying, espe-
ially as many lies are told internally and unconsciously. If we move
vith discernment, we can learn a tremendous amount from how and
vhen lies are told.

Honesty

The intention to be honest can reflect an earnest effort to move with
he sense of truth. Yet often, when someone says: "To be honest with
ou..." you could be suspicious. Are they admitting to lying until that
moment? Are they trying to get your attention because what they're
bout to say must be taken as absolute truth? Are they searching for
ntimacy or legitimacy? Often when someone says "Honestly" they're
bout to admit the shadow side of a contraction, the underbelly of feel-
ng or emotion which is rarely shown. They seek admission without
ondemnation, because honesty is generally graced with social approval.

Honesty can carry a sense of vulnerability and the fear of rejection. It
eems to take courage to be honest, even internally. It can sting, feeling
naked and exposed. Above all, honesty tends to move us into the area
of uncertainty, not-knowing, and the doubting of habituated beliefs
bout ourselves, others and the world. This is because the 'known' con-
ent of the mind is inherently dishonest, existing in a cloud without
clear anchorage in the truth of living experience in the moment. Simi-
arly, the structures of our beliefs are often inherited, based on an evo-
ution of survival patterns. They are not truths, but deeply ingrained
hought forms used to structure experience. It can be deeply honest to
admit that in absolute terms, we know nothing at all.

Honesty involves releasing our hold on the deceptive forms of mind in
which we are caught. Many of the contractions described in this book
nvite this kind of honest, inner inquiry through an opening of the sense
of truth. Honesty involves the unpeeling of layers of illusion.

Often, self-deception at the deeper layers becomes increasingly simpl and irrational. This is good. The simpler the illusion, the easier it is t release it. For example, in the statement: "I have to do everythin alone." These are core beliefs worked with by teachers such as Byroi Katie. Such beliefs are formed by hypnotic, repeated lies, and realizin, this can disable whole fields of mental illusion, clearing the way fo conscious awakening. Yet the sentient content of the lie held in con traction beneath the layer of conscious mind is still active. It still need to be allowed, felt and released, even after the surface lie has been un done.

Truth: Nondual Quality

From one perspective, all communication simultaneously involves botl lying and honesty. Words, thoughts and physical mannerisms can only point towards a truth that is vastly pre-lingual and which exists behinc all conditions of time and space. Language is descriptive, it's not defin itive: it seeks to express or hide truth, but it cannot claim to be the origin of it.

As the truth has been misconceived as an objective 'thing' which is the opposite of a 'lie', we have by degrees suffered a disconnection from the inherent sense of truth. Truth has been a whip that has hurt us. It has been an artifice that has been objectified, leased, pawned, borrowed anc sold to the highest bidder. It is logical that by degrees, we stoppec believing in truth and submitted to the never-ending story of illusion Yet in doing this, the Separate Self has created its own state of existen tial isolation.

All forms of perception can at best reflect the truth of form, in all its indeterminate beauty. This reflection carries a sense. It can involve goosebumps, or sudden calmness. It can feel like a cause-less awakening or a deep connection and reunion. Research by Leanne ten Brinke ai

ιe University of California found that our unconscious ability to detect
es by far outperforms the lie-vetting strategies of the conscious mind.
ιtuition from the gut has a greater sense of truth than all the criteria
f our critical thought processes. The sense of truth can be somatic,
·om the lower regions of the body: what some have called 'gut feeling'.
ome refer to the 'Still Small Voice' – a voice of benevolent neutrality
rising from the stomach that speaks its words irrespective of the argu-
ιents of mind. We would do well to listen to it.

ßreakage of form, or processes of destruction, will often expose deeper
ιyers of truth through the gaps. Sometimes, we will have clients who
re engaged in self-destruction driven by the sense of truth. There is
pace for honor here. Often in cases of severe addiction or mid-life crisis,
he drive towards the inner truth surpasses all instinct to preserve form.
·he drive is that: "Even if I die in this, I will be honest until I can rest
ι truth".

n some processes, the drive towards truth can leave an aftermath of
)etrayal. The pursuit of more essential truth can break many contracts
hrough the explosion of many contractions. It can wreck the founda-
ions of the past and expectations of the future. Yet, at the same time
ruth brings an increasing sense of power and freedom.

ntuitively, we can sense that the truth will cut through fear. Yet be-
ween the truth and the conditioned mind, there are clouds of dread
ιnd paranoia. The truth can't be grasped, kept, dictated or controlled:
t's not a fixed thing. It can only be experienced in moments of clarity
)r deep recognition in which the truth in us recognizes the truth in
orm. Truth is not found in what is known, it's sourced in the knower.
Ve don't 'speak the truth', rather, we are the truth speaking.

Truth is a Nondual Quality which can be sensed, experienced or em-
)odied through the surrender of form to the needs of the whole at any

moment in time. Every form is inherently true, just as every form i inherently empty. Truth is form, and form is truth: yet none of it ca be held, caught or prescribed. When we try to seize the truth, we ar left with the truth of seizure. When we try to reject the truth, we ar left with the truth of rejection. The sense of truth is in direct alignmen with the clarity of consciousness. The less content, the greater the pre cision and the higher the resonance of truth. This resonance brings vi tality, purpose and direction.

The sense of truth guides us to the reverberations of a contraction, a the way to the release of trapped vitality back into the flow of life. I opens a deeper form of communication that is found in energetic reso nance. The mind listens to words, the heart listens to feelings. The bod listens to the truth of resonance. The expression and reception of trutl is primarily experiential, which means it can manifest only in the her and now. In the words of Dōgen: "If you are unable to find the trutl right where you are, where else do you expect to find it?"

Contemplations

1. Close the eyes and relax the body. Tell yourself an outright lie, as i it were true. Notice and blend with the energy of the lie. Let it expand Repeat with an honest statement. Again, notice the Felt Sense of hon esty, including any ingredients of fear, anger, stress or sadness.

2. As you move throughout the day, try to notice external stimuli with out naming them with a thought. If you see a tree, look at the form without naming it. If you hear a sound, experience the sound withou naming.

3. With eyes closed, move your attention to the center of the body and contemplate the darkness. Try to relax into seeing, without distraction By releasing any stimuli or thoughts that appear, fall back as the seer

he origin of seeing. Whatever appears in perception, disregard it, as it
s a momentary reflection, not the truth of what you are.

Form does not differ from Truth

And Truth does not differ from Form.

Form is Truth and Truth is Form.

32 Sanity, Insanity & Insight

The partner of sanity is insanity.

Insight has no opposite.

In insight, insanity and sanity are one.

"It is no measure of health to be well-adjusted to a profoundly sick society."

JIDDU KRISHNAMURTI

The judgement of sane and insane depends on a deeper investment in the maintenance of a Separate Self, including a separate mind. The edict continuously censors each mental movement and behavior to ensure brand loyalty to the 'sane'. Within the insane we can include all forms of originality and non-conformity which threaten convention.

Consider a time when you were dismissed with one of these pejoratives: silly, ridiculous, irrational, senseless, foolish, idiotic, crazy or mad. How

id it make you feel? What happened to the freedom of your mind? Do
ou ever use those pejoratives towards yourself?

n our outer and inner discourse, we generate a lot of threats through
he power-structure of conditioned 'sanity'. The intention is to frighten
he mind into a certain form. These prohibitions, restraints and con-
ractions are initiated in childhood and their effect can be hypnotic.

f insanity is in the air, the Separate Self will try to ensure this insanity
s blamed on 'the other'. If someone else is the insane one, the Separate
Self can feel that it is sane. It gains entitlement and legitimacy. It be-
omes 'right' while the other is 'wrong'. The criteria of sanity are widely
used as a formula for power abuse. This can move according to the toxic
ormula that you're either with me or against me. If you have a different
perspective, then you're crazy; you have no right to a voice. The label
of insanity is a dark way to disempower any opponent, especially when
here is a recruitment of social consensus.

Sanity and insanity are highly charged judgmental terms that limit the
possibilities of form and transformation. This is partly because contrac-
ions are formed out of fear of insanity. These terms assume precondi-
ions of mind: that it's a fixed entity in the head with only one
dimension of programming. The duality ignores the dimension of higher
mind. All activity of mind, whether thoughts are congruent or confused,
s witnessed. We might 'go crazy', but we see ourselves doing crazy. We
might suffer dementia, but we witness it happening. This dimension of
oversight is also the perennial Source of insight. Insight oversees and
penetrates the deeper formulas of form, including mental form. In this,
t is the Nondual Quality that will support the mind in navigation from
confusion to clarity and from dissonance to a more liberated form of
harmony. This insight is a vital resource to be recruited when our client
enters periods of mental imbalance, especially when the fear of insanity
is behind that imbalance.

Insanity

Contractions around insanity are not only socially affirmed but also a often part of our genetic inheritance of trauma. Our survival respon system at a cellular level is literally coded through epigenetics to avo the label of insanity at all costs. Insanity can be feared as a fate wor than death; such is the nature of this traumatic wounding. We not on fear the label of insanity, but also the whole atmosphere. The atmo phere of insanity can at once repulse and compel us. This could tak the form of anxiety around the whole area of mental illness, or even polarity, as a determination to become a mental health professiona Such epigenetic traumas literally shape our psyche on all levels.

When we sense the atmosphere of insanity, we can find that it has man flavors. It has a reverberation of horror, abandonment, neglect, be trayal, delegitimization, cruelty and abuse. This is the haunted atmo phere of Bedlam – expressing the suffering underbelly of the collectiv psyche: the skeleton in the family cupboard that everyone pretends isn there; the shared lies shielding murder, child-abuse, rape; dirty secret arising from the subconscious with apparently insane form.

Mental illness is fundamentally a physical illness. It is the embodie enactment of trauma. Yet often it doesn't receive the compassion o support that naturally arises with other physical afflictions. Too ofte the horror of insanity is based on witnessing the insane person from th outside. There's a resistance to imagining how the world is experience from the 'insane' person's point of view. If we did, we might becom aware that there's as much insight occurring when the mind is out o balance, as when we are 'sane'. Even in states of psychosis or dissocia tion, we witness how the body and psyche is moving and the treatmen it receives. For better or worse, we gain insight into the nature of th mind.

When it's not possible to integrate experience, then the experience becomes mentally forbidden and the pain contracts as separate from the whole. This contraction needs to be defended. The very approach of consciousness towards the contraction can set off the sentient alarms. Yet the contraction presents a limitation – a kind of psychic slavery to the imperceivable nightmare. It reverberates with the craving for release. At a certain stage, the contraction unfolds anyway, through the psyche and onto the environment. It 'plays out' with lack of proportion in the wrong contexts. The psyche is screaming trauma, and often the social response is to exclude through medication. The internal shame or pain of rejection then becomes external, as communication breaks down and eyes are averted from the insane person. In the field of mental disorder, we tend to punish the scream of trauma with more trauma. Where the voice needs to be heard, we dismiss it as nonsense. Where the body needs to throw off its psychic slavery, we restrain it. Where the mind has fallen into confusion and helplessness, we deny it authority. Where the biochemistry has moved into imbalance to try to find deeper balance, we dose the scales with imprecise drugs and risk lifetime dependency to force a superficial balance as soon as possible.

We not only fear insanity, we shame, condemn, exclude and punish it. This has generated an atmosphere of insanity that is suffused with the energy of trauma. Contemplate the mood around a Victorian mental institution or the nightmare of Bedlam to get a sense of the dread field around the insane. The label 'Insane' comes with a dark cloud of rejection, exclusion, condemnation, disenfranchisement, abandonment, betrayal and death.

The art of psychiatry is born to be a merciful one, in which danger and suffering are reduced and time and space are created for the person to return to a degree of balance. When an individual is caught in trauma and is acting out on the environment, they are seeking the resolution on the outside which they can't find within. Yet this disruption to

conformity can be unendurable for others. When the destructive forc
of trauma is releasing in physical form, there is a need for a protecte
environment. There is no question that at this stage, the facilitation c
a secure, healing space with stable routines, can support the releas
Yet more than ever, there is also a need for respect, honor, and th
restoration of the authority of individual experience, in order to acces
the powerfully healing Nondual Quality of insight. There is method i
every madness. By respectfully but firmly withdrawing the projecte
madness 'outside', it's possible to gain insight into the methodology o
the 'inside' of the psyche.

This can be extra complicated where the trauma has been around th
Nondual Quality of care. When care has been abused, the individua
can be enraged by care. Care can be held responsible for injustice, rape
violation, betrayal, oppression and any other horror. Care has becom
associated with abuse. Indeed, the decision not to care anymore, coul
even have been the lynch pin that, when removed, caused the collaps
of the mental fortress of sanity. In this, caregivers can be perceived a
the greatest liars and tricksters – the predators in a hell zone of trauma
The same is true around the abuse of freedom, where the individual i
unable to appreciate that the time and space to relax could suppor
their mental wellbeing. Instead, they can feel enslaved, possessed anc
helpless.

When pain reaches out to seek relief, this can also bring in the elemen
of substance abuse. Drugs and alcohol can react with prescription psy
chiatric drugs introducing an unpredictable cocktail of biochemistry
Physical addiction and dependency on outer substances to treat inne
states of suffering has its own whiplash, reducing the personality to the
suffering of craving and the temporary relief of that horror. The genera
confusion between addiction and mental disorder means that therapeu
tic options tend to be undermined or abandoned. In general, issue

round addiction need to be addressed first. Only later is it possible to gain insight and work with the underlying trauma and contractions.

Often, the combination of addiction with mental disorder is a lethal one and care becomes a palliative process: accompanying the person through the downward slide of self-destruction. Trauma seeks to recruit others into its universe. This will include family members, friends and even random people. Guilt would have us join our beloveds in hell if we are not vigilant. Yet the attempt to comfort suffering by also suffering will multiply suffering. The move must be to a shore outside of the trauma zone – to a less conditioned space that can allow freedom of form and the freedom to suffer. When we can stay in that space, irrespective of the trauma of our beloved, we hold that space for them: the traumatic zone loses its absolute grip on reality.

The challenge is to allow the continuing connection and one-ness through the Nondual Qualities, while maintaining a vigilance about boundaries. Indeed, the more we put boundaries, the more we can allow peace to be present even as the war of self-destruction rages. We might not be able to 'save' our client, but we can refrain from blocking the care; we can suffer the pain in the love; and we can come to peace with the soul's journey, however horrific it might seem from the outside.

Sanity

The first layer of mental disorder is reflected through our judgements about mental disorder. We grasp towards sanity and reject insanity. We warn and threaten ourselves and others with the condemnation of insanity. We experience shame at the slightest hint of mental disorder. We dread that our mind will betray us, and that sanity will be abandoned. Yet the degeneration of mental functioning is an inevitable part of the aging process. Our minds are tools for reflection, they are not the Source of all we are.

Clinging to sanity involves a constant conformity to pre-given model of behavior and thought. It creates an exaggerated dependency on th imagined opinions of others. In striving to stay sane, we increasingly drown in a sea of projection. We may appear sane, but we have the gun of insanity held to our heads, choking our voice and amputating ou authenticity.

Contractions around sanity can feature as a compulsive worry abou what others think, splitting the psyche through the need to constantly wear a mask to control imagined reactions. This is because sanity is so often featured as stability, predictability and conformity. All three de pend on a perfect placement of the person's behaviors within the field of expectation of the environment. In some cultures, for example women seeking education can be labelled crazy; homosexuality is seen as mental disorder; and spiritual awakening is seen as 'losing it'. Wher you think differently from others, you leave the safe territory of sanity The known, familiar, predictable forms are sane, the unknown is crazi- ness.

Yet the word sanity, on inquiry, pretty much defines itself according to its opposite. If there was no 'insanity', sanity itself would lose its con- text. We should be grateful to the insane for defining our sanity.

At a deeper layer, the very ability of the brain to evolve and heal itself depends on movement beyond the road most travelled in the neural networks of the brain. At times, this means we break out of known, familiar thought patterns. This mental evolution releases the grip we have on our contractions. When the mind confronts its own freshness, there can be a feeling of strangeness or alienation, as if the world and the phenomena of the self were viewed for the first time. In this mental space, underlying wounds or traumas can finally begin to express. We might begin to mentally process through imagination and lingual xpression some of the horrors that were prohibited. We might seem nsane, yet beneath the apparent insanity, a deeper sanity is emerging.

nsight: Nondual Quality

nsight into our True Nature can enormously support healing processes hrough mental contraction, from the inside-out. In this, the miscon-·eived agenda of healing, fixing and conforming the person to the out-,ide world takes a secondary place to the more essential needs of the)syche to move into harmony with the whole. When we can suspend udgements in our inner world around sanity or insanity, a skylight)pens in the ceiling of the mind through which insight shines. We begin o see and feel the insanity in our sanity and the sanity in our insanity.

The quality of insight moves beyond the grasp of personhood with a :uriosity that penetrates the forms of mind as they dance through du-lity. It brings a sense of space and a freedom from the dictates of time. This allowance of time and space through the suspension of judgement neans the mind can relax and open. Neuroplasticity – the brain's ability :o heal itself – increases.

When we believe in a separate 'Me', there will be the perfect 'Me', and ts shadow. We will be slaves towards a sanity we can scarcely find, and victims of an insanity that often feels like home. When we begin to abide in a space beyond the tyranny of judgmental mind, then a cen-tered insight emerges by itself. This insight is always here, whether we are sane or insane. It witnesses our craziness and our conformity. It allows action and reaction, mental freezing and over-stimulation, non-sense, absurdity and gravity, seeing what works and what doesn't.

Insight means we simply stop believing in the thoughts and images in-side our heads. This means they lose their definitive grip over who we think we are and what we expect ourselves to be. Through the disinvestment of belief in mental processes, these processes get space to play out according to the logic of the contractions they reflect. Insight moves through this spaciousness into a reflection of deeper layers of feeling, stress and pain. Insight can move from the pain in the body upwards or the repeating thoughts of mind downwards. Sooner or later it penetrates the heart and releases its deeper holdings.

Insight is here as an infinite resource to all of us, whether we are sane or insane. It will inevitably come forward around the time of our physical death. But we don't have to wait until then to access it.

Contemplations

1. Contemplate an insane person. Blend with the atmosphere of insanity and notice how your body reacts. Let the atmosphere expand, paying attention to any emotional ingredients. Take three conscious breaths and let yourself rest in the silence beneath thought.

2. Take a situation and find where you hold the stress of it in your body. Move attention to the center of the head and imagine light there. After a while, move your attention again to the Felt Sense in the body where the problem was. Wait and allow any insight to emerge.

Form does not differ from the Insight

And Insight does not differ from Form.

Form is Insight and Insight is Form.

33 STUPIDITY, SMARTNESS & GENIUS

The partner of stupidity is smartness.

Genius has no opposite.

In genius, stupidity and smartness are one.

"Talent perceives differences; genius, unity."

WILLIAM BUTLER YEATS

The duality of stupid and smart is deeply engrained as a parameter of judgement and condemnation in our conditioning, educational systems, survival codes and our estimation of worth. The strive to be smart and the wounding around the feeling of stupidity is such that it breeds both arrogance and ignorance on multiple levels, freezing form, bypassing living connection, sabotaging communication and feeding into the vortex of despair.

The 'stupid' wound hooks into many traumas through guilt, shame and beliefs in punishment or misconceptions of 'Karma'. The stab of rejection and the physical threat of being stupid freezes neural connections causing rigidity of thought, confusion or mental black-out. These phe nomena loop back to affirm the sense of stupidity. The effort to b smart is often no less stupid. Plots, plans, manipulations and strategie to win in any situation feed an egoic mask that is often oblivious to it own transparency. In the agenda to be smart, we are often blinded t the transparency of our schemes to others and the absurdity of th pretense.

Estimations of stupid/smart are often given weight by judgements o our learning abilities. These learning abilities are measured within th very small frame of what is fundamentally an alien system of readin and writing and mathematics. Later, it is based on the ability of th brain to hold facts – to know abstract information: names, places, date Difficulties in taking on these fundamentally unnatural systems of lar guage can have a variety of causes – from biochemical, to psychologica

There can be a genetic inheritance that produces another kind of neura connectivity, or it can be due to physical accident, medical operation or even deeper freedom of spirit. Yet it's all called Dyslexia. As on expert in the field told me, conventional approaches to dyslexia are "Like diagnosing a headache and giving one solution – pain-killers, whe in fact there can be a myriad different causes and treatments."

The measurement of stupidity and smartness fundamentally depend on the belief that the mind is a physical object contained within th head in the form of a brain. This brain can work well or badly. Som people are blessed with good brains that make them intelligent, other have disabled brains and they are stupid. The intelligent ones survive and the stupid ones – left unprotected – will go down. It's 'survival c the fittest' and the battlefield is inside our own heads. This belief nar rows the mind and blocks consciousness with a slavery to thought pro cesses. Thinking becomes the bottom line of reality, and feeds into value system based on winners and losers; success and failure i xpression and manifestation into the world. If you're stupid you have o right to exist, if you're smart, you could be king of the castle (for a hile). Competition plays out and collaboration diminishes. Compari- n between separate selves becomes the measurement of status, legiti- acy, entitlement and in the end the right to be alive in time and space. tupid people should shut up. Smart people lead the way.

he objectification of the Separate Self and the championing of the parate brain has led us to label certain people as 'genius'. Yet the ord genius itself belies its Nondual nature. There is no such thing as a genius', yet there are manifold channels of genius, including every hysical form. When the mind and brain can relax within and beyond he contraction of lingual thought, beliefs and imagination, the mind egins to open. In opening, the compulsion to action or doing subsides to receptivity. Even on the level of neurochemistry, this relaxation nd lessening of stress hormones allows greater neuroplasticity and con- ectivity.

ree of the agenda to be smart and not be stupid, the mind begins its atural role as an organ of perception, a receiver of impressions. The eeper the relaxation, the wider the opening, and the greater the possi- ility for all neural networks to channel the genius that is alive in every noment of perception.

Genius, like the associated word Genesis, is at the core of creation. Genius arises out of a field of infinite potential manifesting as the intel- igence of life. It can be naughty and playful. It can seem unnervingly nsane. It moves beyond structures of authority, flying through channels f inspiration and aspiration. It moves in alignment with universal need hrough every path of least resistance. In this, the surrender of all we re to be of service to the whole is a first move in becoming a channel f genius.

Stupidity

The feeling of stupidity can be horrific. It can include the horror of exclusion, helplessness, radical diminishment and loss of all self-esteem. As one client who was repeatedly condemned as a child as stupid told me: "It feels like being a lamb to the slaughter." Yet it is not an objective quota of stupidity that limits our freedom of thought, it is our belief systems connected with the body-mind.

When the body-mind is condemned as inadequate by the inner judge on the sliding scale of stupid and smart, it bends over, contracts in pain, freezes and starts to move through a treadmill of despair. Repeating authorities or power structures from our environment, we condemn ourselves as stupid and as this is fearful, we try to hide it through pretense. For a while, these masks of 'smartness' allow a relaxation in the brain, but the Ego is a vulnerable structure, investing vast amounts of energy in keeping up appearances. It is not surprising that this demands that a lot of mental processes then become dedicated to keeping up the mask and watching for threats of exposure.

As the wound around stupidity is often traumatic, when it is triggered we can move into traumatic states of shock. When stupidity has been associated with trauma, can be important to find the inner perpetrator – the internal sabotage mechanism that is still whipping the psyche down under the intangible, gold standard of smartness. Just awareness of the inner conflict and the self-abuse within this contraction opens time and space for genius, in which forms are seen and experienced at origin, out of the genesis of original misconception.

Smartness

Smartness is defined by the relative stupidity of others. We need to see stupidity, to feel smart. We fill our worlds with people where we can ccess stupidity, for the temporary rush of feeling better, smarter and npowered. In this we begin to dread the ones that could make us feel upid. It's a whole battle-game with often deadly consequences.

Vhile being smart or intellectually adept can seem to make life easier, often makes life more complicated. When we can move out of smart-ess and get feedback on our intelligence it provides a feeling of ac-eptance and power. This feeling doses the area of rejection with opioids hat are literally the neurochemical painkillers in the brain. Unfortu-ately, tolerance to opioids can increase, meaning we need ever higher oses to get the temporary effect of euphoria.

martness requires the isolation of conditions and context. That is, we an only be smart about a given situation or a specific time and space the 'problem'. To be smart, smartness also demands neutrality, which an mean a disconnection from feelings, emotions and sense perception n the here and now. When the head is cut off from the heart and body, t has freedom 'to think'. This is the inherent sabotage in smartness: he very environment on which it seeks to enact its smart plans is walled ut of living perception and reduced to a set of superimposed parame-ers within the mind. Therefore, characters from Soap Operas take valks alone to 'sort my head out'. Once the head is sorted, the environ-nent can be sorted too, through the dictation of 'smart' plans and trategies. Ultimately, it's a fool's game.

The 'smartness wound' can occur where intelligence has been abused to vin a right to exist, or to be seen or heard. Dependency on being smart an bypass the deeper pain and insecurity of the psyche, dosing the liscomfort in the depths with a wash of opioids. If we are clever, we are ccepted. If we can throw out many complicated words, explanations nd justifications, we will be 'OK'. We will outwit the battle of life. Vhile this could supply short-term fixes to psychic survival, it rests on the perception that life is a battle. Life is at war with life. The system is attacking itself.

No degree of recognition and affirmation of intelligence can take away the pain of rejection and the suffering of disconnection in the heart. Intelligence as a form cannot create, dictate or control love, peace, unity or any Nondual Quality. It can only honor and reflect that which is at the origin of any form, including smart ones.

Smartness brings arrogance and a reflex to condemn stupidity. When the mind is not free but instead is functioning as a psychic defender against deeper pains including its own dirty secret of inherent empty ness, it will use formulations to smoke screen others. Many words, many stories, many speeches and many empires have taken form to separate us from our perceived enemies. Yet a million brilliant statements cannot equal a single moment of blend between one soul and another.

The critical dislocation between head and heart in which the mind assumes domination over the whole and appoints itself as the defender against all threats, inevitably leads to stupidity. The mind is simply unable to outsmart the life, of which it is just one transient and temporal expression.

The greatest relief in any intellectual inquiry can be when we realize how misconceived we have been, and we experience stupidity in its purity (the 'dumb donkey' feeling). A vast sense of living humility releases the mind of its former constraints. This is the great peace that emerges when the mind prostrates in humility and wonder at the genius of all that is beyond the parameters of perceptive limitation.

On the level of the brain, we will always be stupid, whichever way we turn and however we endeavor. At the same time, we will always display miraculous intelligence, precisely according to the conditions of the brain at any given moment in time and space.

Genius: Nondual Quality

Surrender to the deeper needs of the whole allows the channeling of genius which is at core to the whole. Its source is always imperceivable, beyond knowledge and radically free of dualistic limitation. Genius can only be seen or experienced by the expression of Nondual Qualities into the world, often through other qualities. For example, the quality of harmony could be expressed through the musician in one way, or through the athlete in another. The expression and reception of quality are both ways to move through genius. We channel genius whether we are the actor or the receiver, the speaker or the listener – the experience of the quality of genius is the same in real time.

Genius is holographic, found in every moment of form and each second of perception. For many, it will be easier at first to see the genius in the beauty of a flower than the misshapen lips after a Botox treatment, but genius is there, nevertheless.

As inherent to consciousness, genius can never be elsewhere. It's inherent connection to truth makes it deeply attractive. It operates according to the principle of universal need. Both need and truth will draw us into the depth of perception beyond superficial judgements.

Genius is always alive, right here, in the consciousness of whatever. Vast amounts of knowledge, training, vocabulary and refined neural networks will not change the quality of genius. The simple mind will be like a river where the water meets the sea directly, with astounding simplicity and clarity. A complicated mind (often called intelligent) will be like a delta. The water will move towards the same ocean, while displaying more possible routes, pathways, landscapes and ecologies. The water is the same, as is the ocean.

The belief in the Separate Self dictates that genius must be either inside ourselves (mine) or somewhere outside of ourselves (in the 'other'). Yet genius is ubiquitous in the miracle of each moment. The way to access genius is to allow it. When we recognize and take in genius, we become genius, we express genius, we channel genius. Perhaps the way the flow of genius moves through our form involves unique colors, pathways, expressions and combinations of qualities. When we can refrain from judging, we are the only ones in any moment that can allow this unique expression to occur. Who are we to deny it?

Both smartness and stupidity are contractions occurring in the brain because of a disconnection from the heart and the body. In disconnection, thought forms float in seeming separation, dislocated from the here and the now. When we are disconnected from the here and now, within our bodies and within our environment, we are disconnected from the whole which makes us tremendously unsafe.

Genius takes form out of a deeper layer of need – the need of the whole. It expresses in ways that the intellect could never oversee, based on vast quantities of sensory information in real time, much of which is not consciously processed. It is attuned to past, present and future and arises out of the collective field of infinite potential. It flowers into form wherever it is allowed. Allowance requires opening and opening requires relaxation.

Each contraction mentioned in this book will have its own expression of genius. Each requires relaxation of the whole to open. Relaxation requires the release of the conditions of space and time. The contraction has all the space and all the time to be – the fullest right to exist. It also needs all the permission to marinate, and all the space to spontaneously express. Each contraction will tell a tale of genius, an area of mastery, expressing a direct path to the Nondual Source of all we are.

When we can allow genius, we do not speak, we are spoken; we do not think, we are thought; we do not compose, we are composed; we do not create, we are the creating; we do not live, we are the living.

Contemplations

. Close your eyes and become aware of your breathing, letting it be relaxed as possible. Any thought, image or sensation that comes forward, let yourself silently reply: 'I don't know'. Notice the effect of the admission and softly let the field of 'not knowing' expand through and round the body.

. Take any part of the physical body and let your consciousness move there as if this body part were the source of all genius. Stay connected with the Felt Sense of the body part, absorbing the resonance of genius.

Form does not differ from Genius

And Genius does not differ from Form.

Form is Genius and Genius is Form.

34 MOTHER, FATHER & CHILD

The partner of mother is father.

The child has no opposite.

In the child, father and mother are one.

"Cause only a fool lean upon his own misunderstanding.
What has been hidden from the wise and the prudent,
been revealed to the babe and the suckling."

BOB MARLEY

All of us are children to a mother and father. The child often
expresses the Nondual Qualities most needed in the blend between mother and father. We will often find that the parents
contain two sides of a contraction and that the associated Nondual
Quality is embodied in their child. For example: a mother who experiences a lot of shame can be attracted to a partner who expresses disgust.
The child born to them could have a strong quality of purity – that
inherent quality out of which both shame and disgust take form. This
rough formula offers insight to the formational years of the child's

syche and can give direction in terms of the needed bridge to liberation
or the child, as the mother and father are fully alive in them, regardless
f the degree of contact.

ften, the evolution of mastery in form around Nondual Qualities will
ave a thread that continues through generations, both through mater-
al and paternal lines, and dancing between the genders. We will find
milies that express degrees of mastery around the Nondual Quality of
eedom, for example, often with repeating themes of slavery and liber-
tion, until the True Nature of the quality irrespective of form is liber-
ted.

he child in us is a sacred resource, access to which often gets lost
uring the intense years of puberty. Because of this disconnect from the
re-pubescent child, we often relate to our inner child as if it were an-
ther person, like a character in a story. Great shifts occur when the
lient can access experiential memory and experience themselves as the
ame 'one' as the child, rather than as a detached witness. This kind of
egression involves direct re-experiencing of intimate atmospheres.
hese atmospheres will also be pre-natal, as the first impressions and
iochemical stress patterns arising in awareness in unity with the
other occurred inside the womb.

Mother

he somatic template of the feeling connection to our inner mother is
ourced in the spectrum of qualities and contractions alive in our own
hysical mother at the time of pregnancy and in infancy. While con-
entional schools of psychology will rarely admit that pre-lingual and
re-natal experience affects the psyche, in Nondual Therapy, these early
ibrations in awareness are found to be formational. These are the es-
ential atmospheres of home, the moods and attitudes that form states,
eemingly inseparable from all experience.

As these primal vibrations are both the background and soil to all othe
experiences, they play a formational role through each contraction
While we can penetrate them at any moment, it is through the libera
tion of the Nondual Quality of pure, unentangled awareness that the
emerge to the foreground. When these subtle mists are realized as nor
absolute, there can be a liberation of many contractions.

Such core atmospheres resonate with contractions around the Nondua
Quality of home (where the duality of familiarity and strangeness move
in contraction). They form as filters over consciousness itself, like th
proverbial rose-pink sunglasses, or the perception of the world throug
clouded windows. Indeed, post-awakening, many will report the tempc
rary lifting of these filters. Everything seems more alive; light seems t
have greater purity; and colors are more vibrant.

When we are in the womb and in early infancy, we are in biochemica
unity with the mother. It's not only the conscious patterns of stres
that form the patterns of our psyche, but also the subconscious vibra
tions. In this, the full blend with the energetic patterns of the mothe
is also a blend with the mother's mother and onwards, each womb con
taining the next. Because we are in an energetic unity with the mother
the child-mother relationship reflects an essential layer of healing. In
deed, it could well be that the incidence of our conception relates to
precise resonance of Nondual Qualities, and a need to liberate them.

The formation of the psyche in utero is based on patterns of stress
harmony and dissonance. These patterns are identified as 'reality' b
the unborn child. The mother is not separate, but she is the gateway t
the physical life and in this, her energy and atmosphere defines th
physical universe.

After birth, the psyche continues to be formed by patterns of harmon
and dissonance, with an increasing emphasis on patterns of separation

irth, the great rupture from the mother's body, is followed by reunion, ut within this unity there is already a distance and the possibility of oss. The patterning of separation and disconnection is already forming he borders and sensitivities of the Separate Self, and the child's later bility to stay in unity regardless of spatial distance. The first patterns f dissonance or separation are experienced as the agony of rejection. This pain can be so uncontainable that an energetic freeze forms directly round the purity of love that connects mother and child. This can nean that later on, vibrations of that frequency can trigger reflexes of epulsion and compulsion. Subconsciously, we can be triggered by a eeling quality which we fear – in the form of a kind of intimacy that eels dangerous. Beyond rationality, enemies form in the social field, imply because of this resonance with the early thwarting of motherly ove.

Much has been written about the Mother Wound and the complex of dynamics for daughters in finding form in later life. Issues of loyalty nd betrayal can feature strongly as the daughter chooses to express er freedom into the world where the mother remained enslaved. Reection of daughters by mothers and vice versa can take tangible form s daughters strive to form happy relationships (or choose to leave unappy ones) or endeavor successful careers. Complications around the Mother Wound can be even worse for males. Daughters can sometimes etain the sense of unity with the mother even while moving into separate form, without feeling they are betraying the mother by espousing different patterns.

However, males have a more complicated relationship within the collective trauma of gender separation, or what some call patriarchy. In a way, the baby boy is already 'other' to the mother before he makes a move. This can mean that he symbolizes the perpetrator, abuser, or the external authority for the mother, and therefore she can subconsciously see him as an object in the way of her personal freedom (or an object

which needs to deliver to her the 'male' fulfillment that she lacked i
life).

From the moment gender is declared the male is delineated as separat
from the mother and begins to be psychologically formed in the role c
the 'other' sex. This existential guilt in their being the essential caus
of disconnection from the mother (universe) can widen the dimensio
of despair suffused with a sense of unconditional condemnation. As
male they can experience a despair in not being able to fulfill th
mother's subconscious conditions on unity. There can be a sense of be
ing eternally 'never good enough'. As a successful male (becoming th
oppressor), they betray her, and as an unsuccessful one they disappoin
her. They are damned if they do, damned if they don't: perpetuall;
barred from the unity they crave with the mother. This can lead to
sense of unworthiness or inner evil, that disqualifies them from feelin;
at one with the physical universe. For every human, the mother is i
first physical manifestation of the universe.

In many instances, we are talking about a whole category of Inheritec
Trauma. To the post-traumatic slave syndrome, referred to in the chap
ter on Freedom, we could add post-traumatic gender syndrome. It's no
too long ago that our mothers could have been incarcerated as insan
simply because their husband wanted a divorce. Imprints of a socia
field in which loss of a husband meant loss of livelihood, poverty anc
shame still plays out in many partnerships. A single woman is desig
nated a threat to family units, and a childless woman is either pitied o
socially estranged. These dynamics of oppression continue in many
places in the world in physical form, and everywhere else energetically
They affect both mother and father, as well as the mother and fathe
energy within ourselves. The healing opportunity is found in the birtl
of every fresh form – in every child. Every child is a beacon of Nondua
Qualities and every child still lives at the core of each one of us.

Father

While the mother is the connection to the Source, universe; or final relaxation, opening and receptivity, the father is the active principle: he represents 'the world'. He is the visible template for activity, manifestation, authority, law and for 'reality' itself. Out of unity with the mother, the father is the first significant 'other'. He stands for safety and protection and is often the bottom-line for the physical survival of the family unit.

The father's patterns of judgement can seem to be absolute and can form beliefs around the nature of God the father (the fearful one, the absent one). These beliefs can be somatic, emasculating the son and robbing the daughter of her natural movement through time and space. Contractions around the Nondual Quality of authority express through the duality of conformity and rebellion through every movement into the 'outer' world as well as in patterns of intimate relating.

This contraction affects the flow of expression and by default the ability to receive. To say it simply, contractions around fatherhood directly affects our ability to manifest, to take form, and to dance in the world of duality. While the Mother Wound spirals around the horror of separation, Father Wounds typically resonate around the pain of condemnation.

Child: Nondual Quality

The Nondual Quality of the child has been reframed in current conditioning to the point of abuse. Dominant forms of conditioning rest on the premise that the child is a kind of untrained mammal, whose brain is inherently hollow. Left untamed, this mind will lead to bestiality – unbridled sexuality, violence, untold social offences and destruction. Similar misconceptions surround the Nondual Quality of the child as

we infuse our concepts around freedom. These misconceptions rest o
the premise that our True Nature is intrinsically cruel. Yet the child
the pinnacle of our evolution, where Nondual Qualities shine nakec
infiltered by the legacy of trauma. Children are our teachers and a
living gateways to Source. There is nothing 'childish' about the child.

The mind of the child is akin to what Zen Buddhism has called 'Begir
ner's Mind'. Unfettered by the conditioning of past, present and future
free of the agenda of perception that distorts consciousness with expec
tation, the child's senses open directly on the world with a freshnes
that is beyond selectivity. The child does not seek to make sense o
what he or she sees. Rather, the child is the sensing itself.

In this chapter, we have touched on some of the afflictions connecte
to the male and female aspects of ourselves, as reflected through th
father and the mother. These afflictions play out through limitations o
movement through the world of duality. For example: they can bloc
the cycle of receptivity and expression; they can create filters of atmos
pheric states of consciousness itself (such as an attitude of negativity)
At a very fundamental level, the suffering between male and femal
aspects of ourselves blocks our naturalness: meaning our freedom to 'be
whatever we are at any moment.

These core colorings and patterns of the psyche can feel heavy, yet th
child is not residing in them. In childhood, these patterns of lonelines
and intimacy, abandonment and possession, strangeness and familiarit
are surface textures to a universe filled with Nondual Quality. For th
child, the storyline caught in time is mostly an abstraction. The habit
of time, story, expectation, history, agenda and excuses are learnec
later. The child resides as the undivided, spatial, Nondual Quality o
pure awareness. Within this awareness there are patterns of dissonance
rejection, stress, loss and discomfort. Yet this dissonance is relating to
the world of form, a form of the psyche that is hardly developed and is

not yet taken as absolute. The personality of the child is still a playground, just as even his or her name is a label that needs to be learned. The child is natural, open and free.

The perspective of the child is often one that brings shame. To call someone 'childish' is to insult them. It seems we live in a culture where maturity is often determined by the degree of contraction and separation from the Source of ourselves as well as from each other.

The reunion with the inner child as a resource and guide is an important part of every process of freedom from contraction. The child within cannot be bypassed. The popular focus on childhood trauma is incomplete without resourcing and honoring the inner child as a spiritual master, experientially alive with pure Nondual Quality. The child is not only an object that needs to be healed, it is a vital resource at the formational basis of the psyche. Every stage of development or liberation includes the Nondual Quality of the child. Alive as the perfect blend between male and female aspects, the Nondual Quality of the child can be the key that unlocks freedom of form through releasing the dualities of push & pull, male & female, creation & destruction at a Source level. Unfiltered perception as experienced by the inner child is our first and last resource in the human life cycle. We would do well to rest in it.

Contemplations

1. Close your eyes and imagine one of your parents is standing behind you. Connect to the Felt Sense of their presence and notice any reactions in your body to being watched by them. Introduce the other parent and repeat. Lastly, do the same exercise with both parents at the same time. Notice any effects.

2. Close your eyes and consider how it feels to be falling asleep. Now, imagine yourself as a young child trying to fall asleep. Look into the darkness inside and notice it's the same one then as is here now. Let any childhood memories come forward freely, affirming that you are the same one now, as then.

Form does not differ from the Child

And the Child does not differ from Form.

Form is the Child and the Child is Form.

35 SILENCE, STILLNESS & EMPTINESS

The partner of silence is stillness.

Emptiness has no opposite.

In emptiness, stillness and silence are one.

*"Only when you drink from the river of silence shall you
indeed sing. And when you have reached the mountain
top, then you shall begin to climb. And when the earth
shall claim your limbs, then shall you truly dance."*

KHALIL GIBRAN

Knowledge rests on understanding. Understanding rests on experience. Experience depends on a priori awareness. It is the Nondual Quality of awareness that allows experience to arise, ake form and transform. All experience – whether it be thought, image, feeling, emotion or physical sense perception – is a form of vibration. It s a kind of music. The pre-requisite of all music is silence. The Nondual Quality of Silence allows vibration to take form. Silence is the quality that underlies the duality of loud and quiet.

Vibration is a frequency, which means it is movement. All movement i
made possible through the Nondual Quality of Stillness, which precede
underlies and continues within all manifestation. Stillness is the qualit
that underlies the duality of activity and receptivity.

These two Nondual Qualities of Silence and Stillness are not the same
although they are fundamental to all form, just as every form is a man
ifestation of configurations of time and space. Silence pertains more t
the dimension of mind, and stillness to the dimension of feelings an
emotions.

When we allow ourselves to fall back into the Nondual Quality of Emp
tiness, then Stillness and Silence are liberated to dance through th
therapeutic encounter, as needed. All three Nondual Qualities are fun
damental to the liberation of contractions.

Silence

Volume, quality and rhythm are all functions of how silence expresse
through denser vibration. This silence is here as a fundamental part o
all we are. Silence is another way to refer to the infinity within us, th
listener. As we listen to the silence, we can notice it has its own languag
– the language of more subtle vibration, or finer melody moving somat
ically, beneath the grasp of conscious control, towards harmony.

Sharing silence can awaken contractions precisely according to what i
needed at any moment. When we are silent together, it becomes unclea
where our private silence ends, and the silence of the other begins. Th
boundaries of the Separate Self begin to reverberate, perhaps wit
shame, denial or a fear of intimacy. Contractions awaken. In sharing
silence, a communication arises which is beneath the dictates of th
conscious mind.

efore, between, behind, above and underneath the formation of every
ought is silence. Without silence, no thought, no vibration, no form
uld come to be. Without silence, thought would not be possible at all.
lence is not a dense nothingness, and it's not an absence of sound or
sence of thought. It is the subtle soil out of which every sound, each
btle vibration arises, takes unique form, and into which it rests.

ilence has quality. From the denser silence of resistance through to the
inner silences of non-verbal atmospheres, it is a language in itself:
eneath the time-based polarities of the thinking mind. In silence, there
re no borders, just gradations, slopes, rifts and valleys. In silence, there
inherently no disconnection.

lence is an invitation to unity, which is why we can so often feel
shamed when silence is here between us. What is this shameful silence?
it the shame that is unclothed when the borders between the private
side and the public outside are touched? Is it the pain of exposure of
layer of resistance to being here as one, together in peace? Can this
ame of silence teach us where we are not free to be? Is shame not also
lent? Where does the silence of shame end and the silence of love
egin? Who could say where the silence deep inside ourselves is separate
om the silence out there, which we can hear with our ears? Where
oes private silence end and melt into the boundless, natural, universal
ilence?

Vhen we listen to the silence of another, we listen at a layer deeper
han their words. We can hear the anger behind the obligation of kind-
ess. We can hear the language of personal survival speaking through
vords that pretend togetherness. In the silence, we can sense the fear
nderlying the most enraged diatribe, or the insecurity beneath the em-
owered dictation of what is 'right' and what is 'wrong'. When we listen
o the silence, rather than the words or the voice, we can sense the

causal layers of the energy alive behind all forms of expression. Silenc needs no translator as she speaks. Words are optional.

Many of us are formed by a silence that has been used as a weapon t try and annihilate our souls. We are the children that should be see and not heard when our father speaks. The babies that impoverishe their families and bothered them with questions. We are the wome that when they expressed themselves were castigated, imprisoned, hu miliated and condemned. We are the minorities who should not attrac attention and be silent to survive. We are the injured ones, who learne that if we don't keep our silence, we could die, through the consequence of expression; at the same time that silence is akin to death (when a falls silent, there is no life).

One tragedy of the dynamics of power and abuse that have left thei footprints on our personalities is that the magnificent resource of silenc has been barred from our perception. Where might is right, because i can beat you up, exclude you and rob your body of air, there we fin that silence, or silencing is used as a weapon. And the experience c silence gets encoded as punishment.

Stillness

Like silence, stillness is shared with a client, not through word or con cept, but through transmission. Stillness can paradoxically become clea where there is a lot of movement. Have you noticed the sense of stillnes before a storm? Or the stillness at the site of a car accident?

Stillness is an accelerator of transformation, as it releases our attach ment to form – paradoxically, the greater our ability to rest in stillness the more freedom we have in speed (moving very fast or moving ver slow). Experience gets liberated to find its own rhythm. Stillness give us the ability to relax our tendency to try and control experience base

n our fears. Through the quality of stillness, we gradually learn to
elax in freedom, as the body, psyche, and mind have their own in-built
,rotection mechanisms. They don't need to be dictated.

t's important not to confuse stillness with the act of freezing, or lack
,f activity. Stillness is a perennial backdrop to all movement – which
an take form as a high frequency of consciousness. In this way, it in-
ites a sense of safety amid the relativity and perpetual movement of
ll form.

Emptiness

Emptiness is not void of content but teeming with life and infinite pos-
ibility. Emptiness is empty only of separation. It acknowledges the
ure inseparability of all forms – even subtle ones - and as such is the
source of all the qualities of our True Nature. All that can be thought,
elt or experienced is fundamentally empty, in that it has no independ-
nt existence from the whole.

All that is limited in time, or confined in space, is non-absolute; whereas
ut of perception through emptiness, all this is seen. Emptiness will
elease even the subtle agenda to 'stay aware' or to keep silent or still,
pening an even deeper dimension of freedom in form, through which
ll dualities can dance without the intrusion of judgement. Indeed,
within emptiness, even the movement of the mind through dualistic
structures of judgement is liberated, as non-absolute.

Through emptiness, the qualities of silence and stillness refine, support-
ng the therapeutic process according to the highest authority – which
s the intelligence inherent to the process itself.

Contemplations

1. Listen to the silence inside the head, irrespective of thoughts. Listen to the silence around noises far away, irrespective of those noises. Listen to the one that is listening.

2. Relaxing the body, use your conscious attention to imagine you are drawing a circle of light around the body. As your consciousness moves notice a center point of attention which remains unmoving, and perhaps also an awareness around that center point and throughout the greater space.

3. Closing the eyes, attend to any phenomena (thoughts, sense perceptions, subtle energy, feelings) arising or passing through conscious awareness. Relaxing into the pull of gravity, agree to release all phenomena to its own flow. Focus on the space between phenomena and let yourself merge with the space.

Form does not differ from emptiness

And emptiness does not differ from Form.

Form is the emptiness and emptiness is Form.

PART III

A CURIOUS UNIVERSE

*"When we look deeper, the reality is, that we are all one.
And we are all trying to establish this at-one-ment. When
the qualities of two persons blend, they are in a state of at-
one-ment."*

BOB MOORE

Georgi Y. Johnson

CHAPTER 1: BEYOND FRONTIERS

"The less that we're involved in the therapeutic resonance, the more of it there is... Now there's not necessarily a therapist and a client. That doesn't mean that there's not therapy taking place."

ADYASHANTI

Out of the duality of therapist and client, healing is emerging. Evolutionary, transpersonal and unconditional, this healing will always liberate part of the whole. It is wise for a therapist to identify techniques for personal use that support centering in the here and now and resting in pure awareness. This awareness is outside of specific identity, shape, form or feeling. It's like resting in the space behind and between objects, the silence beneath and between sounds and the stillness within all movement.

We shouldn't wait for an enlightened endpoint to dedicate ourselves to service to the whole. This is withholding, pending future spiritual attainment; it is a contraction based on the belief that fulfillment resides in the future; it evades the tremendous healing possibility of the here and now. Many will consciously or unconsciously hold back out of fear of rejection. This fear especially is deeply invested in the Separate Self – in the belief that it's 'Me', the personality that is the Source of healing (with 'my' love, 'my' peace, 'my' freedom etc.). When the separate 'I' is there as the therapist, we are narrowing the channel of Nondual Qualities. Everything has consequence, and for better or worse, the result will fall to the burden of the Separate Self. We begin to be limited by the dictates of contraction It's when the therapist and client dissolve that healing is happening at it depth.

When the therapist still holds this belief in the absolute separate 'I' the personal entanglement and agenda intensify. The universe, the Source c all identity, the origin of consciousness, the miracle of being together be comes obscured by an agenda to be personally successful.

Quality Whiplash

When we open in service to the whole, there'll always be a play of ac ceptance and rejection. We could find ourselves vulnerable, exposed, ig nored, persecuted, shamed, ridiculed or glorified. When we get hurt in ou work with others, the pain will be precisely in an area of contraction wher the healing process is shared. Clients need to reject, as nearly all of us ar wounded in this area. We are wounded not only in being rejected, but als in our right to reject what's not right for us. Just the freedom to reject without consequence, can have liberating effects on the psyche. A goo precept in dealing with the minefield of rejection is to wed ourselves to th service of the whole. This means that even if we feel ourselves despised, w dedicate that experience to the service of the whole. This is not theoretica. Every experience arises according to need, and in this, every experience i of service to the whole. Let the personality be rejected. Let it be plagiarized crucified and eulogized. It never was who you really are. The healing pro cess was never about who you are.

After opening as a channel for Nondual Qualities, we can sometimes expe rience a personality whiplash. Suddenly, we're clamoring for appreciation There can be a deep sense of inner lack, or barrenness. In stark contrast to the high of quality expression, we can suddenly experience ourselves a rotten. We might experience anger and resentment, wanting to blam someone for something that is somehow not good enough. The personalit tries to cash in on the glory of the universe that just flooded through it. I ants to take control, and to be rewarded as the source of that glory. The ind wants to get on the bandwagon too. It seeks to make sense of it – to ut it into a story – to delegate the living miracle of the client into a 'case udy' that proves the therapist's effectivity and brings legitimacy. This is ie re-emergence of the 'Despicable Me'. The personality is back and it's ot happy about the party that went on in its absence. How is that even ossible? It was Me. I did that. I helped him. It all came through Me. If iey feel better, it's because of Me. I am the superior/inferior therapist. I m the source of all of this. This is My space, and that's My client. What bout Me? On the one side, the personality is screaming for attention, on ie other side appears to be an abyss. We can feel confusion as to who we re, what we are and where we are. But we can't bridge that gap with the eparate Self.

'he re-emergence of the Separate Self after a therapy session or group can e like a brief encounter with the Dark Night of the Soul. The 'normal' ersonality can be shaken and desperately seeks affirmation. Because this an be irrational, emotions get inflated. It's important to develop an ability ɔ ride out the personality whiplash with peace and patience and not to ivest too much in the possible confusion of the psyche. The dust will settle eautifully, all by itself.

'rom where does this need arise if not from the contractions in the psyche f the therapist that still seeks liberation? Healing is happening. It's un-onditional. The psyche of the therapist is no less deserving of freedom han the psyche of the client. Even before the therapeutic connection was pened, the psyche of the therapist was inseparable from the psyche of the lient. It was out of this inseparability that the conscious encounter merged in the first place. The light of awareness shines on contractions of ɔoth therapist and client, without discrimination. The wind blows and all he leaves quiver. There is no therapeutic immunity to evolution.

Vhen we begin to move with the transformative power of Source unity, it an also be beneficial to adopt an attitude of humility. This supports the freedom of the psyche to release its stress, confusion and imbalance and t return to harmony outside of the therapeutic context. Called b Adyashanti "A ferocious humility," this attitude eases the transition be tween service to the whole and 'regular' life. It releases the tendency to b reactive and to grasp towards personal survival.

Nondual Therapy goes beyond the Separate Self, which means beyond cl ent and therapist, teacher and student, superior and inferior, active an receptive. The liberation of the qualities of our True Nature in the her and now through layers of contraction – mental, energetic and physical involves an ongoing practice of relaxation and release. This is a therapeuti paradigm shift. In the words of Spiritual Teacher Jennifer Welwood: "Ou wound is not what happened to us in the past; it is that we were unable t stay connected with our deeper nature in the face of what happened to u in the past. This understanding allows us to directly relate to our probler in present time, which is a disconnect from the truth of who we are. It als helps us avoid the common therapeutic pitfall of fixating on the part in way that solidifies rather than liberates."

The prerequisite of every therapeutic meeting is the open and unconditiona energetic connection. This loosens the energetic container of the Separat Self, which means that we become more empathic. In this way, we ca intimately experience the resonant effects of contractions carried by ou clients.

There is some confusion about empathy. Empathy is not to grasp at th suffering of another or to exaggerate it. Remember, we are the reflectio through which the client can model the possibility of enduring the unen durable or containing the uncontainable. We are evolving to move ever out of the contraction of Good Versus Evil, through the Nondual Qualit of discernment which is a mental relaxation in pure perception. This mean that while fully sharing the experience, we neither grasp it nor push i away. We relax within it, without denying its pain or grasping towards it rewards. We stay in uncontracted awareness in the here and now gardless of the horrors that are expressing. This spaciousness also makes very experience of suffering relative to any other, thus disinvesting it of s authority and power over the client's direction. We can pick up the xperience and share it with the client, but we must also know how to put down and/or return the authority to them.

he art of therapy is to learn to allow these uncomfortable energies to love unconditionally, and even invite them to become more potent: for xample, to allow anger at the anger. To experience the purity of that nger even without a reason or without a context. When we come across a ontraction in which we also have personal difficulty, it's important to feel ne freedom to take the process slowly, even in slow motion, and with an pen curiosity to explore the phenomena with the client together. Even esistance has a feeling resonance: explore it. All of this is possible when e can learn to disinvest from the belief in the Separate Self, moment by loment.

s spiritual teacher and Nondual therapist Ellen Emmet writes: "When we pen deeply to our direct experience here and now, we may see that we low as the ever-flowing movement of experience and that at the very same ime we rest as something that never comes and never goes and which aturates every movement of experience with its loving substance."

very feeling, emotion and experience is available to us at any moment. Vhen we empty ourselves to move into a shared process with a client, we ill encounter all the energies alive within the client – conscious and unonscious. This means that in the rape victim, we will also meet the rapist; n the martyr, we will also meet the hatred; in the surrendered we could neet the victory cry of war.

Dread Attacks

Those who have undergone a spiritual awakening often experience sudden ttacks of formless dread. This dread can be sensed by all species of life. It is the human conceptualization of future horror – a debilitating blend c fear and anger, formlessly threatening the unspeakable. Where we are nc free within ourselves, this dread will awaken the pain of contraction. It agenda is to reinvest the mind with the belief in control over reality. If w ignore this temptation to believe in the autocracy of conscious though then the expansion to experiential spaces beyond the low murmur of drea is possible. Anything in us that could be threatened, is not who we trul are. When the suffering of dread arises, it can serve as a scan to show u where we are still contracted, where we still deny aspects of experience, c where we lose our freedom. This is true whether the dread is generatin internally or is channeled towards us by another person.

Many have advised methods to protect ourselves against bad energies. Ye much of this is futile. In allowing ourselves to be emptied out completel by energetic attack, without entanglement, we allow a process of purifica tion and emptiness itself to become a lived experience of zero-distance ful fillment and freedom. Zero distance is an effect of unconditioned awareness Just as awareness becomes unbounded, stretching into infinity, it also un obstructed. With pure awareness, we are able to pass the split of subjec and object inherent to perception and 'become' that which is perceived without being possessed by it. Dread thrives in the rift between subjec and object. When we are utterly able to allow experience at zero distance dread dissipates. Having said this, we live in what can be experienced a dreadful times, and it's not always possible to move out of the paradign of time, space and fear. We see the effects of dread in the field when w find ourselves with bent head, hidden face, crossing our legs, wrapping ou arms over the solar plexus. When the experience of dread in the field be comes uncontainable, it can be a support to:

1. Rest in mindful breathing (breathe in the freshness of the Now, anc breathe out the sense of dread). Notice that the experience of dread is never there on the in-breath. Notice also that breathing is a baromete of the amount of psychological stress running through the system. We

momentarily stop breathing or our breath becomes shallow when a contraction emerges.

2. Find rhythm. It can be through listening to music; tapping the fingers or feet; or squeezing a part of the body rhythmically. Dread gets its power in the field of illusion out of real time and space, and it threatens us primarily through its sinister lack of form. When we use rhythm, we structure the energetic field in the here and now. Dread cannot be sustained in this.

3. Become empty. Release all agenda to do anything about whatever the dread is suggesting is wrong. Connect from the existential emptiness in ourselves to the emptiness in the other. The human organism is an open channel. If we let it, any energy entering us can just as easily exit to the universe through the back door of the psyche.

Part of the client's process can be reflected through undercurrents of thought appearing in the therapist's head. For example: "I am special; Everyone hates me; I want to kill myself." The degree to which this bothers us directly reflects latent patterns of identification and brings opportunities to disinvest from the thinking mind and to invite somatic contractions to relax.

Everywhere that we suffer in the therapeutic process is an invitation to wider expansion and deeper liberation through the soft dissolution of freezes in our True Nature. As therapists, we have agreed to lift the veils of denial and to allow suffering. This allowance of suffering depends on our unfiltered awareness. When we stay as pure awareness, the organic movements of contraction, expansion and contraction are liberated. We are free to focus, concentrate, or to broaden all horizons without the need to dictate from the mind, or to submit to the dictations of form. In allowing suffering, suffering loses its leadership over the process, and like a forsaken child, it begins to come home to the Source unity out of which it was born.

CHAPTER 2. I AM HERE: MIND, HEART & BODY

"What has happened cannot be undone. But what can be dealt with are the imprints of the trauma on body, mind, and soul: the crushing sensations in your chest that you may label as anxiety or depression; the fear of losing control; always being on alert for danger or rejection; the self-loathing; the nightmares and flashbacks; the fog that keeps you from staying on task and from engaging fully in what you are doing; being unable to fully open your heart to another human being."

BESSEL VAN DER KOLK

Each form is a form of contraction. It is not inherently separate from the whole, yet it is a contracted part of the whole. The whole is itself formless, a flow of manifestation in which phenomena emerge and pass away in naturalness within a seamless evolution towards harmony.

s we address areas of contraction in mind, heart and body, the opening
the three dimensions of perception beyond contraction presented in the
ook I AM HERE, can be a powerful part of the integrative healing process:

1. The awakening of mental consciousness from the contraction of repeating thought patterns, beyond the parameters of linear time;

2. The allowance of unconditional feeling awareness, behind and beyond
contractions in feeling and emotion, beyond the parameters of space;

3. The allowance of perception through emptiness, behind and beyond
all limitations in form.

very contraction will have roots in these three dimensions of perception.
or example, a contraction of guilt can be temporarily released through
onsciousness of a thought form, but the Felt Sense of guilt will remain,
erhaps even coming to the foreground as it has no mental container or
istification. The Felt Sense of guilt can be released, but still the legacy of
ne contraction can be present in the body, for example, in a reflexive
ightening of the shoulder muscles on one side of the body, or in cravings
or substances that historically gave relief.

he book I AM HERE – Opening the Windows of Life & Beauty, gives a
etailed description of these three windows of perception: consciousness,
wareness and emptiness. None of these existential windows can be left out
i the full circulation of form through the evolutionary cycle.

Vhen a contraction has released through all three layers, perception
hrough emptiness becomes more consolidated. There is a clarification of
ense perception, as the client literally comes to life through sensing more.
he opening of sense perception is an effect of the ability to relax, relaxing
inconditionally into the emptiness of the unknowable and imperceivable.
Vhen we relax, we open; when the body relaxes, our senses open. All sense
erception is fleeting and infinite in its possibility. Its speed is very high.

The mind creates an appearance of stability out of rapidly changing sens perceptions.

The opening of the dimension of feeling awareness is perhaps the least ex plained part of all healing work, yet it's the direct bridge between min and body. The liberation of that which can sense our True Nature is crit cal. Sublingual, the dimension of awareness is found in the unconditiona use of the Felt Sense. Feelings are not fixed objects, and when we feel phenomenon, we can only become the phenomena. So, the dimension c awareness is about the freedom to flow through, within and as anything i perception, without separation. It's about merging with what is, becomin it, and being the phenomena without fear of getting caught there.

The dimension of consciousness is more related to mind and visualizatior This the seat of the witness, on the perimeter of the psyche. Timeless, it' both the source of time and exists as eternity beyond all forms of time. It' the silence between thoughts, and the silence beneath thought. It is deepl creative, yet also creates illusion. As such it can interfere with wholenes and naturalness and is behind much of the evolutionary process. Conscious ness is often invested in the story, and the story is not ultimately real: i can only be descriptive or playful. Every story arises out of a priori expe rience, and experience is formed by energetic contraction. Stories are als illusory in that they take on a definitive beginning, middle and end. Non dual Therapy is more concerned with the moment before the beginning anc what happened after 'The End'.

The three layers of perception are reflected in the classical trilogy of mind heart and body. Each of these layers has its own language. Each will hav its own way to express a contraction. Each layer is interrelated with th other two. Yet the layer of feeling awareness – the Felt Sense – has bee therapeutically most neglected. This is the bridge between body and mind the domain of energetic contraction that must be loosened to allow th release of both physical and mental contraction. When the heart is closed severing the connection between inner and outer world and solidifying a

438

elief in the absolute separation of self from 'other', then the contraction will seek release through mind (mental instability), through the body (disase) and through the outer world (physically acting out). Yet our restance to attend to our feelings and emotions is huge and socially nforced. The release of this bottleneck in pure awareness is a large part of ne endeavor of Nondual Therapy.

Consciousness & Mind

'rom a Nondual perspective, humanity is presently evolving out of the asic, dualistic mental conditioning of binary mind (from either-or to and-nd). As we evolve out of this either-or mental software, a wider and more nclusive aspect of mind comes into play which is free of expectation and udgement and that can perceive without contraction. The ability to wit-ess the either-or of thought as non-binding makes it easier to let go of the tory of the Separate Self, which facilitates healing and transformation.

Vhen the witness position is uncovered beyond the cycles of linear time, he either-or code of limitation is broken but not lost. These binary func-ions of mind continue to be of strategic value in structuring, planning, playing and decision making, but they lose their emotional charge. Freed f the pressure of personal survival, thinking becomes playful, informed hrough the consciousness liberated of mental conditions.

Conventions assume that the brain is a container of a certain amount of ntelligence, knowledge and thinking ability. It assumes that the effort of he brain, together with education, is what determines the output of the ame brain. This is not brain science, but the science of belief. The belief hat the brain is inherently separate from the general field of brains and ninds, is like expecting a laptop to resource Google without connection to he internet.

Putting the materialist belief in the brain's separation aside and opening he treasury of modern neuroscience, it becomes increasingly evident that the brain is more a reflector of experience than a generator of it. The brai would seem to be a primary sense organ, receiving information from mu tiple dimensions, by its openness.

Like the eyes that will not see the forest when they are clouded with im aginary shadows, the brain's ability to perceive or reflect experience ge restricted by stress, emotional contraction and psychological trauma. Eve what we would conventionally call 'memory' (what we chose to rememb of any event) is a contraction based on grasping, in which unconditiona memory of the experience is censored.

The more the mind disinvests from habitual thought reflexes and inherite structures of belief, the better it functions. It opens like a sense organ t channel a purity of impressions. Insight emerges, expressing through th unique forms of the individual mind. It's not by chance that many unedu cated, 'unintellectual' Nondual teachers suddenly find themselves able t discuss both philosophy and science at a high level. Both thought program and conceptual programs have been liberated with the realization of th illusion of the Separate Self. Free of the 'Despicable Me', unbridled by fea of error, every brain can reflect the wonder of the cosmic dance throug duality.

Awareness: Felt Sense

On the level of awareness, Nonduality is about opening the channel to allo those sentient Nondual Qualities such as love, care, and peace, to resonat through all the layers of form. By allowing the infinity of awareness, w allow the refinement of feeling, and the feeling of feeling – the sentien deepening into the Source of all we are. This is the dimension of Being that precedes, underlies and survives all activities of mind.

Much has been written about spiritual bypass. This can involve escapin painful feelings through the temporary relief won through the notion o spiritual 'transcendence'. But this kind of spiritual bypass is unsustainabl ıd leads to denial of the living inheritance of the psyche. We could also y to avoid intimacy with the suffering within the psyche through stories ɔout our contractions. These stories can support a feeling inquiry, but ɩey can also become strategies of evasion. Consider this: we are unqualified ɔ tell any story about a contraction without first experiencing what it is ɩade of. How can we be an authority on a feeling that we haven't really ɡreed to feel? This is where the silence, stillness and emptiness of the ɩerapist can be a powerful encouragement to stay present to the Felt ɛnse.

Vhether our conscious emphasis is through the body or mind, there is ɩterally no escape from feeling the feelings. Sentient awareness is often ɩndeveloped due to the state of our conditioning and education. This is ɹreventing healing and driving us into the wilderness of thought, physical ɩistraction and symptomatic medication. The opening of sentient aware-ɛss (that source within us which is able to 'feel a feeling') is central to ɛvery healing process. It's only through feeling the feelings that we can ɩtegrate them. It's only through the direct experience of contracted energy hat painful experience can be transformed from trauma to resilience.

Vhile the conscious mind will often grasp the least horrific side of a con-ɾaction, the deeper healing is found in the shadow of the conscious form. Iere, the dance of duality comes to the foreground as every form contains ɔs opposite. For example, when we have a belief: "I am generous", and ɩdhere to that belief with religiosity, the shadow belief "I am miserly" is hat which is growing, fed again and again with each affirmation of gener-ɔsity. The Felt Sense of miserliness in turn feeds the conscious belief "I am ɛenerous". Freedom is lost, as the identity of generosity becomes a major ɩmitation on expression and comes into conflict with all those experiences ɹhere meanness could have been more appropriate.

Ɉo form moves without a shadow, and the shadow is often found in the ɔontraction of that which must never be felt. Nondual qualities open the ɩrena in which the dance of duality can happen in freedom, energized by

the quality. For example, within an atmosphere of gratitude, it becom
much easier to be generous or miserly as needed, in real time.

Emptiness: Sensation & Body

All experience has a biochemical form. Take stress for example, it is see
physically as the movement of cortisol and other stress hormones. The
hormones effect our health. The parts of the contraction we refuse to fe
will become embedded in the physical body, affecting our physical wel
being and moving us out of balance. The body stores energetic contractior
that have been rejected from sentient awareness. For example, the pain c
grief can show up as pain in the back, for which there seems to be n
objective medical cause. The body keeps the score. This means that man
of our core, unconscious fears and unprocessed emotional conflicts are foun
deep within the cells of the body.

Perception through emptiness is about the direct experience of being phys
ically alive. The relaxation into emptiness has the power to liberate th
psyche from fears of death, sexuality, insanity and disease. When we pe
ceive through emptiness, we consolidate as the existential source of all per
ception. This source is continuously perceiving through the transience c
all phenomena. Phenomena (whether thoughts, feelings or physical man
festations) are all caught in time (with a beginning, middle and end) an
bound in space (contracted). The blend of time and space, through the pu
of gravity, is that which allows form. When we penetrate the impermanenc
of all form, that which is impermanent loses its illusory authority Tha
source of perception within is revealed as a dimension that is at source eve
eternity and infinity.

At the same time, however, this emptiness is where we throw (in our illu
sion) our worst fears. It is the home of that which is denied, repressed an
rejected inside us. Therefore, the Dark Night of the Soul can be experience
as such an existential horror, while at the same time it offers the greates
existential opportunity. When we find ourselves adrift on the dark water

our unconscious, we are one step away from setting ourselves free from ur worst nightmares, somatic contractions that have perhaps been with ur families for generations. In this, every movement into the Dark Night the Soul, although it could be a time when the individual person feels ost condemned, is actually a voyage of service to the whole. The therapeutic need to support others in the wilderness has implications far beyond ie individual client. The very presence of another human being with an pen awareness and unconditioned mind in the Dark Night already exposes ie fallacy of the Dark Night's greatest weapon – the belief that the individual is irrevocably separate from the whole.

he demons of the emptiness distract us from the awesomely familiar and idlessly resourceful intimacy of the perennial presence of the formless in ll we are, and this is a tragedy. As spiritual teacher and psychotherapist ennifer Welwood writes in the book The Sacred Mirror: "To our psyche . Emptiness appears as any experience that threatens or disrupts whatever orm we are trying to hold onto at a particular moment. Any experience iat we don't want to have, anything that's not the way we're trying to et it to be, becomes an emptiness experience for us."

erception through emptiness is initiated through direct contact with the ore reality of the bones of the physical body. This is partly because in the hysical dimension, there is a vast polarization between substance (atoms which are fluctuating, compact energy) and the vast emptiness out of which hey arise and into which they disappear.

)f the myriad celestial dimensions being accessed through meditation and nergy work, the evolving physical body is the most precious and relevant, s it is the container of all experience. This body is born, grows in our wareness, ages, and gently decomposes back to earth. The individual body ; a direct channel of information between dimensions of form. Through he body, consciousness awakens, and consciousness accelerates transformation. It's an opportunity not to be wasted.

On the level of body, Nonduality is about incarnation. So many of our fea
relate to the resistance to being in a body. A process in which we realiz
the emptiness of all form opens a wider vista of freedom, as all forms ar
realized as inherently empty and inseparable from the whole and therefor
we (as the whole) will never get stuck or trapped. This applies also to tl
body, which while appearing fundamentally untrustworthy (it gets ill an
dies), at the same time appears as a kind of prison that we might nev
escape. Through processes of emptiness, the body can be experienced as a
impermanent phenomenon and as a purposeful manifestation: a living op
portunity for expression, not a curse.

Thought contractions (the suffering of the binary mind); sentient contrac
tions (conflicting feelings and emotions); and physical contractions (dis
ease in the body) are causally interwoven.

The genetic programming of the body holds the blueprints of our person
ality, as well as the experiential archive of our ancestry. This is not a fixe
structure. Tinier than DNA, epigenetic tags or mini, biochemical contrac
tions of our DNA are released through relaxation. They unfold in the sen
tient space of awareness. In this dimension, sound and vibration affect
matter – including the subtle vibrations of Nondual Qualities. When ther
is a release of an epigenetic contraction over our DNA, there are reverber
ations throughout the psyche. Nondual Qualities are also released. Th
acceleration in transformation – the rapid change – loosens the grip of th
psyche as we find ourselves resting in the change-less space of uncondi
tioned awareness through which all change occurs. In this, the body offer
the master-keys of healing. The only way to realize the unbinding imper
manence of form is to be able to fully experience it without denial. We ar
ultimately not our bodies, or our personalities, but the way out is through

The interaction between the three layers of perception, consciousness
awareness and perception through emptiness is perpetual and interdepend
ent. Imagine you have a repeating thought echoing through the chamber
of your mind: "I am unlovable". Whatever the historic source of thi

rogram, it is setting the terms and conditions of thought. Inevitably, this thought contraction will be found reflected in a contraction of feelings and emotions – it will determine the nature of experience. The thought sustains the energetic contraction. However, when we switch from conscious mind to feeling awareness, we begin to invite those contractions to unfold, regardless of thought. The Felt Sense of being unlovable comes forward into an awareness that inherently contains unconditional love. A healing process begins.

Contracted areas of non-feeling are found in physical locations in the body: perhaps in the chest area, or the shoulders and back of the neck. The cells themselves are contracting which means they become less responsive to stimuli. This decreases blood flow and generates more areas of physical stress where the body tries to rebalance the energetic load. All of this is also requiring energy, which pulls perception away from the feet and the hands as they are most sensitive. Clumsiness follows. The environment itself seems to echo the message: "You are unlovable."

With all this incoming data, the mind continues to repeat its mantra, because there is still more control and apparently less suffering in the horrible mantra in the head than the actual experience of rejection. At the same time, the thought "I am unlovable" is bound up with the even more horrific possibility "I am lovable". How would that be? To be vulnerable to love, to be acceptable as a clumsy fraud, and to suffer the grief that is here in the inevitable loss of every form? The greatest defense against this wounded, complicated love from the outside, could well be to dictate that the shop is closed. Not lovable.

In this contraction of love, the living body itself – the sensory gateway to the experience of life – gets disconnected from the head due to the hypnotic effect of one thought form: "I am unlovable." 'The World' appears as a loveless road to nowhere. The inner world is also no source of love for the unlovable. Love is banished inside-out. The whole psyche begins to shut down on life, outwardly and inwardly, attempting to lock down its fundamental vital resources. When the psyche lacks vitality, illness and/or accidents happen. The face contorts with contempt and aversion. This signals a refusal of care and compassion - until some consciousness enters the home of that body that cares enough to suffer the healing process. The lovable-unlovable story is a love story – a love story that tells of where the mind, heart and body are insisting on separation from the whole. It's all about the pain of rejection, but who is rejecting who?

Alive in and of itself, the body as energy is the energetic savior of what has not been processed through awareness. Embedded in the core of our cells are our basic lessons and learnings about survival as a human mammal. Also, embedded in the body are our traumas – not just the ones in this lifetime but also those of our ancestors. All the wisdom of the physical universe can be found in our bones. Nothing gets lost. What we fail to process through the transformer which is our personal patch of the human psyche will be processed through the collective psyche. In this, healing is not a choice, but an inevitability, and supporting others in healing is not a ticket to goodness or superiority, but a rational prerogative in the interests of the true, undivided self.

The emptiness of the body isn't a hell-zone: it's alive with formless Nondual Quality, a field of infinite probability and limitless potential. Even the separate body is an interacting temporary formation out of the one body of the earth. Its seeming separation is illusory. Every particle of this experienced body is resonating in surrendered harmony as part of the body of the whole. The physical dimension is not a prison, or something to be feared or denied. It's not a 'thing' at all, but a living experience, or the experience of the living. In the words of Bessel van der Kolk, author of The Body Keeps the Score, "The greatest sources of our suffering are the lies we tell ourselves." Fulfillment, happiness, ease and peace comes with embodiment of all we are and all we are not, as imperfectly perfect, dynamic manifestations of the whole.

♯

Chapter 3: I Am That

"Realize once and for all that neither your body nor your mind, nor even your consciousness is yourself and stand alone in your true nature beyond consciousness and un-consciousness. No effort can take you there, only the clarity of understanding. Trace your misunderstandings and abandon them, that is all. There is nothing to seek and find, for there is nothing lost. Relax and watch the "I am". Reality is just behind it. Keep quiet, keep silent; it will emerge, or, rather, it will take you in."

NISARGADATTA MAHARAJ

Nondual Therapy is emerging to address the collective need to unwind conditioning and to move into increasing degrees of alignment with our True Nature. In this work, we present qualia of consciousness – or Nondual Qualities – that offer energetic pathways to release contractions in the psyche. These Nondual Qualities are defined as intrinsic to all experience: they are always here, and are timeless, infinite and unconditional.

Nondual Qualities are not endpoints but entry points, with the precise healing elixir needed for any afflicted state of being. They don't conclude a process as they are beyond conclusion but can initiate transformation. One quality can of itself reveal many other Nondual Qualities. While these qualities of our True Nature can be enticing, it's important to note, that they are still just forms of experience. As much as anything, the Felt Sense of these qualities is determined by the contraction that has unfolded. How we experience freedom, for example, is at first determined by the nature of the prison we were in before. Only later, does the experience evolve into a seamless unity with the whole.

All transformation is a function of the allowance of the nervous system and involves its reprogramming as well as the evolution of thought forms and the opening of new dimensions of mind. As such, the nerve system deserves the greatest respect and patience. Here, the default positions are relaxation, silence, stillness and emptiness. Filling in the gaps with ungrounded stories, or encouraging a client to do so, threatens to obstruct the process of liberation and provide an escape route from deeper liberation. When we fall back into our source unity, this doesn't have to be a supernatural state. Rather, it has the quality of naturalness and groundedness. There is a reduction in fear and stress; an easiness in letting go; and a freedom to both take authority and at the same time to allow multiple perspectives. It can be noticed in gradual changes such as increased vitality; an easy emotional intelligence; less stress; freedom of mind; and the ability to center.

The more the therapist can relax into the unconditional, Source unity that precedes even consciousness, the more the flow of healing is liberated through the array of Nondual Qualities. Interference is less needed as the contractions reveal their own remedies.

Our default position is pure relaxation in the existential continuum. The more we are consolidated in this Source unity, the more we can listen openly and unconditionally, without judgement or agenda. 'That' (a term arising from the book I Am That, by Nisargadatta Maharaj) is prior even to True Nature and to all Nondual Qualities. As such, when we surrender into That, all Nondual Qualities are free. A simple rule would be to say

1at if you can sense it, feel it, think it, touch it, it's not That. The only 1ing to be said about this existential Source unity is that we will never /ade it. Likened to the eye that cannot perceive itself, it's the Source of .l perception. Its stability, power and freedom are beyond measurement. 's formless yet stronger than anything in sight. It's the source of longing et it's the space of all belonging. It's as powerful as the wind in its effects, et like the wind, it remains invisible.

1 therapy, 'That' supports the ability to be able to let go, let be and be 1r real. It allows the release of agenda and the spontaneous emergence of 'rue Nature. This includes even the agenda to rest as pure awareness or 1e stay in the here and now. It requires no effort as it presents an absolute 1d pre-given Source unity.

Vhen we remember, we bring parts of our experience back into 'That'. Vhen we forgive, we return to 'That' which was given before. When we elease, we surrender all our experience into 'That'. 'That' is the center-oint of relationship and is inseparable from all relationships. Inviolable as ource, it supports the same inviolability in the client, allowing a flow of ransformation to occur beyond judgement in the evolutionary, healing pace between 'That' and 'That'. Through 'That', we can become truly nconditional, which means beyond the restraints of time and space, and his is the most powerful support possible for our client.

n the words of Nisargadatta: "There are no conditions to fulfill. There is othing to be done, nothing to be given up. Just look and remember, what-ver you perceive is not you, nor yours. It is there in the field of conscious-ess, but you are not the field and its contents, nor even the knower of the ield. It is your idea that you must do things that entangle you in results f your efforts – the motive, the desire, the failure to achieve, the sense of rustration – all this holds you back. Simply look at whatever happens and now that you are beyond it."

CHAPTER 4: THERAPEUTIC TECHNIQUES

"From this experience of pure spaciousness therapists can authentically question the structure, the texture, the nature of someone's suffering in a way that begins to dissolve a contracted and self-serving interpretation of the present moment. If a client stays intimately connected with a therapist who is in this state, they have no choice but to observe the evaporation of their problem."

PETER FENNER

Nondual Therapy is not about what we do, but more about what we don't do. We're not making a better personality, but rather unmaking personality. It's less about the emergence of form and more about the disappearance of form. The personality is a 'doer' and a 'fixer'. It's an active expression into the 'outer' world. Receptivity is the end of personality. We can only receive the other, where we are 'not' through the spaces between all the concepts, ideas and feelings about who what and where we are as a Separate Self. It's enough to be still, silent and receptive.

It's enough to connect without therapeutic agenda. Being here is already a powerful, living miracle.

All the Way Home

When working with contractions there are two poles to the process, both of which are equally important. Contractions occur where we freeze experience, we refuse to go all the way. Sometimes, we follow the client all the way into Source Unity, through an incremental realization of non-identity. Sometimes, we will be led to the core of the contraction – to the fullness of the experience in its potency. Expressed verbally, this can present a big difference. One moment it can be "Anger is here, you are not your anger," and at another time it can involve looking for the point of pure singularity with the trapped emotion. "I am anger; anger is absolute. This anger fills the whole universe." Both will facilitate freedom. We are as much constrained by our refusal to experience an emotion, as we are by our inability to realize we're beyond it.

It's important to follow the client in this. Let them determine the direction. If you notice that although they are resting in formless awareness, the guilt thing keeps coming back again and again, it's not resolved. It's time to fully become the guilt – to experience it in every shade and contour, without any excuse. Just this conscious movement into the contraction releases a corresponding energy of expansion. That means that the contraction can now be experienced as a much broader feeling – not localized to a spatial area of the body. This new space can allow a client to access the purity of the experience of guilt - perhaps showing them that this experiential phenomenon of guilt (in them) is not ultimately separable from the sense of guilt in anyone else.

If you notice that the client is caught in a program of identification with the contraction, however, the opposite movement could be needed. Ignore the contraction, go for the fullest experience possible of being in the here and now, in the wonder of pure awareness, without stories, issues or agenda. For example, they can see the blue sky. If their awareness is in the sky, then are they also the sky? Can they let their awareness be infinite like the sky, as the sky?

There are no mistakes with this. Just trust the intelligence within the process of the client. Always take that extra moment and that extra space. Don't assume they've answered when the universal question from the core of your client is still unfolding.

Sentient Geography

Where possible, let the client locate contractions in their body, or in the space around them. You'll already get a sense of their psychological geometry in their body language and posture. What's behind them and what's in front? What's far away from the body and what is closer to the skin or inside? Let the client experience the motility of energy.

Many will have no idea that what feels like a physical pain in the body, will begin to transmute when you move your awareness to it. The shifting of pain from part of the body to another as a response to our conscious attention can give us an energetic insight into the pattern of emotional conflict. This shows up as a pathway of pain within the physical body. For example, the physical pain in a muscle can spread across the shoulder, together with a sense of irritation; awareness of the irritation can spur a sudden stabbing pain in the left kidney, which in turn (when allowed into awareness) could reveal a deep discomfort with an area of natural expression or release. Awareness will invite a contraction to tell its story, and it will do this through the Felt Sense of the body.

It's also important to bring the principle of freedom of movement all the way to the physical body. When we are in contraction or trauma, part of the body freezes. The traumatic experience involved a restraint on movement (whether physically, psychologically or mentally), and this restraint in movement shows up in therapy. Already when the client finds she can 'move' attention to areas of contraction, the principle of free movement is energetically restored. When in addition, they are encouraged to physically move (for example, to stamp the feet), it signals to the psyche that the old context of the contraction is no longer true on a physical level. There is a

hysical container that is not limited or frozen. This in turn supports en-
rgetic movement, which supports freedom of mind.

s mentioned in Section I, the human form manifests through natural du-
lity. Be aware of this. For example, if a contraction is focused on one side
f the body, attend to the opposite polarity. When there is a freeze in the
ft hip area, for example, what is happening in the right? Is the right
umb, sending all the nervous responses to the left? Or is it overexerted to
ompensate the left? There will always be a reflection on the opposite side,
nd each side is born to support the other, so recruit that support. These
ualities will reflect with right and left, in front and behind, up and down.
hey will also reflect in terms of content or story. For example, a refusal
o believe in a god above the head, could reflect in authority complexes
rith the father behind the back. A difficulty in expression will connect
rith a refusal to hear something. Ask questions, and let the client ask
ogether with you. Let curiosity guide the process.

ess is More

ilence between people can evoke an atmosphere of shame. Speaking can
e a way to maintain separation and control and in this, silence can be
oth confrontational and deeply healing. When there is silence, refrain from
lling it, until words come of themselves. Let yourself sense into the at-
osphere of the silence, without drawing conclusions. Give time and space
or silence, so that energetic contractions around the Separate Self between
ou and your client can awaken. Let silence be a default, even exploring
rith the client the feeling quality of the silence. For example, if it is a
ervous or uncomfortable silence, invite them to take more time and space
o relax into it.

tillness is also an excellent default position. When we share stillness with
ur client, the time-based story which has limited the client's freedom loses
s exclusive grasp on reality. Stillness is more powerful than all stories, as
t is the very facilitator of all movement, happening and transformation.

Beneath the clinging to what has happened, and what has been done c not done, and the anticipation of what needs to be done, or what coul happen, is the client's agenda to stay in the trance of the story.

Stillness has a powerful energetic resonance that will awaken that sam stillness in the client, regardless of the story they are telling themselve: Contrary to popular belief, stillness is also an initiator of movement.

Within the context of less is more, it is also important to remember th holographic principle. Every detail of the client's expression will tell th story of the whole energetic life journey, when we give it space and tim For example, when we ask how they feel, they can at first say that the feel 'nothing'. Give them time and space. Move with curiosity and softnes together with them. Take even one particle of this 'nothing' and explore i together. There is no such thing as 'nothing'. The 'nothing' is pregnan with everything that has been denied.

In our agenda to fix problems, to do the right thing as a therapist and t succeed, we risk robbing experience of time and space. The deprivation c time and space is precisely that which causes the formation of a contractio in the first place. The feeling of no time and no space is directly asking fo time and space. Within the here and now, time and space are eternal an infinite. Stress is unnecessary.

Sensory Experience

All experience is form in transformation. This experience arises out o awareness – it is awareness with quality. Pure awareness precedes, under lies and continues beyond each differentiation into experience. Awarenes is like the space between objects that allows them to appear in differentia tion. Even the 'elsewhere' or the past or future time is here in and a awareness.

While being inextricable from pure awareness, experience is also alway happening through our senses – our capacity to feel. To sense anything ae spaciousness of awareness is needed a priori. Only with space can we pen to harmony. Only with time can impressions occur according to the rogression of the melody. When we move into the here and now, our senses pen to the resonance of life as a direct response to the allowance of space nd the presence of time.

'et our many senses – such as sight, sound, smell, touch and taste – do ot only turn outward, they also turn inward. They are open channels of onsciousness and in this, it is through our sensory response mechanism hat we can feel the density of contractions, the relief of spaciousness, the ull of love, the omnipresence of care or the vitality of truth. In this, the ensory impressions of the client, both outer and inner, form a navigational ompass to the process of the client.

Vhen we meet a contraction, we can sense a density or heaviness. This lensity will have a separate form within the whole. It will have a texture, olor, smell, taste, sound and atmosphere. The same contraction will have s own sensory intelligence. It might be fearful, foreboding or annoyed just y the approach of consciousness. This is a sensory and energetic corre-pondence – between the contraction and the whole – that can be deeply lealing. The whole dialogue is an experience, and the experience is arising n unbounded awareness in which the client and therapist are one.

Releasing Pronouns

n seeking to possess a personality, we become possessed by our personality. 'ersonality is composed of a pattern of identification, and these formations f identity are held and maintained by the conscious mind. When we name omething, we feel we have power over it. When we name ourselves, we eel we have some control over the mystery of who we are. When we name listurbing emotions, there is a movement of recognition and emotional re-ponsibility, but this is just the first stage, a stage which can become a rap.

There are underwritten limitations to talking about "my anger", "my jea ousy" or "my love". What follows can be an imprisonment in unwante states of Being. Therapeutically it can be worthwhile to play with thi pronoun. For example: "He is angry with me," can be turned around wit the question: "Are you angry with him?" or "Where does the feeling of hi anger end and the feeling of your own anger begin?" After playing with th pronoun over the illusory borders of the Separate Self, the space t acknowledge that "Anger is happening" or "Anger is here" can arise in th field. Anger is an energetic resonance that moves between people. It i never really possessed by anyone.

As we begin to experience energetic resonance as impersonal, many layer of fear, shame and guilt around the emotion can be released. In the sam way, the tendency to blame the 'other', or to put them at cause of th direct experience is relieved. Difficult feelings or emotions gain the spac outside the story to be experienced with softness and curiosity in freedom beyond judgement.

Inquiry & Paradox

Inquiry is an integral part of psychotherapy and psychoanalysis. In Non dual Therapy however, the inquiry tends to run deeper into the truth o who we are, resting in an experiential knowing of our True Nature as wel as an insight into the self-defeating, paradoxical nature of belief. The Work as introduced by Byron Katie, is a powerful tool of self inquiry and is highly recommended for therapeutic use. At the same time, it is necessary to acknowledge the energetic substance of contractions at the formationa layer of beliefs. Contractions in feeling and emotion have layers and uniqu ingredients with their own need for process time and the allowance of space for expression. When a belief is released, there can be an open vulnerability which when ignored, threatens to breed more beliefs. Honor, care and trus are needed to encourage space for the healing process to spiral through cycles of transformation (returning to the same themes again and again from deepening perspectives) according to the intelligence of need.

he foundational structures of beliefs, however, generate a strong force. he best way to decrease our compulsion toward mind control is to use ought itself to expose the fallacy. This is because mind is inherently born be of service. When through its own logic, the mind becomes aware of e self-defeating effect of its controlling strategies, it can feel empowered ough to release old patterns of thought.

here are many paradoxical belief structures on which a large part of hu- an striving and suffering is based. Many of these beliefs are based on ort-term gratification rather than on long-term nurture. To put it an- her way, they are often based on wants (grasping and aversion) rather 1 deeper need. Here are some examples:

1. Fear tells us to avoid future fear, based on fears from the past.

2. We close our senses to feel safe, and in doing so, blind ourselves to risks in the environment.

3. We cling to what we know, to avoid the Source of all knowledge, which is that which is not yet known.

4. We repress life to survive life.

5. We expect to know how to swim before entering the water.

6. We strive to become someone else, to become accepted as who we are.

rue Nature as Resource

here will be clients of all kinds. Some, for no apparent reason, will have ich a severe addiction to the personality, including all its suffering, that ere is very little space to maneuver. Even a real-time experience of the oundless can send them scrambling back in a panic to bolster habitual atterns of anxiety. Working with a contraction can be difficult. As soon s a contraction is accessed, they embody it, reflecting a poverty of space in awareness. Such clients can show a lot of impatience with the proce and will constantly demand results. They are perennially disappointed, y they still come back for more.

In this, the onus is on the therapist to relax even more deeply into the True Nature, releasing all agenda of success. The therapist becomes a open channel of stillness, peace, care or belonging which by degrees ca loosen the grip of personal possession. Patience – a natural effect of con nection with our own timelessness is fundamental. We are not in control where, when or how a client awakens. The unfolding is so much bigger tha the context.

Other clients will be post-awakening. The tremendous experience of libe ation from preconceived limitations can open the senses. When our sens open, there is a direct invitation for contractions to unfold in consciousnes This is where a process of self-realization begins, in which the client neec support and affirmation in the allowance of all they carry in the psyche t begin reuniting with True Nature. The process of self-realization involve realizing the illusory nature of our habitual reality. It is not just for sator it is for every moment of living experience. When it is done on a person scale, it continues through ancestral layers and the transpersonal.

In Nondual Therapy, some processes can move very fast, especially thos where the client arrives on the verge of medication, reaching out from th Dark Night of the Soul. The fundamental realization of the fallacy of th concept of separate existence becomes the initiator as contractions fall lik dominos through a process of increasing stability and consolidation in th formless Source of Being.

At all stages and with all clients it is important to identify Nondual Re sources – those qualities which are available to experience in any momen – and to connect them with areas of suffering. The connection can b through pendulation, or through direct transmission of the Nondual Qual ity towards the contraction. Also, we can become sensitive to the cor Qualities or learnings around which a client's universe is spiraling toward eedom in form. In this, the thread of learning (for example, around the uality of Innocence) will span generations and will be reflected in the lend of the client's parents. With the quality of Innocence, the mother ould be the accusing one, and the father the one with a blockage around uilt. They conceive a child with a strong quality of innocence directly out f the somatic resonance of need. Again, we will see that the areas where ne client has the greatest issues, are the areas where the quality shines rightest. This is part of the evolutionary service they carry as pure aware-ess in this life cycle.

Nondual Resources do not only include the qualities as sensed in human orm, and it is often very important to put down the suffering structure we all humanity and to relativize it be drawing on Nondual Resources as ound in nature and as nature. The split from our True Nature is reflected s a direct separation from physical nature. In this, the planet, trees, ani-nals, rivers, flowers, oceans and infinite expanse of air are all Nondual Qualities, part of the living mystery of that which is at cause of our most ntimate layers of experience.

"Please call me by my true names, so I can hear all my cries and laughter at once, so I can see that my joy and pain are one."

THICH NHAT HANH

###

Georgi Y. Johnson

INDEX OF QUALITY CONTRACTIONS

Perception: **Chaos**, Order
Child: Mother, Father
Choice: Suffering, Resistance
Clarity: Confusion, Agenda
Evolution: Competition, **Collaboration**
Community: Comparison, **Collusion**
Community: Comparison, Collusion
Community: **Comparison, Collusion**
Compassion: Fear, Anger
Evolution: **Competition**, Collaboration
Enthusiasm: **Compulsion**, Obsession
Salvation: **Condemnation**, Redemption
Authority: **Conformity**, Rebellion
Clarity: **Confusion**, Agenda
Congeniality: Guest, Host
Connection: Loneliness, Intimacy
Consciousness: Light, Darkness
Perception through Emptiness: **Consciousness**, Awareness
Honor: Pride, **Contempt**
Rhythm: **Contraction**, Expansion
Helplessness: **Control**, Submission
Nurture: **Craving**, Repulsion
Transformation: **Creation**, Destruction
Empathy: **Cruelty**, Self-Pity
Curiosity: Expectation, **Disappointment**
Miracle: Blessing, **Curse**
Consciousness: Light, Darkness
Life: Birth, **Death**

Protection: Attack, **Defence**
Authenticity: Pretence, **Delusion**
Direction: Desire, **Denial**
Movement: Speed, **Density**
Journey: **Departing**, Arriving
Interdependence: **Dependence**, Independence
Relaxation: Stress, **Depression**
Direction: **Desire**, Denial
Need: **Despair**, Hope
Transformation: Creation, **Destruction**
Inspiration: **Devotion**, Inquiry
Direction: Desire, Denial
Curiosity: Expectation, **Disappointment**
Discernment: Good, Evil
Wellbeing: Health, **Disease**
Purity: Shame, **Disgust**
Beauty: Like, **Dislike**
Synchronicity: **Dissonance**, Harmony
Merging: **Domination**, Subordination
Earth: Heaven, Hell
Ease: Effort, Tiredness
Ecstasy: Specialness, Renunciation
Ease: **Effort**, Tiredness
Essence: Personality, **Ego**
Empathy: Cruelty, Self-Pity
Emptiness: Silence, Stillness
Friendliness: **Enmity**, Alliance
Enthusiasm: Compulsion, Obsession

Equality: Superiority, Inferiority
Essence: Personality, Ego
Esteem: Injustice, Illegitimacy
Eternity: Nostalgia, Longing
'*THAT*' (Nisargadatta Maharaj):
Eternity, Infinity
Identity: **Everyone**, No-one
Form: **Everything**, Nothing
Space: **Everywhere**, Nowhere
Discernment: Good, **Evil**
Evolution: Competition, Collaboration
Reality: **Existence**, Non-existence
Existence: Presence, Absence
Curiosity: **Expectation**, Disappointment
Experience: Expression, Impression
Experience: **Expression**, Impression
Survival: Success, **Failure**
Home: **Familiarity**, Strangeness
Frequency: **Fast**, Slow
Child: Mother, **Father**
Compassion: **Fear**, Anger
Feeling: Sensitivity, Numbness
Wholeness: Male, **Female**
Flow: Action, Reaction
Form: Everything, Nothing
Freedom: Slavery, Liberation
Frequency: Fast, Slow
Friendliness: Enmity, Alliance

Patience: Anticipation, **Frustration**
Fulfilment: Loss, Gain
Play: **Fun**, Naughtiness
Now: Past, **Future**
Fulfilment: Loss, **Gain**
Genius: Stupidity, Smartness
Discernment: **Good**, Evil
Gratitude: **Greed**, Poverty
Gravity: Time, Space
Gratitude: Greed, Poverty
Joy: **Grief**, Preservation
Congeniality: **Guest**, Host
Innocence: **Guilt**, Accusation
Happiness: Sadness, Negativity
Synchronicity: Dissonance, **Harmony**
Love: **Hate**, Sacrifice
Body: Head, **Heart**
Wellbeing: **Healing**, Disease
Body: **Head**, Heart
Earth: **Heaven**, Hell
Earth: Heaven, **Hell**
Helplessness: Control, Submission
Here: Inside, Outside
Change: **Holding**, Withholding
Home: Familiarity, Strangeness
Truth: Lies, **Honesty**
Honor: Pride, Contempt
Need: Despair, **Hope**
Congeniality: Guest, **Host**

Awe: **Humiliation**, Adoration
Humility: Jealousy, Idolatry
Identity: Everyone, No-one
Humility: Jealousy, **Idolatry**
Esteem: Injustice, **Illegitimacy**
Connection: Loneliness, **Intimacy**
Reflection: Memory, **Imagination**
Experience: Expression, **Impression**
Interdependence: Dependence, **Independence**
Equality: Superiority, **Inferiority**
Infinity: Less, **More**
'*THAT*' (Nisargadatta Maharaj):
Eternity, **Infinity**
Esteem: **Injustice**, Illegitimacy
Innocence: Guilt, Accusation
Inspiration: Devotion, **Inquiry**
Insight: Sanity, **Insanity**
(*Sacred*) *Safety*: Security, **Insecurity**
Here: **Inside**, Outside
Insight: Sanity, Insanity
Inspiration: Devotion, Inquiry
Interdependence: Dependence, Independence
Inspiration: Devotion, Inquiry
Togetherness: Recruitment, **Isolation**
Humility: **Jealousy**, Idolatry
Journey: Departing, Arriving
Joy: Grief, Preservation
Learning: Teacher, Student
Center: **Left**, Right

Infinity: **Less**, More
Freedom: Slavery, **Liberation**
Truth: **Lies**, Honesty
Life: Birth, Death
Consciousness: **Light**, Darkness
Beauty: **Like**, Dislike
Connection: **Loneliness**, Intimacy
Eternity: Nostalgia, **Longing**
Fulfilment: **Loss**, Gain
Love: Hate, Sacrifice
Trust: Betrayal, **Loyalty**
Wholeness: **Male**, Female
Manifestation: Affirmation, Negation
Reflection: **Memory**, Imagination
Mercy: Misery, Torment
Merging: Domination, Subordination
Miracle: Blessing, Curse
Mercy: **Misery**, Torment
Infinity: Less, **More**
Child: **Mother**, Father
Movement: Speed, Density
(*Unconditional*) *Release*: **Murder**, Suicide
Nature: Shock, Trauma
Play: Fun, **Naughtiness**
Need: Despair, Hope
Manifestation: Affirmation, **Negation**
Happiness: Sadness, **Negativity**
Identity: Everyone, No-**one**

Silence: **Noise**, Quiet
Reality: Existence, **Non-existence**
Eternity: **Nostalgia**, Longing
Form: Everything, **Nothing**
Now: Past, Future
Space: Everywhere, **Nowhere**
Feeling: Sensitivity, **Numbness**
Nurture: Craving, Repulsion
Source: Subject, **Object**
Enthusiasm: Compulsion, **Obsession**
Perception: Chaos, **Order**
Unity: Self, **Other**
Here: Inside, **Outside**
Bliss: Pleasure, **Pain**
Passion: Boredom, Addiction
Now: **Past**, Future
Patience: Anticipation, Frustration
Peace: Surrender, War
Perception: Chaos, Order
Perception through Emptiness:
Consciousness, Awareness
Essence: **Personality**, Ego
Play: Fun, Naughtiness
Bliss: **Pleasure**, Pain
Care: **Possession**, Abandonment
Gratitude: Greed, **Poverty**
Power: Abuse (Perpetrator), Victimhood
Existence: **Presence**, Absence
Joy: Grief, **Preservation**

Authenticity: **Pretence**, Delusion
Honor: **Pride**, Contempt
Protection: Attack, Defense
Sexuality: Push, **Pull**
Purity: Shame, Disgust
Sexuality: **Push**, Pull
Silence: Noise, **Quiet**
Flow: Action, **Reaction**
Reality: Existence, Non-existence
Authority: Conformity, **Rebellion**
Stillness: Active, **Receptive**
Togetherness: **Recruitment**, Isolation
Salvation: Condemnation, **Redemption**
Reflection: Memory, Imagination
Responsivity: **Refusal**, Vulnerability
Belonging: Acceptance, **Rejection**
Relaxation: Stress, Depression
Ecstasy: Specialness, **Renunciation**
Nurture: Craving, **Repulsion**
Choice: Suffering, **Resistance**
Responsivity: Refusal, Vulnerability
Rhythm: Contraction, Expansion
Center: Left, **Right**
Love: Hate, **Sacrifice**
(***Sacred***) ***Safety***: Security, Insecurity
Happiness: **Sadness**, Negativity
Salvation: Condemnation, Redemption
Insight: **Sanity**, Insanity

(*Sacred*) *Safety*: **Security**, Insecurity
Unity: **Self**, Other
Empathy: Cruelty, **Self-Pity**
Feeling: **Sensitivity**, Numbness
Sexuality: Push, Pull
Purity: **Shame**, Disgust
Nature: **Shock**, Trauma
Awareness: Vibration, **Silence**
Silence: Noise, Quiet
Emptiness: **Silence**, Stillness
Freedom: **Slavery**, Liberation
Frequency: Fast, **Slow**
Genius: Stupidity, **Smartness**
Softness: Strength, Weakness
Source: Subject, Object
Gravity: Time, **Space**
Space: Everywhere, Nowhere
Ecstasy: **Specialness**, Renunciation
Movement: **Speed**, Density
Stillness: Active, Receptive
Emptiness: Silence, **Stillness**
Home: Familiarity, **Strangeness**
Softness: **Strength**, Weakness
Relaxation: **Stress**, Depression
Learning: Teacher, **Student**
Genius: **Stupidity**, Smartness
Source: **Subject**, Object
Helplessness: Control, **Submission**
Merging: Domination, **Subordination**
Survival: **Success**, Failure
Choice: **Suffering**, Resistance
(*Unconditional*) *Release*: Murder, **Suicide**

Equality: **Superiority**, Inferiority
Peace: **Surrender**, War
Survival: **Success**, Failure
Synchronicity: Dissonance, Harmony
Learning: **Teacher**, Student
Balance: **Tension**, Attention
'***THAT***' (**Nisargadatta Maharaj**): Eternity, Infinity
Gravity: **Time**, Space
Ease: Effort, **Tiredness**
Togetherness: Recruitment, Isolation
Mercy: Misery, **Torment**
Transformation: Creation, Destruction
Nature: Shock, **Trauma**
Trust: Betrayal, Loyalty
Truth: Lies, Honesty
(*Unconditional*) *Release*: Murder, Suicide
Unity: **Self**, Other
Awareness: **Vibration**, Silence
Power: Abuse (Perpetrator), **Victimhood**
Responsivity: Refusal, **Vulnerability**
Peace: Surrender, **War**
Softness: Strength, **Weakness**
Wellbeing: Healing, Disease
Wholeness: Male, Female
Change: Holding, **Withholding**

About the Author

Georgi Y. Johnson graduated from Oxford University with a determination to explore the mysteries of perception through mind, heart and body. Together with her partner Bart ten Berge she has an international teaching and healing practice in Nondual Therapy and Spiritual Psychology. Georgi's other books include I AM HERE – Opening the Windows of Life & Beauty. Georgi's poetry is featured in several anthologies of spiritual poetry, including: Into the Further Reaches and Diamond Cutters. Georgi and Bart live in Israel and together have ten children. You can watch an interview with Georgi on Conscious TV here: http://conscious.tv/single.php?vid=4753209717001.

More information:

info@iamhere.life

http://www.IAmHere.Life

htttp://www.NondualTherapy.Life

Made in the USA
Columbia, SC
07 November 2020

24096965R00254